Norman
14 June 1983.

CHANGE AND CONTINUITY IN SEVENTEENTH-CENTURY ENGLAND

Change and Continuity in Seventeenth-Century England

Christopher Hill

Weidenfeld and Nicolson
London

Weidenfeld and Nicolson Limited
11 St John's Hill London SW11

ISBN 0 297 76822 0

Printed in Great Britain by
Morrison & Gibb Ltd
London and Edinburgh

To the memory of
Margaret James and John Buckatzsch

Contents

Preface

The seventeenth century is an age of intellectual and political giants, who carried on a long and unbroken warfare. It will always be studied. It is the favourite topic or theme of writers. But as it has been hitherto written, it is nothing but the record of their drama, the estimate of their characters, who were the agents of this colossal strife. To me the century has another and a very different aspect – the history of the people, whose fortunes have hitherto been passed over in silence.

> J. E. Thorold Rogers, *The Economic Interpretation of History* (1909), p. 5. First published 1888.

The essays in this book were written separately over the past dozen years or so, but they deal with a single theme, or group of interrelated themes. They circle round the English Revolution of the seventeenth century, of whose crucial significance a French historian has recently written:

> 'The leading political power of Europe in the first decades of the eighteenth century is also the society which has broken with traditional principles, rejected divine-right monarchy, absolutism and arbitrary government . . . England has overcome the internal crises of the seventeenth century and represents not only a specific political force but also another sort of society, victorious because different.'*

This difference in English development from that of most continental nations resulted from the seventeenth-century English Revolution; the essays in this book explore from different angles the reasons for and consequences of that all-important event in our history.

A main theme in all of them is the interrelationship between

* R. Mandrou, *Louis XIV en son temps, 1661–1715* (Paris, 1973), p. 544; cf. 27-8, 377.

material and intellectual aspects of the Revolution, between economics, politics and ideas. Chapter 1 considers attempts to impose the ideology of the economically advanced areas of England on the backward North and West, and the paradoxical backlash from the North which followed: chapter 2 is a case study of a Welshman in London. Chapter 3 tries to suggest some ways in which protestantism facilitated acceptance of new ideas and practices; chapter 4 to show how the content of old ideas might be transformed by social pressures. Part III looks at the radical critique of the three traditional professions, divinity, law, medicine, emphasizing especially the social attitudes which underlay ideological attack. Part IV deals with class divisions in ideas. (Chapter 11 strays beyond the chronological limits of my title, but its theme is linked to that of other essays in this section.) Finally Part V tries to see the convergence of continuity and change in the post-revolutionary world of Sir Isaac Newton, and to use this too to place the English Revolution in its historical context.

Too many people have helped in the writing of this book for me to thank them all. The notes acknowledge the debts of which I am most conscious. But I should like to thank particularly Mr John Addy, for casting light on dark corners, Professor Frank Manuel, whose Fremantle Lectures on the religion of Isaac Newton I was privileged to hear and to have the opportunity of discussing; Joseph Needham for help with his distinguished predecessor William Dell; Dr Kenneth Morgan and Professor Glanmor Williams in respect of Arise Evans; Mr Conrad Russell and Professor C. M. Williams for guidance and advice about the many-headed monster; Professors André Parreaux and Ivan Roots, Mr Quentin Skinner and Mr Charles Webster. I must also express my gratitude to the Hobhouse Memorial Trust Committee for inviting me to deliver the Hobhouse Memorial Lecture in 1969 (chapter 4) and to the Society of Apothecaries, who invited me to give the Gideon Delaune Lecture in 1973 (chapter 7). I thank the University of Texas for an invitation to participate in the Tercentenary Congress which celebrated Newton's Annus Mirabilis in 1966 (chapter 12), and the participants in those discussions; and Johns Hopkins University for asking me in 1970 to give a James S. Schouler Lecture, reprinted here as chapter 5.

Mr Andrew Foster very kindly helped with the proofs. My wife and my pupils contributed more than they or I know, but none of them is to blame for the final result.

Some of the essays have been substantially rewritten, apart from those which were originally review articles. Here I have confined myself to factual corrections, minor additions and the restoration in chapter 9 of matter in my original draft which was not printed. Nor have I attempted to rewrite chapter 3: I should want to do so at greater length if at all. Spelling and punctuation have been modernized throughout, except in titles of books.

The dedication records a continuing debt to two friends, one of them also a colleague. Both died tragically and prematurely, but not before they had opened up new areas of research which historians are still exploring. An awareness of the pioneering significance of their work was forced on me again and again whilst writing this book.

Acknowledgments

Acknowledgments are due to the following publishers for permission to reprint material:

To Messrs A. and C. Black and to the Council of the Royal Historical Society for the two pieces which combine to make chapter 1 in this volume; to the Cambridge University Press for chapters 3 and 10; to Messrs Routledge & Kegan Paul, Ltd, for chapter 4; to the Johns Hopkins University Press for chapter 5; to the *History of Education Quarterly* for chapter 6; to Random House, Inc., for chapter 8; to *History and Theory* and to Wesleyan University Press for chapter 9; to *The Times Literary Supplement* for chapter 11; to the *Texas Quarterly* and to the M.I.T. press for chapter 12.

Abbreviations

The following abbreviations have been used in the notes:

C.S.P.	*Calendar of State Papers*
C.S.P.D.	*Calendar of State Papers, Domestic*
C.J.	*Commons' Journals*
D.N.B.	*Dictionary of National Biography*
Ec. H.R.	*Economic History Review*
E.H.R.	*English Historical Review*
Hist. MSS Comm.	Historical Manuscripts Commission
L.J.	*Lords' Journals*
P. and P.	*Past and Present*
T.R.H.S.	*Transactions of the Royal Historical Society*
V.C.H.	*Victoria County History*

PART I
Changing Relationships: London and the Outlying Regions

Puritans and 'the Dark Corners of the Land'[1]

The service these two fruits of the bishops' government have done: profaneness hath made a general averseness to reformation; and ignorance with the help of that hath furnished the King with an army against the Parliament, fetched from the barren mountains of Wales, Cornwall and the North, which were kept sure without the means of knowledge, as a fit reserve for such a time as this. I speak of the common sort of soldiers, many of the rest have too much knowledge and too little conscience.

[Anon.], *The Mysterie of Iniquity yet working in the Kingdoms of England, Scotland and Ireland* (1643), p. 14.

I

The century between Reformation and Civil War saw a slow but steady expansion of the cultivated area of England – by bringing new lands under the plough in outlying regions like Devon and Cornwall, Cumberland and Westmorland; by extension of cultivation to forests, wastes and common lands; and by drainage. The same century also saw an expansion of the area of London's trade, and of London influence. Corn and dairy products were being shipped to the capital from Yorkshire, Durham and Northumberland.[2] London merchants began to purchase wool direct from North Wales, Wiltshire and the West Riding.[3] Welsh cottons and cattle depended on the London market: early in the Civil War the gentry of North Wales petitioned the King for safe conduct across the fighting lines for their herds.[4] Merchants in Shrewsbury and Hereford kept up trading connections with the capital throughout the Civil War: Worcester merchants tried to do the same.[5]

These two social movements ultimately had the effect of civilizing the outlying regions, of bringing them into closer contact with the metropolis and its standards. 'Their constant converse and traffic with London,' said Richard Baxter of Kidderminster's weavers, 'doth much promote civility and piety among tradesmen.'[6] But the extension of London influence proceeded slowly, silently, unobtrusively, until expedited by the events of the Interregnum which forcibly united England. The North and West were turbulent areas, where loyalty to the local feudal lord still counted for more than loyalty to the distant sovereign at Westminster. No sixteenth-century monarch ever visited the North, the South-West or Wales: the Stuarts passed through the North of England on their way to or from Scotland, but Charles never visited the principality from which he took his title – until driven there by civil war. The North and West were also papist areas. When contemporaries thought of the remoter regions, they did not say that the North and West should be opened up to cultivation or to London traders. They said that the gospel should be carried into those dark corners of the land. 'When I come out of the country hither to the City,' said a preacher at Paul's Cross in 1571, 'methinks I come into another world, even out of darkness into light; for here the Word of God is plentifully preached.'[7] Puritanism spread along the trade routes, with market towns as its outposts in the North and West; merchants played a big part in spreading it. There is a certain parallel between the extension of London's trade and the extension of Puritanism. But this would have seemed a mere coincidence to the men of the sixteenth and early seventeenth centuries. My object is to consider attempts to evangelize the outlying areas, culminating in Parliament's Commissions for the Propagation of the Gospel in Wales and in the four northern counties.

II

The problem of the North and West of England was with the Tudors from the beginning, and it was intensified by the Reformation. Opposition to Henry VIII's divorce came especially from these outlying regions.[8] In the Pilgrimage of Grace and the Cornish Rising of 1549 religious and social causes were inextricably mingled: but clearly the protestantism of the capital increased its unpopularity with the outlying regions. The existence of the Council of the North and the Council in the Marches of Wales (not to mention the abortive Council of the West) shows the continuing awareness of governments that there were special problems in these areas. The frequency with which bishops were appointed to the presidency of the Council in the Marches, and the Council's attention to religious matters, suggests that the absence of religious revolt in Wales did not mean that there was no tension between the old and the new in the Principality.

In 1551 six itinerant ministers were appointed to tour in rotation Wales, Lancashire, Yorkshire, the Scottish borders, Devon and Hampshire; John Knox and Edmund Grindal were among their number.[9] The revenues of Manchester College were devoted, *inter alia*, to the maintenance of ministers whose task was to go round the countryside preaching. Haweis, who knew the evidence better than most, thought that itinerant preachers played an important part in consolidating the Reformation.[10] In June 1560 the Lord Treasurer wrote to Archbishop Parker that he had moved the Queen to appoint three preachers for the diocese of York, and two more for Durham.[11] Four months later Parker told Cecil that it was false economy not to appoint bishops in the North. Vacant sees might enrich the government, but the absence of reliable agents and propagandists would weaken it. 'Whatsoever is now too husbandly saved will be an occasion of further expense of keeping them [i.e. the people of the North] down if (as God forfend) they should be too much Irish and savage.'[12] The Rising of 1569 showed how right Parker was. The rebels had mass said daily wherever they went, and Philip II told Alva to stand ready to intervene.[13]

On the eve of the rising the Council of the North had informed the Privy Council that in several northern churches there had been no sermon for years; most ministers were unable to preach and the people were hopelessly backward in religion. This backwardness, however, proceeded from ignorance rather than from wilful disobedience. The Council had ordered preachers in cathedral churches to turn themselves into itinerants: Justices of the Peace were ordered to collect audiences for them.[14] Grindal, who became archbishop of York in 1570, explained to Elizabeth seven years later that 'by preaching ... due obedience to Christian princes and magistrates is planted in the hearts of subjects ... Where preaching wanteth, obedience faileth.' What had caused the loyalty of London

> 'but the continued preaching of God's Word in that City? ... On the contrary, what bred the rebellion in the North? ... One poor parish in Yorkshire, which by continual preaching had been better instructed than the rest (Halifax, I mean) was ready to bring 3 or 4,000 able men into the field to serve you against the said rebels.'[15]

On the nature of the problem all were agreed. The ministry in Durham was said in 1560 to be 'barren and destitute of a sufficiency of worthy men'.[16] The bishop of Carlisle in 1561 described his clergy as 'wicked imps of Antichrist, for the most part very ignorant and stubborn, past measure false and subtle'.[17] Bernard Gilpin, 'the Apostle of the North', said in 1552 that 'a thousand pulpits in England are covered with dust.' Some churches 'have not had four sermons in these fifteen or sixteen years'. Under Elizabeth he used regularly each year to visit 'the most neglected parishes in Northumberland, Yorkshire, Cheshire, Westmorland and Cumberland', preaching to large crowds in churches or barns.[18] When Grindal entered his northern province in 1570, he told Cecil that 'this seemeth to be, as it were, another church, rather than a member of the rest'. Among the 'remnants of the old' he observed that holy days and feasts were still celebrated; beads were told; 'they offer money, eggs, etc. at the burial of their dead.'[19]

In 1599 we are told of the diocese of Carlisle that fear of oppressive landlords and poverty of livings prevented the spreading of the gospel. The majority of the clergy were unable even to read English clearly and distinctly. Three years earlier English and Scottish commissioners had decided to ask their respective governments for 'God's ministers of the Word to be planted at every border church, to inform the lawless people of their duty'; but in 1599 many border churches still lacked anyone to celebrate divine service, 'save only certain beggarly runners who come out of Scotland'. In Durham, too, 'vagabond Scots who dare not abide in their country' were serving chapels in the 1560s; thirty years later there were 'scant three able preachers to be found in the whole county'.[20] Birdsall, where Henry Burton was born in 1578, was 'an obscure town in Yorkshire, and the more obscure as having never had a preaching minister, time out of mind, long before I was born, nor (for aught I know) to this very day' (1645).[21] This may help to explain Burton's radical puritanism. William Bradford the Pilgrim Father was born in south Yorkshire in 1590. The villagers whom he knew as a boy were, we are told, totally ignorant of the Bible. In Cumberland 'the poorer sort' were 'pitifully ignorant of the foundations of Christianity'; in Northumberland there were men who had never learnt the Lord's Prayer.[22]

When John Penry, another radical Puritan, sought help from Queen and Parliament for the evangelization of Wales, 'the most barren corner of the land', he said in 1587 that for one Welsh parish that had a quarterly sermon, twenty had none. There was not a parish in Wales 'where for the space of six years together, within these 29 years, a godly and learned minister hath executed the duty of a faithful teacher'. Apart from 'some few gentlemen or such like, . . . the rest of our people are either such as never think of any religion, true or false, plainly near-atheists, or stark blinded with superstition.' Some were near-papists, saying 'it was a good world when a man might have a pardon for his sins . . . for . . . 4d . . . If they meet with any who can write and read, they will demand of him whether he can teach them ever a good prayer against such a disease in man or beast.' Others listened to 'our swarms of soothsayers and enchanters', who walk with the fairies. Penry doubtless exaggerated; he thought a belief 'that the Lord is bound to save all men, because they are his creatures', no less erroneous than belief in the Virgin's power of intercession, and 'the cause why our people make but a mock of sin'.[23] But on his main point – the scarcity of preaching in Wales and the consequent irreligion of the people – he is confirmed by many sources, including his arch-enemies the bishops.

At the beginning of Elizabeth's reign there were only five preachers each in the dioceses of Llandaff and St Asaph, two in Bangor.[24] There were nine in St David's in 1569, fourteen in 1583.[25] 90 per cent of the clergy in North Wales were returned as unable to preach in 1567.[26] 'Ignorance continueth many in the dregs of superstition,' said Bishop Robinson of Bangor that year.[27] On Sundays and holy days, we are told of North Wales about 1600, 'the multitude of all sorts of men, women and children' used to meet to hear 'their harpers and crowthers sing them songs of the doings of their ancestors.'[28] In 1582 the bishop of St David's reported that the preachers in his diocese were very poor, the people greatly infected with atheism and wonderfully given over to vicious life.[29] Conditions had improved by 1603, but in that year there were still only fifty preachers for 192 cures in Llandaff.[30] Chief Justice Lewknor spoke in 1601 of 'great backsliding in religion, . . . especially in the confines of the shires between England and Wales, as Monmouth, Hereford and Shropshire, and the skirts of the shires of Wales bordering upon them'.[31] Two years later Sir William Meredith referred to the lack of preaching in the Wrexham area, which was likely to continue 'unless it please God to move the heart of our King to look into and reform the most lamentable and desperate estate of all the churches of North Wales'.[32] In the Golden Vale there had been 'not two sermons . . . this 500 years, unless by chance', said Rowland Vaughan in 1610; and in the hundred of Weabtree there was not a preaching minister in 24 parishes.[33] The phrases ring out with sad iteration in Bishop Bayly's report on his visitation of Bangor in 1623: 'But two sermons . . . this twelvemonth'; 'no sermon . . . this five or six years'; 'no quarterly sermons'; 'no sermons'; 'no sermons at all'.[34] So there was much evidence to justify the Principal of Jesus's statement to the House of Commons, in 1626, that some churches in Wales 'have not had a sermon in them this nine years, scarce prayers'.[35] 'Half understood relics of the missal and breviary', Professor Dodd sums up, 'survived in the home for generations after they had been banished from the church.'[36]

As late as 1635 the bishop of St David's 'complains . . . that there are few ministers in those poor and remote places that are able to preach and instruct the people'. Three years later the bishop of Bangor moaned that he was compelled to ordain 'weak scholars or none', since 'all clergymen of hope and worth seek preferment elsewhere.'[37] There were over a thousand parishes in Wales, a member of Parliament alleged in 1640, and not thirteen preachers who habitually preached and catechized in the Welsh tongue.[38] In 1646 both Walter Cradock and Vavasor Powell asserted that there were not so many conscientious and continual preachers in the Welsh language as there were counties in Wales.[39] Although the Welsh members of Parliament nominated eight divines to the Westminster Assembly, only one of them was a Welshman holding a living in Wales: he was later cited as a delinquent and deprived.[40]

For the Marches we may quote Baxter, who says that the Shropshire of his youth in the 1620s 'had but little preaching at all'. There were only three or four preachers near where he lived, to a dozen or more non-preachers.[41] In 1641 it was reported from Herefordshire that there were 'but twenty constant preachers' in 225 churches and chapels.[42] The county abounded with 'insufficient, idle and scandalous ministers', said a petition to the House of Commons in 1642, 'whereby the people generally are continued in ignorance, superstition and profaneness', the natural seed-bed of popery.[43] In Cheshire, too, there were few constant preachers: the godly came six or seven miles to hear Samuel Clarke preach, and maintained him by voluntary contributions.[44] In 1622 the bishop of Chester referred to the 'dry and barren soil' of his diocese.[45] In the archdeaconry of Staffordshire in 1584 scarce one clergymen out of 150 was fit to preach.[46] At Kendal the Marian altars were still standing in place in 1578. In Boroughbridge Deanery, at Hunsingore, pre-Reformation 'superstitions in burying the dead' remained in use in 1595. Thirty-eight years later rush-bearings were still practised in parts of the West Riding, with crosses and crucifixes carried round the villages.[47] John Aubrey tells us of 'sin-eating' and other pagan customs in Wales and Herefordshire, and Arise Evans confirms him.[48] Lancashire was famed both for its popery and for its witches. In Ben Jonson's *The Sad Shepherd* the witch has a northern accent; in *The Devil is an Ass* Satan declared that second-class agents would do to promote his cause in Lancashire and Northumberland, so easy was the conquest of those counties.[49]

The survival of popular superstitions in the dark corners of the land, and the protection of popery by some of the big landed families, became especially dangerous as seminary priests and Jesuits began to carry on active propaganda – concentrating, as Burghley noted in 1586, on areas in which there was least

9

preaching.[50] At the beginning of Elizabeth's reign Nicholas Sanders had told the Vatican that the most remote parts of the country were those least inclined to protestantism. He named Wales, Devon, Westmorland, Cumberland, Northumberland.[51] In the 1560s William Allen and Thomas Vaux, two Lancashire men, were re-entrenching recusancy in their native county; in the 1580s John Bost did the same for Cumberland and Westmorland. In Durham the 'best houses' protected seminary priests.[52] In 1585 Robert Parsons told the Pope and Philip II that the northern counties were especially Catholic, and that all Wales would rise up to assist a Spanish invasion.[53] Nearly 60 per cent of the students registered at St Alban's College, Valladolid, between 1589 and 1603 came from Wales, Herefordshire, Staffordshire and Yorkshire.[54]

A Welshman, Thomas Salusbury, was executed in connection with Babington's Plot in 1586. Next year a Stanley, a Salusbury and other Welsh conspirators persuaded their fellow-countrymen in the English service in the Netherlands to betray Ostend to the Spaniards. Their correspondence was conducted in Welsh.[55] Some of the conspirators later transferred to Essex's service, and in 1601 there was considerable support for Essex from the Catholic lesser gentry of Wales and Herefordshire. Sir Gelly Meyricke, who had organized this Welsh support, was among those executed.[56] In 1605 Catholic disturbances started in a village near Hereford in which – as the vicar admitted at the previous visitation – no sermon had been preached for the best part of a year. After order was restored, the bishop of Hereford and the Justices of the Peace were rebuked by the government for the lack of good teaching and preaching in the county.[57]

In the North, too, preaching was regarded as an antidote to popery and rebellion. Papists flourish in country districts 'for want of that teaching which is in good towns', William Bradshaw observed. The rebellion of 1569 occurred in areas 'where the gospel is not effectively preached'. Lancashire gentlemen who in 1604 petitioned in support of Puritan preachers claimed that 'by means of their good doctrine and example we have found it more easy to contain the common people in the duties of their subjection and loyalty to the supreme power'.[58] In 1614 clothiers of Halifax boasted that they contributed generously to their ten preachers and that the town had no papists.[59] Next year the four thousand inhabitants of Pickering, Yorkshire, complained that their rector, the absentee bishop of Bristol, provided no sermons. The Privy Council took the matter up, 'considering how busy the priests and Jesuits are in these days, especially in these parts, not only labouring to corrupt His Majesty's subjects in their religion, but also infecting them with such damnable positions and doctrine touching their allegiance unto His Majesty's sacred person'. The bishop pleaded that he had no legal obligation towards the parish, but in vain: he had to replace his non-preaching vicar by a man who preached weekly.[60] The failure of the Tudor church to evangelize Ireland made Catholicism a national religion there, with deep popular roots: Ireland remained an open door to Spanish or French invasion. The same thing might have happened in Wales, the North and Cornwall if more effective action had not been taken in those areas – largely by private initiative.[61]

III

In 1580 Robert Hitchcock, in a pamphlet advocating government support for the fishing industry, suggested that eight principal ports – London, Yarmouth, Southampton, Hull, Newcastle, Chester, Bristol, Exeter – should be given a specially privileged position and each made responsible for a group of counties. (It will be noted that the hinterland of the last five of them includes many 'dark corners'.) Each town should appoint 'one honest, virtuous, discreet and learned man' as a preacher who 'shall travel continually, as the Apostles did, from place to place, preaching in all fishing towns and decayed towns'. The preachers should have £100 a year each for three years: the object of this capital investment was 'to root out idleness, the mother and breeder of vagabonds'.[62] This rather simple emphasis on the usefulness of religion in promoting labour discipline frequently recurs. I have quoted elsewhere some passages which illustrate it.[63] A century later Zachariah Cawdrey, advocating the propagation of the gospel in America and Africa, wrote: 'This course would be a key to let in the English merchant further than ever yet he hath pierced into the knowledge of the commodities of those vast inland countries:

and so truth and trade would mutually make way for one another, to the just glory and advantage of the English nation.'[64] We should not read similar *naïvetés* of cynicism back into the activities of those who worked so hard to propagate the gospel in the dark corners during the preceding century; but the words of this respectable Cheshire divine are a warning that motives can sometimes be mixed.

Three of Hitchcock's ports were in the North: none in Wales, though Bristol and Chester would no doubt have looked after preaching there. In Yorkshire, Lancashire and Tyneside there were industrial areas which were also Puritan areas (Halifax, Manchester, Newcastle-on-Tyne) from which ministers could set out to evangelize the dark corners. There were towns in the Welsh Marches (Worcester, Hereford, Shrewsbury, Chester) in which Puritans were to be found, and from which Puritan ideas infiltrated. All the origins of nonconformity in Wales are associated with border counties (Denbighshire, Monmouthshire) or with Pembrokeshire, closely connected with England by trade. Puritanism spread along the trade routes to Bristol and Chester, and then to Wales,[65] just as in Yorkshire it advanced along the Great North Road.[66] But Wales lacked urban areas in which protestantism was sufficiently strongly rooted to act as diffusion centres. Language acted as a further barrier. On the coast, in the Marches and in market towns, English preaching was understood. But must the rest of Wales, Penry asked, 'be subject to the curse because they understand not the English tongue?'[67]

IV

In 1585, when the Puritan John Udall was silenced at Kingston-on-Thames, the Puritan Earl of Huntingdon, then President of the Council in the North, persuaded him to come and preach in Newcastle.[68] The previous year, when Huntingdon was trying to get good preachers for all market towns in Yorkshire, he lamented how much remained to be done. Some thought (though his lordship was 'not of that mind altogether') that the universities 'have not store of preachers to send forth'. 'God increase the number', he piously concluded.[69] Penry's emphasis was different. He estimated that in the thirty years since

Elizabeth's accession 3,400 scholars had graduated from one of the two universities, of whom 400 could have been usefully employed in Wales; whereas in fact 'we have not twelve in all our country that do discharge their duty in any good sort.'[70] Supply was one obstacle to expansion of preaching. The universities increased their output of graduates in the late sixteenth and early seventeenth centuries, but by this time the bishops were looking coolly on such Puritanical spirits as those whom Grindal had imported to evangelize the dark corners of the diocese of York. In 1577 Aylmer suggested to Burghley that Puritans like Charke, Chapman, Field and Wilcox should be transferred to Lancashire, Staffordshire, Shropshire and other barbarous counties to draw the people from gross ignorance and popery.[71] By the seventeenth century such a humane and practical proposal would have been unusual in a bishop. It was the old-style Calvinist Thomas Morton who used difficult Puritan ministers for work in the remote and disaffected regions. When bishop of Coventry and Lichfield he sent Anthony Lapthorne from Lichfield to Cannock Chase, 'the most profane and barbarous parish within that diocese'. Later when Morton was bishop of Durham he transferred Lapthorne to a Northumbrian parish where there had been no preaching for forty years and one churchwarden did not know the Lord's Prayer. There Lapthorne's labours were 'not unprofitable'.[72]

A second obstacle to a preaching ministry was the ubiquity of impropriations, in which only a small allowance was made to the minister. In many Welsh parishes, we are told, tithes were worth £100 a year, but the curate was paid a mere £6 6s. 8d. The same reason was given for the lack of a learned ministry in Cumberland, Westmorland and Durham.[73] In the province of Canterbury 40 per cent of the livings were impropriate; in York 62·6 per cent.[74] In Llandaff over half the benefices were impropriate.[75] Many of these impropriations were royal. Their abundance in Richmondshire and the consequent lack of preaching there was worrying Burghley and Walsingham in 1580,[76] but as so often the financing of the court was an obstacle to reform. Impropriations also financed the hierarchy, so the higher clergy were ambivalent in their attitudes to an extension of preaching. Two of the archbishop of Canterbury's three impropriations in Lancashire were 'as far out of order as the worst in all the county', the bishop of Durham told Parker in 1564; but there is no evidence that the archbishop did anything about them.[77] The revenue of the cathedral and chapter of St David's derived almost entirely from tithes; and it was by no means unique.[78]

'If impropriations and non-residencies were not tolerated,' Penry suggested, 'a teaching minister in Wales might live well by the church.' At least impropriators should contribute one-tenth of their revenue to a preaching minister. Vicars should farm royal impropriations; ministers should not be deprived for Puritanism, and Welshmen holding English benefices should be sent home. If the government showed it meant business, and if the advantages to be gained from a preaching ministry were once appreciated, 'our gentlemen and people . . . would be soon brought to contribute.' Until good ministers were established in every parish, the people should be encouraged to go outside their own parishes to hear sermons, and to receive the sacraments from a preaching minister. (This, as Penry very well knew, was encouraging them to break the law.[79]) Penry's appeal was to the secular power – to the President of the Council in Wales and to Welsh Justices of the Peace, to the Queen, the Privy Council and Parliament. He despaired of the bishops, themselves mostly non-resident pluralists, and trusted to see Christ's church 'flourish in Wales, when the memory of lord bishops are buried in hell whence they came'.[80]

The secular power did little about reform. In 1581 the Earl of Derby and the Bishop of Chester were asked to appoint some learned and godly ministers to repair to the dark and disobedient corners.[81] Eighteen years later four Queen's Preachers were established in Lancashire, with an income of £50 apiece, paid from recusants' estates. In some parts of the county these preachers had to be protected by the High Commission before they dared to show themselves.[82] Lancashire, Fuller acutely observed, was 'a frontier country . . . of papists and protestants, where the reformed religion had rather a truce than a peace'.[83] A petition of 1603 tells us that the preachers resided 'in the most backward parts of our country, for the needful instruction of the simple and ignorant in the knowledge of their duties to God and Her Majesty'. The bishop of Chester put them 'in every part of the county where there are most recusants', and especially 'in

Her Majesty's impropriations, which I thought deserved first her bounty'. At least one of the original preachers had Puritan leanings, but as greater emphasis came to be placed on conformity than zeal, so the King's Preachers deteriorated in quality. Bishop Bridgeman thus described *those whom he had appointed*: one had been deprived of his living for simony and was probably of unsound mind; another was a common haunter of ale-houses, an excessive gamester, a fearful blasphemer, a night-walker, dueller and blackmailer, who 'hath had four young wives, who died soon after their portions were spent'. He had one bastard and four legitimate children, who were left to beg because their father did not maintain them. A third thought hell a mere delusion, invented to oppress and torment the consciences of men. It was only sensible of him to sell his preachership as soon as he got a good offer.[84]

In November 1640 Cornelius Burges summed up for the House of Commons:

'King James indeed took commiseration of the gross ignorance of multitudes in the North parts of this kingdom, and sent some preachers at his own charge among them . . . But what through the unsettled wanderings, idleness, the superficial and unprofitable performances of some of these preachers, and what through the supine negligence of some in authority who should have looked better to those itinerary ministers, most of that labour and charge was little better than lost. For some of you know that in no parts of the kingdom hath there been such an increase of papists as in those very corners where that slight means was used to reduce men from popery.'[85]

Bacon recommended to James I that the Lancashire system of itinerant ministers should be extended to 'other corners of the realm', the preachers to be rewarded with liberal stipends.[86] But this interesting anticipation of the Rump's Committees for the Propagation of the Gospel was not acted upon. At the Hampton Court Conference the dark corners were discussed, and James announced his intention of placing good preachers in districts containing a concentration of popish recusants – Wales, the northern borders and Ireland. He promised that no severe measures should be taken against Puritan ministers in Lancashire (and only there), because of their usefulness as preachers.[87] But although a government committee was set up for the propagation of the gospel, the bishops appear to have prevented any effective action being taken. Nothing came of the discussion unless it was a Welsh translation of the homilies, published in 1606.[88]

This was an ironical response to Penry's plea for a state-subsidized version of the whole Bible.[89] A translation of the epistles and gospels had been made in 1551, of the whole New Testament and the Prayer Book in 1567, but into a Welsh which most congregations found difficult to understand. In 1588 William Morgan, later successively bishop of Llandaff and St Asaph, published a complete translation of the Bible. But this was a bulky and expensive folio: it was not until 1630 that two London merchants of Welsh origin, Sir Thomas Middleton (a former Lord Mayor) and Rowland Heylyn (a former sheriff of London), paid for the printing of an edition of handy size, which 'for the first time brought the Scriptures to the homes of those who could meet the cost [5*s*.] and had learnt to read'.[90] Myddelton and Heylyn also financed a 'remarkable output' of 'devotional and instructional literature in simple Welsh', which included *The Practice of Piety* and other treatises inculcating, in Professor Dodd's words, 'the middle-class virtues of sobriety and thrift, humility and self-denial, respectability and Sunday observance, in place of the aristocratic and military virtues favoured by that relic of pagan vanity and vainglory, the bardic order'.[91] This outburst of activity from the London printing presses coincided with the period when the Feoffees for Impropriations were trying to supply preachers for 'the barren places of England'.[92] Heylyn was one of the Feoffees; another was John White, a lawyer from Pembrokeshire. The publication of the cheap Welsh Bible was clearly part of a concerted policy, in which merchants took the lead.[93]

The Feoffees were inspired by John Preston, and he was acutely aware of the problems of the North and West. In a sermon preached before the House of Commons in 1625 he asked: 'Is it not a lamentable case to see how many perish for want of knowledge in Wales, in the Northern counties and in many places besides? . . . Where doth popery abound so much as in the dark places of the kingdom?'[94] The Feoffees' activities lasted for only eight years, and were to some extent guided by chance: by the availability of impropriations or patronage in areas known to the London merchants, lawyers and ministers who made up their number; or to their friends. In 1613 (before the formal existence of the Feoffees) Alderman Heylyn had bought an impropriation in Shropshire and used it to set up a lectureship at St Alkmund's, Shrewsbury: two protégés of the Feoffees subsequently held this lectureship.[95] The Feoffees were accused of spending money on lecturers in London rather than on 'those dark and far-distant corners where souls were ready to famish for lack of food of the Word';[96] and there is no evidence that they paid special attention to Wales. Nevertheless, it is significant that of the thirty-odd ministers whom they appointed or to whom they gave augmentations, nearly half were in Wales or on its borders (six or seven in Shropshire, three in Stafford-shire, one each in Pembrokeshire, Radnorshire, Worcestershire and Gloucestershire).[97] The suppression of the Feoffees by Laud in 1633, like the execution of Penry at Whitgift's insist-ence forty years earlier, showed that neither government nor hierarchy would help to evangelize Wales.

The Feoffees were only the most self-conscious and organized form of a movement of long standing. It was the custom of London merchants born in the same county to get together to promote preaching or education in their native county. Those of Lancashire origin supported five or six preachers in places 'where there was neither preaching nor means to maintain it'; and there are many other examples.[98] But under Laud such meetings and contributions were forbidden. Gatherings of Londoners to discuss how 'to set up the light of the gospel in all the dark places of your county', 'to set up weekly lectures . . . in places most destitute of the gospel', were resumed only after 1640.[99] Many London trading companies had also taken an interest in the dark corners – for example, the Mercers, to whom Richard Fishbourne left money in 1625 to endow preaching in some northern counties where they 'find most want of preaching of the Word of God to be'. The Mercers established lectureships at Hexham and Berwick-on-Tweed.[100] The Haberdashers settled an augmentation on the living of Bunbury in Cheshire, a great centre of papists and of wakes. They claimed the right 'to place and displace' the minister, 'without any respect of episcopal jurisdiction'. They introduced 'novelists' and 'unconformable' ministers.[101] In the diocese of Carlisle there were two lecturers, maintained 'partly by a Londoner . . . and partly by the benevolence of Dorchester and Lyme'.[102] In 1631 the Reverend Peter Simon was accused of fomenting revolt in the Forest of Dean and preaching the equality of all mankind; it emerged that he had been presented to his living by the Haberdashers' Company, under the will of one of their members who was a Welshman by origin.[103]

Professor Jordan's researches now enable us to document the effects of this activity, at least for Yorkshire and Lancashire. There the proportion of charitable endowment devoted to religious uses in the period 1480–1660 far exceeded the nation's average. The endowment of lectureships was greater in those two counties than in any others studied by Professor Jordan, outside London.[104] In Lancashire 41·79 per cent of all charitable funds went to education; in Yorkshire 31·12 per cent. This was mainly due to large benefactions from London merchants, which changed the 'whole social and religious structure of a county like Lancashire' and gave important help to Yorkshire, as both counties were slowly drawn up to the educational level of the southern counties.[105] In this charity Professor Jordan notes the minor role of the clergy: bishops, Parker had explained to Cecil in 1563, were now too poor to endow schools.[106] It was London merchants who took the lead in watering their 'native barren soil'.[107] In Lancashire 28 per cent of the county's total charitable endowment in Professor Jordan's period came from London; 12 per cent in Yorkshire. 43 per cent of London gifts to Yorkshire were for schools, accounting for more than a quarter of the capital with which a system of education was created there in this period. There was a particularly heavy concentration of large benefactions in the years from 1600 to 1630.[108]

Yorkshire and Lancashire were perhaps more fortunate than their northern neighbours. A petition of 1631 from Sir Richard Graham says that the poor inhabitants of Cumberland could not say the Lord's Prayer: their utter ignorance of God led them to indulge in all manner of lewd vices. 'At the last gaol delivery those felons that were going to be hanged begged that their children might be brought up in the fear of God, the want whereof brought them to that untimely end.'[109] The mayor of Sunderland in a petition to Parliament of 1640 said: 'We are a people who have been destitute of a preaching ministry – yea, ever since any of us who are now breathing was born'; and he associated the ten or twelve adjoining parishes with the statement.[110] Even in 1657 a work whose object was to introduce the culture of the South to the barbarian North said of Northumberland, Durham, Westmorland and Cumberland: 'These counties, recorded for honour, have not been yet worthy to be branded with anything that could truly stick to them so much as the present want of studious gentlemen.'[111]

Professor Jordan's conclusions apply also at least to the Marches of Wales. In a block of five counties extending from Lancashire to Herefordshire forty-four grammar schools were established by Londoners in his period. 'These were regarded as counties of marginal opportunity . . . which must be brought level . . . with the whole of the nation.' 'In will after will eloquent reference is made to the needs, the shortcomings and the poverty of these "rude", "popish" or "ignorant" reaches of the realm.'[112] Lancashire, Yorkshire and Wales between them account for 14·5 per cent of all London charities in England and Wales outside London and Middlesex, 27·5 per cent of all London educational endowments and 17·7 per cent of all religious endowments.[113]

The cultural gap between North and South was widened, Professor Stone has suggested, by the lack of private schools in the outlying regions comparable to those run by clergymen in the South and East.[114] In 1622 John Brinsley dedicated a book to the President of 'the ignorant country of Wales', among other 'governors to whom the . . . care of schools for the inferior sort is assigned', including those of the Virginia and Somers Islands Companies. The 'inhumanity' of 'barbarous nations' sprang from 'their extreme ignorance of our holy God and of all true and good learning'. The secular authority should help to remedy this situation by promoting religion and education.[115] Sir Benjamin Rudyerd repeated the argument – and echoed Preston – when in the House of Commons in 1628 he said that 'there were some places in England which were scarce in Christendom, where God was little better known than amongst the Indians.' He defined these areas as 'divers parts of Wales' and 'the uttermost skirts of the North, where the prayers of the common people are more like spells and charms than devotions'.[116] 'We have Indians at home – Indians in Cornwall, Indians in Wales, Indians in Ireland', said 'an eminent person' two decades later when the conversion of the American Indians was under discussion.[117] John Dury had expressed scepticism about such schemes as early as 1636 when writing to Hartlib. 'Is not there more hope to do good to Christianity in building up the waste places here and hereabout in Europe than in laying new foundations without settled ground?'[118]

V

I have not hesitated to quote literary evidence and petitions on the condition of the dark corners. Such sources no doubt exaggerate; nevertheless, there is significant agreement between bishops and Puritans. Moreover, for our purposes, what men thought is almost as important as what actually existed; and Professor Jordan's evidence shows that many people, merchants and Puritans especially, took action to spread preaching, education and Bible-reading. It seemed to John Pym's friend Richard Sibbes, the great preacher of Gray's Inn, and to many like him, an urgent practical task 'in all the dark corners of the land to set up lights that may shine'.[119] The ignorance of these corners seemed an insult to God, a menace to the souls of men and a political danger in that survivals of popery and superstition there offered a basis for revolt or support for foreign invasion. Before the Civil War the task of enlightenment could be undertaken only piecemeal, by private enterprise. Penry's eloquent appeals for state action fell on deaf ears; and in the 1630s even private enterprise was actively discouraged.

The controversy over Sunday sports perhaps takes on a different appearance if we think of it as a struggle between the ethos of urban civilization and the ethos of the dark corners. It was the poorer Welsh members of the Shearmen's guild in Shrewsbury who rioted in 1588 to defend a maypole which the municipal authorities had prohibited.[120] The Welsh were often denounced for their horrible profanation of the Sabbath 'by using unlawful games even in the time of divine service, and that oftentimes in the very churchyard'.[121] Under Elizabeth the

Council in the Marches had been authorized to enforce the statutes against unlawful games. But in the seventeenth century the government threw its weight on the other side. James I's Declaration of Sports was issued in connection with events in Lancashire – a county where one of the King's Preachers found that 'profane pipers' kept people from church by piping during service, and were almost as great a hindrance as popish priests and gentry; a county, too, notorious for its witchcraft, which contemporaries attributed to Welsh influences as well as to lack of preaching.[122] Papists in Lancashire, said the Reverend John White, were the ringleaders in riotous, drunken and seditious assemblies, profaning the Sabbath by quarrels, brawls, stage plays, church ales 'and all heathenish customs . . . The people . . . in other parishes where the gospel hath been taught' were 'reduced to civility'.[123] The reissue of the Book of Sports in 1633 resulted from events in Somerset, like Lancashire an outlying but a clothing county in which the old and the new were in conflict. Walter Cradock and William Erbery were among the Welsh clergy ejected for refusing to read the Book.[124]

Meanwhile Laud suppressed the Feoffees for Impropriations and hounded down those Puritans who were most anxious to undertake itinerant preaching. In the diocese of Coventry and Lichfield there was a 'running lecturer' who conducted preaching tours 'to illuminate the dark corners of that diocese'. He was suppressed in 1633, Charles I commenting approvingly to his archbishop: 'If there be dark corners in that diocese, it were fit a true light should illuminate it; and not this that is false and uncertain.'[125] But no true light took its place: the corners remained dark. The reply to Charles was given by William Wroth of Llanfaches, Monmouthshire, 'the Apostle of Wales'. Called upon by his bishop to explain why he infringed the canons of the church by preaching out of doors, he replied: 'There are thousands of immortal souls around me, thronging to perdition; and should I not use all means to save them?' Wroth founded the first separatist church in Wales.[126]

Everywhere we meet the same official lack of enthusiasm, especially after the accession to power of Archbishops Laud and Neile. In Lancashire the King's Preachers lost their evangelical fervour. In the diocese of York not enough preachers were being licensed to keep monthly sermons going in each parish.[127] Even the practice of conniving at Puritans who were spreading the Gospel into obstinately papist regions was abandoned under Neile. One wonders, in retrospect, how far this tightening up was influenced by the infiltration of Scottish Presbyterians, and especially by the Scottish troubles after 1637.[128] In that year Stephen Marshall, continuing unofficially the activities of the Feoffees for Impropriations, passed £50 from Lady Barnardiston (daughter of a Lord Mayor of London) to Anthony Thomas, 'who lectureth in Wales . . . in the Welsh tongue, of which he [Marshall] says there is great necessity'. The ecclesiastical authorities did not see the necessity and Marshall was dismissed only after he had received 'many admonitions'.[129]

In December 1633 Henry Jacie, writing from his Yorkshire living to John Winthrop, recalled sadly the days when an archbishop of York (Grindal) had actually favoured preaching. 'We had need stand as much in the gap as we can,' he said, 'though we be not without some danger for it. Blessed be God, there are divers such in this cold climate of Yorkshire and Northumberland, people, ministers, gentlemen . . . Pray for us.'[130] Within a year Jacie had been deprived 'for not using the ceremonies'. In 1639, when he was minister of an underground Independent church in Southwark, his congregation sent him to help Wroth to gather a church at Llanfaches.[131]

Bacon, in a defence of the Council in Wales, had remarked that 'all who know those parts must acknowledge that the power of the gentry is the chief danger of the good subject there.'[132] Many of the leading families were Catholic.[133] The earls of Essex in Pembrokeshire were rare exceptions: their influence, together with the trading connection with Bristol, helped to keep the county on Parliament's side in the Civil War.[134] The Parliamentarian Middletons, descended from a Lord Mayor of London, were surrounded by royalists in Denbighshire, though the Puritans of Wrexham looked to them for support.[135] (Wrexham's Puritanism derived from the endowment of a preacher in 1603 by Sir William Meredith, who also had interests in the City.[136]) In Herefordshire Sir Robert Harley's 'planting of godly ministers, and then backing them with his authority, made religion famous in this little corner of the world'. But the Harleys were unpopular in their county.[137] In Northumberland in 1635 John Blakiston invited the Puritan William Morton to a lectureship in these 'bad and barren parts'.[138] Most often Puritanism was introduced into the dark corners from outside, as when Sir Francis Barrington of Essex presented Puritans to his living in the East Riding of Yorkshire in the hope of 'awakening those drowsy corners of the North'.[139] When there were insufficient livings to maintain preaching ministers, recourse was still had to the device of supporting itinerants, as the Earl of Huntingdon had done in the North under Elizabeth.[140] In the bishopric of Durham in the 1630s one Banks refused the offer of a chapelry at twenty marks a year, preferring, it was alleged, to 'go abroad seeking out knots of Puritans and be a preacher at large, receiving present pay.[141] In George Walker's *Exhortation for contributions to maintain preachers in Lancashire* (1641) strong emphasis was laid on the provision of sermons by itinerants.[142] A petition from the county of the same year attached more importance to a re-distribution of church revenues to the advantage of the less well-paid clergy.[143]

VI

The Civil War confirmed the worst forebodings of those who had agitated for the evangelization of the dark corners. The gentry and clergy of Wales were royalist almost to a man. Not one pamphlet sought to explain the Parliamentary standpoint in Welsh. There had been alarm about the possibility of a Spanish landing in Wales in 1587, 1597, 1598, 1599, 1603 and 1625; in 1641 a story that Welsh papists were being armed as a preliminary to a Spanish or other foreign invasion passed into English popular mythology.[144] The main strength of the Parliamentarian armies came from the South and East of England, especially from godly and self-respecting volunteers in the urban and Puritan areas. But there were pockets of support for Parliament in the North and West. 'In whatever considerable village there was a Puritan preacher,' says the historian of Puritanism in Lancashire, 'he found adherents to the parliamentarian cause among the yeomanry and traders of his neighbourhood.'[145] There was spontaneous support for Parliament in the Forest of Dean, where in 1631 Peter Simon had preached the equality of all mankind.[146]

Puritanism taught men to stand on their own feet: it established a higher duty to God which could override feudal loyalties.[147] At the beginning of the Civil War the earl of Derby raised three regiments of foot and three troops of horse among his tenants, dependants and friends in Lancashire; in the East Riding Sir Marmaduke Langdale, and in South Wales the Marquis of Worcester, raised regiments in the same way.[148] In such areas men who made some conscience of what they did were a minority. 'The common people addicted to the King's service,' wrote the contemporary historian of the siege of Gloucester, 'have come out of blind Wales and other dark corners of the land.'[149] Wales was 'the nursery of the King's infantry', the magazine whence 'all His Majesty's provisions of victuals and men do proceed'.[150] They also came from the North and Cornwall, with still blinder Ireland and the Highlands of Scotland as ultimate reserves: ''tis the dark and ignorant places of the earth', said a Worcerstershire divine, 'which are habitations of cruelty and rebellion.'[151]

If only the light of the gospel had shone more brightly in those regions, the King might never have managed to raise an army at all – as indeed had seemed unlikely before his tour of the North in the summer of 1642. It is hardly surprising that, once the war was over, and the power of great magnates like Derby, Langdale and Worcester was broken, the time seemed ripe to evangelize the royalist areas once for all.

VII

From the earliest days of its existence the Long Parliament showed great interest in the problem of the North and West. If MPs were ever in danger of forgetting it, preachers of Fast Sermons would remind them. Cornelius Burges, preaching on Queen Elizabeth's day, 1640, complained that the King's Preachers had not done their job in Lancashire.[152] Twelve days later John Gauden called for 'good and painful preachers in the dark and obscure places of our land' to batter down and demolish the adverse party.[153] Both of these were influential preachers. In December 1640 a committee was appointed to inquire into the shortage of preaching ministers, and to consider some way of removing those who were scandalous – what later became famous as the Committee for Scandalous Ministers. It included Sir Robert Harley, long a patron of Puritans in Herefordshire, and all the MPs for Wales, Northumberland, Cumberland, Lancashire – the only areas so heavily represented.[154] Next year the Committee on Preaching Ministers authorized Walter Cradock and other ministers to preach in Wales.[155]

Another influential divine, Edmund Calamy, told the Commons in December 1641, that 'those places which are rudest and most ignorant, . . . and where least preaching hath been, are the greatest enemies to reformation'. He called for the setting up of a preaching ministry thoughout the kingdom, 'that the light of the Gospel of Jesus Christ may shine in the dark corners of the land' – with, he added prudently, a competent maintenance for such ministers.[156] The demand was repeated by Thomas Goodwin, Obadiah Sedgwick and Thomas Hill, the latter calling for itinerant preachers 'to enlighten the dark countries'.[157] After that I can only list references to the subject by preachers of Fast Sermons. Andrew Perne and Francis Cheynell in 1643: 'is there not a Babylon in the North and another in the West?' the latter asked.[158] In 1644 John Greene and Henry Hall ('prodigious ignorance, next to barbarism', like those 'that live in the wild deserts of America'), Gaspar Hickes (who put in a special plea for the dark places in his own county of Cornwall), Henry Scudder and Thomas Thorowgood.[159]

The preachers were echoed by other propagandists – Lord Brooke ('scarce any ministers in whole shires, as Cumberland, Westmorland, Northumberland and especially Wales'), John Milton and George Walker in 1641.[160] In 1642 Nehemiah Wharton, after hearing Obadiah Sedgwick preach, added his own plea from Hereford for the sending of 'some faithful and painful minister'.[161] John Geree in 1641 and Hugh Peter in 1646 looked back to 'that famous, ancient, glorious work of buying in impropriations, by which work 40 or 50 preachers were maintained in the dark parts of the kingdom', and called for a resumption of its activities.[162] Freeholders in Yorkshire and the north parts of the kingdom petitioned in 1641 for the establishment of universities in Manchester and York. 'We have been looked upon as rude and almost barbarous people'; it was essential that 'a learned and painful ministry' be established in order that the North may not 'be instruments of any irreligious and unreasonable design for the overthrow of religion and liberty'.[163]

In March 1644 the Westminster Assembly appointed a committee to select a suitable person to translate its Directory into Welsh.[164] Three months later the Commons appointed a Committee to provide ministers able to preach in Welsh, for the Parliamentary armies as they advanced into Wales.[165] Sir Thomas Middleton – son of the ex-Lord Mayor of London who had financed the translation of the Bible into Welsh in 1630 – who appropriately commanded the army which conquered North Wales, was empowered to replace scandalous ministers by religious and learned men.[166] An ordinance of 28 March 1646 provided for the maintenance of preaching ministers in Herefordshire.[167]

Parliamentarians had always claimed that one of the objects of invading Wales was 'to plant the Gospel among the Welshmen'. Large numbers of Welshmen captured at Naseby were exposed to a sermon preached in Welsh by Walter Cradock. Five hundred of them were persuaded to take the Covenant and volunteer for service in Ireland. After the war was over, Morgan Llwyd, Ambrose Mostyn and Vavasor Powell were appointed itinerant ministers for North Wales, an appointment regularized in June 1648. They received £100 a year each.[168] In August 1645 the House of Commons sent Henry Walter, Walter Cradock and Richard Symonds to South Wales to preach 'itinerantly' in Welsh, also at £100 a year each, to be found from the revenues of the bishops, deans and chapters of Llandaff and St David's.[169] Preachers in South Wales and Monmouthshire also received money from the sequestrated estates of the catholic Marquis of Worcester.[170]

In 1644–5 there had been a revulsion of feeling against the royal forces in Wales and its Marches: armies of clubmen helped the Parliamentarian generals to finish off the war, as they did in Devon and Somerset.[171] This reinforced feelings among supporters of Parliament that the common people of Wales were 'but a seduced ignorant people': the words are attributed to Oliver Cromwell.[172] 'At length the moles have eyes,' wrote *Mercurius Britanicus*. In August 1645 the House of

Commons ordered that Parliament's case should be explained to the people of South Wales. Parliament was also confident that the people of North Wales, although not so active in rejecting the royalists, could be won over by propaganda. It ordered a declaration to be drafted 'to inform them aright of the Parliament'.[173] *The Parliament explained to Wales* was published in 1646 by John Lewis, who claimed to be 'the first of my country that did publish anything in order to the Parliament'. His book was dedicated to Sir Robert Harley, Sir Thomas Middleton and John Glynn, all MPs. Since Lewis was later one of the Commissioners for the Propagation of the Gospel in Wales, his book neatly links the Propagators with pre-1640 attempts to spread light in the dark corners of Wales.[174]

So by the end of the Civil War it was being assumed, as a correspondent with the army besieging Carnarvon put it, that Parliament 'will take care to send a powerful ministry so soon as North Wales is totally reduced', since 'the country towns hereabouts have been quite without all manner of preaching almost.'[175] 'Doubtless we are deep enough in their [the Parliament's] thoughts,' John Lewis agreed; 'and . . . they do mind our happiness more than we do ourselves. The only compendious way to make us happy is to have the Gospel come amongst us . . . It will presently purge church and state.'[176] 'Churches . . . will be your strongest castles, if you furnish them well with ministers', Henry Palmer told the House of Commons in September 1646, after describing counties, especially northward, 'that have been for many generations . . . a howling wilderness', with 'scarce a sermon preached among them in many miles compass, ever since the reformation'. This 'kept them in a way of rebellion still, and of late they have proved rebellious against you'. The House must 'send spiritual commanders among them', with a large maintenance.[177] By 1645 a new note creeps into the Fast Sermons, stressing the scarcity of ministers in the North and West, which can be met only by better maintenance, or by the use of itinerants, by greater liberty of preaching to those who scruple Presbyterian ordination, and by reform of the universities.[178] Serious attempts were already being made to provide ministers for Northumberland and Durham.[179] Sir John Bourchier in April 1647 asked Fairfax 'to stretch out the utmost of your power that the Gospel may flourish' among the 'ignorant and sottish people' in 'this your blind county' of Yorkshire.[180] From 1646 onwards petitions flowed in to the London classes asking for ministers to be sent to the former royalist areas of Wales and the North, over which God had now cleared up 'those misty clouds of affliction and oppression'.[181] They were answered by petitions from London citizens on behalf of the propagation of the gospel, and continuing references to the subject in Fast Sermons.[182]

The time seemed ripe; and the political as well as spiritual advantages of evangelizing the dark corners were clear. 'The people are desperately ignorant and profane abroad; and from profane priests and ignorant people, you know the other party have fomented this war, and may begin it again, if the Word prevent not the sword.' So Hugh Peter told Parliament, the Lord Mayor and Aldermen of London and the Assembly of Divines in 1646, reminding them that he had formerly been an active associate of the Feoffees for Impropriations.[183] He had found the Marches of Wales 'ripe for the Gospel'.[184] John Owen, himself of Welsh origin, made the point to the Commons in the same year: 'Doth not Wales cry, and the North cry, yea and the West cry, "Come and help us. We are yet in a worse bondage than any by your means we have been delivered from. If you leave us thus, all your protection will but yield us a more free and jovial passage to the chamber of death".'[185] Cradock hammered the argument home in a sermon preached before the Commons in July:

> 'And what if you should spend one single thought upon poor contemptible Wales? It's little indeed and as little respected, yet time was the enemy made no small use and advantage of it ... Is it not a sad case that in thirteen counties there should not be above thirteen conscientious ministers who in these times expressed themselves firmly and constantly faithful to the Parliament, and formerly preached profitably in the Welsh language twice every Lord's Day?'[186]

(We note in passing Cradock's simple assumption that regular preachers would of course be constantly faithful to Parliament.) In *The Parliament explained to Wales* John Lewis complained of 'that swarm of blind superstitious ceremonies that are among us, passing under the name of old harmless customs' – worship of saints, pilgrimage to wells, superstitious veneration of chapels. It 'is still to this day undispelled, and hinders us from the primitive light of the Gospel'.[187] The task of enlightening Wales was therefore a dual one: darkness had to be dispelled as well as truth preached.

For this preaching *in Welsh* was essential. But there were grave obstacles. Livings in Wales were desperately poor. Parliament did much to end pluralism, to divert the revenues of sinecures to preachers, to augment stipends and to find Welsh preachers. The practice of reducing royalists' composition fines on condition that impropriated tithes were made over to the minister of the parish greatly increased the maintenance available for many ministers, especially in the North and West.[188] But the Army was a competitor for sequestrated impropriations: some time before 1650 three royalists' livings in Pembrokeshire were assigned to Colonel Horton's brigade.[189] Finance was crucial to the provision of preaching: only after Pride's Purge were dean and chapter lands sold and £20,000 a year made available for this purpose.[190] But the nature of the preachers was also at issue: so long as it was assumed that they must be ordained ministers, preferably university men, the supply fell short of the presumed demand. In 1646 William Erbery alleged that so far from orthodox preaching being extended into the North and West, Puritan ministers from those areas 'are gone to fat parsonages from whence malignants have been thrown out'. 'These old waste places' would have to be evangelized not by 'those who call themselves ministers' but by 'those whom the people shall call ministers' – i.e. by unordained itinerants. His charge is confirmed by *The Scottish Dove* in 1645; his solution foreshadowed controversies which were to split the radicals.[191]

Hugh Peter had a simple and traditional solution, which he put forward on every occasion: itinerant preachers. These, he thought, should be established by the state in all parts of the kingdom, especially in the dark places. 'What you have gotten by the sword must be maintained by the Word.' The Westminster Assembly, by concentrating on creating presbyteries in London, was tackling the problem from the wrong end, he thought.[192] What Britain most needed was 'justice, charity and *industry*,[193] the only upholders of that flourishing neighbour-

nation, the Netherlands'. A preaching ministry was the way to
attain all these desirable objectives. 'How long therefore shall
I entreat some three or four itinerary ministers in a county?
. . . How easily might the land be (in some measure) reduced to
God and their own civil interests, if provision was laid in of
this kind?' A college should be set aside, at Oxford perhaps, to
train 'godly youths out of shops' to act as travelling preachers.
A committee should be set up to approve preachers who
'cannot answer the narrow examination of an Assembly', even
though 'they should fall short of arts and tongues'.[194] Itinerants
were advocated by the Fifth Monarchist *Certain Queries* of 1649,
and by *Mercurius Politicus* in November 1650. Itinerants in the
North, the latter said, 'would do as much good service to the
state as a regiment of soldiers in a shire'.[195]

A year later Peter proposed that tithes should be pooled, and
was more specific about the central examining committee
which he had in mind. No doubt recalling the Feoffees, he said
it should consist of 'godly men, ministers, gentlemen and
others', and should test would-be itinerants, of whom two or
three should be sent to every county.[196] In 1651 he proposed that
each university should maintain at the public charge 'able, fit,
godly and learned men', who would travel through the country
settling all religious disputes and disposing of errors.[197] Peter
was to be an enthusiastic supporter of the Propagators of the
Gospel in Wales, and actively assisted them in Pembrokeshire.[198]
He thus forms another link between the Propagators and the
pre-1640 attempts to evangelize the dark corners.

In fact missionary enterprise started in Wales and the North
as soon as the war was over: it rapidly got out of the control of
Parliament and the Assembly of Divines. The New Model
Army spread radical religion into the areas it occupied.
'Having marched up and down the kingdom, to do the work
of God and the state,' William Dell said in 1646, 'we have met
with many Christians who have much Gospel-light . . . in such
places where there hath been no Gospel-ministry.'[199] 'Emissaries out of the sectarian churches,' Thomas Edwards noted
in the same year, 'are sent to infect and poison . . . Yorkshire
and those northern parts, . . . Bristol and Wales.'[200] In many
areas they were welcomed by previously existing underground
congregations like those described by Dell. 'In some parts

where the Gospel came,' declared Vavasor Powell, 'they far and near pressed to hear it, night and day.'[201] Walter Cradock, in a sermon preached in 1648, said:

'I have observed and seen, in the mountains of Wales, the most glorious work that I ever saw in England, unless it were in London. The Gospel is run over the mountains, between Brecknockshire and Monmouthshire, as the fire in the thatch. And who should do this? They have no ministers; but some of the wisest say that there are about 800 godly people there, and they go from one to another . . . Shall we rail at such, and say they are tub-preachers, and they were never at the university?'[202]

Peter and Cradock posed the question that Wales and the North were setting. 'Tarrying for the universities' in the decades before 1640 had left the problem of preaching in Wales virtually untouched. Even the generous augmentations of the forties and fifties did not furnish many livings rich enough to attract graduates. In any case there were not enough Welsh-speaking graduates. One of the ministers ejected by the Propagators admitted in 1650 that scarcely one in fifteen of his clerical contemporaries could read and write Welsh.[203] So there was a case for pooling parochial funds in state-controlled livings, and for employing non-graduate Welsh speakers – if anything was to be done to evangelize Wales at all. Preaching the Gospel in the dark corners was a tough job, which called for many enthusiastic participants. But enthusiasm was what the Parliamentary Presbyterians and the Westminster Assembly most dreaded, since it was most obviously to be found among the sectaries and in the New Model Army. 'Godly youths out of shops' were not to everybody's liking: yet how else could preaching ministers in sufficient numbers be provided? 'Shall we rail at such, and say they are tub-preachers, and they were never at the university?' The Presbyterians, like the bishops before them, inclined more and more to shelve the problem. Yet its urgency was underlined by the second Civil War, when the royalist forces were based on Wales and Scotland. The problem was tackled only after Pride's Purge.

In 1650 'the Parliament of England, taking into serious consideration the great duty and trust that lies on them to use all lawful ways and means for the propagation of the Gospel of Jesus Christ in this Commonwealth', set up Commissioners for the Propagation of the Gospel in Wales and in the four northern counties. This was an attempt to carry out the policy which three generations of earnest Puritans had dreamed of, prayed for and worked for.[204]

By these acts Parliament attempted to do for preaching in the dark corners what the generals had done for the Army in 1647: to take over and canalize a rank-and-file movement which they could not supress and with whose objects (if not with whose methods) they to some extent sympathized. Even the Petition of the Six Counties of South Wales, a fierce attack on the activities of the Propagators, agreed that the Act for the Propagation of the Gospel 'filled all the inhabitants of Wales with joy and gladness'.[205]

VIII

On 22 February 1650, the Act for the Propagation of the Gospel in Wales was passed, 'according to the plan laid down by Hugh Peter'.[206] Since the livings at Parliament's disposal – church and crown livings, and sequestrated livings of royalists – could not all be filled with learned and Welsh-speaking ministers, their revenues were to be pooled. In each county a group of itinerant ministers was set up, at £100 a year each, with the further inducement of a pension of £30 a year for widows. In addition the use in their own neighbourhood of gifted lay preachers was authorized; these received £17–24 a year. There were seventy-one commissioners, all laymen, including significantly few representatives of the old ruling families but most of the local Parliamentary officials. But the commissioners were by no means a revolutionary body. A majority had been royalists and churchmen before 1646, and conformed after 1660. Two were executed as regicides, but Colonel Philip Jones, the leading Welshman on the commission, cooperated in bringing about the restoration, retained the lands he had acquired during the interregnum, and was High Sheriff of Glamorgan in 1671.[207] The commissioners had power to examine and where necessary eject the incumbents of Welsh livings, for delinquency, scandal, malignancy or non-residence:

pluralists had to opt for one of their livings. There were ejected 278 ministers in all, some of them because they could not preach in Welsh.[208] Twenty-five ministers (six of them itinerants) were named as approvers or triers of ministers and schoolmasters.

Even more significant were the political powers entrusted to the commissioners, which strongly recall those previously wielded by the Councils in Wales and the North. So do the reasons given for granting these powers. 'The remoteness of the said counties from the courts of justice at Westminster occasioneth many acts of high misdemeanour, oppression and injury to be committed there, which often times escape unpunished.' The commissioners were therefore authorized to hear complaints of such offences, to call the parties before them, and 'with the consent of both parties . . . to hear and determine the same'. This was particularly designed for the protection of 'persons well-affected to the Parliament', who could not afford to travel to London to seek redress. The only appeal from the commissioners lay in religious matters to Parliament's Committee for Plundered Ministers, in civil matters to its Committee of Indemnity.

For three years the Committee for the Propagation of the Gospel remained 'the real government of Wales',[209] which enjoyed complete independence in religious matters. But the independence was relative, since a majority of the commissioners, headed by Major-General Harrison, commanding the army in South Wales, were English.[210] The chief Welsh Propagators 'were men who, through a forced sojourn in England' during the war 'had come into contact with the fertile thought of a new liberty', rather as Penry had done in his day.[211] Dr Richards speaks, perhaps a trifle strongly, of 'the peculiarly English atmosphere of the Puritan conquest of Wales, with the hordes of English officials who infested the country'. 'A jury will do no good in that county [Cardiganshire],' said Colonel Philip Jones in June 1651, 'where little of the Gospel hath yet been.' So he advocated a court martial.[212] The propagation of the Gospel meant also the extension of English law, order and civilization. Whether we give the main credit to the Propagators or not, after their régime Wales and the North gave no more political trouble: when in 1651 Charles II swung westwards to Worcester, no recruits rallied from the nursery of his father's infantry. Wales and the North were finally integrated during the interregnum into the civilization which was extending from London over the whole country.

'Hath any generation since the Apostles' days had such powerful preachers and plenty of preaching as this generation?' asked Vavasor Powell.[213] Powell himself – the 'metropolitan of the itinerants' – often preached in two or three places a day, especially at 'fairs, markets or any great concourse of peoples'.[214] Even so some areas were left uncovered. For the Commission lasted only three years. In August 1652 the Declaration of the Army to Lieutenant-General Cromwell had put propagation of the Gospel first in its demands.[215] Cromwell must have favoured bills for continuing the authority of the Propagators, despite allegations that Harrison was using the Commission to enlist four thousand men for his own purposes. One of these bills was rejected on 1 April 1653, and an order was made for replacing the twenty-five approvers or triers by more 'moderate' men.[216] This was one of the reasons for the dissolution of the Rump on 20 April. The dissolution was welcomed by some at least of the commissioners; Vavasor Powell and his party, Thurloe said three years later, 'were the occasion of destroying the Rump'.[217] As with the events of Thermidor, the fall of the Rump was brought about by a temporary coalition of right and left. On 25 April, immediately after the dissolution, Cromwell urged the Welsh commissioners to continue their work.[218]

'God did kindle a seed there indeed hardly to be paralleled since the primitive times,' Cromwell said of Wales under the Propagators. He was speaking to the Barebones Assembly, and he continued:

> 'What discountenance that business of the poor people of God had (who had men watching over them like so many wolves ready to catch the lamb as soon as it was brought into the world), how signally they [the Rump] trod that business under foot, to the discountenancing of the honest people and the countenancing of the malignant party . . . The state of that business of Wales [seemed to Cromwell] as plain a trial of their [the Rumpers'] spirits as anything.'[219]

When we try to assess the achievements of the Propagators

we must take into account not only the ecstasies of Vavasor Powell and Oliver Cromwell but also reports like that accepted by the sober lawyer Whitelocke, that in September 1652 'there were 150 good preachers in the thirteen Welsh counties; most of them preached three or four times a week. In every market town there was placed one schoolmaster, and in most great towns two schoolmasters, able, learned and university men.'[220] Among the successes of the men who ran the Propagation, we must count the dissemination of the Bible in Welsh. In seven years from 1647 to 1654 three editions of the New Testament (over three thousand copies) and one edition of the Bible in Welsh (up to six thousand copies) were distributed.[221]

The Committees for the Propagation of the Gospel then were the culmination of two or three generations of Puritan aspiration and effort. This tends to be forgotten by those who dismiss the Welsh Propagators as 'a knot of Tammany demagogues'.[222] Inevitably, the operation which they had to perform was political as well as religious: the areas concerned were those which had needed to be governed by the special processes of the Council in Wales. The noted preacher Rice Williams of Newport commanded a party of soldiers which searched Walter Powell's house in Monmouthshire for arms in January 1650.[223] The Propagators' task was doubly difficult in view of hostility from London as well as from Wales. Both the Propagators and frightened conservatives looked on the Welsh campaign as a model which could be extended to other regions: from June 1650 to its dissolution the Rump was continually discussing 'the advance of the Gospel in all parts of this Commonwealth'.[224] The Propagators were feared less because of their methods of overcoming tough resistance in a tough area than because it was feared that those methods might be extended to the rest of Britain.[225]

The case against the Propagators has frequently been disproved,[226] yet it goes on being repeated. It is based largely on the evidence of Alexander Griffith, a clergyman who had the misfortune to be deprived of two livings (for immorality) by the bishops before 1640, and to be ejected by the Propagators on the same grounds, though in 1650 the charge of drunkenness was added.[227] His is not the most reliable testimony. The Propagators handled large sums of money, and in accordance with seventeenth-century custom accusations of corruption were laid against them. But peculation was never proved, despite repeated attempts. Some of the Commissioners – e.g. Colonel Philip Jones – seem to have thrived during their period of office. But at least one – Major John Sadler – was in such abject poverty in October 1659 that he was granted a pension of £8 a year by the JPs. It ceased of course at the Restoration.[228] In August 1654 Cromwell set up commissioners 'for taking an account of the moneys received' by the Welsh Propagators, and their accounts were allowed and passed a year later. Nevertheless the House of Commons in October 1656 created a commission of its own to examine the disposal of moneys by the Propagators of Wales and the four northern counties. The matter was raised again in the Commons in February 1659.[229] A very strict inquiry held after the Restoration by the commissioners' fiercest enemies could produce no scandals.[230] Even Anthony Wood only says that Vavasor Powell and the agents of the Propagation 'had the disposal of above £40,000 *per annum*', leaving his readers to draw conclusions.[231]

To the accusations of peculation social sneers were added, and there is more truth in them. After 1649 control of local affairs, in Wales as elsewhere, passed to more extreme Puritans, yeomen and tradesmen who held the lower commissioned ranks in the Army.[232] The traditional ruling gentry either withdrew or were removed (in so far as they had not already been extruded as royalists). 'Wales during the Propagation régime was governed by a military middle class.'[233] 'The gentry and all the considerable persons of Wales [are] dejected and oppressed,' said a pamphlet of 1652.[234] Alexander Griffith was horrified at oppression when it was directed against 'a gentleman of good estate and quality, and some time a Justice of Peace'.[235] 'By means of Harrison,' a letter from Glamorgan said in 1653, 'all the honestest, ablest and most understanding gentry are put out of commission.'[236]

But the most serious allegations were those affecting the itinerants. Clement Walker said in 1649:

'These wandering apostles are to preach anti-monarchical seditious doctrine to the people (suitable to that they call the present government) to raise the rascal multitude and schismatical rabble against all men of best quality in the kingdom, to draw them into associations and combinations with one another in every county and with the army, against all lords, gentry, ministers, lawyers, rich and peaceable men, and all that are lovers of the old laws and government, for the better rooting of them out.'[237]

That was the authentic note of alarm felt by conservatives, and set the tone for the stories which were repeated so frequently later.

Some of the itinerants could not read or understand English.[238] Their enemies complained of men who were 'continually thundering out in the ancient British tongue'.[239] There were never enough preachers, and some of them were enthusiastic young craftsmen and ex-soldiers who preached in English. The churches in Wales, the future Earl of Shaftesbury told Parliament in 1654, were all unsupplied with ministers except a few 'grocers or such persons' put in by the Propagators.[240] Vavasor Powell admitted to one weaver, one smith, two or three officers. In the mouths of opponents this became the unqualified generalization: 'soldiers and unordained tradesmen'.[241] The grand jury of Montgomeryshire – i.e. the gentry of the county – in April 1652 dismissed the itinerants *en bloc* as 'a few illiterate poor traders'.[242] Nevertheless, the Barebones Parliament extended the itinerant system to Herefordshire, also plagued by shortage of ministers.[243] George Griffith, Post-Restoration Bishop of St Asaph, indulged in what seem today rather unpleasant sneers at Powell's weakness in Latin and his ignorance of university rules for disputation. When Griffith and Powell debated in 1652, 'the better sort' wanted them to speak in Latin, the majority demanded English. Griffith thought the object of this was to arraign him 'before an ignorant multitude'.[244]

We can see the other side of this medal in Morgan Llwyd's denunciation of woe to the 'evil gentry, licking the sweat of the poor, making your tenants groan'. His attack was extended to lawyers, priests, beggars and ignorant labourers.[245] William Erbery defended the poor against the rich;[246] Vavasor Powell attacked lawyers and spoke up for the people against the government.[247] The 'richer sort' of his followers were soon to disavow his Fifth-Monarchist views.[248] Another of the approvers was denounced in 1659 as 'a Leveller', anxious to imitate John of Leyden.[249] Such accusations of social revolution must be related to the mounting social conservatism of the years after 1653.

We should be especially wary when reading post-Restoration accounts like that by Bishop Lucy of St David's, who alleged that churches in Wales 'have had no divine duty' for years together.[250] In many churches in this diocese, its bishop told Laud in 1634, the chancels had been pulled down or allowed to fall, 'leaving them so open and cold, as that the people in those mountainous parts must endure a great deal of hardness'.[251] But the itinerants' habit of preaching in the open air sprang not only from the deplorable state into which the churches had fallen. It was also a matter of deliberate policy, to counteract the Welsh superstitious regard for church buildings.[252] Whether it was successful or not is another question. In 1652 John Taylor the Water-Poet observed that 'in many . . . parishes in Wales . . . they have neither service, prayer, sermon, minister or preacher, nor church door opened at all, so that people do exercise and edify in the churchyard at the lawful and laudable games of trap, cat, stool ball, rackets, etc., on Sundays.'[253]

In the North the Commissioners for Propagation were responsible only for Cumberland, Westmorland, Northumberland and Durham. Yorkshire and Lancashire were excluded from their purview, presumably because urban-Puritan bases already existed there: all that was needed was freedom of propaganda. In Cumberland and Westmorland, on the other hand, 'the whole gentry are malignants, delinquents, papists, popish or base temporizers', declared John Musgrave in 1650 – a not entirely reliable witness. He estimated the number of gentlemen in the two counties who 'have proved cordial to the state' at less than ten.[254] Parliament took over payment of the four King's Preachers, and augmented their stipends: the augmentation lapsed in 1660.[255] There were similar augmentations to other stipends.[256] There was also much church-building, mostly at government expense, in Lancashire, Yorkshire and Northumberland.[257] The Commissioners encouraged preachers to come to the North, inserting one into the Mercers' lectureship at Hexham.[258] The first well-considered plan for improving and effectively supporting the parochial institutions of Yorkshire, we are told, was that framed by the Commissioners, whose recommendations were carried out gradually and piecemeal during the 150 years after the Restoration.[259] In Durham itinerants continued to function: Durham College provided stipends for two of them.[260]

To set against the hostile verdicts of conservatives we may cite the Congregational churches in the North, who in October 1653 said that the Committee for the Propagation of the Gospel had 'proved the greatest blessing that ever the North had'. 'Had not their commissions so soon expired, all places might have been well provided for ere now.'[261] Similar bodies were contemplated for other outlying areas. A committee for the propagation of the Gospel in Cornwall was proposed in 1650.[262] Prodded by John Owen, the Rump in March 1649 had passed an Act for the Better Advancement of the Gospel in Ireland – a year before it set up the Commissions for Wales and the North. By this Act 300,000 acres of former church lands were reserved for the support of a preaching ministry. The Commissioners sent into Scotland in December 1651 were instructed 'to endeavour to promote the propagation of the Gospel there, and the power of true religion and holiness', with a competent maintenance for ministers. In April 1658, £1,200 was made available for planting the Gospel in the Highlands, as the best way to plant civility there.[263] John Tillinghast looked even further afield, envisaging the sending of itinerant missionaries to India and Turkey as well as to the equally dark areas of Northumberland or Cumberland.[264]

What remains after we have sifted and discounted the accusations against the Propagators is the disunity among supporters of Parliament which their régime expressed and continued. The Leveller dream of political and judicial de-centralization could have no place in the thoughts of the Propagators, operating from on top and dependent on support from London. The local backing that they won necessarily remained restricted. On the other hand, by the years 1650–3 the idea of itinerants roused alarm in the minds of more conservative supporters of Parliament. The Ranter Lawrence Clarkson, who proclaimed the godliness of adultery, was an itinerant. The Ranter Abiezer Coppe, who announced that sin and transgression were finished, was an itinerant. William Franklin, the familist rope-maker who claimed to be the Messiah, was an itinerant. George Fox, who in these years was sweeping the North in a whirlwind campaign, was an itinerant. James Nayler, who in 1656 was to rouse a national scandal by re-enacting at Bristol Christ's entry into Jerusalem, was an itinerant. The antinomian and subversive views of such lower-class preachers reproduced on a much larger scale the heresies of the itinerant King's Preacher in Lancashire in James I's reign, and of Peter Simon in the Forest of Dean under Charles I.[265] These had been isolated individuals, easily identified and dealt with. But by the early 1650s it looked more like a mass movement.

The radical groups in the North and West established contact with London. In 1649 emissaries were sent from Glamorgan to the London Baptist Society, in the hope that labourers would be sent 'into those dark corners of the land'.[266] Many of the London gathered churches, Baptists and Independents alike, in fact sent missionaries to Wales and the North.[267] The Quaker Children of the Light first flourished in the dark corners of Yorkshire, Cumberland and Westmorland which even the Propagators missed. From 1654 onwards, as conservatism triumphed in the South and East, itinerant Quakers – yeomen, craftsmen, ex-soldiers, 'the dregs of the common people', Ephraim Pagitt called them in 1654[268] – alarmed respectable opinion by organizing missionary tours to evangelize southern England, Cornwall and Wales. In 1656 Richard Davies was told of 'a sort of people come up in the North, called Quakers'; two years later a Quaker came to settle in Davies's 'dark corner of North Wales'.[269] Some of the Welsh itinerants joined the new movement.[270] Merionethshire, of which John Jones had asked in 1651, 'Is that county denied the tender of Gospel mercies?', later contributed more to the ranks of Quakerism, in relation to its population, than any other Welsh county.[271] The Quaker Edward Burrough in 1655 exulted in this demonstration of the victory of the Gospel in the North: 'and thou, O North of England, who art counted as desolate and barren, and reckoned the least of the nations, yet out of thee did the branch spring and the stem arise which

gives light unto all the regions round about.'[272] Parliamentary
debates in 1656 show that the respectable classes reacted very
differently to a movement which seemed to reproduce some of
the least desirable ideas of Levellers, Ranters and Welsh
itinerants. 'Those that come out of the North are the greatest
pests of the nation', said Samuel Highland; 'the Diggers came
thence.'[273]

A moderate man like John Lewis thought in 1656 that too
much emphasis had been laid on preaching, to the exclusion of
other ordinances; and perhaps the attack (of which he originally approved) on traditional customs, festivals and set prayers
had been too savage.[274] John Owen in the same year deplored
'the unhappiness of almost all men running into extremes',
which had 'disadvantaged the advancement of the Gospel', so
that the whole work was almost cast to the ground.[275] Erbery
also believed that there had been too much discussion, which
had led to divisions and confusion among a people unaccust-
omed to it.[276] Erbery even joined in the social sneers, when he
referred to 'such itinerants, who make a trade of teaching: only
what formerly he sold in a shop, is now set to sale in a pulpit'.[277]
But Erbery's criticisms came from the left, not from the right.
What outraged him was the Propagators' acceptance of payment from tithes, after so many of them had denounced
hireling ministers before 1650. He welcomed rather 'the
whirlwind from the North', where 'John's spirit' was rising
with the Quakers in the North of England and in North
Wales.[278] Itinerant ministers were put forward as an alternative
to the tithe system by William Sprigge, Fellow of Durham
College, in 1659.[279]

This brings to the surface a dilemma which had long lurked
in the background of radical Puritan thought – their attitude to
the state and their willingness to use Beelzebub for the purpose
of casting out devils. Penry in 1587 had appealed to the secular
power against the bishops, and in 1593 he made a frank attempt
to bribe the Earl of Essex by offering him the plunder of the
Church.[280] But those were dark days. In the intoxication of the
early fifties, 'those halcyon days of prosperity, liberty and
peace',[281] the millennium seemed too near at hand for such
compromises to be necessary. As the case of Erbery shows,
disestablishmentarianism was already becoming an ideology

41

among Welsh radicals. Not everybody was as satisfied as Hugh Peter with a situation in which 'the state pays them, and thus they have a dependence upon the state'.[282] Too many of the professors showed spiritual pride and worldly-mindedness, said John Miles in 1656, 'while they associated themselves with the rich and honourable, despising the poor'.[283] Even Vavasor Powell was horrified at the way in which some of his allies enriched themselves. In 1654 he 'told the sword-men . . . that the spirit of God was departed from them; that heretofore they had been precious and excellent men, but that their parks and new houses and gallant wives had choked them up.'[284]

So the enthusiasts who had taken up the task of preaching fell out among themselves. But they could not afford disunity. Beelzebub was still necessary. The Commissioners were trying to do too much too quickly, perhaps aware that their time was short. The attempt to impose English standards aroused hostility, and did not last long enough. As soon as the preachers ceased to itinerate we hear again the familiar complaints: 'Here are very few good ministers and schoolmasters'; for 'want of able preachers . . . these people will some of them become heathens', something which Major-General Berry 'knew not how to remedy'.[285] There was still 'a great famine of the Word' in Wales in 1658.[286] Oliver Cromwell told a committee of Parliament that the garrison at Hereford must be kept up because Wales 'for religion and other things [was] not so well qualified as would be desired'.[287]

The correspondence of John Jones shows with great clarity the dilemma of the godly minority who hoped to Christianize Britain through army rule – a dilemma which existed in its most extreme form in Wales. No amount of electoral qualifications, Jones thought, would 'persuade a people sensible of their present burdens, and not of the reasons and necessity of them, to choose those persons that laid the burdens on them ... What interest in England is like to carry the universal vote?' he asked. 'If the hearts of the people be generally for the present government and governors, what need armies and garrisons to be kept on foot?' This appalling frankness led him to a conclusion similar to Cromwell's 'What's for their good, not what pleases them', though the paths of the two men were soon to diverge. 'I had rather do a people good though against their wills', Jones continued, 'than please them in show only . . . Let the Commonwealth have some time to take root in the interests of men.'[288] It is the recurring dilemma of revolutionary minorities, stated by Rousseau in the doctrine that it may be necessary to force men to be free. The dilemma was especially painful for a Welsh Puritan, acutely conscious that his party was a tiny minority, dependent on English support. If God's cause was to be forwarded at all, it *must* be against the wishes of the majority of the population.

In the South and East of England the nomination of delegates to the Barebones Assembly, some from the Independent churches, could be defended as no less democratic than the old franchise: it merely brought a different minority to Westminster. But this could not be argued for Wales. Even after 1660 Vavasor Powell himself claimed only a score or so of gathered churches in Wales.[289] So it is hardly surprising that Harrison in London and Jones in Ireland should discuss who were suitable nominees 'to serve on behalf of the saints in North Wales'.[290] Saints were so few that they must have almost selected themselves. It is difficult to see anything sinister in this correspondence.

Most of all perhaps we should emphasize the educational activities of the Commissioners. Sixty or more new schools were started in market towns in Wales, free, and some at least of them open to both sexes: the first provision for education ever made by the state in Great Britain. In Northumberland and Durham fifty-eight towns received provision for education.[291] There was also a considerable expansion of schools in Yorkshire, Lancashire and Cheshire.[292] When we recall the virtual exclusion of the lower classes from grammar schools founded under the Tudors and Stuarts – an exclusion contrary to the intentions of the founders – we get some idea of the revolutionary nature of the Commonwealth's educational innovations. Before 1640 schools had been subject to strict ideological control by the hierarchy; but there is no evidence of interference with existing schools by the Propagators, or of ejection of schoolmasters.[293]

Hugh Peter proposed that universities to train godly ministers should be set up in Cornwall, Wales and Yorkshire, the three darkest corners of the land. William Dell echoed the call.[294]

There were local demands for a university from Yorkshire, Lancashire and Wales. John Lewis supported the idea of a college or two in Wales, subordinate to Oxford and Cambridge.[295] It was no doubt under Peter's influence that Cromwell wrote to the Speaker in March 1650 advocating 'a college for all the sciences and literature' at Durham, which 'may much conduce to the promotion of learning and piety in those poor, rude and ignorant parts'.[296] But when the decision was finally taken to establish a university at Durham, the Propagators had gone, and 'learning and piety' were not the only considerations. Durham University, wrote Robert Lilburne to Thurloe in January 1655, 'will much affect the inhabitants of that poor county and city to [Oliver Cromwell] and the government'.[297]

IX

In 1660 all but one of the sixty new Welsh schools came to an end.[298] So did Durham University. So did the augmentations to ministers' stipends. As with so many of the ideals of the Puritan revolutionaries, the achievement fell far short of completion. Yet the revolutionary decades saw a great expansion of sectarian activity. The national sectarian organizations established during the revolutionary decades survived the dark generation of persecution which followed the Restoration; through these links ideas and mutual influences passed backwards and forwards between the capital and the former dark corners of Wales and the North. On the other hand, the movement to form voluntary associations of ministers (of which Baxter's Worcestershire Association is the best known) found its main strength in the outlying regions.[299] This 'Presbyterianism from below' helped to prepare for the restoration of a less tolerant state Church. So both in producing the Quakers, and in producing the most organized reaction against them, the dark corners were now a beacon for the rest of England.

The sword which the Propagators brought into Wales left deep and lasting divisions. The gentry, even the Parliamentarian gentry, hated the methods and social doctrine of the itinerants no less than did the university-trained clergy. Yet the Gospel could not have been propagated in Wales by traditional means. In so far as it was propagated, the work was done by 'tradesmen', by men less formally educated perhaps than the incumbents of the established Church, but better able to speak to their compatriots and less concerned about a living in the financial sense. The sectarian churches took over where the Propagators left off. By 1660 the Gospel had penetrated into most corners of England and Wales, inadequate though the achievement would have seemed to John Penry or Hugh Peter or Vavasor Powell. Puritan preaching had extended laterally, into the North and West; it had also, thanks to the sects, extended in depth, to social strata previously left untouched. In Wales nonconformity lost its alien quality, but it became a lower-class religion. Before the Civil War there had been no protestant nonconformity in Pembrokeshire. After it, the working and middle class were largely dissenters: but the squires, whether Tory or Whig, were churchmen almost to a man.[300] Dissent after 1660 was not a political conspiracy, as some bishops and MPs believed, or pretended to believe: the dissenters themselves had abandoned policies of violence. But dissent still remained a social phenomenon, and its social overtones still disturbed the respectable.

After the Restoration Thomas Gouge – son of the Feoffee for Impropriations – resumed the work of the Propagators. He was described for his pains by the Bishop of Bangor in 1666 as 'an itinerant emissary of the leading sectaries', and in 1672 was excommunicated by the Bishop of Llandaff for preaching without a licence. But Gouge – an occasional conformist himself – went very prudently to work, made his peace with the bishops and secured the cooperation of some Anglicans. ('How shall we Welsh bishops look if we refuse to take part?' one of them asked, with reference to Gouge's scheme for reprinting the Bible in Welsh: so much at least had been gained by the ending of the Anglican Church's monopoly.) Gouge organized a trust, which included Stillingfleet and Tillotson; he distributed the Book of Common Prayer in Welsh, and *The Whole Duty of Man*. Eight thousand copies of the Welsh Bible were printed, of which a thousand were given to the poor, and the others sold at 4*s*. apiece, 'much cheaper than any English Bible ... of so fair a print and paper'. Gouge collected money for education in Wales, especially from 'that perpetual fountain of

45

charity, the City of London, led on and encouraged by the most bountiful example of ... the Lord Mayor and Court of Aldermen'. More important perhaps, Gouge received 'large and bountiful contributions' from 'the nobility and gentry of Wales and the neighbouring counties': many Welsh towns were stirred up to emulate this activity, until some 1,500–2,000 children were being taught to read each year.[301]

But despite Gouge's caution, hostility remained, and his 300–400 reading schools seem to have come to an end after his death in 1681.[302] The distribution of Welsh books continued; but the main result of their circulation was an increase in dissent in Wales, said an Anglican sourly in 1697. ('If the growth of dissenters in Wales be an effect of the increase of knowledge there, we can't help that,' Calamy commented. The desirability of keeping the lower classes in a state of ignorance was a popish, not a protestant, doctrine, he hoped.[303]) The propagation of the Gospel was still a sword to divide. When Gouge's edition of the Bible ran out, it was Oliver Cromwell's friend, the Whig Lord Wharton, together with 'ministers and citizens of London', who financed the printing and distribution of a new edition.[304] Once the Toleration Act had given freedom of action to dissenters, it was only a matter of time before the majority of the Welsh people was won for dissent – though by the Baptists, Independents and Quakers, not the Presbyterians.[305] Already Wales had become a secondary sphere for the propagation of the Gospel. Robert Boyle indeed contributed to the republication of the Bible in Welsh; but he also sponsored translations into the languages of Ireland, North America, India, Malaya, Turkey.[306] Zachariah Cawdrey was advocating the propagation of the Gospel in America and Africa when he wrote the passage quoted on pp. 11–12 above.

So the illumination of the dark corners came ultimately by private enterprise. Yet state action between 1640 and 1653 was as important in the extension of London civilization over the whole of England as it was in transforming agrarian relations (abolition of feudal tenures, land confiscations) and foreign policy (Navigation Act) and finance (excise, assessment). Private enterprise could consolidate once the obstacles had been removed which had baffled generations of effort: bishops, prerogative courts. The Commissioners for Propagation acted as a sort of Council of the North, a Council in Wales, in reverse: even after they were abolished the field was left open to voluntary effort, thanks to the failure to restore prerogative courts and High Commission, and above all to the change in the climate of opinion which made even bishops reluctant to proceed to extremes against Thomas Gouge. Wales, the North and Cornwall went straight from Anglicanism (or indeed popery) to the sects, with little Presbyterianism except in the old frontier country of Lancashire. In this evangelizing effort, merchants cooperated with Puritans; the ideals of the latter were curiously blended with the interests of the former.

By the end of the seventeenth century the 'civilizing' process, in England and Wales, was for all practical purposes complete. In 1688–9, 1715 and 1745 there was no significant support for the Jacobites from the former royalist areas of the North and West. Though Sacheverell in 1710 won cheers and votes in Wales and on the Welsh border, in Devon and Cornwall,[307] military backing for Jacobitism came only from the dark corners of the Scottish Highlands and Ireland. These areas were first effectively conquered by English arms in the 1650s, and the propagation of the Gospel there was seriously envisaged; but they had not been brought into London's orbit by 1660. In Wales nonconformity established itself as an indigenous religion, like popery in Ireland and Presbyterianism in the Scottish Lowlands; but at the price of perpetuating a split in Welsh society. The extension of English influences among the common people of Wales was not primarily the work of the Anglican Church, to which the mass of the gentry adhered. For this outcome the credit, or the blame, must go chiefly to the Propagators. For in their brief years of rule they carried out in a way that could never be reversed some at least of the tasks which Penry and the Feoffees for Impropriations had set themselves and which the bishops had before 1640 always been able to frustrate.

47

2
Arise Evans:
Welshman in London

Our northern and Welshman when they come to London are very
simple and unwary, but afterward by conversing a while and by the
experience of other men's behaviour they become wonderful wise
and judicious.

> T. Wright, *The passions of the minde*
> (1601), Sig. A 4, quoted by D. B. Quinn,
> *The Elizabethans and the Irish*
> (Cornell, 1966), p. 13.

I

Arise Evans, in so far as he has any historical importance at all,
is a figure in English history. He lived in England most of his
life: he wrote in English. Christened Rhys, his acceptance of
the anglicization of his name to Arise is symbolic. His career
may tell us something about relations between Wales and
England in the seventeenth century: it may illustrate that
transition from what we call backwardness to what we call
modernity which fascinates historians today. Wales, as we saw
in the last chapter, like the North of England, was thought of
as one of the dark corners of the land, isolated from the national
culture which developed during the sixteenth century by the
extension of the London market, London religion and London
ideas generally over the whole of southern and eastern
England.

Rhys Evans was born in Merioneth in 1607, in the parish of
Llangelynin, a mile from Barmouth.[1] He was, he tells us, the
son of Evan the son of Rhys the son of Owen the son of Rhys
the son of Evan the son of David the son of Rhys the son of
Griffith the son of the Red Lion the son of the Ren.[2] His father

was 'a sufficient man of the parish', who gave the poverty-stricken curate a little tenement to live upon, and regularly entertained him at his own table; for the living was a lay impropriation, and the curate had to subsist on a small stipend.[3] The curate in return looked after Rhys's education. Rhys's father died, however, before he was seven years old, leaving him nothing. His mother soon married again. In 1616, at the age o-nine, Rhys was apprenticed to a tailor of Chester, long imporf tant as a market for North Welsh cloth.[4] But within a couple of years his master was bankrupt, a victim no doubt of James I's disastrous personal intervention in the affairs of the cloth trade. Rhys returned to his mother, whose second husband had died. When she married a third time and moved to Wrexham – a market town, engaged in the manufacture of flannel and of iron – Rhys accompanied her. We may speculate about the effect of all these upheavals on a young boy's mind, but we have no evidence. Nor can we assess the influence on him of the Puritanism of Wrexham, associated with Walter Cradock, Morgan Llwyd, Sir Thomas Middleton and John Jones. The last-named, a freeholder of Merioneth by origin, rose as a Parliamentarian leader through association with Wrexham and the Middletons in London.[5] Our hero was to claim acquaintance with him.

We do not know enough about migration inside Britain during the sixteenth and seventeenth centuries, that epoch of rapidly expanding population. There was clearly a great deal of it, affecting all social groups, with towns like London, Bristol and Southampton, together with the two universities, acting as mixing-pots. Craftsmen's sons went to London to seek their fortunes; the victims of agricultural change who found it impossible to hold on to their plots of land took to the road in search of survival in some great city, often ending as vagabonds. So did the victims of industrial unemployment, now at the mercy of national market fluctuations. In 1621 we are told of three Merionethshire parishes, with three hundred and more inhabitants who formerly lived well by clothing but are now 'come to begging'.[6] The population of Merioneth, Evans's county, was increasing more rapidly in the late sixteenth and early seventeenth centuries than that of any other Welsh county.[7] There was no Welsh county, it has been said, where in the early seventeenth century there was such reverence for literature and education as Merioneth. Although in 1651 John Jones thought that religion fared badly in his native county, it later contained the greatest proportion of Quakers to population of any Welsh shire.[8] Merioneth was beginning to feel the pull of English culture as well as of the Chester and Shrewsbury markets.

The central role of London in English cultural life can be illustrated by taking the very greatest names of the century and a half after the Reformation. William Shakespeare was the son of a burgess of Stratford-on-Avon, who came to London via the theatre. Thomas Hobbes, fatherless son of a glover of Malmesbury, and Isaac Newton, posthumous son of a Lincolnshire yeoman, came via the universities. From the beginning of Elizabeth's reign Shrewsbury School was helping to anglicize the sons of the Welsh gentry. At Oxford the principalship of New Inn Hall was held by nine Welshmen in succession during the fifty years after 1536; Jesus College was founded in Oxford in 1573. Although at Cambridge Welshmen were specifically excluded from Caius College, along with the 'deformed, dumb, blind, deaf, lame, mutilated' and those suffering from contagious diseases, there were many Welshmen at St John's, and the teaching of law at both universities was very nearly a Welsh monopoly under Elizabeth. By 1587 All Souls College was 'almost subverted as to its government by the troublesome Welsh scholars'. Thomas James, Bodley's first Librarian, was a Welshman.[9]

But no doubt, as soon as one considers it, the contribution of Wales to the remarkable flowering of English culture in these centuries, to the national mix, was at least as important as what Welshmen got out of it. In the 150 years after the Union of Wales and England persons of Welsh origin were extraordinarily important in English history. If we think of the Tudors themselves, the Cecils, the Herberts, the Cromwells, the Devereux Earls of Essex, the Somersets Earls of Worcester, the Middletons; or of secondary figures like William Thomas, Sir Roger Williams, Sir John Davies, Judge Jenkins, Sir Thomas Morgan, John, Michael and Philip Jones, it is clear that the political and social influence of men of Welsh origin was greater than at any period before the age of Lloyd George, Aneurin Bevan and Arthur Horner. Perhaps even more significant in the sixteenth and seventeenth centuries were the predecessors of Dylan Thomas – Donne, the two Herberts, the Vaughans, John Davies of Hereford, and Traherne also from the Welsh borderlands.[10] Inigo Jones is said to have been of Welsh descent. Men of Welsh origin are conspicuous in the field of science and mathematics, of alchemy and astrology.[11] If we think of religion, there were those who made a career in the Church of England, like Richard Davies, Bishop of St David's, the best-selling Lewis Bayley, Bishop of Bangor, Archbishop John Williams, who never lost his Welsh accent even when Keeper of James I's Great Seal, and who survived to claim kinship with Oliver Cromwell in 1647.[12] Among many more radical religious figures there were John Penry, Roger Williams of Welsh origin, John Owen of an old Welsh family; there were Walter Cradock, Morgan Llwyd, Vavasor Powell, William Erbery. There were prophets like Arise Evans.

All of these, whether or not they matter in Welsh history, are very important in the history of England. The contribution of Wales (as of the dark counties of the North) to English metaphysical poetry, to science, mathematics and radical religion in England, is unmistakable. This cultural influx may have been a bad thing for Wales. But it was certainly very good for England. To pick out the elements which mattered most in this cross-fertilization is difficult. Perhaps the longer survival of communities in which agrarian magic still meant something may have contributed both to the Welsh mathematicians and scientists and to the prophecies of Arise Evans; perhaps the more democratic structure of these communities may have helped the Welsh, together with 'the Northern Quakers', to radicalize English religion.

II

In the early 1620s Evans was apprenticed again in Chester, to his old master's father-in-law. This man took to calling him Arise, a habit I shall follow. It was probably in Chester that Arise made his first recorded venture into prophecy, announcing that woe would come to England on the second Thursday after Midsummer Day, 1623. It is always unwise for a prophet to fix precise dates – a lesson Arise never really learnt – and Evans tells us that he lost credit when nothing seemed to happen on the fatal day. But he discovered later that something had in fact happened: 'upon that very Thursday in that very year Oliver Cromwell presented a petition to King James touching the Fens in Lincolnshire and about Ely ... and as soon as King James took the petition his nose fell a-bleeding, that he swore it was an ill omen, saying if he could tell how, he would hang that fellow that had given him that paper'. The fire between king and country, Evans said in 1659, began that very day, and so the prophecy was fulfilled. There is no other evidence to suggest that Cromwell was interested in the rights of commoners in the Fens as early as this, before he had moved to Ely; but I suppose it is not impossible that Arise may have picked up some garbled story in Oliver's entourage which, as we shall see, he later frequented.[13]

After completing his apprenticeship, we must suppose, the young Evans set out for London, where he arrived in 1629. In his first four years there he began to prosper as a tailor. He lived in the parish of Blackfriars, under the ministry of the Puritan William Gouge. In March 1633 Arise was much impressed by hearing a stranger preach on the subject of Jacob wrestling with the angel; twenty years later he remembered this preacher saying that God did delight to have us strive with him in prayer, and was willing to be overcome. Arise now started to have many visions, prophesying destruction in the near future to king and kingdom. Many regarded him as mad, including his employers, who dismissed him. His landlord, thoroughly frightened, turned him out of his lodgings. His period of prosperity came to an end. Friends advised him to keep his mouth shut on subjects which should properly be left to the clergy. But Arise was under strong internal compulsion to declare his message. He wrote to the King, denouncing Queen Henrietta Maria and urging Charles to stand up against popery. He went to the royal palace at Greenwich and handed the King a message from God. What strikes us is the relative tolerance with which this slightly barmy young Welshman was allowed to pester the Court with petitions, on one occasion staying there two days, lobbying bishops and learned doctors, who took refuge in flight and barricaded their doors against him.[14]

So Evans tried an even more dangerous approach, or so he claimed on many occasions well after the event. He went to see the Earl of Essex, hero of the Londoners but not of the Court, in order to tell him that he would be general of all England in command of a party that was to execute judgment upon the Court. Essex, Arise tells us, took him into his private room and heard him with delight. He tipped him, but did not take him seriously, and his attendants made fun of it all. I find it very difficult to believe that Arise did in fact deliver such a message, in any comprehensible form. The future Parliamentary general would hardly have made light in public of anything so clearly treasonable. Essex got rid of Arise by sending him on to Lord Brooke, another opposition peer; but Arise could not swallow Brooke's hostility to the Church of England, and left him in dudgeon. In the summer of 1634 Evans's friends got him out of London and back to Wrexham. There he continued to spread his message, but only his elder brother was convinced, or pretended to be; his parents brought the local clergy to reason with him. Finally he was shut up as mad and dangerous; God, he tells us, fed him in a cloud.[15]

He must have recovered slightly, for he succeeded in persuading a lady to marry him, on the enviable condition that she would never contradict him: perhaps his relations arranged this as a therapeutic measure. At all events, by 1635 Evans was back in London, for he could not rest until his message had got through to the higher powers. After spending his first night lying in the street, he took work as a tailor until he was turned out of his lodgings again. The porter at Somerset House refused to receive any more letters. But Arise persisted, and in August he was arrested. This may have been his object, for he at once submitted a document for Secretary Windebanke: 'You are the King's Secretary and I am God's Secretary.' In this he prophesied that the King would die by the hands of his enemies, and that kingdom, church and nobles would be destroyed and all turned upside down. Windebanke, Evans tells us, asked him to pray for them all, and especially for the King. But he was put into close imprisonment at the Gatehouse, where he came into contact with the Puritan martyr John Bastwick, who however failed to respond to Arise's overtures.[16] There is no evidence of any contact between Arise and the

Lady Eleanor Davies, who soon joined him in the Gatehouse. She was another prophetess (not Welsh) who had made her reputation by announcing in June 1628 that the Duke of Buckingham's time was not till August: he was assassinated on 23 August 1628. She also told Queen Henrietta Maria in 1627 that she would be happy for sixteen years, 'and that is enough'. Men noticed that too sixteen years later, when the Queen was on the run in 1643. In 1633 Lady Eleanor had printed in Amsterdam verses predicting the violent overthrow of Charles I. She was arrested and tried before the High Commission, where a main part of her defence turned on the anagram of her maiden name: Eleanor Audeley, Reveale O Daniel. This however was turned against her when one of the Commissioners, who had been doodling quietly, produced a rival anagram: Dame Eleanor Davies, Never so mad a lady.[17]

Arise remained in the Gatehouse for two years, during which period his visions continued. He was finally released because certified mad – more fortunate than Lady Eleanor, who was sent to Bedlam. Arise returned to Wrexham, where he remained uneventfully for four years. But with the approach of civil war the pull of London proved too strong. In December 1641 he was back in Blackfriars, working occasionally as a tailor. By this time he had many small children, which added to his financial problems. In November 1643 he went to remind the Earl of Essex, now General of the Parliamentary Army, of his prediction nine years earlier; but Essex dismissed him. Evans was again a communicant at William Gouge's parish church in Blackfriars. He was still having visions, and soon got involved in religious controversy, disputing both with Anabaptists and other sectaries and with the now dominant Presbyterians, whose downfall he later claimed to have predicted.[18] He attracted the attention of the heresy-hunting Thomas Edwards, to whom it was reported that Arise claimed to be Christ.[19] He was arrested again, and when questioned told the Deputy Recorder 'I am the Lord thy God: thou shalt have none other God but me'. Several Presbyterian divines tried to help him. Christopher Love, originally one of William Erbery's converts, came to see him. Gouge too rallied round, and Arise was persuaded to sign a recantation, on the strength of which the ministers tried to get him certified and sent to Bedlam; but the

Deputy Recorder preferred to send him to Bridewell, though apparently only for a short term.[20]

In the summer of 1647 Arise decided that the Independents were preferable to the Presbyterians – though this may be the hindsight of 1652. Hearing a very good report of Oliver Cromwell's accessibility, Arise went to his house in Drury Lane and was taken into the dining-room with Ireton and another member of the family. He stayed till midnight. Evans's support for the Army lasted till the autumn of 1647, the period in which the Independent Grandees were negotiating with the King. After Charles's flight to the Isle of Wight in November Arise began to criticize the Army, and in June 1648 he publicly defended the King's party in his employer's house. The consequence, he tells us, was that one of his children fell and broke its right arm: this discouragement decided him to be more careful. He disapproved of the King's execution, but was silent for a long time. In 1649 he had a vision telling him that after Oliver Cromwell England would have a king again. Next year Evans went through France to Rome in a vision, and 'a voice came to me saying, So far as thou art come, so far shall Cromwell come'. Like many others, Arise claimed after the event to have predicted Charles II's invasion of England in 1651, and its unsuccessful outcome. He was present at Christopher Love's execution on the eve of the Battle of Worcester. Evans took the Engagement to be true and faithful to the Commonwealth, and at this time was in touch with the influential Colonel John Jones of Wrexham (already a regicide, soon to become Oliver Cromwell's brother-in-law) 'he being very loving unto me'.[21]

In 1652 Arise Evans published his first work, *A Voice From Heaven to the Commonwealth of England*. In this he called on Parliament and Army to restore Charles II, lest foreigners do it. Charles, he said rather surprisingly, was the Messiah destined to convert the Jews and lead them back to Israel. Charles I had been the third person of the Trinity, taking precedence over the Holy Ghost. (Either Evans or someone else had made this point earlier, for the author of *Light Shining in Buckinghamshire* referred in 1648 to Charles I 'their third person of their Trinity', next under God and Christ.) In 1653 Arise described Charles II as 'a child of God and appointed to be the most eminent servant of Jesus Christ in all the world'.[22] 'I am a man to whom God hath given foreknowledge', Arise announced, 'which I declare with all humility, love and respect.' He was pestering the authorities again, trying to use Colonel John Jones to convince the Council of State of his bona fides. He submitted a petition to Sir Gilbert Pickering for Oliver Cromwell, and he gave an exposition of Amos 8 and 9 to Hugh Peter and Cromwell. 'Many of our ministers make but a jest of Master Hugh Peter's preaching', Arise noted; 'but I tell ye, ye may all go learn to preach of him . . . He may be turned to the right way'. Arise discussed with Peter the possibility of tolerating Cavalier religious meetings.[23]

'I see a black day coming upon you', Arise warned Parliament in December 1652 – right for once, since Oliver turned them out of doors on 20 April 1653, 'much about the time' that Evans was telling Elias Ashmole that the Parliament's 'time was short and it was even at the door'.[24] In May, just after the dissolution, Arise twice petitioned Cromwell and the Council of the Army to restore Charles II – urged to do so, he says, by men of all sorts of judgments. 'If the King comes in by the sword', he told the soldiers, 'you will become slaves and force him to use tyranny.'[25] The Council were so impressed by one of these petitions, Arise thought, that they did not molest him at all though he disputed in favour of Charles before them all for four hours on end. He claimed to have argued many times with officers at Whitehall, enjoying the protection of those who spoke for liberty of conscience.[26] In 1653 Arise published two autobiographical tracts, whose object was to demonstrate his skill as a prophet. Most of our information about him is perforce drawn from these not entirely satisfactory sources. Unfortunately for him, in the second of these pamphlets he committed himself to the prediction that Charles would be on the throne of England before the end of 1653.[27]

He had some difficulty in laughing this off when it failed to happen. In 1654 he explained that Charles had not been restored yet because Oliver Cromwell and his party had had the sense to pay more respect to Arise Evans's prophecy than the King's party. And in any case it was a Romish error to think that 1653 ended before Christmas Day 1654.[28] In 1655 he argued retrospectively that the prediction had been fulfilled by the establishment of Cromwell as Lord Protector in December 1653, for the Protector is king by proxy. ('I must be for His Highness the Lord Protector', he had written in 1654, 'because I see God is for him.'[29]) After the restoration, when Oliver as *locum tenens* for Charles II was not a popular idea, Evans tried a different explanation. Cromwell commissioned Monck to Scotland in 1653: Monck was to be the agent of the Restoration, but it would not have been prudent to reveal earlier that Arise had advance information of this![30] In 1655 Arise urged Charles to secure his restoration by marrying one of Cromwell's daughters. Oliver, after all, was descended from the ancient British kings (Cadwallader and Blethin ap Cynvin, Prince of Powys) as well as from the royal house of Stuart on his mother's side.[31]

This pamphlet, Arise claimed after the Restoration, very much annoyed Cromwell, because any talk of a marriage alliance with the Stuarts made his own party jealous of him. Though Arise later claimed that Oliver 'came to speak with me and used me very familiarly', in 1654 he complained on many occasions that the Protector's attendants prevented him 'having such conferences with you as heretofore I have had' before the proclamation of the Protectorate. Oliver was kept close prisoner by flatterers, just as the late King had been. Not even his innumerable writings, Arise grumbled, were delivered any longer.[32] But a journalist's anecdote of September 1655 suggests there was still a friendly relationship. It tells of Evans 'going for the Bath', meeting Oliver near Hampton Court.

O.C.: 'Where away, Mr. Evans?'
A.E.: 'To the Bath, my Lord.'
O.C.: 'But what's the reason, Mr. Evans, you wear a sword? Prophets are not to wear such weapons.'
A.E.: 'To keep the wolves of the time from my legs, my Lord.'
O.C.: 'And who be they?'
A.E.: 'Soldiers.'
O.C.: 'Oh, you think you shall have a king still?'
A.E.: 'Yes, my Lord, and I am assured of it.'

His Highness, we are told, 'smiling parted with a compliment'.[33]

Evans was again in financial difficulties, he tells us in 1652 and later – old, sick, unable to work. He had spent all he had in writing and printing on behalf of the King, and was brought low in every way – friends forsaking him, work proving difficult to get. 'Divers persons of quality', he says, 'paid me royally for my former book, else I had not been able to subsist.' But 'all that I had from them for books these three years did not amount to' £50.[34] I shall consider later who these 'persons of quality' may have been.

In 1656 Arise made some more cautious and more successful prophecies – that Charles II would be restored without bloodshed within five years, and that some regicides would be executed. But in the same pamphlet he declared that the Jews would return to Palestine under the banner of Charles II, who 'is he whom you call your Messiah'. 'All these late transactions in England,' he told the Jewish people, 'came to pass only for your sake'[35] – one of the few interpretations of the Civil War that has not yet been taken up by a modern historian. In 1659 Arise put forward constitutional proposals of his very own, which I shall consider later.[36] In the year of the Restoration he published *To the Most High and Mighty Prince Charles II . . . An Epistle*, in which he claimed a reward for services rendered. He was still poor, and jeered at by the sectaries because of his lack of recognition. His wife and family had suffered greatly from mockery because he had been unable to explain the true significance of his prophecy about Charles's restoration in 1653.[37] So far as we know, he received no reward. He died some time after the Restoration, we do not know exactly when.

III

Endearing though Arise Evans is, he was clearly mentally abnormal. But we can learn from him perhaps something about the (relatively) common man and his attitudes towards religion, the Bible, politics, at one of the very few times when we can hear him speaking in his own voice. Before 1640 we have to rely on the distorted evidence of heresy trials, witch trials, accounts of peasant revolts from the pens of those who applauded their suppression. There is virtually no hard information about what the majority of the population was thinking. So it is worth using every scrap of evidence thrown up in the revolutionary decades, when discussion suddenly became free and when printing was still a cheap enough process for almost anyone to be able to get his views published. Some most surprising views appeared in this period, of great interest to the sociologist and perhaps the psychologist as well as to the historian: they can help to throw light backwards and forwards on to darker periods as well as illuminating the 1640s and 1650s themselves. Using them for this purpose has its dangers. Norman Cohn tried the technique in his *The Pursuit of the Millennium*, which seems to me to suffer from a fundamentally unsympathetic attitude to all radicals, whom he regards as psychological cases, rather as some psychiatrists in the USA and USSR think agitators and dissidents need adjusting to their society. We might more profitably reflect on London in the 1630s and 1640s as a training school in radical politics, not unlike most universities today. Arise Evans's contemporaries included the apprentices John Lilburne, Gerrard Winstanley, Nicholas Culpeper, William Kiffin.

Arise Evans tells us, for instance, that his approach to the Bible changed in London in the pre-revolutionary decade. 'Afore I looked upon the Scripture as a history of things that passed in other countries, pertaining to other persons; but now I looked upon it as a mystery to be opened at this time, belonging also to us.'[38] This attitude must have been shared by many victims of economic or political crisis, who turned to the Bible for immediate guidance in those perplexing decades. The 1640s and 1650s were indeed the great age of mechanick preachers – laymen interpreting the Bible according to their untutored lights with all the confidence and excitement of a new discovery. 'I am as the Paul of this time', Arise claimed; 'he was a mechanick, a tent-maker, Acts 18.3. I am a tailor.'[39] There were many such.

In the seventeenth century the Bible was the accepted source of true knowledge. Everybody cited its texts to prove an argument, including men like Winstanley and Hobbes who *illustrated* from the Bible conclusions at which they had arrived by rational means. Simpler men believed the Bible to be divinely inspired, and applied its texts directly to the problems of their own world and time with no idea of the difficulties of translation, nor of the historical understanding required. So Arise thought that Revelation 8 and 11 gave an account of the English Civil War, that chapters 8 and 9 of Amos set down all that came to pass since the beginning of the Long Parliament; in Amos 9.1 the lintel at the door, which must be smitten that the posts may shake, can therefore only refer to Speaker Lenthall.[40]

But these untrained minds included a George Fox and a John Bunyan. They were grappling with the problems of their society, problems which called urgently for solution, and they were using the best tools they knew of. More respectable Puritan divines had cited the Bible against bishops, against persecution, against tithes. The Evanses studied it very carefully, if less skilfully, in order to understand and so be able to control what was going to happen. They may well have felt that they had been at the mercy of events for too long. The Civil War period gave a forum to what was almost a new profession – that of the prophet, whether as interpreter of the Bible or of the stars. With the breakdown of the censorship, 'the malice of the clergy' could no longer prevent publication of astrological books as it had done before 1640.[41] There was an outburst of publication of prophecies, old and new.

Mr Lamont has recently reminded us of the millenarian enthusiasm which gripped large numbers of perfectly sane supporters of Parliament in the 1640s. Biblical chronologists, Presbyterian preachers to Parliament, John Milton, Sir Henry Vane, all believed that the millennium was coming in the near future.[42] Students of biblical prophecy were attempting to create a *science* of prophecy: this interested minds of the calibre of Napier, Joseph Mede, Henry More and Isaac Newton. The attempt did not succeed, any more than Hobbes's attempt to found a scientific political theory. But there is nothing inherently more silly in either attempt than in Boyle and Newton taking alchemy seriously, or Dee and Richard Overton taking astrology seriously.[43]

'These revolutions and changes', Evans wrote in 1652, 'came to pass even to fulfil the words and promises of God.'[44] It is therefore very important for us to grasp the role of prophecies in popular psychology, to take them seriously. Evans himself was steeped not only in the Bible but also in Welsh prophecies. In his early twenties he spent three months in Coventry *en route* for London, studying an old chronicle 'that shewed all the

passages in Britain and Ireland from Noah's flood to William
the Conqueror'. He got by heart the most material passages.
Brutus, Joseph of Arimethea and Merlin figure in his pamphlets. He quotes Grebner and Francis (? = Roger) Bacon's
prophecies.[45]

Arise Evans, it must be admitted, was not always a very good
prophet. But he had his own critical standards of a sort.
Visions and revelations must not be followed if they contradict
the Bible.[46] He even submitted himself to the test of experiment,
as when in May 1653 he offered as a sign that Charles II would
be restored before the end of the year the fact that it would
rain (more or less) on all the following seven Sundays – which,
he assures us, it did, though in the very drought of summer, at
a time when there was hardly any rain on weekdays.[47]

Arise Evans regarded himself as a cut above astrological
quacks, quoting the one who prophesied a fine day on one side
of the street and rain on the other, so as to be sure of being
right. 'It is usual for thieves to go to cunning men or astrologers' to learn whether they will be hanged or not.[48] Evans's
relationship with Parliament's favourite astrologer William
Lilly fluctuated wildly. In 1652 he quoted him with approval.
Next year and in February 1654 he criticized him. But later
that year a pamphlet by an anonymous astrologer, *King Charls
his Starre*, was published. In this Arise Evans's prophecies were
praised so extravagantly that many contemporaries thought
that only he could have written it. After this Arise decided that
astrologers – and particularly the author of *King Charls his
Starre* – were 'far more excellent, meek and wise-spirited men
than the proud Presbyterian ministers' who opposed them.
Astrology is lawful, he decided, so long as astrologers study the
Scriptures as well as the stars. Lilly shared Evans's dislike of
Presbyterians, and *King Charls his Starre* spoke favourably of him
too. But two years later Arise declared that Lilly 'knows nothing,
nor ever did know anything but as the Parliament directed
him to write'; though by 1660 he seems to have been on better
terms again with him.[49]

Wales played its part in Arise's mental make-up. He quoted
Welsh on many occasions – perfectly correctly, I am assured.[50]
Christopher Love won his confidence when he visited him in
jail in 1646 by speaking Welsh to him. Mountains loom large

in his symbolism: he thought Cader Idris the highest hill in the world.[51] Cader Idris played for him a part similar to that of Pendle Hill on the Yorkshire–Lancashire border for George Fox – a mountain of vision from which a specially prepared promised land was viewed.[52] Arise accepted many traditional superstitions. He believed that God would grant whatever one asked of him at sunrise on Whit-Sunday, though he only recalled trying it once at the age of fourteen. He thought you could counteract witchcraft by drawing blood from the witch. On occasion he let himself be guided by opening the Bible and lighting on a text at random.[53]

In one pamphlet, but only in one, Arise Evans makes great play with Saxon-British antagonisms, stressing the Trojan origins of the Britons/Welsh, who were Christians above a thousand years before Christ was born. The Britons were held in great slavery from the reign of Edward I to Henry VII, cruelly used by the English, who destroyed their ancient records, tried to extinguish their ancient language and so make the prophecies and promises written in it ineffectual. But the Welsh preserved their language and enough of their writings until finally Henry VII came to the English throne because he observed the prophecies. 'The generality of the people of this land are Britons (or Welsh as we now call them) by descent.' But this was no racial theory to unite the common people against the foreign invaders, such as the Leveller theory which called on descendants of the free Anglo-Saxons to revolt against the Norman yoke of king and aristocracy. For Evans it was always the nobility who fled to Wales. Now in 1659, he said, it is time for Englishmen to stop despising the Welsh and to consider their prophecies, 'that ye may as Britons be made partakers of the blessing with us, denying your English or Saxon interest, for surely the Saxons shall vanish as God hath determined it by our prophecies'. 'Therefore you brave Britons, stand up for Christ's kingdom.'[54]

Despite his Welshness, despite his opposition to the republican régime, Arise declared in 1652 that 'the elect are nowhere else but here in England, and so tied to this place that if the faith of God's elect were destroyed here, there should be none saved'. 'God hath a special regard to England', he repeated in 1653 – words worthy of English patriots like Milton and Cromwell.

Arise wanted Parliament and army to restore Charles II in 1652 lest foreigners do it.[55]

Evans's main interest for us lies in his royalism. Most of the mechanic preachers were radicals, opposed to the church establishment which thought that laymen should not preach.[56] But though Arise, as we shall see, was critical of many aspects of church and state before 1640, in the 1650s he was a staunch monarchist and episcopalian. Church government, he wrote in a highly traditional passage, 'is the foundation of all governments . . . for by church government men are brought to be of one mind and of one spirit, to unity and peace'. He made a very sensible plea for organs in church, against those Puritans who would have removed them. As a child what 'first brought me to be well-affected to coming to church', he recalled, was music: children are not interested in a man talking literally above their heads whilst they have to sit in silence. True religion Evans defined as that of Edward VI, Elizabeth, James I and Charles I. 'Except the protestant religion [i.e. episcopalianism] be established here again', he wrote in 1654, 'there is no hopes that the next generation will be but atheists.'[57] This was a conclusion not altogether lacking in shrewdness if we consider the tendency towards rationalism in radical ideas among Diggers, Ranters and early Quakers.[58] It was a conclusion which drove many to support the restoration of episcopacy in 1660.

Arise himself preferred not only Episcopalians but Papists or Independents to Presbyterians. In 1652-3 he was in favour of the retention of tithes and so of a state church.[59] In 1653 he called for restitution of church property and of the traditional government in consultation with bishops. Presbyterians were, he thought, by then 'so sensible of their errors' that 'many of their ministers and ringleaders do begin to creep toward the bishops' good old way': yet it would be folly to trust them. They worship the Dragon and the Beast, he insisted in 1660.[60] One of the subjects which Arise seems to have discussed with Hugh Peter was an offer made by Parliament to let Archbishop Laud go to New England with Peter.[61]

Arise Evans seems to have attended Anabaptist meetings from 1643 onwards, especially those of Thomas Lamb in Bell Alley, Coleman St, and later those of Peter Chamberlen. He

left the Anabaptists some time in or before 1651 and decided
that there was 'no truth among the sectaries'.[62] In 1653 he
attacked Christopher Feake, John Simpson and other Blackfriars Fifth Monarchists; he refuted William Aspinwall's *A
Brief Description of the Fifth Monarchy*.[63] As late as 1655 Evans
still thought the necessity of rebaptism was 'a truth', though
later he defended infant baptism. He disapproved of the
'incivility' of Quakers, but he spoke favourably of Menasseh-
ben-Israel.[64] By 1652 he came to think that the Rump of the
Long Parliament was the Beast of Revelation 13; next year its
successor the Barebones Parliament seemed to him the image
of the Beast. The mystic numbers 666 could be interpreted as
'the weal publike of England' (i.e. the Commonwealth) or
'in the true ancient Welsh or British language' as Delwan
Lloiger, England's idol, which was the same thing. They could
not refer to William Laud since he added up to 667. But
'though Antichrist for the present plant his tabernacles here,
yet he shall vanish speedily.' The Fifth Monarchy would
shortly be set up under the rather unexpected person of
Charles Stuart.[65]

Nevertheless there are moments of shrewd common sense.
Arise quoted with approval the suggestion that 'this word
godliness will shortly become the mark of the Beast'. He
observed grimly that the Apostle's command 'be not forgetful
to entertain strangers, for some thereby have entertained
angels unawares' (Hebrews 13:2) was out of date: the rule now
was that strangers should be carried to Bridewell; if an angel
came nowadays that is where he would be lodged.[66] 'The
Cavaliers are they that relieve the Lazaruses of our times, and
the Presbyterians do not only deny them relief but also afflict
them sore in Bridewells'[67] – no doubt a recollection of Arise
Evans's own period in Bridewell during the Presbyterian
ascendancy. There is a passage in his *Epistle . . . to Charles II*
which is so good that one wonders whether Arise really wrote it.
He is describing Presbyterians and sectaries.

'They are very just in their dealings, true in their promises,
they will not swear, lie or be drunk; and excellent qualities
they have in their dealings between man and man, only they
will deal so hard that a poor man cannot get water to his

hands by them; but they pay just, and you shall not find the least sin in them, for they sin not by retail but by wholesale, . . . their consciences being nice and curious in small matters and not at all in great things.'[68]

If Evans did write that, I suspect he learnt it from the likes of John Penicote, the very honest godly man of Blackfriars who turned him out of his lodgings in 1635.[69]

Arise Evans's royalism and episcopalianism makes his analysis of the causes of the Civil War especially interesting. Before 1640 'the Court of England (as most courts are) was grown very corrupt'. He gave as examples the Overbury poisoning case, the Book of Sports, refusal to consider an Anabaptist petition of 1633 and the execution of a young man in 1634 for poisoning his master. The latter two were relatively unpolitical incidents, important for him because they occurred at a time when Arise was getting interested in London politics. He laid considerable emphasis on the Book of Sports and royal anti-Sabbatarianism: 'King James destroyed his throne by making a law to profane the Sabbath'. Even in 1655 Evans told Charles II that the Queen Mother 'must leave idolatrous superstition and all other sins attending courts . . . behind her' if her son was to be restored.[70]

'These miseries', Arise tells us of the pre-1640 period, 'did spring from the covetousness of some clergymen' – pluralists, non-preaching curates. 'In the late King's days all the ministers sought after church livings, to the end that they might follow the gentry rather than the ministry, so that they forgot to preach.'[71] This produced a Puritan reaction – hireling lecturers, wolves in sheep's clothing: 'to fill their bags they will flatter the people, and preach them all to be saints, forsooth, that follow them'. At his lower level Evans echoed Chillingworth's impartial denunciation of scribes and pharisees on the Parliamentarian side, publicans and sinners on the royalist: 'While the one part of the parish are drunk at the ale-house and on the Sundays run into all manner of uncivilities for want of sober godly preaching . . . the other part with immoderate teachings do run in spiritual whoredom and drunkenness.' Puritan preachers won fame by attacking bishops, were persecuted by them and so won still greater reputation. This poisoned the whole kingdom. When Parliament met in 1640 'the Puritan and hireling ministers of London etc. began to stir up the City against the King and bishops'. 'How thirsty were the Presbyterian ministers for the innocent Bishop of Canterbury and other men's blood.' The guilt of the King's execution too lies ultimately on the Presbyterian clergy and on those City authorities who stirred up tumults to put pressure on Parliament in 1641. 'Where are the great ministers that preached the people into tumult and rebellion?' Arise asked in 1653. 'Do they not stink now in the nostrils of those whom they preached up?'[72]

Nevertheless, Evans recognized, popular support for Parliament in the early 1640s was a reality, and sprang from prewar experience of Court corruption, the covetousness of the rich, their hardness of heart towards the poor, deceit of the people and neglect of them in the worship of God. This led to a general rising throughout the land and the complete overthrow of the King's party. The Parliamentary Army won not only because it fought better in the field but also because it behaved so much better in the counties. Unlike all previous armies, the New Model was not recruited from jails and the lowest sort.[73] Arise thoroughly disapproved of the swearing and debauchery of the Cavaliers, and of their vindictiveness.[74] The royalist irreconcilables who in the fifties wanted Charles II restored by violence were 'bloody men', who felt oppressed 'first, because their means is taken from them, so that they cannot commit such sins as they would do if they had plenty of money; secondly, because they are restrained from their courses of sins by these men now in power, more than they were formerly', and are themselves kept out of power.[75] It was to the credit of Parliament that 'a petty constable shall in all places and at all times [this is 1653] order a lord by birth that is unruly'. The king and nobility of England had been destroyed by their sins.[76]

Yet Arise Evans also criticized the corruption of which so many contemporaries accused MPs under the Rump, referring to 'the seeming godly man's self-interest in the world', and to 'the deceitfulness of riches gotten in this time'.[77] 'Do you think,' he asked, 'that such men, raised to such high places, who have not means of their own sufficient to maintain their greatness, will not have it out from the people' – by raising their children, friends and relations to all places of profit? 'Truly it were a shame for them if they did it not', Arise continued in an interesting comment on popular standards in his day, and what was expected of ruling persons. 'I am confident that if ye were in their place ye would do no less, although the country should still suffer by it.' The country would continue to suffer until king, nobility and gentry were restored to power, 'for they have great revenues of their own, by which they are able to bear such places of authority and govern the people at their own proper charges'.[78] Evans called for an account from committees and trustees for the sale of confiscated lands, by whom the Commonwealth had been cheated. If they were made to disgorge, taxes might be reduced. Better still, if the lands had never been sold, the Commonwealth could have used the income from them to pay for its wars, as Elizabeth used to do. Evans regarded the Rump's war against the Netherlands as 'hurtful to England'.[79]

Yet on the whole Arise Evans preferred Independents to Presbyterians. 'Some of your intentions and meanings are good', he reassured the Rump in 1653. For 'valiant Cromwell' he always had a soft spot, as one who 'was not a bloodthirsty man', and moreover 'was not proud but one that did receive instructions many times from mean men' – a rare quality, as Arise found from his own experience. Evans has an interesting analysis of Cromwell's behaviour in 1647–9, when he could neither do much for or against Charles I 'but as the stream of the Parliament, Army and people went then, so must he go or be disabled'. Others more guilty try to put the blame for the King's execution on the Lord General. Even if he was guilty, 'divine providence so ordered the matter that it was his place, for he was a servant in it to the Parliament, to the Lord General Fairfax, to the Army and to the people': if he had not acted many others would have done so.[80] One wonders whether in this we do not hear an echo of what Cromwell himself said in those long conversations which Arise describes. 'The King and all the nobles in England', Evans declared in 1655, 'could not have done so much right to the Commonwealth or crown of England as His Highness the Lord Protector did.' This was part of Evans's attempt to persuade Charles II to come to terms with Cromwell, who could have taken the crown himself, and whose refusal manifested to Arise that Oliver really acknowledged the King still. 'Neither you nor all Europe', he rightly told irreconcilable royalists, 'shall be able to bring them down by force.' All Englishmen will rise against a foreign invasion. The only hope of a peaceful solution is for Charles to offer a general pardon to all and to 'join your royal self to His Highness the Lord Protector and his Council'.[81]

Arise Evans was inconsistent. In 1653 he expressed a preference for the rule of the aristocracy rather than that of the lower classes. But if harm came to the Parliament, 'we the poor are like to suffer with you' – unless peace were made with the King.[82] In 1659 he wrote a pamphlet quite unlike anything else in his writings, in which he put forward 'a system never yet tried, . . . the only way for settling the Good Old Cause'. This was by establishing a poor man as king. 'Jesus Christ is for a single person and not a free state (as you call it) . . . But he would not have the great and rich to be his kings, but would have the poor and low exalted to the throne.' Formerly, Arise wrote, 'the Scripture was engrossed . . . in great men's hands, so that they might do as they pleased with the people that knew little or no Scripture'. But with the invention of printing and freedom to read the Bible, 'knowledge is increased among the people, and shall increase; so that they will not be ruled by the kings set up after the manner of the Gentiles any more'. 'Here is the Good Old Cause that God raised our Army to stand for.' It is the only time Arise uses the language of democracy and appeals to the rank and file of the Army or to the Good Old Cause. If 'your head officers . . . stand between you and it', Arise called on the rank and file to depose them – in the spirit of Wildman in 1647. 'The noble spirits of the under-officers and Agitators doth all', Evans declared.[83]

His king was to be chosen by lot – a poor but literate and industrious godly man, over fifty years of age, who was not worth £5 nor was £5 in debt, but who had been forced to accept alms. (He had thought of using the oldest inhabitant of the Charterhouse – 'it would save the trouble of electing the king' – but there might be cheating, and anyway election by lot is best since it leaves the choice in effect to God. Arise may have expected that God would allow the lot to fall on him, since he was qualified in other ways.) The king should have sole power, accountable to no man; and £100 a year for his maintenance. All writs should run in his name, and he should call six-monthly Parliaments every three years. The Protector (Richard Cromwell by this time) would however also continue to rule, becoming hereditary; but every third year the Protector should render account before king and Parliament. The Protector would hear complaints in public once a week, giving judgment within seven days; if he failed to do so he would be called to account by king and Parliament. MPs would be over fifty years of age, fearing God and loving the poor: any contentious hypocrite who was elected should be expelled. No officeholders or officers should sit. The king chosen under this scheme should always be known as King Charles – perhaps a way of realizing Arise Evans's prediction that Charles would be restored. Evans still believed Charles Stuart to be the best of all kings, but 'his resolution is not right, for he would come in and settle all things as formerly we had them; therefore he cannot prosper'.[84] A king chosen under this scheme, 'being old and poor', will protect both great and small. There will be no temptation to treason, for who would want such a crown? A perpetual succession is provided for by lot. In such a king Jesus Christ comes to reign on earth.[85]

It was a lunatic scheme, of course, especially when put forward by a hitherto consistent royalist, one year before Charles II's restoration. But it is perhaps not all that much less realistic than Milton's *Ready and Easie Way to establish a free Commonwealth* of 1660, which is taken seriously. At least Evans was shrewd enough to see that the only power capable of introducing his scheme was the junior officers, Agitators in the Army and others still loyal to the Good Old Cause. And the idea of making the job so unattractive that it ceases to be an object of competition is not a bad one. One wonders whether Arise Evans had somehow heard of Cyrano de Bergerac's *Les États et Empires du Soleil*, written about 1650 but not published until 1662. In the sun birds choose for their king 'the feeblest, gentlest and most peaceful, ... so that the humblest could avenge himself if the king did him any wrong'. Even so the king was changed every six months, and could be recalled or indeed executed if he failed to satisfy his subjects.[86] In a country whose traditions include *le roi d'Yvetot* this may have been less eccentric than Arise Evans's pauper king. It seems wildly unlikely that the worlds of Cyrano and Arise could ever meet; but the coincidence in time of the two schemes is striking.

IV

If Arise Evans had lived in the twentieth century he might have been an influential political journalist, guiding as well as commenting on events. Something like that clearly was his aspiration. 'The King should have taken some notice of me', he complained in 1654. 'I am more able to do him good ... than all his friends besides, because the spirit of prophecy moveth all the wheels or generality of the nations to act and pray for him.' In 1654 and 1655 Arise urged an alliance between the House of Cromwell and the House of Stuart and a general pardon, since there was no possibility of a lasting settlement based on force.[87] At least three other prophets were proclaiming a union between Oliver and Charles at this time – Elinor Channel (whose prophecy Arise Evans published), Walter Gostelow (who praised Arise) and Mr J. Sanders of Harburn near Birmingham.[88] Anyone who spoke well of Cromwell, Arise declared in 1654, was slighted; booksellers cannot dispose of books which praise him. 'Since the last Parliament disowned you', he told Oliver in the spring of 1655, '(whom we looked upon as honest men) all do disown you.' Regarding Oliver as Samson, he said of the future Major-Generals 'these colonels dally with you, but in the mean time they cut off your locks in the Army; and they know already that they have more of the Army on their side than you have'. On the other hand, 'why should a man pay for 30,000 men', when he could have King Charles for nothing?[89]

In 1660 Arise claimed to have used policy as well as prophecy in writing his books: some things were put in on purpose to make the sectaries read them.[90] In this he succeeded, even if his intentions were not as subtle as he claimed. At least one future Baptist came across Arise's books 'at a neighbour's shop' in Bristol in 1654, and was worried by his attack on Puritans, 'justifying himself by many circumstances related in his book'.[91] From 1653 onwards Evans's pamphlets were regularly quoted at length in royalist news-letters: Elias Ashmole mentions him with respect, Cromwellians thought him worth attacking.[92] 'Why am I so pestered with the people that I cannot rest', Arise asked in 1654, 'but all the day long answer them?' One suspects the usual illusions of grandeur of the author when he continues 'And why are my books gone over all the earth, and translated into all languages, and are so famous that I am troubled to answer men that come from Turkey, from Italy, from Germany, from Spain, yea from all parts of the world where Englishmen go?' Modestly he attributed this to the fame of Charles II rather than his own.[93]

In 1655 a fellow-prophet Walter Gostelow (who had got to know Arise as they both hung about the Protector's court) gives a more plausible picture. Whilst praising Evans as a man the English public was unworthy of, a good man who 'hath . . . endured so much and almost worn himself out that you might turn and live', he admitted 'yet him you asperse, too many of you miscalling him mad, foolish, babbling mistaken fellow'. Gostelow agreed with Arise in advocating a restoration of bishops and of Charles II in alliance with the Protector: though Gostelow, whose kinsman was secretary to the Earl of Cork and who himself claimed connections with Lord Broghill, thought it was the Lady Elizabeth Boyle 'whom God Almighty hath set apart and chosen' as Charles II's Queen. He also believed that Oliver Cromwell would never die.[94] In a letter published in 1659 another journalist observed that Arise Evans's former predictions had been strangely successful and that 'he is not half so much laughed at as he was at first'. This, and Evans's immunity from molestation, led the journalist to speculate whether the Welshman was not 'privately cajoled by some stars of magnitude'.[95]

It is a question we may ask ourselves. The main internal evidence lies in the marked contrast between the sheer lunacy of some of Arise's writings (which I have tended to be sparing in quoting) and the hard-headed common sense often contained in the same pamphlet. The constant features of what we may call the sane Arise Evans are a settled desire to see Charles II restored, not by royalist violence or foreign conquest but by agreement with Cromwell and his Council. This is combined with steady denigration both of the Presbyterians as the real instigators of the Civil War, and of royalist intransigents. Now this is a line which might appeal either to moderate royalists as a tactic to subvert the Commonwealth and Protectorate; or to those whom Dr Pearl calls 'royal Independents', those who had always wanted a monarchical settlement and deplored the extremes of radicalism forced on the Army leaders by Presbyterian intolerance and rank-and-file pressures.[96]

Can we find any trace of such men behind Arise Evans? It is hard going once we try to get beyond the to me weighty internal evidence. Here are such clues as I have been able to find. In 1655 Arise said that 'divers persons of quality paid me royally for my former book', which was probably *The Bloudy Vision of John Farley*. The unique feature of this book is that it reports someone else's vision. Farley, Evans tells us, was a gentlemen of Wallington (Wellington?), Shropshire, who 'was not factious on any side' during the Civil War. He wished to remain neutral but was plundered by both parties. He mortgaged his estate and farmed another gentleman's lands in Wales until the cost of maintaining his wife and eight children forced him to give up. He went to London in 1652, but could get no help there, and finally emigrated to Virginia. He had his vision in London in January 1653. Evans published it after his departure. The vision, as interpreted by Arise Evans, was of a violent overthrow of Parliament and a restoration of monarchy. Arise (or one of his friends) hoped that the publication might act as a warning 'that this sad distressed nation is once again to suffer by the sword if there be not speedily a peace made' with the King.[97]

In this tract Farley's vision is sandwiched between passages defending Evans's reputation as a prophet, criticizing the more extreme aspects of the Rump's policy but praising others, and especially praising Oliver Cromwell. And one unusually fierce note: 'How justly hath God struck Milton blind for writing against the King's book.'[98] Was there a Farley, or is the account fictitious? If Farley existed, he has left no trace in the records that I can find.[99] Did Arise think up the story, or did someone else? Evans was hardly the man to invent visions for other people. Whether true or fictitious, the Farley story was well calculated to appeal to moderates on either side. Farley entertained no spirit of revenge, Evans tells us; no hostility towards the Parliamentarians. News of the existence of the Farley manuscript, Evans says, 'came to the ears of the royal party, and then I was sought out and sent for by persons of quality'.

Of these he names only 'a gentleman of Gray's Inn, William Satterthwayt', who offered to pay for the printing. He can be identified as Clerk of the Nichills in the Upper Exchequer from at least 1650 to 1658.[100] A man whose interest in Farley's manuscript was roused because he was of the royalist party would scarcely pay for its printing unless he had some say in its contents. Many, Evans tells us, helped him with money, but besides Satterthwayt he mentions only Mr Samuel Starling. This was presumably the brewer who in 1648 was supplying beer to the navy. Alderman in 1661, sheriff 1661–2, Lord Mayor 1669–70, he became Sir Samuel in 1667 and died in 1674. After the Restoration he gave moral support to the respectable Presbyterian minister Zachary Crofton;[101] but in 1674 he was vigorous in enforcing the laws against radical dissenters, 'contemning all danger for the safety of His Majesty's government'. Just the sort who would have been a cautiously moderate royalist in the 1650s. His widow married George, fourth Viscount Grandison, of an impeccably royalist family. Pepys describes Starling as very rich and so mean that when thirty men saved his house during the Great Fire of 1666 he gave them half a crown between them. He too would hardly have financed Evans without expecting some return.[102]

On the other side Evans never had so much as 2s. in money from Oliver Cromwell, he tells us.[103] He had, or claimed to have, close relations with Hugh Peter and Colonel John Jones of Wrexham.[104] Neither of these would have approved of Evans's political line after 1653. The only other clue I have come across concerns Arise's changing attitude towards Speaker Lenthall. In 1652 (as we have seen) and again in 1659 he spoke disrespectfully of him, differentiating in the latter year between 'Bampfield's Parliament' (under Richard Cromwell) and 'Prynne's Parliament' (the Long Parliament including the secluded members) on the one hand, and 'Lenthall's Parliament' (the Rump) on the other: the latter, Arise thought, was interested only in retaining church and crown lands. But after the Restoration Evans spoke up warmly for Lenthall and clearly tried to influence Charles II in his favour. Lenthall 'always had a good heart towards your majesty'; 'Lenthall and

73

I have been God's instruments to turn this stream another way'. 'What could Monck have done without Lenthall?'[105] But how exactly Lenthall used Evans, if at all, is not clear.

If it were not for the hostile reference in his 1659 pamphlet, we might have supposed that Lenthall and Evans were in touch from 1653 onwards, Lenthall being certainly on the conservative wing of the Independents. He had made his pile by then, and would want a settlement which would guarantee him against his Presbyterian, royalist and republican enemies, and allow him to keep his winnings. The one man towards whom Evans was especially vindictive in 1660, calling for his execution, was Thomas Harrison, the man who turned Speaker Lenthall out of his chair when the Rump was dissolved in April 1653. In 1655 Arise had listed the Independents' demigods as Harrison, Feake, Vavasor Powell, Rogers, Simpson – all men of the radical wing of the Independents, opponents of the Protectorate and so *a fortiori* of any monarchical settlement.[106] But all this is mere speculation. We should have to dismiss *A Rule from Heaven* as the product of Arise's unaided efforts at a time when he despaired of a moderate solution – as on internal evidence we well might.

V

I do not wish to exaggerate the importance of Arise Evans. He is a tiny footnote to history. I have quoted some of his shrewder insights into the society and politics of his day, his gossip about Oliver Cromwell, Hugh Peter, William Lenthall and others of the great upon whom he forced himself. His pauper king, if not a remarkable contribution to political theory, is at least intriguingly original. He gives us grounds for speculating on the relations of Welsh to English culture, not least in his vision of the majority of Englishmen as Britons: his English patriotism, given this background, perhaps fits into the realities of Anglo-Welsh relations in the century and a half after the Act of Union. Evans's career as a prophet no doubt owed a good deal to his Welsh background; but there were other prophets at work in the revolutionary period who were not Welsh, and a study of any one of them may help us to grasp the importance of prophecy – biblical, astrological or Merlinical – as a motive

force for the common people in the revolution. The vision o
Arise Evans as a political journalist born too soon, and his
possible exploitation by royalist moderates or Independent
monarchists as a political stooge, reminds us that though Evans
lived through what used to be called the Puritan Revolution,
the Popish Plot came only just over a decade after he disappears
from the scene. In this religion was shamelessly and blatantly
used for political purposes.

Finally we may reflect on this society, still so primitive that
the royal touch cures scrofula, the King's Evil; and mild
mental abnormality is still regarded as somehow sacred. In the
cruel and brutal world of mid-seventeenth-century England
men were hanged, drawn and quartered for having the wrong
ideas. Only fifteen years before Arise came to London an
elderly clergyman had been tortured and sentenced to death
for having in his drawer a sermon which had never been
preached and which he had no intention of publishing. But
Arise could hang about Charles I's court for days on end, and
deliver a message from God to the King that he and his kingdom were to be destroyed. Meanwhile bishops ran away at the
sight of him and the royal Secretary of State asked for the
prayers of 'God's Secretary'. In the 1640s he got only a brief
term in Bridewell for telling the City's Deputy Recorder that
Arise was the Lord his God. He called on Oliver Cromwell
and stayed till midnight, he pestered the Council of State
with demands that they restore the son of the King they had
executed, and republican officers defended him in long arguments at Whitehall. The Commonwealth did not even imprison
him as Charles I and the Deputy Recorder had done. The holy
imbecile clearly had a great deal of licence. But – and it is a
big but – only when he is an isolated individual. Ten years after
Arise was accused of claiming to be Christ, James Nayler rode
symbolically into Bristol on a donkey, with women strewing
palms in his path. Whether Nayler was less unbalanced than
Arise Evans is an open question. But Nayler was a leader of the
Quakers, a democratic movement whose rapid growth was
frightening the men of property in the mid-fifties. The whole
House of Commons spent six weeks denouncing Nayler with
hysterical frenzy, and he was flogged and branded with a
brutality from which he never recovered. Notwithstanding a

reference to his 'disciples' in 1655, Arise Evans had the good fortune to have few followers.

Our last glimpse of him is highly symbolic, and may give us a clue to the fundamental reason for his royalism. Some time in the summer of 1660 he intercepted Charles II strolling in St James's Park. Perhaps he hoped to extort a reward at last, perhaps he hoped that the royal touch would cure the skin disease which had been spreading over his face in the preceding years, 'so that it was not only nauseous to view but very fetid of smell'. When Charles was told who it was kneeling before him, he gave Arise his hand to kiss; but the latter refrained because his mouth was sore. Instead he rubbed his nose, variously described as 'fungous', 'ulcerated and scabbed', on the royal hand until it burst open and poured forth its contents. At that one royal touch 'the evil humours that did disfigure my face very much was gone'. Elias Ashmole, who saw him two days later, confirmed that he was cured.[107] So the holy healing king and the holy afflicted man his servant, who claimed to have done so much for his restoration, met for the first and last time. Charles II had been restored, one MP said, because we need 'a king with plenty of holy oil about him'. So the false, synthetic, shored-up past met the true past in St James's Park. Charles sauntered on, thinking no doubt of his chemical experiments, or of the ideas of Thomas Hobbes, as well as of Mistress Barbara Palmer. Arise Evans was left on his knees, thanking God. His cure was often quoted in the folklore that gathered around the King's Evil.[108] So far as we know Arise Evans received no other reward.

Writings of Arise Evans

A Voice From Heaven to the Common-Wealth of England (1652).

An Eccho to the Voice from Heaven (?1653; Preface dated 19 December 1652).

To His Excellency the Lord General Cromwell and his Honourable Council of the Army (16 May 1653).

Same title, second petition, 20 May 1653.

The Bloudy Vision of John Farley (1653).

The great and bloody Visions Interpreted by Arise Evans (1654), a shorter version of the preceding pamphlet.

A Declaration of Arise Evans (9 February 1653–4).

The Euroclydon Winde Commanded to cease (1654).

A Message from God . . . to his Highness the Lord Protector (27 June 1654).

The Voice of Michael the Archangel To his Highness the Lord Protector (1654, after 29 September).

The Voice of the Iron Rod to the Lord Protector (1655).

The Voice of King Charls the Father to Charls the Son (1655).

Mr. Evans and Mr. Penningtons Prophecies (1655).

Light for the Jews (1656).

A Rule from Heaven (1659).

To the Most High and Mighty Prince Charles II . . . an Epistle (1660).

[Anon.], *King Charls his Starr* (1654). MS note in Bodleian copy attributes to Arise Evans.

PART II

Change in Continuity: Some Fundamental Ideas

3
Protestantism and the Rise of Capitalism[1]

Man looketh on the outward appearance, but the Lord looketh on the heart.

I Sam. 16:7.

If . . . the motive is generosity, or to give to the Church, and if any prize is really incidental – and the man's main object is fellowship and giving to the work of Christ – then that would seem to be right. It is a question of taking it back into the conscience of each person and examining the motive in that way.

The Rt Rev G. F. Allen, Bishop of Derby,
on the lawfulness of using football pools, raffles
and games of chance to raise funds for the church
(*The Times*, 9 November 1959).

I

It is nearly fifty years since historical thinking in this country was stimulated by the publication of Professor Tawney's *Religion and the Rise of Capitalism*. Most historians would now accept the existence of some connection between protestantism and the rise of capitalism, though Professor Trevor-Roper is a conspicuous exception. But there is little agreement on the nature of the connection. Seventeenth-century protestants themselves emphasized the fact that godly artisans had been the backbone of the Reformation, and that protestantism in its turn had proved to be good for trade and industry; and they were right on both points. Nevertheless there are still untidinesses at the edge of the thesis. The object of this article is to try to clear away some of them, by developing hints given by Professor Tawney himself.[2]

81

One criticism, levelled especially against Weber, is that he made inadequate chronological distinctions, illustrating the causal influence of protestantism in moulding 'the capitalist spirit' by quotations from seventeenth-century writers; even Professor Tawney relies largely on Baxter and Bunyan in his discussions of English Puritanism. Another criticism is that some of the countries in which Calvinism developed in its classical form (Scotland, Hungary) were economically backward; many aristocratic supporters of, for instance, the French Huguenots, were not at all bourgeois in origin or outlook. A third criticism is that Weber and Tawney emphasized points of doctrine which would not have seemed central either to the reformers or to their critics. Protestant teachings on usury, callings, treatment of the poor, and so forth, were peripheral: granting that individual protestants contributed to the rise of a capitalist ethic by what they said on these subjects, it still has not been shown that protestantism as such is associated, either as cause or effect or both, with the rise of capitalism. If connections are to be established, they must be sought in the central doctrines of the reformers, those which most sharply differentiated them from their Roman Catholic contemporaries. And then we have to face a fourth objection in the fact that the reformers thought they found their doctrines in the New Testament and St Augustine. Are we to regard these writings as emanations of the capitalist spirit? If not, why not?[3]

II

The central doctrine of protestantism is justification by faith. The central target of the reformers' attack was justification by works. We must begin here.

When protestants criticized the doctrine of justification by works, they were not saying that charitable works should not be performed. They were attacking the purely formal routine actions by which many Roman Catholic theologians taught that merit could be acquired – telling of beads, saying of paternosters, giving of candles. Luther distinguished between 'two kinds of works: those done for others, which are the right kind; . . . and those done for ourselves, which are of smaller value'.

'We wear and consume our bodies with watching, fasting and labour, but we neglect charity, which is the only lady and mistress of works . . . Paul not only teacheth good works, but also condemneth fantastical and superstitious works.'[4] 'Fixed holidays and fasts, fraternities, pilgrimages, worship of saints, rosaries, monasticism and such-like' were the 'childish and unnecessary works' which the Confession of Augsburg denounced in 1530 as having been exclusively emphasized by popular Roman Catholic preachers. Tyndale, Foxe and other early English reformers delighted to draw up lists of these superstitious works, by which, they did not fail to point out, the church invariably drew money from the pockets of the faithful.[5]

These 'extern matters and ceremonial observations, nothing conducing to any spiritual purpose' were what the reformers had most of all in mind when they denounced 'works'. In discussions between protestants and papists in England in 1559, the former singled out for criticism the sermon on Candlemas Day, in which 'there is also a history of a woman which never did good deed, but only that she had continually kept a candle before our lady', in return for which Mary saved her from hell. 'What occasion of dissolute life and sin may be ministered to simple people by these and an infinite number of such like fables, it is easy to perceive.'[6] The protestant objection was to mechanical actions in which the heart was not involved.

Where 'good works' in the wider sense were concerned – acts of mercy or charity – a protestant thought that *what* a man did was less important than the spirit in which he did it. Justification by works led to a formal righteousness: by performing a round of good works, one bought oneself off from the consequences of sin. Grace came through the sacraments, through the miracle of the mass. Penance was imposed by the priest: it could be performed without true inner penitence. But protestants thought the effectiveness of the sacraments depended on the moral state of the recipient. Man was justified by faith alone: by turning towards God with the full consciousness of his moral being. He was saved not by his own righteousness, not by his own efforts, but by the righteousness of Christ imputed to the favoured few whom God had chosen. Once a protestant had acquired this sense of unity and close personal relationship with God, his attitude towards the world, to sin and to repentance was transformed. The goodness of an action depended not on what that action was (the pagan philosophers had attained to moral virtue) but on the conviciton, the love of God, which inspired it. 'Christ is eaten with the heart', said Cranmer in debate before Protector Somerset. 'Only good men can eat Christ's body.'[7]

On Luther's visit to Rome, as he climbed Pilate's stairs on hands and knees, repeating a paternoster on each stair and kissing it, he wondered if this really did release souls from Purgatory. From Erasmus's Greek Testament he learnt that 'penetentiam agite' meant not 'do penance' but 'be penitent'. This he described as a 'glowing' discovery. In his consciousness of sin, Luther had come to hate the God whose commandments he could not keep: until his outlook was transformed by the Pauline sentence 'the just shall live by faith'. Henceforth, for him, external ceremonial, outward actions, were contrasted with internal conviction, a change of heart. God ceased to be an enemy to be propitiated: works flowed from grace, but man was not justified by them. He had been justified long before, or else his works were worthless. A good man made a good work, not a good work a good man. Faith was 'nothing else but truth of the heart'.[8]

This insistence that each believer should look inward to his own heart contributed to give protestantism its fundamentally individualist bias. Papal doctrine since the fourteenth century had postulated a common store of grace, accumulated in the first instance by Christ, and added to by the merits of saints, martyrs and all who performed more good works than were necessary for their own salvation. Monks and chantry priests, by dedicating their whole lives to religious exercises, built up a superfluity of 'works'. 'This treasure', said the Bull Unigenitus in 1343, 'is . . . entrusted to be healthfully dispersed through blessed Peter, bearer of heaven's keys, and his successors as vicars on earth . . . to them that are truly penitent and have confessed.' Individuals could draw on this treasury of grace only through the mediacy of priests, whose authority came through the hierarchy from the Pope. Indulgences, sold by papal permission, were cheques drawn on the treasury of merits: they could shorten time in Purgatory, for the dead as well as for the living. Thus good works were bought and sold, said Luther.[9]

Justification by works, then, did not mean that an individual could save himself: it meant that he could be saved through the Church. Hence the power of the clergy. Compulsory confession, imposition of penance on the whole population – the majority of whom were illiterate – together with the possibility of withholding absolution, gave priests a terrifying power. Obedience to the Church was an obligatory part of the virtue of humility. If she [the Church] shall have defined anything to be black which to our eyes appears to be white,' said St Ignatius, 'we ought in like manner to pronounce it to be black.' Protestants would inculcate such blind faith in no earthly institution or man, but only in God; and fortunately God's pronouncements were more subject to argument than those of the Church. Even the Bible was checked by what the Spirit of God wrote in the believer's heart.[10]

Justification by works means that salvation out of communion with the Church was unthinkable. For the reformers, the direct relationship of the soul to God was what mattered: the priest, the Church as an institution, were quite secondary. So from the very beginning the protestant revolt against the Roman Church was from the nature of its theology an individualist revolt. That of course was not how Luther and his contemporaries saw it. They began by criticizing specific abuses – sale of indulgences, commutation of penance. But even when they went on to attack confession and monasticism, their starting-point remained the same: a rejection of outward ceremonial enacted without a change of heart. Here is Luther on monasticism:

'Hitherto it hath been the chief holiness and righteousness . . . [for a man] to run into monasteries, to put on monkish apparel, to be shaven, to wear a hempen girdle, to give himself to fasting and prayer, to be clothed with hair-cloth, to lie in woollen garments, to observe an austere manner of living, and in fine, to take upon him monkish holiness and religion; and thus, resting in a show of good works, we knew not but we were holy from top to toe, having regard only to works and the body and not to the heart, where we were full of hatred, fear and incredulity, troubled with an evil conscience, knowing almost nothing rightly of God . . . But there

85

is another righteousness which God esteemeth and accepteth which also we must consider; it consists not in a grey garment nor in a black or white cowl, but in a pure conscience .. When the heart is pure, the house is unto it as the field, and the field as the house; the market is as much esteemed as the monastery; and on the contrary, neither remaineth unto me any work, place or garment which I count profane; for all things are alike unto me, after that holiness hath full possessed my heart.'[11]

Luther thus ended the dual morality, not merely by bringing the ascetic out into the world, but by telling him that his standards were all wrong. Monastic routine could be imposed only on men and women who did not know the direct relationship to God which Luther had experienced and taught. Once the heart was changed, it would leap beyond the formal confines of monastic restrictions into Christian liberty. 'He that bideth in the world, as the monks call it', wrote Tyndale, 'hath more faith than the cloisterer: for he hangeth on God in all things.'[12] For Christians no action can be casual or perfunctory: the most trivial detail of our daily life should be performed to the glory of God, should be irradiated by a conscious cooperation with God's purposes. This was not originally to sanctify the life of all laymen: on the contrary Luther held that the world belonged to the devil. But the true Christian could live in the devil's world without being of it because of his saving faith.[13]

But my motives, my intentions, the spirit in which I perform an action, are within my control. Philosophically, protestant theologians believed that the inclination of one's will toward God came from outside, from God; practically, as moralists they emphasized the careful scrutiny of motives, the conscious attempt to see that one's will was tuned in to the divine harmonies. 'Impenitence is the unpardonable sin', declared Luther, for whom faith was 'the most difficult of all works.' Faith without a desire of repentance is as worthless as repentance without faith, wrote Calvin. No priest can search the secrets of my heart.[14] 'Is there any angel,' asked the Homily Concerning Prayer, 'any virgin, any patriarch or prophet among the dead, that can understand or know the reason of he heart?' The question expected the answer No. I, and I alone, can know whether the illuminating contact with God has been established. If it has not, all the priests and all the ceremonies in the world will not establish it. Compulsory confession cuts across the individual's direct relation to God; it is 'both tyrannical [to the sinner] and insulting to God, who in binding consciences to his Word, would have them free from human rule.'[15] For the godly, morality should be self-imposed: unquestioning obedience to the priest was a positive hindrance.

Protestants thus had a new measuring-rod. Duties, Calvin declared, are estimated not by actions but by motives. 'There is nothing which God more abominates than when men endeavour to cloak themselves by substituting signs and external appearance for integrity of heart.' To wear mourning apparel from mere social convention, without feeling real grief, was evil and hypocritical. Scholastic sophists, Calvin continued, 'talk much of contrition and attrition, torment the soul with many scruples, and involve it in great trouble and anxiety; but when they seem to have deeply wounded the heart, they cure all its bitterness with a slight sprinkling of ceremonies.' 'There is nothing which gives men greater confidence and licence in sinning than the idea that after making confession to priests they can wipe their lips and say, I have not done it.'[16]

Bishop Fisher regretted that he was not left time enough between condemnation and execution to perform so many good works as he believed to be necessary to salvation. Such good works no doubt included frequent repetition of the Lord's Prayer. Luther prided himself on having freed people from this mechanical repetition of the paternoster in the gabbling manner which has given the word 'patter' to the language. 'Neither words nor singing (if used in prayer)', said Calvin, 'avail one iota with God, unless they proceed from deep feeling in the heart.'[17] The Preface to the First Prayer Book of Edward vi complained that when men attended services in Latin 'they understood not, so that they have heard with their ears only: and their hearts, spirit and mind have not been edified thereby.'

Ceremonies are of value only in so far as they contribute to this edification of the believer, helping him to understand the act of worship he is taking part in. Hence Bible and Prayer

87

Book in the vernacular; emphasis on preaching rather than on prayer and sacraments; music must edify and not distract – hence metrical psalms and hostility to organs, polyphony and choristers, dislike of images and gaudy churches. All these sprang from the same concern with turning the heart of the worshipper towards God. The same principle opened the way to many of the heresies of later radical protestantism. The attack on set prayers, the desire of laymen to pray and preach, are natural extensions of Lutheran principles.[18] So was adult baptism.[19] So was Milton's demand for divorce where religious temperaments were incompatible.[20] Laud's attempt to revive ceremonies flew in the face of this long tradition. 'The matter is not great which way we turn our faces, so the heart stand right', Raleigh had written in a phrase he later made famous at his execution. The chapel of Emmanuel College, its former Master told Laud, was 'consecrated by faith and a good conscience', and so did not need the ceremony of episcopal consecration.[21] Many came to think tithes and the Sabbath mere ceremonies. And, since no one can judge the heart of another, we have in Luther's teaching the germ of the most subversive of all heresies, religious toleration, horrified though Luther would have been at the thought.[22]

It took time for such conclusions to be drawn. But in a society where custom and tradition counted for so much, this insistence that a well-considered strong conviction overrode everything else had a great liberating force. We see more clearly by the light of grace than by the light of nature, Travers told Hooker. We must, of course, take care that our inner light is not darkness. 'Beware of thy good intent, good mind, good affection or zeal, as they call it,' Tyndale warned. 'Labour for knowledge, that thou mayest know God's will.' So inquiry, searching the Scriptures, was stimulated. The godly man looked beyond ceremonies and sacraments to the thing signified, 'and will not serve visible things', for that was idolatry.[23] As soon as protestantism established churches, it had itself to face the dissidence of dissent. The Calvinist discipline was one method of curbing the exuberant consciences of laymen, rather more doctrinally satisfactory than Luther's reliance on the secular arm. The Anglican *via media* left room for men to have it both ways. 'There is no religion where there are no ceremonies,' said

Archbishop Bancroft. 'The more ceremonies, the less truth', said the Puritan Greenham.[24]

Luther had started more than he knew when he laid it down that the heart decides for itself. 'A man can form his own rule and judge for himself about mortifying his body.' 'Neither pope, nor bishop, nor any one else, has the right to impose so much as a single syllable of obligation upon a Christian man without his own consent, . . . for we are free from all things.' This Christian freedom makes us 'kings and priests with power over all things'.[25] The important thing is not that Luther made such remarks, though that mattered; but that an anarchy of individual consciences flowed from the logic of his theological position. 'To have faith', added Calvin, 'is . . . to possess some certainty and complete security of mind, to have whereon to rest and fix your foot.'[26] That is what protestantism gave to the sixteenth-century man of scruple, tormented by a sense of his own sinfulness: an inner calm and self-confidence, intermittent perhaps, but firmly based on moments of elation which, once experienced, marked a man off in his own eyes from his fellows. (Hence the importance of the doctrine that the elect could never wholly fall from grace.) The tension between hyper-consciousness of natural sinfulness and the permanent possibility of God's grace expressed itself in exuberant efforts to do good works, which had nothing in common with formal righteousness. 'We teach,' Thomas Taylor declared, 'that only Doers shall be saved, and by their doing though not for their doing. The profession of religion is no such gentlemanlike life or trade, whose rents come in by their stewards, whether they sleep or wake, work or play.' The godly look often into their account books and cast up their reckonings. 'But a bankrupt has no heart to this business.'[27] For 'the Papal doctrine of doubting of God's love cuts the sinews of endeavour'.[28]

III

Luther was always very unwilling to apply this principle outside the purely religious sphere; yet its extension was inevitable. All action should rest on faith, he told the city of Nuremberg, when it was worried about the lawfulness of resisting the Emperor. Action taken in faith might be good 'even though it

89

were an error and a sin'. 'To steal, rob and murder', Tyndale thought, 'are holy, when God commandeth them.' *Pecca fortiter*: sin may not be sin after all if the heart believes strongly enough that it is commanded by God. And only the individual can decide this. He is therefore placed under a tremendous obligation to make sure that his heart is properly informed – by studying the Scriptures for instance. But in the last resort conscience is the supreme court, from which there is no appeal.[29] Bishop Hall found it difficult to determine 'whether it be worse to do a lawful action with doubting or an evil with resolution', since that which in itself is good is made evil by doubt. Oliver Cromwell was sure he should not accept the crown in May 1657 'because at the best I should do it doubtingly. And certainly what is so done is not of faith', and consequently is 'sin to him that doth it'.[30]

The danger of antinomianism always lurked behind Lutheranism and Calvinism. 'Whatsoever thou shalt observe upon liberty and of love, is godly,' said Luther, 'but if thou observe anything of necessity, it is ungodly.' 'If you have the true kind of Christian love and faith, everything you do is of service. We may all please ourselves what we do.' Calvin agreed that, with safeguards, 'the consciences of believers may rise above the Law, and may forget the whole righteousness of the Law.' 'The elect, having the Law written in their hearts, and loving it in their spirits,' declared Tyndale, 'sin there never; but without, in the flesh.' 'If an adultery could be committed in the faith,' Luther reflected, 'it would no longer be a sin.' Barely a century later Lawrence Clarkson acted on the principle that with God adultery and marriage are but one, 'and that one holy, just and good as God'.[31]

But the antinomians were a fringe, and can be disregarded for our purpose. What matters is the main stream of protestant thought. Luther and Calvin set men free from forms and ceremonies, and even from the law. It is essential to understand the release and relief which protestantism brought to ordinary men and women if we are to obtain any insight into the astonishing rapidity with which it spread. The political consequences of looking into the heart, of making integrity of intention the test, are clear. 'If we deposed the said Queen Regent rather of malice and perverted envy than for the preservation of the commonwealth', said Knox, then God would prevail against us even if she deserved her fate.[32] But revolutions made with the right motives are godly. In October 1647 the members of the Army Council sought God in prayer before reporting to one another the inclination of their hearts towards Charles I. Ceremonies are the form of worship laid down by public authority. This authority is held to be inferior to the voice of God speaking within the pure heart. Strafford observed to Laud, of the Puritans, that 'The very genius of that nation of people leads them always to oppose, as well civilly as ecclesiastically, all that ever authority ordains for them.'[33]

Protestantism then was infinitely more flexible than catholicism. Catholicism had the iron framework of the hierarchy, headed by the pope. It had the machinery of confession, penance and absolution, and of church courts and excommunication, not to mention the Inquisition, with which to enforce traditional standards of orthodoxy. Protestantism lacked many of these barriers to change of moral attitudes. Some of the institutions and codes of the past were retained in the Lutheran countries and in the Anglican church. Efforts were made to erect new disciplinary institutions and codes in countries where Calvinism triumphed. Desperate attempts were made to compile a protestant casuistry. But the guides to godliness, the plain man's pathways to heaven, the practices of piety, were perforce addressed to the consciences of lay heads of households. The ministers may have helped such men to discipline and educate their families and employees. But the Roman church was able slowly to adapt its standards to the modern world through a controlled casuistry guiding a separate priestly caste, which wielded the power of confession and absolution. Protestant ministers had to tag along behind what seemed right to the consciences of the leading laymen in their congregations.

It is here, through its central theological attitude, that protestantism made its great contribution to the rise of capitalism. What mattered was not that Calvin was a trifle less strict than the canonists in his approach to usury. What mattered was that protestantism appealed, as medieval heresy had done, to artisans and small merchants, whom it helped to trust the dictates of their own hearts as their standard of conduct. The elect were those who felt themselves to be the elect. What was astonishing was that so many people had at the same time the same miraculous experience of conversion: thanks to God's direct intervention, grace made them free. It would indeed be inexplicable if we could not see that the psychological states leading up to conversion were the effects of a social crisis which hit many unprivileged small producers in the same sort of way. There was no salvation in the old priestly magic, because that no longer gave them any sense of control over the world of economic fluctuations in which they now had to live. Only an assertive self-confidence could do this, and that was so novel that it must seem to come arbitrarily from outside.

> 'Take me to you, imprison me, for I
> Except you enthrall me, never shall be free,
> Nor ever chaste, except you ravish me.'[34]

The social situation set large numbers of men and women seeking answers to similar problems. As, thanks to a Luther, a Calvin, a Zwingli, groups of men realized that 'the object of [Christ's] struggle was to raise up those who were lying prostrate',[35] this in its turn redoubled their confidence. They were the elect, not only because they felt they were, but also because other people, good people, recognized that they were; and shared their views. So, once the religion of the heart spread (and the printing press, that technical triumph of the urban craftsmen, gave it a great advantage over medieval heresies), Lutheranism, and still more Calvinism, was a magnificent bond of unity and strength. Once touched with grace, the small group of the elect felt themselves to be unique, differentiated from the mass of mankind. Lack of numbers ceased to matter: if God was with them, who would be against them? So their numbers grew.

In the last resort, what comes out of the conscience of a man bears some relation to what goes into it: to the social environment in which he lives. Absolute individualism of conscience, paradoxically, means that society has a greater influence on conduct. So protestantism spread as a negative reaction to institutions and practices which large numbers of men and women felt to be abuses. But, for the same social reason, the positive forms which the protest took tended to vary from region to region, and in the same region from class to class. Belatedly, Calvinism tried by organization to impose homogeneity. But once the pamphlets and sermons had encouraged wide discussion of theology and church government, it proved as impossible to maintain unity as it was among English Puritans after 1640 or within the French *Tiers État* after 1789. Unity existed only so long as there was an enemy to be overthrown. After that the voice of God said different things to different people. So the earnest minority which found the eternal decrees and the rule of the ungodly not unacceptable was challenged by those descendants of the medieval heretics who were prepared to contemplate the possibility of all men being saved: who wanted to be freed from the rule of new presbyter no less than of old priest.

From their different points of view both Hooker and Perkins showed themselves aware of this social background. Perkins asked how we should judge what is the measure of wealth which the master of a family may with good conscience seek. His reply was: 'not by the affection of covetous men', but by 'the common judgment and practice of the most godly, frugal and wise men with whom we live'.[36] Hooker wrote ironically that 'whosoever shall anger the meanest and simplest artisan *which carrieth a good mind*, by not removing out of the Church such rites and ceremonies as displease him, "better he were drowned in the bottom of the sea".'[37] Fulke Greville well expressed this sense of permanent criticism in protestantism, its ability to interpret even the Bible, when he made his chorus of priests conclude *Mustapha* with the words:

> 'Yet when each of us in his own heart looks
> He finds the God there far unlike his books.'[38]

For the protestant conscience there were no absolutes, no accepted infallibilities, though each sect as it arose tried to establish them. But there was no final court of appeal, not even the Bible. Even yesterday's conscience might be repudiated today. The religious radicals inherited from the medieval heretics the concept of the Everlasting Gospel, written in men's hearts; more respectable Puritans evolved the doctrine of progressive revelation: both allowed moral standards to be modified as society changed.

93

IV

When the businessman of sixteenth- and seventeenth-century Geneva, Amsterdam or London looked into his inmost heart, he found that God had planted there a deep respect for the principle of private property. The more sophisticated might express this in the seventeenth century by saying that respect for property was a fundamental law, or part of the law of nature (or reason): but it was easier, and more likely to over-bear opposition, to say with Colonel Rainborough in the Putney Debates that God had commanded 'Thou shalt not steal'. Such men felt quite genuinely and strongly that their economic practices, though they might conflict with the traditional law of the old church, were not offensive to God. On the contrary: they glorified God. For here the protestant theologians had sold the pass, by their fundamental distinction between formal and charitable works, and by making the individual heart the ultimate arbiter.

The elect, Luther had said, must perform good works to help their neighbour, the community, the commonwealth, humanity; this prevents the doctrine of justification by faith giving 'licence and free liberty to everyone to do what he will'. Men serve God in their callings, however vile, because they serve their neighbour. 'A cobbler, a smith, a farmer, each has the work and office of his task, and yet they are all alike consecrated priests and bishops, and every one by means of his own work or office must benefit and serve every other, that in this way many kinds of work be done for the bodily and spiritual welfare of the community.'[39] In his teaching on usury Calvin always insisted that men must consider the good of the commonwealth before their own gain. It all depends on the attitude with which we go about our work. George Herbert derived directly from Luther when he wrote that labour was dignified or degrading according to the spirit in which it was done.

> 'A servant with this clause
> Makes drudgery divine;
> Who sweeps a room, as for thy laws,
> Makes that and the action fine.'[40]

The enthusiasm with which English Puritan preachers took up this point shows that it met a real need. It was very arguable that productive economic activity in the sixteenth and seventeenth centuries was a charitable good work in Luther's sense. The protestants' emphasis on hard work, which linked their reprobation of idle monks with their reprobation of idle beggars, sprang from the economic circumstances of the time as reflected in the thinking of bourgeois laymen. When Francis Bacon suggested that the age-old problem of poverty might at last be soluble if the resources of the community, including its labour, were rationally utilized, he was only developing an idea which he might have received from his very Puritan mother.[41] The ambiguity of the word charity helped. The law without charity was nothing worth. Fuller said that Edward vi's charity was no less demonstrated in his foundation of Bridewell for the punishment of sturdy beggars than of St Thomas's Hospital for relief of the poor. Perkins thought the Poor Law of 1597 was 'in substance the very law of God'.[42] Professor Jordan's remarkable book on philanthropy in England shows how in the sixteenth and early seventeenth centuries sober and rational calculation of what was of advantage to the community replaced the medieval ideal of indiscriminate alms-giving. The latter created beggars, and was self-regarding anyway; true charity was to encourage self-help in the deserving.

The preachers, and still more their congregations, might well be genuinely convinced in their hearts that industry was a good work, for the 'common good', for 'the use and profit of mankind'; that negligence in business harms the public state.[43] 'The Lord mislikes the yawning mouth and folded arms, the signs of sleep which commonly follow the careless man, who doth neglect the state and condition of his house and family. But on the other side the Scripture commendeth highly faithful labourers and good and painful people in work.' The words are those of the official translation of Henry Bullinger's *Decades*, required reading for godly protestant Englishmen.[44] It is a duty to God and the commonwealth to use your talents, said John Preston. Provided you do not make gain your godliness, provided you do not seek riches but accept them as the blessing of God if they happen to come – then you may lawfully take care to increase your estate. 'Ask thyself then', said Thomas Taylor, 'what good doth my life to church, to commonwealth, to family, to men?'[45] It was in fact the labour of generations of God-fearing Puritans that made England the leading industrial nation in the world – God, as His manner is, helping those who helped themselves.

Through this emphasis on the inner conviction which inspired actions, bourgeois lay society could impose its own standards. 'God's children look to the spiritual use of those things which the worldlings use carnally', said Greenham. The actions of the Scribes and Pharisees 'were good in themselves, and for others', said Sibbes; 'but the end of them was naught, and therefore both they and their works are condemned.' 'Man may with good conscience', Perkins thought, 'desire and seek for goods necessary, whether for nature or for his person, according to the former rules: but he may not desire and seek for goods more than necessary, for if he doth, he sinneth.' ('The former rules' include the convenient provision that 'those goods without which a man's estate, condition and dignity . . . cannot be preserved' are necessary.[46]) The preachers attempted to spiritualize what men were doing anyway, by telling them to do it for the right reasons. One may suspect that their congregations paid more attention to the general permission than to the careful qualifications with which it was hedged around. 'They are very hot for the Gospel', said Thomas Adams of such laymen; 'they love the Gospel: who but they? Not because they believe it, but because they feel it: the wealth, peace, liberty that ariseth by it.'[47]

Men are too ready to accuse Puritans of covetousness, observed William Gouge: we should be very cautious about this, since we cannot read the hearts of others, or know all the extenuating circumstances. 'Covetousness doth especially consist in the inward desire of a man, which is best known to himself . . . Observe the inward wishes of thine heart. If they be especially for the things of this world, they argue a covetous disposition.' 'When therefore thou thinkest of sparing', Dod and Clever advised, 'let not the greedy desire of gathering draw thee to it, but conscience of well using that which God hath lent thee.' 'Seek riches not for themselves but for God', was Thomas Taylor's simpler formulation.[48] 'We teach you not to cast away the bag, but covetousness', Thomas Adams reassured his City congregation. 'O ye rich citizens', announced Joseph Hall, 'we tell you from Him, whose title is Rich in Mercy, that ye may be at once rich and holy.' When ministers went as far as that, we can imagine the simplifications and self-deceptions of laymen. The Presbyterian preachers, Hobbes noted two generations later, 'did never inveigh against the lucrative vices of men of trade or handicraft'.[49]

The Puritans tried to spiritualize economic processes. God instituted the market and exchange, Dod and Clever assured their large public. 'He would have commerce and traffic to proceed from love', and He favours a fair bargainer. Greenham made unrepining acceptance of the market price evidence 'that thine heart is rightly affected, both to God and to the brethren'.[50] Emphasis on the motive of the heart is the key to the preachers' distinction between 'biting' usury and legitimate commercial transactions,[51] no less than to their distinction between indiscriminate alms-giving and relief of the deserving poor, and to the protestant doctrine of the calling. All stem from the theology of justification by faith. Did adventurers sail to North America, 'to seek new worlds for gold, for praise, for glory?' 'If the same proceed of ambition or avarice', they were warned in 1583, 'it cometh not of God', and will not prosper. But if men are impelled by zeal for the honour of God, by compassion for the 'poor infidels captured by the devil', as well as by desire to relieve the poor of England and advance the interest of their honest and well-affected countrymen, then 'so sacred an intention' gives them the right 'to prosecute effectively the full possession of those so ample and pleasant countries'. 'If we first seek the kingdom of God', wrote Hakluyt with divine simplicity and prophetic accuracy, 'all other things will be given unto us.'[52]

This emphasis on the religious motive for colonization was often repeated. Historians looking only at the result have regarded it as gratuitous hypocrisy. Those who have tried to penetrate the hearts of the colonizers have seen it as a seriously held intention, which for some reason was never carried out.[53] It was rather, I suggest, a necessary part of the thought processes of men whose protestant training made secular pursuits possible only if entered into with the right motive. But the example of colonization shows how easily emphasis on godly motive could

97

become a cloak for economic calculation. Protestants, said a preacher at Paul's Cross in 1581, are freed from the tyranny of the law upon the conscience. Hence we are prone to carnality, since 'we live to ourselves'.[54] Zeal-of-the-Land Busy, when asked about the lawfulness of eating a Bartholomew pig at the Fair, reflected that 'The place is not much, not very much, so it be eaten with a reformed mouth, with sobriety and humbleness.' The sin of Ignorance, Bunyan recorded sixty years later, was that he thought all problems of salvation were answered by saying 'My heart tells me so'.

V

Doctrines emphasizing the motives of the heart, allowing social pressures to influence individual conduct more freely, flourish especially, it may be suggested, in periods of rapid social change, and among those persons most exposed to its effects. Christianity arose in such a period; St Augustine, on whose theology the reformers drew so heavily, also lived in an age when old standards were breaking down; and he too stressed inner motive rather than external action. 'When it is plain to him what he should do and to what he should aspire, even then, unless he feel delight and love therein, he does not perform his duty.' 'If they said that any works of mercy may obtain pardon even for the greatest and most habitual sins, they would be guilty of much absurdity: for so might the richest man for his 10*d*. a day have a daily quittance for all his fornications, homicides, and other sins whatsoever.'[55] There appears to be a permanent tendency for established churches to revert to ceremonial, and for opposition groups to stress the internal element. In the Middle Ages, after the Church had become institutionalized, those who laid the strongest emphasis on the intention, the purity of heart of ordinary lay Christians, were the heretics – Massalians, Paulicians, Bogomils, Albigensians, Lollards – to whom radical protestants from Foxe to Lilburne looked back for the true Christian line of descent. This age-old protest acquired a new significance as educated townsmen, trained by their mode of life in rational calculation and independent thinking, began to challenge the clerical monopoly of education and to assert their own standards of morality. The protestant emphasis on the heart helped to dissolve the hard crust of custom, tradition and authority.[56]

To summarize the argument, then: the appeal to inner conviction, and the rejection of the routine of ceremonies through which the priesthood imposed its authority, could have liberating effects in any society. The hold over men's minds of an established doctrinal system had to be broken before the political and social order sanctified by those doctrines could be challenged. The appeal to the heart was common to early Christianity and many medieval heresies. Its most obvious effects were negative. But, positively, it facilitated the evolution of more flexible doctrines. Since opposition to the Roman Church in sixteenth- and seventeeth-century Europe drew its main strength from the big cities, protestantism could be developed in ways which favoured the rise of capitalism. But there is nothing in protestantism which leads automatically to capitalism: its importance was rather that it undermined obstacles which the more rigid institutions and ceremonies of catholicism imposed. The Reformation mobilized masses of men against the Roman Church and the political authorities which protected it. Initial support for protestantism and especially Calvinism came from the educated minority, largely urban, which thought seriously about problems of church and state. But doctrines evolved by and for the middle class could appeal to other dissatisfied elements in the population, like the gentry of Hungary and Scotland, or the plebeians of the Dutch towns. By the same token, protestant churches were established – in Scandinavia, in central Europe – which made only slight and incidental contributions to the development of capitalism.

The protestant revolt melted down the iron ideological framework which held society in its ancient mould. Where capitalism already existed, it had henceforth freer scope. But men did not become capitalists because they were protestants, nor protestants because they were capitalists. In a society already becoming capitalist, protestantism facilitated the triumph of the new values. There was no inherent theological reason for the protestant emphasis on frugality, hard work, accumulation; but that emphasis was a natural consequence of the religion of the heart in a society where capitalist production was developing. It was, if we like, a rationalization; but it flowed naturally from protestant theology, whose main significance, for our present purposes, is that in any given society it enabled religion to be moulded by those who dominated in that society.

'All external things [are] subject to our liberty', declared Calvin, 'provided the nature of that liberty approves itself to our minds as before God.' But Christian liberty was for the elect only. Professor Brown has argued that later Puritan attempts to spiritualize the market were the opposite of Luther's view that the world was given over to the devil.[57] Yet the transformation was due at least as much to the victories of the protestant outlook in the world as to an abandonment of its theology. When true religion had triumphed, the godly could hardly surrender the world so cheerfully to the devil. In a society run by protestants the ungodly must be disciplined; and the duty of performing good works for one's neighbours became a duty to the community. Hence the overwhelming emphasis of later Puritanism on the religious duties of industry, thrift and accumulation. As the bourgeois virtues triumphed, so the society of largely self-employed small producers was transformed into a society of domestic- and wage-workers, who could be profitably employed only by those who owned capital. In this society the few who climbed the social ladder did so at the expense of their neighbours. So the thought of the fortunate upper ranks came to stress more and more the vices and follies of the poor. Later Calvinism in England became harsher and more hypocritical, because of changes in society which it had helped to bring about.

Professors Haller and Jordan have stressed the importance of the Calvinist discipline and organization in giving a sense of status and self-respect to the unprivileged; and have suggested that Calvinism's spread, and its success in building revolutionary parties, owed more to this than to its theology. But the emphasis on motive also helped the theology to flourish among earnest, sincere and responsible men in any sort of environment; and the discipline, ideally designed for preserving the domination of a small nucleus, was adaptable to almost any form of revolt. The appeal of Calvinism in the sixteenth and seventeenth centuries was no more limited to the urban middle class than that of Marxism has been limited to the urban working class in our own day. In Scotland Calvinism became the bond of union between those who wished to be free of France and the French court, as well as of exploitation by the international Church. It was led by quite different social groups from those which dominated English Puritanism. The ministers were almost its only intellectuals. Because the kirk headed a movement for national independence, Calvinism drove far deeper roots than it did in England, where capitalism and the class divisions which accompanied it were much more developed. So in England, within little more than a century of the Reformation, Calvinists had led a successful revolution but had failed to monopolize state power because they could not hold together the diverse groups which had helped to make the revolution: whereas in Scotland Presbyterianism became a popular religion in the same sense as Catholicism did in Ireland, and in a way that Anglicanism never did in England. There were 'nationalist' elements also in the Calvinism of Transylvania and the Netherlands.

So the fact that strong political feelings, of any kind, could express themselves, and be shared, through the emphasis on the heart, helps to explain the existence of sincere Calvinists among the aristocracy and gentry – themselves experiencing social crisis – in many countries from Hungary to France. But we should not be naïve about this. Calvin deliberately set out to win the support of the high aristocracy in France; and the latter no doubt saw the use for themselves of a tightly-disciplined, wealthy and dedicated urban organization.[58] The godly in England also had few scruples about casting out devils with Beelzebub, in the shape of the Dukes of Northumberland or Buckingham, the Earls of Leicester or Essex.

An age of ignorance is an age of ceremony, Dr Johnson correctly observed.[59] The victory of protestantism helped to end the animistic magical universe, and undermined the traditional popular conception of religion as propitiation. Henceforth God and the individual soul stood face to face. The sense of sin remained, became indeed more overwhelming, because sin had to be grappled with alone. But the sense of sin was now also a sense of potential freedom. No magician or priest or saint could help, but God could. His promises were free and sure. The Puritan remained terribly conscious of his own sinful nature, even whilst he tried, by careful scrutiny of motive, to identify his will with the will of God. 'It does not need modern psychology to enable us to appreciate that the more bitter the internal struggle, the more complete was the assumption of identification with the Will of God in external activities.'[60] The simultaneous conviction of depravity and righteousness does not make the most attractive characters in the world; but it gave a vital stimulus to productive effort in countries where capitalism was developing, at a time when industry was small-scale, handicraft, unrationalized. Successful medieval businessmen died with feelings of guilt and left money to the Church to be put to unproductive uses. Successful protestant businessmen were no longer ashamed of their productive activities whilst alive, and at death left money to help others to imitate them. None were more industrious than those who had abandoned the concept of a work of supererogation.

> 'Not the labours of my hands
> Can fulfill Thy law's demands.'

The paradox of protestantism is that it eternally strives to fulfil a law which it knows to be unfulfillable. The paradox of capitalism is that production and accumulation become objects in themselves, losing sight of the end of consumption: just as the man whom Hobbes abstracted from this society sought power after power, ending only in death. Hobbist man is what capitalist man would have been if he had ceased to worry about his motives. At worst the preachers clothed his nakedness in a fig-leaf of hypocrisy; at best they humanized some industrial relations and directed energy towards public service as well as private profit.

'Reason' and 'Reasonableness'[1]

When all is done, let men talk what they will, reason is an excellent thing if a man can hit on it.

> Joseph Sedgwick, *Learnings Necessity*
> (1653), p. 31.

Revolution is only a necessary re-definition of the reasonable by extremists.

> *The Hornsey Affair*, by Students and Staff
> of the Hornsey College of Art
> (Penguin, 1969), p. 10.

I

The very great honour of the invitation to deliver the Hobhouse Memorial Lecture took my mind back more years than I care to remember, to the time when as an undergraduate of Balliol I had the good fortune to go to political theory tutorials with A. D. Lindsay. He gave me Hobhouse's *Metaphysical Theory of the State* and *Elements of Social Justice* to read. I have not referred to these books very often since, but I still have the copious notes I took from them at that time. I copied out Hobhouse's epigram on the General Will: 'so far as it is will it is not general; . . . so far as it is general it is not will'. I have often quoted it since without I fear recalling its author. Another remark – which I have paraphrased without acknowledgement – was that by a 'free monarchy' James I meant a system in which the king was responsible to no one.[2] Hobhouse was illustrating the different meanings given to the word 'liberty', and this leads on to my theme this afternoon.

The shifting meanings of the word 'liberty' in the seventeenth century were noted by contemporaries. In medieval usage it signified almost a property right, a privilege from which others

could be excluded: the popularity of its modern sense dates
from the Civil War. 'Though the name of liberty be pleasant
to all kinds of people', Edward Hyde confided to his commonplace book, 'yet all men do not understand the same thing by
it.'[3] 'All men have stood for freedom', said the Digger Gerrard
Winstanley in 1649; 'and now the common enemy is gone you
are all like men in a mist, seeking for freedom and know not
where nor what it is.'[4] For most members of the Long Parliament, unlike James I, 'liberty and property' were inseparable.
It was only when men like the Levellers started asking for
'freedom for all manner of people' that their opponents
discovered that 'liberty cannot be provided for in a general
sense if property be preserved'.[5] This would not have worried
Winstanley, for whom true freedom lay 'in the free enjoyment
of the earth' and in the abolition of wage labour.[6]

One of the great needs of historians of sixteenth- and
seventeenth-century England is a chronological dictionary, a
dictionary which would tell us which words changed meanings,
and when; when exactly new words were first used, and when
they came into general currency. Some of these facts can be
dug out of the *Oxford English Dictionary*; but it is a large work,
and a chronological linguistic survey of this period might
produce fascinating results. The historian of our own generation
for example could learn a lot about international relations in
the postwar period simply by looking at the new words which
came into use then, or the new meanings which old words
acquired: A for Aggression, internal; B for Brinkmanship, C for
Confrontation, D for Deterrent, E for Escalation and so on.

Words change their meanings in ways which trap the
historically unwary. When a Parliamentary diarist wrote in
1621 of an enclosure bill, 'it is pretended for the good of the
commons',[7] the modern sense of the word 'pretended' conveys
what he perhaps ought to have thought rather than what he
did think. In seventeenth-century usage it is a neutral word,
signifying 'suggested', 'alleged'. When the poet William
Alabaster looked forward to hearing in heaven the singing of
'Archangels, angels, virgins and professors',[8] he was not paying
tribute to the academic profession. And when Henry Vaughan
sweetly sings 'How fair a prospect is a bright backside' he means
only that it is nice to have a little garden behind the house.

The fashionableness of words like 'anatomy', 'anatomize', in Elizabethan England tells us what an impression this crafts-man's art of surgery had suddenly made on contemporaries. The prevalence of the word 'cantonization' in England in the 1640s and 1650s reveals something of the fears that men felt, lest their hard-won national unity might be lost.[9] The word 'revolution' itself acquired its modern meaning only in seventeenth-century England. Previously it had been a tech-nical term of astrology or astronomy. But when Oliver Crom-well said God's revolutions were not to be attributed to the cunning design of mere human invention, the word had acquired a recognizably modern sense.[10]

The only book I know which meets my demand is Mr C. L. Barber's excellent *The Idea of Honour in the English Drama, 1591–1700*. Examining this key word in its social context, Mr Barber concludes that 'the total changes in usage that have been found represent a major change in scale of values', and are related to social shifts.[11] It is in this spirit, as historian and not at all as linguistic philosopher, that I want to consider 'reason' and 'reasonableness' against the changing background of seventeenth-century England.

II

Men's experience of the world was transformed in the sixteenth and seventeenth centuries. Astronomical and geographical discoveries destroyed the old anthropocentric universe, created new conceptions of size and space. The beginnings of anthrop-ology and comparative religion date from European contact with America and the Far East. Nearer home, economic changes produced moral revolutions. In the fifteenth century, R. H. Tawney observed, the practical man 'had practised extortion and been told that it was wrong; for it was contrary to the law of God.' In the seventeenth century 'he was to practice it and be told that it was right; for it was in accordance with the law of nature'.[12] Hierarchy gave place to atomic individualism. By 1725 the Presbyterian Francis Hutcheson, developing some hints of Thomas Hobbes's, had proclaimed the principle 'the greatest happiness for the greatest numbers'.[13] Divine right had disappeared in most spheres. 'To talk of a king as God's viceregent on earth', said the Tory David Hume in 1741, 'would but excite laughter in everyone.'[14] It had not been at all funny a century earlier. The inherited penalties for original sin were being questioned, just as were the hereditary principle in government and the apostolic succession of bishops. Etc., etc. In almost every sphere new ideas of what was reasonable were creeping in, disseminated by the new craft of printing, by the new protestant emphasis on preaching and education.

The most obvious area in which there were rival concepts of 'reasonableness' is the economic. Richard Capel, writing in 1633, admitted that 'most men do think that they have reason to make the most of their money, and (as yet) will see no reason against it'. The individual businessman's conception of what was reasonable was here setting itself up against the preachers' condemnation of usury handed down from a pre-capitalist society. Similarly, Capel continued, gentlemen 'dare proclaim that they *will* enclose, say all the preachers in the world the contrary, . . . because they think that they have reason to enclose'.[15] In conflicts over manorial custom, the law-courts took the 'reasonableness' of a given custom as decisive. They might introduce sweeping innovations under the guise of enforcing customs.[16] For what was a reasonable custom? Here the views of tenants differed from those of lords. Judges sometimes used the concept of 'reasonableness' to limit the arbitrariness of lords of manors; but some old customs beneficial to tenants could seem very 'unreasonable' to improving landlords in an inflationary age. And, as a pamphlet of 1653 put it, 'the chancellor or judges before whom the reasonableness dependeth to be determined are themselves lords of such copyholders, and biased with their own interest and concernment'.[17] One of the Leveller aspirations in the 1640s was to have customs defined so as to give legal force to customs favourable to tenants.[18]

In New England John Cotton wrote in 1641 that the judges should 'set reasonable rates upon all commodities, and proportionably to limit the wages of workers and labourers'.[19] So the medieval conception of the just price was transvalued. 'Customs are only valid when reasonable', claimed journeymen weavers of London in 1649. They continued: 'nothing in the world can be more unreasonable that that such a number of men as sixteen should have liberty to exercise a power over as many thousands without, nay against their wills, consent or election'. It was 'the perfectest badge of slavery that men can be subjected to'.[20] Others would call this free contract, and see it as in accordance with the law of nature.

Protestant theology was another solvent. The Anglican *Reformation of the Ecclesiastical Laws*, a radical document produced under Edward VI and vainly pressed for by Puritans under Elizabeth, said that although custom and long usage are of no inconsiderable authority, yet they are not so valid that they ought to prevail over reason or the law. Custom was not valid if it conflicted with divine or natural law.[21] 'Hath an ill custom lasted long?' demanded Joseph Hall more brashly in 1605; 'it is more than time it were abrogated.'[22]

Theologians had difficulty in enforcing traditional standards against what their congregations thought reasonable in this changing world. The great Puritan William Perkins was prepared to leave a decision on how much wealth was meet to maintain a man's family (and how much should be spent on charity) to 'the common judgment and practise of the most godly, frugal and wise men with whom we live'.[23] William Ames decided that 'some usury is lawful', and authorized interest-bearing loans if they were made 'out of a sincere intention, as also according to the estimation of honest men, and such as understand affairs of that sort'.[24] It may be doubted whether every businessman who believed he was being sincere and honest would draw quite the same lines as the Puritan Ames. By 1673 Richard Baxter had thrown up the sponge, admitting that 'divines that live in great cities and among merchandise are usually fitter judges' of usury 'than those that live more obscurely (without experience) in the country'.[27] The appeal to conscience is in the last resort an appeal from traditional norms to those evolving as society changes: individual consciences reflect what seems right to the society in which their bearers live. In 1603 Sir John Hayward took it for granted that exchange of commodities was part of the law of nature.[26]

In 1630 the JPs of Oxfordshire raised objections to royal purveyance. The commissioners spoke of 'His Majesty's reasonable prices' for commandeered carts. The JPs suggested that a 'reasonable' price was the market price, but the reply was 'it cannot but be well known unto you that the accustomed rate for His Majesty's service is after 5*d*. a lead for every mile'.[27] Here the conflict is clear and simple: is the traditional price 'reasonable', inflation notwithstanding? Or should the market be the measure of all things? It was not so long before Thomas Hobbes was to define justice itself in terms of the rule of reason that men keep their covenants made. Customs and prescriptions, he thought, were not laws of nature – i.e. were not binding *in foro interno* unless they were reasonable.[28] The important question was, Who decided which customs were 'reasonable' and which not? In the late sixteenth and early seventeenth centuries the common-law judges took this task upon themselves. An Act of Parliament, Sir Edward Coke declared, might be disregarded if it were against 'common right and reason'. But the reason of the lawyers, he assured James I, was not natural reason, but the artificial reason of the law, which only trained specialists could understand. 'Reasonableness in these cases belongeth to the knowledge of the law.'[29] Legal reason, like military intelligence, is a very special subject.

This was a game at which two could play. Of a judge who had voted in favour of Ship Money an MP said 'This judge will have the law to be what to him seems reason; the reason limited to him to judge of is what the common law saith is so, what a statute hath so enacted.' Otherwise it 'must follow, as often as a judge's reason changes, or judges change, our laws change also . . . The excessive growth of courts of reason, conscience, came from great and cunning persons', and was 'the most dangerous and sure ways to eat out our laws, our liberties'.[30] In 1644 Rutherford said that the king was under the law because he was a reasonable creature ruling over reasonable creatures.[31] This is the very spirit of 1688.

Already we are verging on politics. If reason can be applied to criticize custom, it can also be applied to precedents. Thomas Hedley told the House of Commons in 1610:

'Great and general mischiefs to the commonwealth are of sufficient weight to overrule both precedents and judgments, for as no unreasonable usage will be made a custom (pleadable in law) to bind within any manor or town, so no unreasonable usage (prejudicial to the commonwealth) will ever make a law to bind the whole kingdom. For whatsoever pretended rule or maxim of the law, though it be coloured or gilt over with precedents and judgments, yet if it will not abide the touchstone of reason and trial of time, it is but counterfeit stuff, and no part of the common law.'

If precedents bound for all time, 'then the common law could never have been said to be tried reason grounded upon better reason than the statutes'.[32] A professor of Gresham College in 1626 praised Ramus's logic because it 'will not suffer men to continue in error, be it never so old and rooted'; 'some may prefer truth before custom'.[33]

This was far-reaching doctrine, but many echoed it. Bacon, in *De Augmentis*, attacked the worship of precedent, and declared that 'the safest oracle for the future lies in the rejection of the past'.[34] In 1621 James I said he was willing that the House of Commons 'should retain what by law and precedents were due unto them, but touching reason, it was so variable according to several humours that it were hard to know where to fix it'.[35]

In the Commons in May 1641 a member said 'Antiquity without truth (as saith Cyprian) is but ancient error.'[36] It is agreeable that he had to quote an ancient authority in order to reject the authority of antiquity. The Commons themselves had been moving since the 1620s towards abandoning the argument from precedent. 'We have formerly broken precedents on the country's behalf', Sir John Eliot confessed in 1626.[37] Parliament, 'being the sovereign power', said William Prynne in 1643, is not tied to any precedents, but may make new precedents and new laws against new mischiefs, as physicians invent new remedies for new diseases.[38] Milton proudly spoke of setting precedents to future ages.[39] An otherwise undistinguished pamphlet written by three students of Trinity College, Cambridge, to justify the execution of Charles I, brings together a number of hackneyed variations on the theme. 'If we had no precedent, either domestic or foreign, yet the very law of reason and nature were sufficient to clear them in it. As for the laws of the land, they are all subordinate unto this of reason, and must give place to it.'[40]

The Levellers quoted reason against precedent, and argued

that laws were not laws unless they were reasonable. Milton elaborated many times on the theme that 'custom without truth is but agedness of error'.[41] Yet though he wrote so much in favour of reason and against custom, it was Milton who said 'Then reason down, or rather reasonings vain'. It was not merely in matters of economics and law that in the sixteenth and seventeenth centuries men's conceptions of what was reasonable and unreasonable were changing. In deeper philosophical senses there was a shift in the meaning given to the word reason, and in the importance attached to it. One could oversimplify the process by describing it as a transition from old to new reason via a phase of irrationalism.

III

The new unreason of the sixteenth century is most obvious in protestantism; but it also appears in the scepticism of Montaigne and his followers, in the Hermetic or magical and Paracelsan traditions, whose importance in the origins of science scholars are just beginning to appreciate. An earlier scholarly generation demolished the idea that there must have been a conflict between religion and science in the sixteenth and seventeenth centuries, as well as in the nineteenth century: the present generation has established that magic and science were by no means polar opposites at this period.[42]

Professor Haydn, who wrote an excellent book on this subject, lines up Hooker on one side as the classic defender of the old reason, and Machiavelli, Calvin, Montaigne and others on the other side.[43] Whilst not disagreeing with his analysis, I shall try to illustrate it from different quarters. Robert Browne, for instance, father of Brownism, criticized the scholastic logic of the universities because it was all 'in names and words, without any use'.[44] It might be Bacon speaking. Sir Walter Ralegh appealed to a reason not restricted to the wise and learned.[45] George Hakewill appealed to evidence against Bishop Goodman's 'logic rule', to experience against authority.[46] John Selden contrasted 'school reason' with the reason of common sense, based on the evidence of the senses.[47] Descartes virtually equated reason and sense. Puritanism and science shared the same enemies.

Common sense, the senses, evidence, experience, experiment, are the key words on the one hand: logic, authority, tradition, correspondences and analogies on the other. And suspicion of novelty. Joseph Hall thought it a 'greater glory to confirm an ancient verity than to devise a new opinion, though never so profitable . . . I will suspect a novel opinion of untruth, and not entertain it, unless it may be deduced from ancient grounds.'[48] 'Though never so profitable': the pragmatic test of usefulness is common to the opponents of the old reason, both Baconians and those theologians who fill their margins with 'uses' of texts. 'Knowledge without practice is no knowledge', wrote the Puritan author of the marginal headings to Richard Greenham's *Works* in 1612.[49] 'Our best and most divine knowledge is intended for action', John Wilkins echoed thirty-six years later; 'those may justly be accounted barren studies', the father of the Royal Society continued, 'which do not conduce to practice as their proper end'.[50]

Hooker, like Shakespeare, saw degree as a fact of the universe, part of a whole cosmology of correspondences and analogies. Attempts to take degree away were both wicked and irrational: who in his senses would want to untune a string? It was the theory of a relatively static hierarchical society: its rationality made sense to the beneficiaries of that society, but did not seem quite so timelessly unquestionable to others in the sixteenth century. 'The general and perpetual voice of man is as the sentence of God himself.' The operative word is 'perpetual': past consent is present consent. For Hooker right reason exists eternally, whether men perceive it or not: which is why transgressors of it are rightly punished, 'even by human law'.[51] Hooker disapproved of Puritans who 'used reason to disgrace reason', and warned that 'extraordinary motions of the spirit' were very dangerous, especially 'in men whose minds are of themselves as dry fuel, apt beforehand unto tumults, seditions and broils'. Such men he thought were to be found among the lower orders of society. Hooker significantly charged his rival Walter Travers with being 'so inured with the City' that he thought it 'unmeet to use any speech which savoureth of the school'. Travers in his turn objected especially to Hooker's view that sense perception, or what we understand by the light of nature, is more evident than 'that which we see by the light of grace; though it be indeed more certain, yet is not to us so evidently certain'.[52]

The new reason was that of mathematics and experimental science, a very different mental operation from reason working by analogy or by syllogism.[53] Science was popular in London, and Hooker was no doubt right in attributing to Londoners a desire for a break with the scholastic, apparently rational view of the universe as a closed hierarchical system, and the scholastic, apparently rational discourse by syllogism. The levers of change were two bodies of ideas which came up from the underworld of medieval thought, heresy taking shape in protestantism, magic and alchemy taking shape in Hermeticism and Paracelsanism.[54] Each criticized the contemporary rationalism of the universities by claiming to restore an older truth. Protestant heretics used the authority of the Bible against the wisdom of this world which was really foolishness: Hermeticists had their esoteric doctrines, claiming to be the primeval philosophy of ancient Egypt.

One of the features of late medieval nominalism had been its distrust of reason. But for our purposes we can start with the Reformation, with Luther's emphasis on the light of grace against the light of nature, his insistence that God was above human reason, which transvalued so many values.[55] For both Luther and Calvin reason, since the Fall, was an unreliable guide unless illumined by grace. John Knox attacked Anabaptists 'who can admit in God no justice which is not subject to the reach of your reason';[56] in 1619 the Puritan William Sclater demanded, expecting the answer 'No', 'Doth any ask reason of the spirit of God?'[57] On the opposite theological wing Archbishop Laud told Fisher the Jesuit that the 'fundamental points of faith, without which there is no salvation, . . . cannot be proved by reason'.[58]

Protestant irrationalism takes the form of, or is accompanied by, Biblical fundamentalism. Men appeal to the Bible to criticize existing institutions or doctrines. Is the Papacy to be found in the Bible? Are bishops? If not, away with them! Henry Barrow could discover no Biblical authority for the tithe-maintained parish ministers of the Church of England, nor for Presbyterian classes and synods, nor even for Parliamentary authority over the church.[59] In the 1620s George

Hakewill quoted the Bible to refute Bishop Goodman's 'reasonableness', his traditional views about the beginning and end of the world.[60] In the Putney Debates in 1647 Colonel Rainborough failed to find any biblical authority for the existing Parliamentary franchise. From this he concluded, not that there should be no Parliaments, but that the franchise should be widely extended.[61] The appeal to the Bible was negative, critical: positive proposals were based on other criteria – in this case on natural rights. 'That cause,' Hobhouse once said, 'must indeed be desperate which cannot find some Biblical text . . . to twist to its support.'[62]

John Udall in 1588 founded his *Demonstration of Discipline* on Scripture, 'by the light of reason rightly ruled'. But what was right reason? Men deviated to the right hand and to the left. 'Though arguments be never so plain, and Scriptures never so frequent, yet a carnal wretch will carry himself against all, and say "It is not my judgment, I am not of that mind".' The words are those of Thomas Hooker in 1638.[63] In 1643 Sidrach Simpson told the House of Commons: 'In reformation do not make reason your rule nor line you go by; it is the line of all the papists.' Antony Burges in the same year noted that reason 'hath been much extolled by a Socinian party alate . . . We may say of reason, this is right reason to one that is not to another . . . All reason severed from God's Word is corrupt and carnal.' John Bond in 1644, Peter Sterry in 1645 and 1648, echoed this scepticism about reason.[64] And they were right. When John Lilburne in 1649 declared that 'Reason is demonstrable by its innate glory, . . . and man being a reasonable creature is judge for himself',[65] one may suspect that his self-evident reason differed from that of Presbyterian divines.

During the revolutionary decades the Levellers and Milton quoted Scripture against legal precedents almost in the same breath as they quoted reason. The two fuse in so far as the appeal to the Bible is an appeal to individual interpretation. The radicals came to insist that the Bible be interpreted in accordance with reason, or with the needs of society. 'When we are treating of worldly affairs', wrote Henry Parker, 'we ought to be very tender how we seek to reconcile that to God's law, which we cannot reconcile to men's equity; or how we make God the author of that constitution which man reaps

113

inconvenience from.'[66] This is not only to make God after man's own image, but to insist that he be kept cut down to size. 'Every rule and instrument of necessary knowledge that God hath given us', Milton agreed, 'ought to be so in proportion as may be wielded and managed by the life of man without penning him up from the duties of human society.' 'No ordinance, human or from heaven, can bind against the good of man . . . The general end of every ordinance . . . is the good of man, yea, his temporal good not excluded.'[67] The combination of individual interpretation of Scripture with this principle of social utility effectively disintegrates such objectivity as the appeal to the Bible may ever have had, and so disintegrates the only rival authority which protestantism had been able to offer to that of the Pope.

A similar principle could side-step the Bible altogether when it proved inconvenient. We are not to stretch Scripture, John Wilkins told his readers in 1640, 'also to be a judge of such natural truths as are to be found out by our own industry and experience'. The Holy Ghost has left us some work to do.[68] These are extremely sophisticated techniques of evasion; yet the idea goes back to the very beginning of the Reformation, to Calvin's statement that Moses wrote to the capacity of his readers, not as a scholar: and therefore in some cases undoubtedly oversimplified.[69] This was a useful argument for a heliocentric astronomer when asked why the Bible said Joshua commanded the sun to stand still.

If the Bible is *the* authority, to which all men appeal, by which all causes are judged, then it is of vital importance to be sure you have an accurate text, accurately translated. A work of impeccable Calvinist orthodoxy like Thomas James's *Treatise of the Corruptions of the Scriptures* (1612), by its painstaking analysis of texts and exposure of forgeries, in the end shows how very precarious the 'true' text is, how insecure the authority on which so much is based. Biblical criticism in the seventeenth century led towards scepticism and even atheism much more rapidly than did science.[70] As revolutionaries in our own century have discovered, a sacred text which was invaluable at the destructive stage needs official interpreters once society is restabilized. The restoration of the Church of England in 1660 was no less important socially than the restoration of monarchy.

Some have seen a 'holy pretence', a Machiavellian double-talk, in much of the Puritans' use of the Bible.[71] I think this is to attribute too conscious motives to troubled men trying to find guides to living in a world rapidly changing but hag-ridden by authority; where innovation, novelty, were dirty words. Traditional authorities *had* to be found for the untraditional actions forced on men. The Machiavellianism, if any, was unconscious; at worst a utilitarianism, an adaptation of norms to the demands of the environment. In one sense Thomas Taylor was indulging in double-talk when he said it was the duty of good subjects to maintain their own liberties, for obedience to God was liberty.[72] But – apart from possible difficulties with the censor – Taylor was genuinely I think trying to preserve two incompatibles at once. To label this simply 'holy pretence' is to do less than justice to the complexity of the problems involved. Oliver Cromwell's concern, at the crisis of Charles I's fate, lest his 'reasonings may be but fleshly' was surely genuine; 'we are very apt all of us to call that faith that perhaps may be but carnal imagination and carnal reasonings'.[73] *Vain* reasonings down.

As protestants appealed to the Bible, so Hermeticists posed their secret doctrine against the speculations of the schools. Nineteenth-century scholars saw only claptrap and humbug in alchemy and astrology: and there was often much of both. But alchemists and iatrochemists worked directly on nature, experimenting rather than speculating. Some astrologers looked through telescopes. A Bruno was wide open to Copernican ideas because he violently rejected scholasticism and because he aspired to *control* the material universe. The Faust legend (Bruno is hinted at in Marlowe's *Dr Faustus*) captures this arrogant desire of the magus to dominate matter. Yet the way led through experiment. It was a short step for Bacon, who owed so much to the Hermetic tradition, to conclude that in order to control nature we must first obey her, to plead against the secrecy of a coterie of initiates in favour of a public pooling of scientific results: and to pose against the arrogance and individualism of the Faustian magi the humility of scientific researchers, each member of the team of experimenters as good as the next. Scientific truth would emerge from the common sense of the collectivity. Paolo Rossi has argued that Bacon was more conscious of what he was doing to the Hermetic tradition than historians have realized;[74] Miss Yates, greatly daring, has suggested that Bacon's otherwise mysterious and reprehensible failure to respond to mathematics, to the Copernican astronomy and to William Gilbert's work on the magnet, was because for him all three were too closely associated with the Hermetic tradition to be respectable. Kepler was magus as well as astronomer, Dee magus as well as mathematician. Mathematics and mechanics still had magical associations.[75] Dee referred to himself as 'this mechanician',[76] and John Wilkins's *Mathematicall Magick* appeared as late as 1648.

The preliminary work which prepared the ground for the new reason was then everywhere destructive. Protestantism and experimental science destroyed the hierarchical universe. Like the appeal to the Bible, the primitivist appeal to the state of nature had the effect of making a clean sweep of the 'historical conditions in which men lived with all their corporate privileges, customary rights and traditional ties'. It envisaged man as a rational but isolated, atomized individual, set free from society.[77] The appeal to the individual conscience, the religion of the heart,[78] was ultimately an appeal to changing social norms. The appeal to reason became an appeal to a more democratic common sense. Ramus, Bacon and Descartes all emphasized things rather than words, practice rather than theory, experience rather than Aristotle. Bacon attacked the idols of the theatre, products of false reasoning and ignorance of the proper method of using the mind. The new logic was based on experiment rather than disputation, on the senses rather than *a priori* reasoning. Montaigne and Descartes turned philosophy into autobiography, a style it long retained. Locke's *tabula rasa* was the culmination of a series of roundabout attempts to set the mind free from the past with its traditions and authorities, a blank sheet on which experience and experience alone can write.[79]

Once the assumptions behind the hierarchical universe of correspondences and analogies are abandoned, sense impressions, individual experience and scientific experiment become the only means of finding out about the world in which we live. Any experiment is good, Bacon thought, because it is studying God's works. The Calvinist Fulke Greville came near the same position when he said 'the world is made for use', and Donne spoke of the transforming effect of 'our new nature (use)'.[80] William Dell, intruded Master of Gonville and Caius College under Parliamentary rule, was said to use the phrase 'carnal and fleshly' interchangeably with 'unuseful'.[81] 'Things themselves speak to us, and offer notions to our minds,' said Benjamin Whichcote, another intruded Head of a Cambridge house; 'and this is the voice of God.'[82] Gerrard Winstanley extended this to proclaim that God can be known only in nature. It is the devil who tells a man 'he must believe what others have writ or spoke, and must not trust to his own experience'.[83]

The Royal Society wished to establish 'an inviolable correspondence between the hand and the brain', practice and theory.[84] Its philosophy 'must not be the work of the mind turned in upon itself and only conversing with its own ideas, but it must be raised from the observations and applications of sense, and take its accounts from things as they are in the sensible world'.[85] Given the disruption of agreed certainties by the individualist revolts of Luther and Descartes, the object of scientific experiment was to rebuild social truth from below, on individual conviction, on experience. This was not a return to truth handed down from above by authority. Rather we may compare Professor Jordan's charitable merchants, reconstructing the institutions of their society from below, against opposition from the authority of the government, so as to fit them for the world in which they wished to live.[86] Or we may compare the independent congregations recapturing certainty through religious experience shared and discussed. In 1644 William Walwyn had observed, coolly enough, that Brownists and Anabaptists 'are rational examiners of those things they hold for truth, mild discoursers, and able to give an account of what they believe'. Their habit of discourse makes them abler arguers than most.[87] 'Letter learning' or 'university knowledge', said John Everard, was no substitute for the religious experience of those who 'know Jesus Christ and the Scriptures experimentally rather than grammatically, literally or academically'. *Macaria* in 1641 envisaged a 'College of Experience' which would synthesize and test new chemical medicines.[88] The only acceptable form of human knowledge for John Dury was 'that which is immediately deduced from or built upon real and certain experiments, and those so many as to make an infallible universal'.[89] Reason, logic, the syllogism, are fruits of the Fall, wrote a pamphleteer in 1652: Adam's knowledge was intuitive. 'An infidel', he added remarkably, 'is the best proficient in the school of nature.'[90] The Quaker Robert Barclay argued that spiritual and scientific proof were equally certain, that experience was analogous to experiment.[91]

Reason sanctified by grace was *right* reason, as in Adam before the Fall. The radicals of the interregnum attributed this reason of the regenerate to all men, or most men. They denied that academic training was a necessary preliminary. As Perry Miller put it, the new reason is the result not only of a lessening respect for formal logic but also of a lessening sense of the sinfulness of man.[92] So we get Lord Brooke saying that right reason is its own judge.[93] Milton not only opposed reason to the logic of the theologians, but also treated conscience as infallible, equating it with reason 'imprinted on the heart of man by the God of nature'.[94] The Levellers assumed that an appeal to natural law or reason would produce the same answer in the minds of all rational men. What is not reasonable and just is not of God, proclaimed Richard Overton.[95] For Winstanley, more simply, reason is the highest name that can be given to God; it means 'Do as you would be done by', and it led Winstanley to communism.[96] John Cook, in the argument he would have used at Charles I's trial if the latter had pleaded, said that the King was condemned 'by the fundamental law of this kingdom, by the general law of all nations, and the unanimous consent of all rational men in the world, written in every man's heart'.[97] These laws were so obvious that there was no need to lay them down. Similarly a character in Henry Neville's dialogue said that the common law 'is reason itself, written as well in the hearts of rational men as in the lawyers' books'. This was as different from Coke's 'artificial reason', acquired by long and painful study, as was the Reason which the legal reformer John Warr opposed to Form.[98]

But in a bitterly divided society agreement was not so easily to be assumed. 'Right reason! Aye, where is it?' demanded the Master of Emmanuel College in 1656. It had been a point of royalist propaganda to argue that for the Parliamentarians reason was unreason, irrationality reason. Where had reason got the King and his supporters? the Earl of Pembroke was made to ask in a burlesque speech printed in 1647.[99] New definitions had to be found. For Hobbes reasoning was addition: it should therefore be possible – given a 'good and orderly method' – to arrive at mathematical certainty, since each man is potentially rational. But men are ideological as well as rational creatures: when they disagree there is no infallible means of deciding between them. 'Commonly they that call for right reason to decide any controversy do mean their own.'[100] For Hobbes the only remedy for this anarchical situation was the arbitrary fiat of the sovereign. Milton, equally pessimistically, was ultimately and reluctantly driven by the political experience of the revolution to conclude that the rational were very few: self-government was only for the free, the rational. James Harrington decided that 'reason is nothing but interest', and 'there be divers interests and so divers reasons'.[101] Bishop Jeremy Taylor observed in 1660 that reason 'is as uncertain as the discourse of the people', could not establish even the existence of God. Christian revelation must be reason's arbiter. Reason may be employed to criticize custom, but must never be opposed to the Scriptures or to 'proper arguments derived from them'.[102] The Cambridge Platonists set up reason against the inner light; academic education was necessary to interpret the Bible. Right reason and faith are identical: if there appears to be a conflict the reason cannot be right. The individual conscience must be set free from authorities and traditions, but not left to its own unaided devices. Religion must conform to the agreed values of the society.[103] The same point was made even by a Baptist, though a relatively conservative one. Henry Denne, opposing Ranter or Quaker emphases in his flock, said: 'We had not so learned Christ as to be guided by the experience of every person.' Scripture was used to check a deviator's 'fancy, which he called experience'.[104]

Reservations of this sort came to be generally accepted after the political compromise (and restoration of censorship) in 1660. But this was no return to the old reason. Theologians like Bishop Wilkins and Archbishop Tillotson solved philosophical problems by appealing to common sense: truth can be tested only in practice.[105] From Hooker to Locke the meaning of reason had changed. It was no longer systematic logic, but the self-evident truths of common sense and experience. Like Hooker's reason, it was a body of eternal verities. Only now one of these verities was that 'usefulness is excellence'.[106] Reason had been moulded to the needs of society, was no longer handed down from on high, remote, above social needs. (No more had Hooker's reason been: but it represented the needs of a different sort of society.) For Hobbes, injustice was absurdity.[107] It was only among the least educated and most alienated sects that irrationalism continued to be extolled: that reason, which had been God for the Levellers and Winstanley, was identified with the devil.[108]

IV

My argument has been that reason, reasonableness, is a social concept. Reason is 'a public and certain thing', said Chillingworth, 'and exposed to all men's trial and examination.'[109] Public, yes; certain, no – as Chillingworth himself would in fact have agreed.[110] The question was, Whose reason? I suggested that irrationalism, by offering a short cut to certainty, also helped to get rid of scholarly superstitions. Perhaps I may quote a modern anthropologist on an analogous phenomenon. Speaking of adherents of cargo cults in Melanesia, Professor Worsley says: 'The type of social action taken by millenarists, then, does not represent an affectual regression from rational action but a questioning of the validity of this very "rationality".' It marks a break in intellectual continuity.[111]

Both religious heresy and Hermeticism rose from the intellectual underworld of the Middle Ages, expanding as the artisan and merchant class grew in numbers and strength. Lutheranism, Calvinism and Anglicanism tamed and institutionalized protestant heresy, though radical sects survived in industrial areas. Bacon and the Royal Society tamed the Hermetic tradition in England, so closely associated with radical religion and politics. Descartes performed a similar role on the continent. But dangers had been revealed during the revolutionary decades. As contemporaries rightly noted, an appeal to the absolute rights of individual conscience must tend towards anarchy. So many men, so many reasons. The society was more stratified and more competitive than medieval society, in which anyway education was much more restricted; and England had recently been divided by a bitter civil war. There was too a sceptical materialist tradition among lower-class Englishmen.[112] Uninhibited speculation led Winstanley to a kind of materialistic pantheism, the Ranters to reject all conventional religion. When Levellers, Quakers and others proposed to test the supreme truths of religion by physical experiment,[113] uncontrolled freedom of scientific investigation might seem as dangerous as uncontrolled liberty of conscience. Charles II was wise to become patron of the Royal Society as well as head of the Church of England.

The fierce suppression of the radicals after 1660 brutally averted any threat of democracy in the state. It was left to the scientists to fight against the risks of materialism and atheism in philosophy. Yet the settlement of 1660 left its mark on the new concept of 'reasonableness'. To oppose reason to enthusiasm became almost a political slogan. Biographers of Locke now emphasize the Hobbist and authoritarian phase he went through immediately after the restoration. 'By Hobbes out of Hooker' is Professor Macpherson's succinct phrase. Locke incorporated far more of the old reason than – say – the Levellers would have done. Men for him were all equally rational by nature, but the fact that some were less rational than others was inherent in civil society; and so legal sanctions and the spiritual sanctions of the church were required to keep them in order.[114] Locke's *The Reasonableness of Christianity* brought reason and revelation into harmony. The principle of utility begs a number of ideological questions: useful for whom, for what? Locke's influence was from the first as ambiguous as that of Hegel was to be: his successors included Lockeans of the left and Lockeans of the right.

The scientists were so anxious to disavow Hermeticists and Paracelsans, to establish that science was not dangerous to religion or the social order, that they too made many compromises. Bishops and peers were used as front-men for the Royal Society; a utilitarian emphasis on agricultural and industrial improvements aimed at interesting the dilettante gentry. The educational schemes of the interregnum Baconians were abandoned. The insistence of Cambridge Platonists, Boyle, Newton and so many others that science helped to prove the existence of God is of more than personal biographical interest. It relates to social needs. As Professor Westfall shrewdly observed, the scientists would not have harped so continually on this theme if they had not nourished atheism in their own minds.[115]

Historians have recently devoted much attention to the fascinating personality of Isaac Newton, the gigantic figure who summed up the new reason for the next two centuries. The more they study his unpublished manuscripts, the more they recognize that Newton was not the lofty Olympian figure of eighteenth- and nineteenth-century legend. He was a strained, neurotic bachelor, whose secret life, at the very time he was inaugurating the modern intellectual world, was still rooted in the study of alchemy and biblical prophecy. J. M. Keynes with brilliant insight saw Newton as the last of the magi.[116] Like Locke, he failed to speak out on some crucial issues, especially where the reputation of the Almighty was concerned. Galileo was silenced by the Inquisition: Newton, like Descartes, censored himself. Blake was right to see him as a symbol of repression. Historians of science who ignore the historical context in which scientific ideas appear, emphasizing only the internal intellectual evolution of the subject, are embarrassed by the difference between Sir Isaac's public and private personae, by his strategic silences, by the strong ideological element in his thinking about the universe: they can attribute them only to individual psychological peculiarities.

It may indeed be argued that even if Newton's psychological compulsions must be taken into account in explaining how he arrived at his grand synthesis, this is irrelevant to the truth or otherwise of the Newtonian system: as irrelevant as Luther's alleged anal eroticism to the origins of protestantism. What matters is the acceptance of the idea by large numbers of men and women who presumably did not share all the symptoms of Luther and Newton. But there may be deeper links between the individual psychology of the thinkers and the society which accepted the thought. So Professor N. O. Brown has argued for Luther: so Professor Manuel has hinted for Newton.[117] Their repressions may tell us something about the society which accepted them. Now that twentieth-century science seems again to be trying to escape from the constraints of a rationalism inherited from the past, it may be legitimate for the mere historian to recall what happened last time.[118]

'The mind of man', Bacon wrote in 1605, 'is far from the nature of a clear and equal glass, wherein the beams of things should reflect according to their true incidence; nay, it is rather like an enchanted glass, full of superstition and imposture, if it be not delivered and reduced.'[119] Bacon assumed that he could appeal to the collective activity of plain blunt scientists against the superstitions and impostures of the academic establishment. He did not envisage a time when – too successful – scientists would themselves be members of this establishment, exposed like the rest of us to its idols of the theatre. Nor did he foresee a time – science too successful again – when manipulation of men's minds by control of education and the mass media would be at least a theoretical possibility. We are not yet in the brave new world: we are still some years from 1984. But when one hears for instance respectable academic psychologists diagnose critics and rebels in our society as 'maladjusted' and in need of treatment or – even more sinister – manifestly badly educated – the seventeenth-century historian is likely to feel for his *Areopagitica*, to assert the inalienable right of man to be irrational in the eyes of academic pundits. If anything can be learnt from my story it is that it is unsafe to assume *a priori* that ideas are necessarily true because they have been accepted for a long time; that new reason is likely to appear unreason to established academics; and that even when it really is irrational, it could just possibly be a better way to truth than our old reason.

PART III

Continuity in Change: Divinity, Law, Medicine

The Radical Critics of Oxford
and Cambridge in the 1650s[1]

It is one of the grossest errors that ever reigned under Antichrist to affirm that universities are the fountain of the ministers of the gospel.

William Dell, *The Stumbling Stone* (1651),
in *Several Sermons and Discourses of William Dell*
(1709), p. 403.

I

In the seventeenth-century English Revolution fundamental questions were asked about most exisiting institutions, including the universities. Criticisms of Oxford and Cambridge at this period are normally discussed in the context of the curriculum and of the history of science. English universities were notoriously backward in mathematics and science. Seth Ward, John Wallis, John Pell, John Milton, all left the universities and went elsewhere to acquire 'the superstitious algebra and that black art of geometry'.[2] The same was true of astronomy and medicine: 'one had as good send a man to Oxford to learn shoe-making as practising physic', declared the great doctor Thomas Sydenham, who fortunately himself lacked a university education. The important scientific and mathematical work associated with the names of John Dee, William Gilbert, Thomas Hariot, Jeremiah Horrox, William Oughtred, John Wallis and William Harvey went on outside the universities.[3]

From Bacon onwards the universities were under attack; the criticisms rose to a crescendo during the Revolution. John Hall in 1649, Noah Biggs in 1651, John Webster in 1654 – their strictures and demands are quoted by all historians of science and of the universities. There was a breakthrough in the 1650s, when a group of scientists gathered at Oxford, and for a brief period science seemed to have got a foot in the door, though the activities of these individuals received little or no encouragement from university officialdom. A critic like John Webster thought that nothing significant had changed; he was answered reassuringly if tendentiously by Ward and Wilkins, moderate reformers who were embarrassed by Webster's maximum programme.[4]

If Oxford and Cambridge had been institutions whose main concern was to serve the secular and economic needs of society, the demands of the modernizers would have been irresistible. But they were not. The main function of the universities was generally agreed to be the production of parsons. From the sixteenth century onwards gentlemen in increasing numbers were spending a year or two at the universities, but they normally left without taking a degree. Some might have dilettante scientific interests, though even Seth Ward thought this would not extend to dirtying their hands with chemical experiments.[5] In any case their interests and needs were peripheral to the main function of the universities. Thomas Hobbes stated flatly that 'the universities are the fountains of the civil and moral doctrine, from whence the preachers and the gentry . . . sprinkle the same upon the people'; 'the instruction of the people dependeth wholly on the right teaching of youth in the universities'. 'A university is an excellent servant to the clergy.'[6] Hobbes's antagonist Bishop Bramhall agreed, observing that the attack on the universities was part of an attack on the clergy.[7] It is controversies over this function of the universities that I wish to discuss.

With the post-Reformation emphasis on preaching as the clergy's principal task, their education became of special importance. The state church was a vast opinion-forming machine, comparable to press, radio and television today. During the century between Reformation and Revolution, church and universities had been reduced to dependence on the crown. Oxford and Cambridge ceased to be effectual self-governing corporations in the medieval sense. The colleges replaced the universities as the main centres of teaching, and the rule of the resident masters of arts was replaced by an oligarchy of heads of colleges. Direct government pressure influenced academic policy and appointments. Seventeenth-century university reformers wanted to reintroduce greater self-government into Oxford and Cambridge. Puritans before 1640 criticized the type of clergy produced by the universities, the inculcation of Laudian, authoritarian ideas.[8] So, inevitably, the meeting of the Long Parliament in 1640 seemed to herald change. As early as December 1640 the House of Commons set up a committee to consider abuses in the universities. A year later the House found it necessary to deny 'that we intend to destroy or discourage learning; . . . it is our chiefest care and desire to advance it'. They announced, however, their intention 'to reform and purge the fountains of learning, the two universities, that the streams flowing from thence may be clear and pure'.[9]

During the Civil War the universities as such took no significant part in national politics, but there is no doubt about their royalist sympathies. The universities, wrote the official historian of the Long Parliament in 1647, 'were of all places most apt to adhere to the King's party, esteeming Parliaments, and especially this, the greatest depressors of that ecclesiastical dignity, in the hope of which they are there maintained'.[10] Oxford was the King's military headquarters during the war. Cambridge had been reduced to submission by one of the earliest military exploits of Oliver Cromwell. Neither university was able to show any independent political initiative. From 1604 onwards Oxford and Cambridge were each represented in Parliament by two members, normally selected in practice by heads of colleges. In the Long Parliament John Selden (Oxford) and Nathaniel Bacon (Cambridge) were active down to 1648, but after Pride's Purge in December of that year they slipped into the background.[11] During the period in which university reform was most actively discussed, Oxford and Cambridge were in effect unrepresented in Parliament.

After Parliament's victory in the Civil War, purges of the universities naturally followed, to subordinate them to the new rulers of the state. Some radical supporters of Parliament had seen a more fundamental link between universities and royalism. Thus the Leveller William Walwyn asked in 1644 'whether the party who are now in arms to make us slaves consists not chiefly of such as have had esteem for the most learned arts men in the kingdom?[12] 'Scholars are our jailors, said Nicholas Culpeper. But times of knowledge will come.[13]

But these were extremist positions. Most members of Parliament, most Presbyterian and Independent divines, accepted the existence of a state church: they simply wanted to put it under new management. This was true even of a militant Independent like Hugh Peter, who proposed that half Cambridge's colleges should be set aside for the sole purpose of training ministers;[14] or of a Fifth Monarchist like John Spittlehouse, who wanted colleges to teach foreign languages to students who would then become missionaries.[15] With the collapse of episcopacy and church courts at the very beginning of the Revolution, however, the problem suddenly ceased to be merely one of controlling the state church and became whether a state church should exist at all. In this new freedom religious sects sprang up everywhere, especially in towns, rejecting any national disciplinary organization. They stressed the autonomy of each congregation and elected their own ministers, often not ordained clergymen at all but 'mechanick preachers', laymen of the middle and lower classes.[16]

> For human arts and sciences,
> Because you dote on them,
> Therefore the Lord will others teach
> Whom you count but laymen.

So sang the prophetess Anna Trapnel.[17] Such preachers earned their living by labouring six days a week, or were maintained by voluntary offerings from their congregations. They had no use for, and rejected on principle, the tithes which went to maintain the parish clergy.

Tithes, the compulsory payment of 10 per cent of each man's earnings to a parson in whose appointment he normally had no say, had long been under attack from religious radicals. A survival from a predominantly agricultural society, they were especially difficult to collect in towns; they led to unedifying quarrels, and they bore especially heavily on smaller men in the countryside.[18] Many Puritans anxious to retain a national clergy would have preferred some less contentious form of maintenance – a stipend paid by the state, for instance. But short of this, there was general agreement that tithes and a national church stood or fell together. To suggest, as sectaries did, that all ministers should depend on voluntary contributions was tantamount to suggesting that most ministers should starve. One might be in favour of this or against it, but all agreed that this was the case.[19]

So the 'mechanick preachers' presented a double threat to the state church. On the one hand, unordained ministers, who had been to no university, would lack the training, the indoctrination, which ensured that quarrels among the clergy, however bitter, never called in question the existence of a national church. On the other hand, if tithes ceased to be paid, there would be no jobs for graduates to go to; there would be no uniformly trained ministry capable of receiving instructions from above, to act as a relatively united opinion-forming body. There would be no central control over the thoughts of the masses of the population. The heresies which proliferated in the 1640s – again especially in urban centres – convinced conservatives that such control was absolutely necessary. A state church, universities and tithes must all be preserved. 'No universities, no ministry' was the theme of the Presbyterian Thomas Hall and others: no learning, no confutation of heresy.[20] Professor Kaminsky has shown how the emergence of Taborite revolutionary theories drove most of the reformist Prague Masters back to a defensive conservative position. Something very similar happened to Presbyterians in England in the 1640s.[21]

Moreover, an important part of the revenues of both universities and of their constituent colleges consisted of impropriated tithes – tithes which had been paid to monasteries before their dissolution at the Reformation, and which were now often received by laymen or institutions performing no pastoral functions. When James I at the beginning of his reign promised to restore royal impropriations to the church and urged universities to do the same, he was lectured by the bishops, who convinced him that such misguided zeal would be fatal to the financial stability of the universities. For many gentlemen too, impropriated tithes formed a significant part of their income; not to mention the fear often expressed in the 1640s, that those who refuse to pay tithes today will refuse to pay rent tomorrow. Property interests linked the state church, universities and a section of the ruling class. About 1654 Francis Osborn referred sardonically to a man who was 'an impropriator, and so will be true to the priests' interest'.[22]

The link was recognized by conservative contemporaries. Any treatise of the time which starts as a defence of learning is certain soon to get round to defending tithes.[23] 'When they commend learning', observed Walwyn, 'it is not for learning's sake, but their own; her esteem gets them their livings and preferments, and therefore she is to be kept up, or their trade will go down.'[24] Earlier clerics had defended pluralism as necessary to learning.[25] Now not only plural claims to tithes but tithes themselves came under attack. Milton thought the abolition of tithes essential to liberty of conscience.[26]

I must define the word 'radical'. I use it to describe those who rejected any state church: both separatist sectaries, who opposed a national church on religious principle, and others – Levellers, Diggers, Fifth Monarchists, Ranters, etc. – whose opposition was part of a more general political, social and economic programme. I distinguish them from the more conservative supporters of Parliament, whether episcopalians, erastians, Presbyterians or Independents, who approved in principle of a state church, and from those Baptists who were prepared to accept it in practice.

For the radicals, a state church, tithes and the universities seemed to go together. They did not want to destroy the universities: they wanted to change their function, to secularize them, to end their role as a factory of divines, who by academic training and source of income were inevitably bound to the *status quo*. Introducing more science into the universities was very much a secondary consideration for such reformers. But once the universities had been secularized, and existed to serve the commonwealth rather than the state church, then the utilitarian arguments of the scientific reformers were acceptable to anti-clerical revolutionaries, many of whom wanted to expand the number of universities once they had been reformed, and to increase the number of scholarships.[27] The separatist William Hartley explained in 1651 that he and his like wanted the universities well regulated, not abolished. 'For human arts, who esteemeth them more than those termed separatists?' Human learning is good in its sphere, though it 'in itself gives no more light than spectacles to a blind man'.[28] Once the universities had been new modelled, the millenarian Mary Cary declared, then those who wished to study any of the liberal sciences might do so at their own charges.[29] Nor were the scientific reformers themselves disinterested in religion: one of them, Samuel Hartlib, denounced the universities' 'show of upholding the name of learning, without any engagement towards the public concernments of the commonwealth of learning or of the church of God in the communion of saints'.[30] There was a convergence.

For the radicals the crux was the universities' role as a fountain of ministers for the state church. The accusation of wishing to destroy learning[31] has deceived some historians, but it is no more true than that most student revolutionaries today want to destroy the universities. The enemy was the close if invisible link which bound the ideologists produced by the universities to the values of the society in which they functioned. Seventeenth-century radicals had a word for it: the universities were antichristian.

This word calls for a moment's digression. Sixteenth-century protestants inherited from medieval heretics the idea that the Pope was Antichrist. This belief became almost the official doctrine of the reformed Church of England, taught by archbishops and bishops from Cranmer to Abbot, as well as by Puritans. Antichrist was associated especially with persecution of the godly, the use of political power in ecclesiastical matters: separatists came to regard bishops and the church establishment as antichristian. Other Puritans continued to hope for reformation. But ultimately they lost confidence, first in bishops, then in the king who supported them, finally in Parliament itself, which wished simply to replace a repressive Laudian church by a repressive Presbyterian church. Radicals came to think of any state church, and the ideology which went with it, as antichristian. Gerrard Winstanley, the Digger, so described the class and property relations which the state church shared and justified. The Taborites, we recall, in 1419–20 had denounced the Masters of Prague University as satraps of Antichrist, and Luther had similar thoughts about the academics of his day. We must bear such senses of 'antichristian' in mind when considering criticisms of the universities.[32]

The view that there should be no separate caste of ordained ministers, that divinity should not be taught in universities, *could* not properly be taught there – these views had a respectable protestant ancestry. The Geneva Bible, the Bible most widely circulated before the Authorized Version, had a marginal note to Revelation 9:3 which equated doctors of divinity with locusts. The first edition of the Puritan *Admonition to Parliament* of 1572 attacked doctors, though this was prudently expunged in the second edition.[33] Separatists like Robert Browne, John Greenwood and Henry Barrow thought universities 'the very guard of Antichrist's throne'.[34] Mrs Anne Hutchinson in New England was said to preach 'better Gospel than any of your blackcoats that have been at the ninny-versity'.[35] Such views were repeated in the revolutionary decades by heretics as diverse as Cobbler How (the unlearned are to be preferred for the ministry before equally gifted learned men),[36] Lord Brooke ('the ways of God's spirit are free, and not tied to a university man'),[37] Roger Williams (God's people do not need 'the university, lazy and monkish', nor its 'superstitious degrees and titles of divinity'),[38] the Baptists Henry Denne ('as soon find' a true minister of the gospel 'in the university of Newgate') and John Horne,[39] the Levellers Richard Overton (whose Mr Persecution had been 'of all the universities of Christendom')[40] and Edmund Chillenden (the spirit is bestowed 'as soon upon a cobbler, tinker, chimney sweeper, ploughman . . . as to the greatest, learnedest doctor in the world').[41] Hugh Peter (the founders of Oxford and Cambridge mistakenly served Antichrist rather than Christ),[42] John Milton ('a fond error . . . to think that the university makes a minister of the gospel'),[43] Robert Norwood,[44] the vegetarian Roger Crab ('the Whore's great eyes . . . are Oxford and Cambridge'),[45] Henry Stubbe, later the enemy of the Royal Society ('antichristian universities'),[46] the Ranter Richard Coppin ('schools of Antichrist'),[47] the Fifth-Monarchists John Spittlehouse and John Canne ('a nursery . . . not of Christ's but of Aristotle's and the state's ministry'),[48] the Quakers Richard Farnsworth ('Antichrist's methodical way in his school'), George Fox ('the Whore set up your schools and colleges . . . whereby you are made ministers'), Samuel Fisher ('learned lieutenants of Antichrist'), and many others.[49]

The essence of this radical emphasis was that God's grace was given direct to his elect: their inner light needed no priestly mediators. This was not always the mere doctrine of individualist anarchism which it appears at first sight. The spirit's message was not self-validating: its acceptability was confirmed (or rejected) by the congregation after discussion, and this congregation was likely to be composed of men and women similar in background, aspirations and needs. There is an analogy between the saint 'speaking experienced truths' to a critical and sophisticated auditory and the scientist describing experiments which can be tested by other scientists.

The execution of Charles 1 in January 1649, followed by the proclamation of a republic and the abolition of the House of Lords, roused radical hopes. But they were dashed by the defeat and suppression of the Levellers in the months which succeeded, and by the apparent determination of the rulers of the Commonwealth to pursue a conservative course. In May 1649, fresh from suppressing a mutiny of Leveller regiments at Burford, Oliver Cromwell assured Oxford University that 'no commonwealth could flourish without learning'.[50] He had just been given an honorary doctorate by the university which had for so long been the King's military headquarters. Next year Parliament augmented the stipends of heads of colleges, the agents of government control over the universities – 'those little living idols or monuments of monarchy', as a contemporary called them.[51] Gowns indeed were 'laid aside' whilst the Army was in power,[52] and hair (which Archbishop Laud had kept closely cropped) luxuriated in Roundhead Oxford. But John Hall in 1649, John Dury in 1650 and Noah Biggs in 1651 saw no hope of fundamental reform from within the universities, and called on Parliament to undertake the task.[53]

In 1653 the meeting of the nominated Barebones Parliament raised hopes for radical reformation of the universities. Pamphlets calling for reform were published throughout 1653 and 1654.[54] Looking back we may judge that all this smoke concealed an absence of flame: the political defeat of the radicals had made real reform impossible. But contemporaries were frightened. The Vice-Chancellor of Oxford referred to 'reports everywhere spread abroad concerning the abolition and destruction of the Colleges'; and there were many more such remarks.[55] The dissolution of the Barebones Parliament in December 1653 made Oliver Cromwell the saviour of conservative society. David Masson was quite right when he wrote, nearly a hundred years ago, 'the Protectorate had come into existence not only in a conservative interest generally, but . . . especially for the preservation of an established church and the universities'.[56] Pamphlets attacked and defended Webster and other would-be reformers of the universities in political terms, as no better than Levellers.[57]

In September 1656 the Lord Protector told his Parliament that 'God hath for the ministry a very great seed in the youth in the universities', thus nailing his colours to a state church; though he added for the benefit of Army radicals that these undergraduates 'instead of studying books study their own hearts'.[58] Oliver's brother-in-law John Wilkins defended the universities *because of* their role in training ministers. In December 1656 John Evelyn heard him preach against ignorant sacrilegious officers and soldiers who would have destroyed learning.[59] Clearly the danger was over.

II

Against this background I want now to look in rather more detail at the views of two of the most radical critics of the universities, William Dell and Gerrard Winstanley.

William Dell, Fellow of Emmanuel College, Cambridge, became a chaplain in the New Model Army. We know little about him except from his own writings.[60] He held political views not far removed from those of the Levellers. In 1646 he married Henry Ireton to Oliver Cromwell's daughter Bridget. In the same year Dell was in trouble with some well-to-do London citizens and with the House of Lords for preaching (to a preponderantly Army congregation) that 'the power is in you, the people; keep it, part not with it'.[61] When invited to preach before the House of Commons in the same year he spoke up on behalf of the poor. He was one of the few so invited to preach whom the Commons refused to thank and did not ask to print his sermon. When Dell did print it they had him up on the mat before them.[62] In August 1647, when the Army marched into London, Dell led the troops in prayer on reaching Westminster. He was attacked by the heresy-hunters Thomas Edwards and Samuel Rutherford.[63]

Dell was apparently a republican earlier than this was fashionable: Charles I was no King to him, he was alleged to have said; Christ was his King. If Venice and Holland could do without kings, he asked, why should not England? He also opposed the House of Lords. In 1654 he campaigned for the election to Parliament of the near-Leveller Colonel Okey, mainly because of his opposition to tithes. In 1657 he agitated against acceptance of the crown by Oliver Cromwell. Two years later he carried the principle of tolerance so far as to allow the tinker John Bunyan to preach at his Bedfordshire living of Yelden; Dell declared in church that he would rather have a plain countryman from the plough speak there than the best orthodox minister in the country.[64] Dell took it for granted that 'every free society hath power to choose its own officers'; *a fortiori* the church, the freest society of all, had this power. Dell was already a notorious radical when in May 1649, on petition from the Fellows, he was appointed Master of Gonville and Caius College, Cambridge – the first married man to hold that position. One of his patrons was Thomas Harrison, the regicide.[65]

Some of his critics alleged that Dell was antagonistic to learning as such. This would be odd in a man who was one of a group which produced an English-Greek lexicon, published in 1661.[66] But the absurdity of the allegation is made clear if we look at his half dozen pages on 'the Right Reformation of Learning, Schools and Universities' (1653). Here he advocated the creation of schools in all towns and villages throughout the nation, where godly men and sober and grave women should teach English and the Bible. In cities and larger towns, Latin, Greek and Hebrew should be learnt. Universities should devote themselves to the liberal arts useful to human society – logic, arithmetic, geometry, geography; and to medicine and law when these had been reformed from their corruptions and disorder 'both for practice and fees'.[67]

Dell's radical political assumptions underlie his approach to university reform. Now that England has become a commonwealth, he argued, and tyranny has been replaced by freedom, Oxford and Cambridge should lose their monopoly. Universities or colleges should be set up in every great city in the nation. The state should allow these colleges a competent maintenance for godly and learned men to teach languages and arts 'under a due reformation'. Undergraduates could thus live at home, and so money would not be needed for scholarships. They should work their way through the university, earning their living in some lawful calling part of the day, or every other day. So twenty times as many undergraduates could attend the universities. After graduating, such men could act as ministers whilst earning their living, and so an end could be put to state maintenance for ministers. If a congregation wished it might support a full-time minister by voluntary contributions, without however calling on the authority of the state. 'This reformed use of tongues and arts justly hath its place in the world.' Even if all men cannot be Christians, yet all can be 'improved in the use of reason and sober learning, whereby they may be serviceable to the commonwealth'. 'Human learning hath its place and use among human things', though it 'hath no place nor use in Christ's kingdom'.[68]

The epigraph to this chapter states forcibly, for the benefit of Dell's Cambridge congregation, the Master of Gonville and Caius's rejection of universities as 'the fountain of the ministers of the gospel'. It was a passage which George Fox quoted with approval.[69] The clergy, Dell thought, should not form a separate caste: 'a poor mean Christian that earns his bread by hard labour is a thousand times more precious than he ["a gentleman, or a knight, or a nobleman or a king"] according to the judgment of God and his Word'. Scholar or clergyman, gentleman or trader, 'if Christ call him and pour forth his spirit on him, that and that only makes him a true minister'. Philosophy, arts and sciences are useless to ministers. The word of God 'cannot be learned as human arts and sciences can . . . by the teaching of men, together with their own pains and endeavours, but only by the teaching of God and his spirit'.[70]

'The word of Christ . . . brings troubles, tumults, stirs and uproars in the world.' 'The rich, wise, learned and honourable' cannot endure this, and look back longingly to episcopacy, when 'all things were well and in good order'. The devil too 'would have all things quiet, that he might keep his possession'. 'The dull and drowsy divinity of synods and schools cannot be the true word of Christ', since the world accepts it. It is 'honoured with degrees and scarlet, and the professors and publishers of it are in credit with men and worldly powers, and receive from them riches, honour and quiet life'. Christ however calls to *his* church 'not the great and honourable and wise and learned, but mean, plain and simple people, . . . base and despised' – 'poor, plain husbandmen and tradesmen' rather than the 'heads of universities and highest and stateliest of the clergy'.[71] 'There is nothing but equality in [God's] church.' Free discussion among equals, Dell argued on Miltonic lines, helps to keep out error, which may easily be introduced 'when one man only speaks'.[72]

Cambridge, Dell told his university congregation, opposed the truth of the Gospel, derided and scoffed at it, relying instead on heathens like Plato, Aristotle, Pythagoras, on the 'cold, vain and antichristian divinity' of Aquinas and Scotus; and on 'the secular arm and worldly power (whom you have seduced for many ages)'. The word of Christ is 'contrary to the philosophical divinity of the schools and university, and the common carnal religion of the nation', reproving and condemning them.[73]

Dell quoted Hus to the effect that 'all the clergy must be quite taken away ere the church of Christ can have any true reformation'.[74] The chief rulers and pillars of the church, 'the most eminent and in appearance most godly and holy and orthodox of the clergy, are above all others most grievously offended at Christ' – now as in his lifetime.[75] In 1653 Dell accused the clergy of aiming to restore Presbyterianism 'if they can gain the secular arm to strengthen them thereunto (of which now they have greatest hopes)'. They want the magistrate to enforce a single national creed devised by 'these men who are in academical degrees and ecclesiastical orders' – 'not for the magistrate's advantage but wholly for the clergy's'. But matters of faith should be determined by 'the congregation of the faithful, and not universities and assemblies of divines'. False prophets are to be found among ordained ministers, especially among 'men of great worth and reputation' who appear to be 'more than ordinarily godly, religious, wise, holy, sober, devout', and who win to their side 'the greatest and highest persons in the kingdoms and nations'. 'For Antichrist could not deceive the world with a company of foolish, weak, ignorant, profane, contemptible persons, but he always hath the greatest, wisest, holiest and most eminent in the visible church for him.' Antichrist 'chose his ministers only out of the universities'. 'The chief design of Antichrist is to seduce the elect, seeing he hath nobody else in all the world that dare oppose him or know how to do it but you.'[76]

He who has not Christ dwelling in his heart, who speaks the words of his own reason, wisdom, and righteousness or other men's, or school divinity,[77] is a false prophet, 'though his knowledge and religion be never so high and glorious, and holy also in the opinion of the world'. They are false prophets even if 'they speak the word of the letter exactly, . . . according to the very original and curiosity of criticism'. 'The word of Christ without the mind of Christ . . . is the effectual operation of error, whereby all hypocrites and false Christians are deceived . . . without all hope of recovery.' A church which has the word without the spirit is Antichrist's church.[78]

False prophets are appointed by men as a result of their own desire and seeking, 'through academical degrees and ecclesiastical ordination'. They 'sprinkle their sermons with Hebrew, Greek, Latin.' They 'will live by the gospel and not by the labour of their hands in a lawful calling . . . They run . . . from a lesser to a greater living, and where they may gain most of this world, there will they be sure to be . . . They especially desire to preach to rich men . . . and care not much to preach to the poor, plain, mean people'. For the sake of worldly advantage, false prophets force themselves upon congregations. They want preaching to be monopolized by those whom the civil magistrate has licensed; all others must be forbidden to preach. True prophets are slandered and persecuted, but are ready to testify to the truth with their properties, liberties and lives; false prophets regard only worldly profit and preferment, accept whatever party shall prevail. They fight against Christ in the name of Christ's church. The godly must separate from the ministry of such false prophets, whatever reputation for godliness and orthodoxy they may have in the eyes of the world. The Bible says nothing about the whole nation being a church. 'Whatsoever a state, an assembly or council shall say ought not to bind the saints further than the judgment of those saints shall lead them.'[79]

The universities are still fundamentally popish, governed by the statutes of their popish founders. The same philosophy and school divinity are taught as in the darkest times of popery. Symbols and ceremonies – hoods, caps, scarlet robes – are all as in popery. Despite the reform of the outward face of religion in England, the universities remain 'the strongest holds which Antichrist hath had amongst us'. Degrees in divinity are antichristian. A Turk or an infidel could take one 'with a little time and pains – and money'.[80] The *system* corrupts even good men who get caught up in it,

> 'as we by sad experience have seen. Many men of great seeming religion, famous for preaching and praying, and reputed pillars in the church, when they have come hither into the university . . . have been entangled and overcome with the spirit of the university and of Antichrist, for worldly honour and advantage sake.'[81]

A university education is useless for a minister who lacks the spirit, superfluous for one who has it. 'Are grammar, rhetoric, logic, ethics, metaphysics, mathematics, the weapons whereby we must defend the gospel?' Dell asked. 'Must that Word be secured by Aristotle which delivers all the elect from sin, death and hell for ever?' The very virtues of the clerical caste, university-educated men learned in philosophy and languages, prevent them from distinguishing between Christ and Antichrist. 'They verily think they oppose and persecute Antichrist himself when they oppose and persecute the faithful people of God.' Subjectively Christian, they are objectively antichristian. Covetousness is the key. Carnal ministers have a numerous (and profitable) auditory because they speak what is in the hearts of worldly people. That is the case for separation, for disestablishment, for ending the training of ministers in 'the antichristian fountain of the universities'.[82]

Dell's theories naturally upset his fellow dons. A young man called Joseph Sedgwick, preaching in Cambridge in May 1653, asked

> 'Is the university stipend, as paid to a divine, antichristian maintenance? Then under what capacity do Mr. Dell and his associates enjoy their places in Cambridge? . . . With what conscience can any Christian knowingly take the wages of

Antichrist? I do not understand much honesty in cheating the Man of Sin of his money.'[83]

Dell did not reply, though he (unlike Sedgwick) surrendered his living at the Restoration rather than conform – when Wilkins and Ward became bishops. 'No man knows the grievousness and efficacy of tribulation, and the weakness and frailty of human nature', said Dell mildly, 'but they who have had experience of both.' But Dell approached Winstanley's more secular analysis when he suggested that the reason why 'all divinity is wrapped up in human learning' was 'to deter the common people from the study and enquiry after it', and make them turn to

'the clergy, who by their education have attained to that human learning which the plain people are destitute of. . . . Then must it sadly follow, that all who want human learning must needs also want divinity; and then how shall poor plain people, who live in lawful callings and have not the leisure to attain human learning, how shall they do to be saved? . . . The necks of the people of the world have never endured so grievous a yoke from any tyrants as from the doctrine and domination of the clergy.'

Not only over bodies and temporal estates: the clergy have also destroyed the people to eternal death.[84]

'When God shall undertake to reform his church', Dell warned, 'all this sort of learning shall be cast out again as dirt and dung, and the plain word of the gospel only shall prevail.' On that day 'the elect shall not stand on compliments, formalities and niceties, nor regard friendship nor enmity; but . . . shall break through all that can be said by the wisdom, policy, prudence and religion of men, and shall execute the righteous judgments of the Lord' on the universities.[85]

Dell was silenced in 1662, though he appears to have been protected by the patronage of Oliver Cromwell's friend, Philip Lord Wharton. In 1667 he planned to fight back by publishing a pamphlet entitled *The Increase of Popery in England* – a tactic which anticipates Andrew Marvell's *Account of the Growth of Popery and Arbitrary Government in England* (1677). In this Dell denounced 'not so much . . . the people as . . . the powers of the nation', who 'have openly renounced Christ', forbidden the preaching of the Gospel, and taken up 'the cruel and murderous religion of Antichrist'. He still hoped for divine intervention.[86] This bold attempt was frustrated. Dell's tract was 'seized in the press'; it was published, posthumously, in the relative freedom of 1681. When Dell died, on Guy Fawkes' Day, 1669, he refused to be buried in the churchyard of the state church.

III

I now turn from the Master of Gonville and Caius to the humbler figure of Gerrard Winstanley, the Digger. Winstanley must have had a grammar-school education in his native Wigan, for he quotes Latin. He came south to become a cloth merchant, and was ruined during the Civil War. In April 1649 he and a group of poor men established a collective farm on common land at St George's Hill, just south-west of London. Winstanley published a series of pamphlets to justify this short-lived experiment. He saw ownership of land as the key to political power: he thought that in consequence of the King's defeat in the Civil War the common and waste lands should be restored to the common people to cultivate. With greater precision than Dell, he depicted the established church and the universities as defenders of existing power and property relations.

'Those that are called preachers . . . seeks for knowledge abroad in universities, and buys it for money, and then delivers it out again for money, for £100 or £200 a year.'[87] In an elaborate metaphor Winstanley depicted evil as 'a mighty spreading tree', covering the earth with its branches

> 'to keep it in darkness and to hide the sun of righteousness from it . . . The universities are the standing pools of stinking waters, that make those trees grow; the curse of ignorance, confusion and bondage spreads from hence all the nations over. The paying of tithes, the greatest sin of oppression, is upheld by them.'

The clergy 'became hearsay-preachers of the Gospel', not from any testimony of the light within, but from book-learning. Yet the Apostles were mechanics, 'fishermen, shepherds, husbandmen and the carpenter's son', who themselves spoke

'as the spirit gave them utterance, from an inward testimony
Yet now these learned scholars have got the writings of these
inferior men of the world (so called), [they] do now slight
despise and trample them under feet, pressing upon the
powers of the earth to make laws to hold them under bond
age, and that lay people, tradesmen and such as are not bred
in schools, may have no liberty so speak or write of the spirit.

'The upshot of all your universities and public preachers . . . is
only to hinder Christ from rising, and to keep Jacob under.
Church and state are in an antichristian conspiracy to keep the
younger brothers servants and slaves. Any who dare oppose the
clergy 'are like to be crushed in their estates by the power o
corrupt magistrates'.[88]
'The university learned ones . . . make themselves minister,
as men teach birds to speak.' 'Under a covetous, proud black
gown' they 'would always be speaking words, but fall off when
people begins to act their words'. The Pharisees still strive to
kill Christ. Pope-like, they silence all who disagree with them.[89]
Unlike Dell, Winstanley thought that even the maintenance of
ministers by the voluntary contributions of their congregation:
was simply a more ingenious and subtle way 'to draw people
under a new bondage, and to uphold the hearsay-preaching
that in time matters may be wheeled about again to advance
the scholars and give them the supremacy in teaching'.[90] After
the Digger colony had been forcibly dispersed, Winstanley
summarized his views in *The Law of Freedom* (1652). In his
utopia one day in seven was still to be set apart for rest from
labour, for mutual fellowship and for education. The minister
elected each year by his congregation (like a tutor in adult
education) had no ecclesiastical functions; his duty was to keep
people informed of current events, to instruct them in the law
of the Commonwealth, in history and in science. The history
was to be slanted to show the benefits of freedom, the evil o
tyrant kings: the science was to cover 'physic, surgery, astrology
astronomy, navigation, husbandry and such-like'. Members o
the congregation were encouraged to contribute, provided they
spoke from experience, not from book-learning or hearsay.
To the complaint that this was a very utilitarian ministry
lacking in spiritual values, Winstanley replied in famous word:

which link the magical tradition of Paracelsans and neo-Platonists with modern science, as so many of his contemporaries among the scientists were doing.[91]

'To know the secrets of nature is to know the works of God; and to know the works of God within the creation is to know God himself; for God dwells in every visible work or body.

And indeed if you would know spiritual things, it is to know how the spirit or power of wisdom and life, causing motion or growth, dwells within and governs both the several bodies of the stars and planets in the heavens above and the several bodies of the earth below; . . . for to reach God beyond the creation, or to know what he will be to a man after the man is dead, if any otherwise than to scatter him into his essences of fire, water, earth and air of which he is compounded, is a knowledge beyond the line or capacity of man to attain to while he lives in his compounded body.

And if a man should go to imagine what God is beyond the creation, or what he will be in a spiritual demonstration after a man is dead, he doth, as the proverb saith, build castles in the air, or tells us of a world beyond the moon and beyond the sun, merely to blind the reason of man . . . A studying imagination . . . is the cause of all evil and sorrow in the world . . . [It] puts out the eyes of man's knowledge, and tells him he must believe what others have writ or spoke, and must not trust to his own experience.'[92]

University divinity is made

'a cloak of policy by the subtle elder brother to cheat his simple younger brother of the freedoms of the earth . . . The subtle clergy do know that if they can but charm the people by this their divining doctrine, to look after riches, heaven and glory after they are dead, that then they shall easily be the inheritors of the earth, and have the deceived people to be their servants . . . Divinity came in after Christ to darken his knowledge; and it is the language of . . . Antichrist, whereby the covetous, ambitious and serpentine spirit cozens the plain-hearted of his portions in the earth.'[93]

'The secrets of the creation have been locked up under the traditional, parrot-like speaking from the universities and colleges for scholars.'[94]

Thus Winstanley, like Dell though on a broader canvas, depicts the universities as tied to the social order; the function of the divines they train is to deceive and silence the people. Before reform is possible, the clergy's 'mouths must be stopped', though 'not by the hands of tyrannical human power', as they have stopped the mouths of others.[95] Winstanley, like Dell, envisaged a future in which the whole educational system should be widely extended, democratized, laicized and made more scientific. This would ensure that 'one sort of children shall not be trained up only to book-learning and no other employment, called scholars', who 'spend their time to find out policies to advance themselves to be lords and masters above their labouring brethren, . . . which occasions all the trouble in the world'.[96] 'The use of human learning in this reformed way' would dissolve the greatest errors of Antichrist, and lead to his downfall.[97] But for Winstanley, more clearly than for Dell, this was part of a general social revolution.

IV

Consideration of the fundamental criticisms of Oxford and Cambridge as 'a fountain of ministers' may help us to understand their role in seventeenth-century English society, better perhaps even than consideration of proposed modernizations of the curriculum. It may throw light backwards and forwards on their unexpressed social role, unexpressed because never challenged except during the revolutionary decades. The shrill cries which the defenders of the universities then emitted show how vital a nerve had been touched.

It would be superfluous to labour modern analogies. The universities of seventeenth-century England were through their ownership of impropriated tithes linked with the prevailing property system – and with what the radicals thought one of its least satisfactory aspects. Their function made them liable to government pressures, and their oligarchical structure facilitated such pressures. The churches today have lost the political power and monopoly position of the seventeenth-century Church of England; but universities still play a part in transmitting the traditional culture, in training the ideologists and the ruling élite of the future. Inevitably they tend to justify the values of the existing society; individuals employed in them may well ask whether they have been as successful as Dell in avoiding becoming 'entangled and overcome with the spirit of the universities and of Antichrist, for worldly honour and advantage sake'.

Where the analogy is incomplete is in our lack of knowledge of what seventeenth-century undergraduates thought. They were of course much younger than today's students. They were either sons of landowners, or scholarship boys from poorer families: the career prospects of the latter, who became gentlemen by graduating from the university, were virtually restricted to the church. If ministers were to be gentlemen, to attain to livings 'full of outward necessaries',[98] *they* could not afford to attack tithes. Nevertheless the Revolution must have had some unsettling effect on them. Dell himself noted that the young, 'as being most free from the forms of the former age, and from the doctrines and traditions of men', were most easily brought over to independency.[99] The Earl of Clarendon, looking back, sourly noted a loss of 'reverence and respect' in all social relations; 'parents had no manner of authority over their children, nor children any obedience or submission to their parents; but everyone did that which was good in his own eyes. This unnatural antipathy had its first rise from the beginning of the rebellion.'[100] But there is a gap in our knowledge here. All we know is that some junior MAs of Oxford – of the same age as today's undergraduates – wanted more university democracy and reform of the curriculum.[101]

Universities were crucial to the ideology of seventeenth-century society. It was not only that they had a monopoly of opinion-forming, training the persuaders. They also embodied and justified fundamental assumptions of the society – that all Englishmen were members of the national church, that only gentlemen educated in the classics might preach, that an ordinary layman must, in Milton's words, 'resign the whole warehouse of his religion' to 'some factor'.[102] They denied by implication the essential protestant doctrine of the priesthood of all believers, or at least appeared to restrict its application to *educated* believers. They had to be overcome before a democratic society could emerge. In fighting against them Dell and Winstanley were working for a more truly human freedom than those who accused them of disruption. Those who defended learning and a civilized way of life also defended tithes, and by implication privilege.

In the seventeenth-century revolution the radical critics of the universities failed as completely as the political radicals: the two failures are of course connected. In 1660 even spare-time scientists like Ward and Wilkins, who had defended Oxford and Cambridge against their more radical critics, were ousted from the universities. The *ancien régime* came back to Oxford and Cambridge if to nowhere else in the kingdom. Modern science had to develop, slowly, elsewhere: in the Royal Society of London, in the dissenting academies. The universities retained their monopoly of training parsons for the state church. The political significance of this changed when that church lost its monopoly after 1689, but the universities were not reformed until the nineteenth century.

Dell, Winstanley and other radical critics were looking forward in the seventeenth century to the modern secular and scientific university as well as to the modern secular state.[103] We must not exaggerate their modernity; yet it is right to recognize the logic of events which made the radicals in the English Revolution adumbrate something of the modern world. The French Revolution expelled priests from the Sorbonne; Oxford and Cambridge were reformed in the nineteenth century, from outside, by Parliament, as seventeenth-century radicals knew they would have to be. Whether we have gone as far as Dell and Winstanley would have wished is another matter. The radicals attacked monopoly and professionalism, in medicine and law as well as in religion.[104] All three have, I suppose, now been thrown open to free market competition, though it is less evident that doctors, lawyers and parsons are the servants of a democratic community in Winstanley's sense. Whether universities can be adapted to serve a democratic community, or are as inextricably trapped in the power and property relations of our competitive society as seventeenth-century Oxford and Cambridge were in their hierarchical society – these are questions currently under debate in most universities of the western world.

6
The Inns of Court[1]

How commonly do they learn to roar instead of pleading!

> Joseph Hall, *Quo Vadis?*
> *A Just Censure of Travel* (1617),
> in *Works* (Oxford, 1837–9), XII, p. 104.

I

In the sixteenth and seventeenth centuries the universities of Oxford and Cambridge trained parsons, and gave a superficial cultural polish to a number of gentlemen. The Inns of Court trained lawyers and likewise acted as a finishing school for gentlemen who had no intention of taking up a legal career. Both the universities and the Inns of Court were attracting the gentry in ever increasing numbers, at least until 1640. Between 1427 and 1540, total admissions to Gray's Inn, the Inner Temple, Lincoln's Inn, and the Middle Temple rose by less than 20 per cent. In the next seventy years they nearly quintupled, and remained at a high level until 1640. The overwhelming majority of those who were thus anxious to avail themselves of an Inns of Court education were members of the landed ruling class. James I's order restricting entry to the Inns to gentlemen by descent was indeed ignored,[2] because in the mobile society of early seventeenth-century England *nouveaux riches* could not be kept out. But the cost of a sojourn at an Inn (*c.* £40 a year minimum)[3] effectively ensured that the privilege was restricted to the well-to-do. Dr Prest's figures demonstrate this social exclusiveness very clearly. Of 12,163 non-honorific entrants to the Inns between 1590 and 1639, 10,761 (88 per cent) were sons of peers, esquires, or gentlemen. Dr Prest, with agreeable modesty and good sense, points out that 'the use of quantitative evidence from a prestatistical age is always a risky undertaking'; but when all allowances have been made there can be no doubt about the significance of these figures. The Inns of Court were much more socially exclusive than Oxford and Cambridge.[4]

These figures are not in themselves startling. There is ample contemporary evidence that in the fifty years before the Civil War lawyers in England were richer and more influential than they had ever been. Sir Thomas Wilson in 1600, George Hakewill in 1627 and Bulstrode Whitelocke in 1649 agreed on the reasons for this phenomenon. They thought that the Tudor peace was principally responsible. Law suits were a continuation of private war by other means: as law and order were extended over the whole realm, so the number of suits increased. 'Peace and law have beggared us all', moaned Sir Thomas Oglander in the Isle of Wight about 1625, urging his son to avoid the lawcourts.[5] King James I and his Irish attorney-general agreed that in Ireland suits 'daily multiply . . . as the country settles more and more in peace and subjection to government'. Dr Penry Williams confirms for Wales the link between the end of private war and an increase in litigation.[6] Whitelocke gave the same explanation for the fact that there were fewer suits in the North of England than in the South. Sir Francis Windebanke, Charles I's Secretary of State, thought that most of the loot from monasteries dissolved at the Reformation went to lawyers; Whitelocke agreed that lawyers throve on the legal disputes resulting from the rapid mobilization of land after the dissolution and from the Englishman's absolute property in his land, including the right to leave it by will. Lawyers looking for business had no difficulty in creating it. 'The greatness of our trade', Whitelocke added, causes 'a multitude of contracts, and these occasion a multitude of law suits', in England as in that other great commercial nation, the Netherlands.[7] The idea of contract is all-pervasive in seventeenth-century thought. For radicals contract was the basis of the state, for Puritans it played an essential part in God's scheme for the redemption of mankind – the covenant theology.

Naturally those who paid the piper called the tune. English law, famous for its defence of property rights, was less careful of the persons of Englishmen. In the decades before 1640 the law was being reinterpreted to the advantage of the commercially-minded, to the disadvantage of government and lower classes alike. A judicial decision of 1568 gave landlords the right to minerals on their land, and so deprived English sovereigns of 'royalties' that their continental rivals enjoyed: the English coal industry, among others, benefited. Another decision of 1605 denied that inhabitants as such had common rights on waste land, and so removed another obstacle to the enrichment of enterprising landlords. The equity of redemption was evolved in the years 1615–30 in order to make it easier for landlords to borrow money for the development of their estates without endangering the interests of lenders.[8] It has been argued that the great influence of Sir Edward Coke stems from the fact that the cases which he reported covered the crucial years 1572–1616, when the common law was being modernized and adapted to the needs of a commercial society.[9] But Chancery too looked especially after the interests of landlords and big merchants.[10]

The conflict of courts in the sixteenth and early seventeenth centuries, of which we hear so much, was in part a struggle of rival groups of lawyers for the profitable business that was going. But it also enabled the unscrupulous to play off one court against another, to drag cases out, to weary the man of shorter purse into surrender. The law's delays encouraged sharp practice, discouraged the straightforwardly honest small trader or craftsman. The cost of a trip to London lasting for several days was prohibitive for a poor artisan or copyholder, to say nothing of the loss of precious working time. Hence the campaign of interregnum radicals for local, decentralized law-courts. This was the atmosphere in which informers were able to carry on their blackmailing trade; and yet without informers, given the absence of a police force, laws could hardly have been enforced at all.[11] The cries from men 'too poor to wage law' against the rich and powerful are too frequent in the sixteenth and early seventeenth centuries not to be taken seriously. Only when a large number of small men banded together was resistance to gentlemanly oppression possible; it was likely to succeed only if by some accident of local politics the support of a rival gentleman was forthcoming. 'Many a man', sighed Richard Stock, 'lives in oppressing and injuring others, his tenants and inferiors; and either there is no civil law against him, or if there be, either his greatness or purse will carry it out well enough.'[12]

All offices are 'in the hands of the nobility', said a French visitor to England in 1597; 'in consequence the people are very hardly treated, and there is no justice where the nobility has any interest.'[13]

Radical critics from More and Starkey in the early sixteenth century to Oliver Cromwell and Gerrard Winstanley during the Revolution denounced the common law as a conspiracy of the rich to keep the poor in due subjection. Hence what was called in 1648 'the general inbred hatred . . . in our common people against both our laws and lawyers'.[14] In his ideal commonwealth Robert Burton the anatomist would have had few laws, plainly set down in the vernacular, with elected judges. Lawyers and doctors should be state-salaried public servants, taking no fees.[15] A surprising number of witnesses give reform of the laws as a motive for fighting on the Parliamentary side in the Civil War. The Leveller campaign to elevate the jury above the judge was an attempt to assert the common sense of small men against the class prejudices of the professionals. Others in the revolutionary decades echoed Burton's call for elected judges, for an unpaid state legal service. Mary Cary wanted to abolish the law and lawyers altogether. For Gerrard Winstanley all that was needed was to make buying and selling illegal: then there would be no need of lawyers.[16]

II

But before 1640 no one doubted the importance of the law, nor the political significance of an ability to manipulate it. 'Every man', wrote Sir Hugh Cholmley 'that hath but a smattering of the law, though of no fortune or quality, shall be a leader and director to the greatest and best gentlemen on the bench' (of JPs).[17] Knowledge of the law helped upward social mobility, or the domination of one's equals. 'To be well read in the law', an enterprising bookseller of Newcastle-upon-Tyne assured potential clients in 1657, 'is the greatest ornament of a gentleman', fits him for the public employments to which he is born. Without a reasonable knowledge of the law any gentleman may lie 'naked and open to the assaults of every base mechanic and troublesome fellow; . . . it's the reason many gentlemen are abused by their vassals.'[18]

A further reason for the especial significance of the law at this period was that the House of Commons was at once a court and the representative institution of the propertied class. It saw politics in terms of antiquarian precedent. The political disputes of the 1620s and 1630s were carried on in legal terms. Charles I's personal rule was 'the only period of English history when the policy of the government has actually been based on historical research'.[19] Against Ship Money, against arbitrary taxation or imprisonment, the Parliamentary opposition stressed the law: 'if you take away the law, all things will fall into a confusion, every man will become a law to himself', said Pym at the trial of the Earl of Strafford in 1641.[20] It is not surprising that the Long Parliament contained an unprecedentedly large number of MPs who had attended one of the Inns of Court – 306 out of 552, 55 per cent.[21]

There seems to be a parallel between the influx of the sons of the gentry into the Inns of Court in this period and their similar appearance in growing numbers at the universities. The question arises, and perplexes historians: what was the educational significance of the fact that so many gentlemen passed through institutions whose principal function was training lawyers and parsons respectively? Opinions differ about the universities: my own view is that educational standards at Oxford and Cambridge were not as high, and certainly not as up to date, as Professor Mark Curtis has suggested.[22] Dr Prest seems to have a similar scepticism about claims that have been made for the Inns of Court as educational centres. He concludes that

> 'judged solely as law schools, the inns of court give little comfort to those who take an optimistic view of the quality of higher education in late sixteenth- and early seventeenth-century England . . . No doubt some exceptionally gifted, industrious and sober youths may have acquired a modicum of legal knowledge during their stay, but the mere fact of an individual's admission to an inn certainly cannot be taken as evidence that he received there a legal education of any kind, or that he had any special familiarity with the theory and practice of the common law.'[23]

This firm conclusion follows forty pages of careful analysis of the legal education available.

Yet, Dr Prest continues, 'the inns were more than law schools'. He is at his most interesting on their role as centres of drama, masque and poetry. The Inns of Court poets include John Donne, William Browne, Thomas Campion, Sir John Davies, Francis Beaumont, John Ford, John Hoskyns, John Marston, Thomas May and George Wither, whom Dr Prest rather harshly describes as a 'third-rate versifier'. But his conclusion is that after the first decade of the seventeenth century, the members of the Inns

'contributed to the arts and sciences rather as consumers and patrons than producers . . . This was partly a reflection of growing specialisation within the legal profession (and indeed all intellectual life), partly a symptom of the general cultural malaise which seems to have set in around the middle of James I's reign: as divisions within society and the state grew more pronounced, the energies which had previously been devoted to literature and scholarship were channelled instead towards political and theological concerns.'[24]

Yet even after they had passed their peak, the Inns 'still continued to provide many a writer with an invaluable start to his career, both as congenial lodgings and anterooms to London's literary society', and 'helped to diffuse the artistic and intellectual effervescence of Elizabethan and early Stuart London throughout the land, to free the arts and sciences from the domination of court and Church (with its agencies, the universities) and hence to mould the distinctive cultural profile of England for several centuries to come'.[25] Even if they did not learn much law, the individual members 'studied astronomy, anatomy, geography, history, mathematics and a wide range of foreign languages in their own time'. This point is reinforced by a valuable study of the libraries of the Inns and their members.[26]

Dr Prest is also healthily sceptical of traditional assumptions about the 'Puritanism' of the Inns of Court. The initial establishment of lectureships at the Inns in Elizabeth's reign, many of which were held by Puritans, 'had owed at least as much to official fears of popery as to the puritanical sympathies of the benchers'. The fierce anti-Puritanism of Whitgift and Bancroft between 1583 and 1610 had its effect. In the seventeenth century Richard Sibbes at Gray's Inn and Thomas Gataker and

John Preston at Lincoln's Inn certainly exercised a Puritan influence, but 'no house maintained an unbroken succession of puritans, while Lincoln's Inn alone appointed a puritan during the years of Laudian ascendancy and non-parliamentary government after 1639'.[27] 'None of the other houses rivalled the puritanism of Lincoln's Inn, either in reputation or reality.' The names of Winthrop, Prynne, Sherfield, Pym, St John, of Feoffees for Impropriations and members of the Providence Island Company, suggest political affiliations; but 'the legal profession was not generally regarded by contemporaries as particularly sympathetic to the puritan cause'. 'Although historians have been impressed by links between the inns and parliament, contemporaries were probably more aware of their connections with the royal court.' But Dr Prest adds that 'while never exclusively puritan in membership or opinion, the societies nevertheless acted as a point of contact in London for puritan gentry and lawyers from all over England, serving to strengthen and extend the network of family and regional connections on which the lay puritan movement was built'.[28]

Dr Prest depicts an interesting generation gap at the Inns that was also a social gap between professional benchers and gentlemen students.[29] Student revolt of one kind or another was frequent, rising to a climax in 1639 which led to government intervention at Gray's Inn, the Middle Temple and the Inner Temple. Dr Prest cautiously says that 'resistance to the benchers' government before 1640 cannot be correlated precisely, either in terms of issues or personnel, with resistance to the king's government after 1640', but notes that the participants included no less than three future regicides, a Parliamentarian judge and a recruiter MP, as well as two royalist officers.[30] Of the benchers, sixty-one supported Parliament in the Civil War, thirty-four the King, and thirty-three were either neutral or unclassified. But as Dr Prest is careful to add, 'no doubt more would have swung to the crown if the inns and law courts had been located in a part of the country which was under royal control when the fighting began'.[31]

Not the least interesting pages of his book are those which analyse the *Vindication of the Professors and Profession of the Law*, published in 1646 by the future regicide John Cook. Its detailed proposals for reform of the common law and of legal education were ignored until the nineteenth century.[32] Once the instruments which enforced royal interpretations of the law – the prerogative courts – had been abolished, the gentry and rich merchants could dominate the legal system, just as they dominated the Church of England once the Court of High Commission had been abolished. When during the interregnum radical demands for law reform seemed likely to endanger property, the 'natural rulers' closed their ranks round the law as it stood. Well-bred men educated in liberal studies, a pamphleteer tells us in 1653, did not speak or write against the law:[33] only the vulgar did that. The law, like the educational system of the Inns of Court, remained unreformed until the nineteenth century; but fear of the social consequences of legal change played its part in bringing Charles II back to England in 1660.

> 'Only armed power can law protect
> And rescue wealth from crowds, when poverty
> Treads down those laws on which the rich rely.'

That succinct summary occurs in Sir William Davenant's 'Poem upon His Sacred Majestie's most happy Return to His Dominions' of 1660.[34] From the later seventeenth century the gentry nevertheless drifted away from the Inns, which lost their prestige as a social centre and reverted to their medieval status as mainly professional institutions.[35] As with the universities, the price of escaping reform was a cosy stagnation.

The Medical Profession
and Its Radical Critics[1]

The true physic . . . is the gift of the most high God . . . It is perfected
and brought to light by practice, not established by human
[institution] but by the institution of God and Nature . . . University
books are not the foundation, but the invisible mercy of God and
his special gift.

> O. Croll, in *Philosophy Reformed and*
> *Improved in Four Profound Tractates,*
> trans. H. Pinnell, 1657, pp. 22–3.

I

It is hardly necessary to say much about the reasons for hostility
towards the medical profession in seventeenth-century England.
The work of Dr Poynter, Professor Roberts and Mr Webster has
made that superfluous.[2] I shall recapitulate briefly.

In London the College of Physicians had, at least in theory, a
monopoly of medical practice. In 1524 there had been twelve
Fellows of the College for a population of some 60,000; 115
years later, when the City's population had increased six- or
seven-fold, the number of Fellows and licentiates of the College
was forty-three. One object of keeping the number of physicians
down was to keep fees up: at 6s. 8d. to 10s. for a visit, only the
well-to-do could afford to call a doctor.[3] Medicine was profitable: a French immigrant was able to lend sums of £10,000
within a few years. Gideon Delaune was said to have died
'worth near as many thousand pounds as he had years'.[4]

Outside London the writ of the College of Physicians did not
run. Physicians in country districts were supposed to be licensed
either by a university or by a bishop. Church courts harried un-

licensed practitioners (i.e. those who had paid no fees) no less than did the College of Physicians – and down to 1640 church courts functioned over the whole kingdom. Archbishop Laud used his metropolitical visitation in 1635 to restrict medical practice to those with degrees. Although some towns (York, Newcastle, Barnstaple, Norwich, Denbigh, Weymouth) followed the example of Geneva and had a physician and/or surgeon paid by the municipality to look after the poor, the numbers of authorized physicians in the provinces must have been at least no more adequate than in London. Reformers from Henry VIII's reign onwards called for free medical services in every town.[5]

Meanwhile most Englishmen could not afford medical advice or treatment. One medical reformer spoke in 1658 of 'the pride and arrogance of our lord-like doctors, . . . their wretched, lazy and unconscionable life, which makes them a by-word to every porter, which they are not at all moved at, so long as they can get money, although with the ruin of families and lives'.[6] We need not believe every word of that, but at least it suggests fairly strong emotions; and the sentiments expressed are not unique. John Robinson, for instance, pastor to the Pilgrim Fathers, referred in 1625 to 'the averseness of many, specially of the meaner sort' to physicians who are 'many times supercilious and neglective of mean persons'.[7]

In so far as the less well-to-do had any medical treatment at all, they got it from surgeons, apothecaries and a nameless host of freelance practitioners, some chemists, some herbalists, some cunning men or white witches, some quacks. The College of Physicians tried to prevent any of these unlicensed persons from practising in London. There was a case for keeping down the number of quacks, though it would have been stronger if there had been more licensed physicians; but of course the College objected most of all to those unlicensed practitioners who were not quacks but had some medical knowledge – especially if they gave their services to the poor gratis.[8] John Cook in 1648 tells us that he could produce over a hundred witnesses to swear that for a quarter of a century Dr Trigg had done good to more than thirty thousand men, women and children around London; but he was a shoemaker, and the College got a judgement against him. Cook said this was not only because he charged little or nothing to the poor but even more because he cured some of the rich whom licensed practitioners had given up for desperate.[9]

The principal doctors of the middle and lower classes were the apothecaries. As pressure from an increasingly prosperous middle class increased effective demand for medical treatment, the College of Physicians became the more determined to maintain its monopoly, which until 1640 was enforced by the Privy Council. The authority of the College was closely dependent on the monarchy and the Church of England. It is not surprising that most apothecaries supported Parliament in the Civil War which broke out in 1642, or that physicians supported the King. Many years earlier Sir Edward Coke had backed up the apothecaries against the College's monopoly. After the collapse of royal government in the Civil War, lawyers were very reluctant to enforce the College of Physicians' monopoly privileges, and church courts ceased to exist. The censorship collapsed, so attacks on the medical profession could be freely published in the 1640s and 1650s.[10]

It may be useful to look at these criticisms in connection with attacks on the other two professions, divinity and law. I start by quoting the Quaker George Fox's *Journal* for the year 1648:

> 'The Lord opened to me three things, relating to those three great professions in the world, physic, divinity (so called) and the law. He showed me that the physicians were out of the wisdom of God, by which the creatures were made . . . He showed me that the priests were out of the true faith, which Christ is the author of . . . He showed me also that the lawyers were out of the equity and out of the true justice and out of the law of God . . . And that these three, the physicians, the priests and the lawyers, ruled the world out of the wisdom, out of the faith and out of the equity and law of God; the one pretending the cure of the body, the other the cure of the soul, and the third the property of the people.'[11]

Fox went on to make suggestions for the reform of all three professions.

The founder of the Society of Friends was not the only one to link the three professions in reprobation. They were regarded by political and religious radicals as privileged monopolies composed of men whose object was to keep knowledge away from ordinary people in order that they alone might profit by it. Nicholas Culpeper, for instance (to whom I shall often refer later) said that 'the liberty of our commonwealth is most impaired by three sorts of men, priests, physicians, lawyers', all of them monopolists. John Cook, lawyer and regicide, whom I shall also mention frequently, spoke of 'three sorts of mountebanks – judges, ministers and physicians – that have but one saddle for all horses'.[12] Samuel Hering in 1653 urged that divines, physicians and lawyers should all be state-salaried officials, not dependent on fees paid by the people.[13] Sir William Petty in 1662 advocated reducing the number of parsons, doctors and lawyers, 'all which do receive great wages for little work done to the public'. Muggleton attacked all three professions.[14] John Heydon wrote that during the Revolution 'porters [would] practice the law, cobblers preach, and stocking-weavers, hatband-makers and smiths etc. pretend to be doctors of physic'.[15] A few years later this was echoed by the historian of the Royal College of Physicians, Christopher Goodall, who spoke of 'a sort of men not of academical but mechanical education', whose aim was to make the faculty of physic 'a prey to ostlers, cobblers and tinkers; hereafter bringing tailors to invade the bar, and jugglers the pulpit'.[16]

The three professions were of course monopolists to differing degrees. Before 1640 the church was a universal monopoly. All English men and women, whether they liked it or not, were members of the state church, liable to pay tithes (a 10 per cent income tax) for the maintenance of ministers whom they did not choose and from whom they could not escape. All English men and women were liable to the penalties of church courts for 'sins' which many did not regard as offences at all. Law and physic were not commodities which all were bound to purchase. Lawyers and physicians sold services which were purchased mainly by the rich: rationing by the purse. But a poor man might get involved involuntarily in a law suit, in which case his interests were likely to suffer if he could not or would not hire a lawyer to represent him. And entry to both professions was restricted; for lawyers by the necessity of entering one of the Inns of Court, in theory open only to sons of gentlemen, in practice also to sons of the rich – a distinction without a difference for our present purposes. The College of Physicians was a small, self-elected body, which itself had the right to forbid competition from those whom it had not licensed.

Whatever the differences, the three professions were often linked, either in common reprobation or in common defence against the onslaughts of the vulgar. Let us look at some of the arguments, starting with the clergy. On them the attack was mounted principally by radical sectaries, using arguments partly theological, partly social. The theological case was simple. Divine grace, not human learning, was the essential for a preacher of the Gospel. Divine grace might be given to un-learned mechanics, as it had been given to fishermen, publicans, tent-makers and carpenters in the days of the Apostles. 'Human learning cannot understand . . . the mystery of the Gospel', wrote John Webster. 'For ministers to be bred at academies, and get orders, licences or seals from human authority, thereby to get fat benefices and rich livings, is to make the ministry a mere trade.'[17] Divinity could not be 'taught' at a university, and it was utterly wrong for a clerical caste to separate itself from the people and demand payment from those who had not called them. University-trained divines, poring over their books, were less rather than more likely to be touched by the Spirit of God than the mechanic preacher who worked with his hands six days a week and on the seventh day discussed theology with the congregation which had elected him, an equal among equals.[18] Now that the Bible was available in English for all who could read, no trained class of specialist expositors was needed to guide the discussions of the congregations.

The argument against professional lawyers was put forward by Levellers, Diggers and other radical political and religious groups. One of the main points made by legal reformers was that the law still needed its protestant reformation, so to speak. Studying the Bible in the vernacular had done much (even if not enough) to diminish the role of a mediating priesthood, who alone had access to and understanding of the sacred scriptures. But lawyers still kept their texts concealed in Norman French and Latin. 'How can that law be called com-mon to all which [the judges] monopolize, engross and ap-propriate to themselves?' asked the Leveller John Jones. 'The true and ordinary judges of the land', he continued, were – or should be – jurors. The Levellers John Lilburne and William

Walwyn, the republican MP Henry Marten, agreed. This was a class issue, Jones insisted: judges were gentlemen, expensively educated at the Inns of Court: jurors were mechanics. The argument is strictly analogous to that which preferred mechanic preachers to university-trained divines. Quarrels should be solved by neighbours, without calling upon, still less paying, professional experts. If there must be a court trial, men should conduct their own defence. Law books should be in English, so that every man can understand for himself the laws of his community: laws must be *known*, not traps. By keeping the laws in French and Latin the judges 'can devise for themselves to mend where they list, which happeneth sometimes for the rich, but rare or never for the poor'.[19] Hence the demand, made by Levellers and Fifth Monarchists, though I happen to be quoting George Fox again, that the law should be 'drawn up in a little short volume, and all the rest burnt'.[20]

If there were to be judges at all, they should be elected, insisted the radicals, including John Rogers, John Spittlehouse and Dr Peter Chamberlen. Walwyn thought that mechanics could do the job adequately, in law as in religion. 'Take a cobbler from his seat', he was reported as saying, 'or a butcher from his shop, or any other tradesman that is an honest and just man, and let him hear the case and determine the same, and then betake himself to his work again.'[21] Gerrard Winstanley, the Digger, more radical still, thought there would be no need of lawyers in his reformed commonwealth once buying and selling had been abolished: 'neither any need to expound laws, for the bare letter of the law shall be both judge and lawyer'. But then Winstanley not only held that the abolition of private property would lead to lawyers becoming superfluous: he also thought that a professional clergy would be unnecessary in a society in which every mechanic was free to preach. In his ideal commonwealth elected ministers were lay educators of their parishioners in science, medicine, history, politics: they superseded parson, lawyer and doctor. Following the trade of lawyer or parson were two of the few offences liable to the death penalty in Winstanley's utopia. The ultimate extension of anti-professionalism was Winstanley's scheme for a citizen army, electing its own officers, ready to act as a check on any who attempted to upset the freedom of the commonwealth.[22]

I am trying to emphasize the close analogy between the case against a professional clergy and the case against professional lawyers: the same men were apt to concern themselves with both issues. The legal reformer, John Warr, for instance, rejected 'the distinction of clergy and laity', just as mechanic preachers did. Many were the radicals in the 1650s who – like Edmund Ludlow and John Milton – joined together 'the corrupt interests of the lawyers and the clergy'. 'Where you find cobblers in pulpits,' wrote John Jones, 'it is because the divines are out.'[23]

Another point linking clerical, medical and legal reformers is hostility to Latin – shared by Culpeper, Webster, Walwyn, Winstanley and Fox. This too had class overtones. Fifty years before the Civil War the statutes of Gresham College had provided that its professors (including professors of divinity, law and medicine) were to lecture, free of charge, in English, so that their London audience would not consist of the learned only. 'Forasmuch as the greatest part of the auditory is like to be of such citizens and others as have small knowledge, or none at all, in the Latin tongue, and for that every man for his health's sake will desire to have some knowledge in the art of physic', the physic professor was told to deal with modern medical theories, not simply to expound Galen or Hippocrates as was done in the universities.[24]

II

We must bear these points in mind when we turn to attacks on the medical profession during the Revolution. Clearly medicine was a less directly political issue than the church or the law. Rejection of a professional clergy, its replacement by mechanic preachers paid by voluntary contributions from their congregations, with no right to tithes – this would have meant the disestablishment of the state church, whose monopoly opinion-forming functions seemed to conservatives essential to social stability, to radicals an instrument of class rule. Abolition of lawyers, as Winstanley saw, could have been realized only if property was also abolished in a communist society; even the subordination of judges to jurors was a specifically social measure. The demand for it arose, John Jones agreed, from 'a general disesteem of gentry more now than from the beginning of the world'.[25]

But if the medical profession was not a political grievance in the way that 'the corrupt interests of the lawyers and the clergy' were, their enemies were also political radicals, who denounced them in similar terms. Noah Biggs, for instance, accused the Galenists of the College of Physicians of 'antipathy' to the Commonwealth.[26] Nicholas Culpeper, republican and radical sectary, who was wounded fighting for Parliament in 1643, made it his life's work to translate medical works from Latin into English. 'I am resolved', he wrote, 'not to give over, until I have published in English whatsoever shall be necessary to make an understanding, diligent, rational man a knowing physician.' His translation of the *Pharmacoepia Londinensis* in 1649 was made 'out of pure pity to the commonalty of England'. The book, he said in his Preface of 1651, 'tends towards the furtherance of a Commonwealth and the pulling down a monopoly'. He made the religious parallel explicit by saying that 'the Papists and the College of Physicians will not suffer divinity and physic to be printed in our mother tongue, both upon one and the same ground'. 'Time was', he argued in 1652, 'when he would have been accounted a monster, and unfit to live in a Commonwealth, that should but have attempted . . . to hide the rules of physic from the vulgar in an unknown tongue.' Yet the College of Physicians, 'such as get their livings under this monopoly', kept 'the rules of physic hid' from the common people 'lest, as they and the Papists say, you should do yourselves a mischief by them, when indeed the truth is (in both cases) their own gain and credit lies at stake'.[27]

'My aim', Culpeper continued, 'is not to make fools physicians, but to help those that are ingenious, rational and industrious, though they have not the knowledge of tongues that were to be desired'. He described one of his books as 'a primer to learn physic by'.[28] *Mutatis mutandis*, the mechanic preachers might have said the same of their sermons; John Lilburne held adult education classes in the law whilst he was in Newgate jail, and hoped that every man might become his own lawyer. Culpeper, one of his probably jealous colleagues tells us, strove 'to make himself famous in taverns and alehouses', like Paracelsus – and, we might add, like many of the mechanic preachers and mechanic lawyers.[29]

As in religion and law, so in medicine, Culpeper held that

there should be no paid specialists monopolizing knowledge. Every man should be his own physician, with the available medical books translated into English to help him, and with knowledge of herbs, diet and simple rules about exercise, sleep, sex, etc. made available to all. He was dealing, let us admit, with a real problem. The College of Physicians restricted the number of doctors available in London, in order to keep fees high. Outside London, episcopal or university licences were (at least in theory) required. Yet even men who could not afford to pay a physician got ill and died. Someone had to cope with their problems and needs. The main alternative resource was undoubtedly the white witch, the cunning man or woman, of whom there was one in most villages. But there was also a great deal of amateur doctoring – by ladies of the manor, by other lay men and women who interested themselves in herbs or in chemical remedies. Henry Best, yeoman of the East Riding of Yorkshire, had many books on physic and surgery in his library in 1617. The Leveller John Wildman studied medicine as a hobby, and doctored himself and his wife.[30]

It was common for ejected ministers to take up medicine – from protestants in Mary's reign through Elizabethan Puritans and Laud's victims to the even larger numbers who turned to a medical career after the great expulsion of 1662 (including radicals like Abiezer Coppe and Paul Hobson). The two professions might be practised simultaneously. The Rev. Timothy Bright was physician to St Bartholomew's Hospital under Elizabeth until he got a rich living. Gideon Delaune's father was minister to the London Walloon church as well as a practising doctor. George Herbert thought medical attention was a proper duty for the parson.[31]

The idea of lay medicine appealed especially to sectarian lay preachers who thought that 'true physic is the mere gift of the most high God'. (I quote a 1657 translation of Oswald Croll,[32] but I might have quoted Van Helmont or many other well-known chemists to the same effect.) Grace, in this view, was no more likely to be found in academically trained doctors than in academically trained divines. Sir Thomas Browne's title, *Religio Medici*, was intentionally a paradox: doctors were expected to be irreligious. John Smyth the Se-Baptist practised physic at Amsterdam,' knowing that a man was bound to use the gifts that the Lord had bestowed upon him for the good of others'. He charged nothing to the poor, half fees to the rich unless they insisted on paying more.[33] Milton observed that Waldensian preachers 'bred up themselves in trades and especially in physic and surgery', so that (like Christ) they 'might cure both soul and body'. George Fox, who had no more medical training than theological, nevertheless was at one time 'at a stand in my mind, whether I should practise physic for the good of mankind, seeing the nature and virtues of things were so opened to me'. He never lost his interest in healing – and was also an amateur lawyer.[34] So the author of *Macaria* in 1641 was not advocating anything sensationally new in suggesting that the jobs of preaching and healing should be combined. But it was a practice which the College of Physicians heartily disliked and which only had a chance of succeeding on a national scale after the overthrow of the monarchy which protected the College.

Hostility to the medical profession, as to the legal and clerical profession, was a long-standing lower-class attitude. John Robinson in 1625 suggested that poverty was not the only obstacle; the poor also suspected that 'the learned' would overreach or neglect 'mean and plain persons', or treat them with condescension. In their preference for cunning men and empirics he saw 'an ambitious desire . . . to advance those of their own order'. Any successes of these untrained practitioners were readily attributed to 'a special divine assistance and helping hand of God'.[35] Robinson's insight here confirms a suggestion that Professor Mandrou has made for France: that licensing was an upper-class affair, unlikely to impress the poor, who had more confidence in the traditional secret folklore of the cunning man than in the university education of Galenic doctors. The historian, Professor Mandrou emphasizes, knows too little of the cultural reality underlying this attitude.[36]

So there is a long tradition behind Culpeper. In the midsixteenth century Andrew Boorde addressed his *Breviary of Health* to 'simple and unlearned men, that they may the better have some knowledge to ease themselves in their distresses and infirmities'. William Bullin and many others under Elizabeth wrote books for 'the poorer sort of people that are not of ability to go to physicians'.[37] 'I saw ancient people coming to me', wrote Culpeper in a famous passage, 'sick and coughing and crying out "for the Lord's sake help us".' He wanted to help such men to help themselves, for many poor people '(to my knowledge) have perished, either for want of money to fee a physician, or want of knowledge of a remedy happily growing in their own garden'.[38]

Perhaps the analogy of modern China may help us to appreciate what Culpeper was trying to do. There, we are told, traditional Chinese techniques have recently been developed side by side with modern western medical practice, because '80% of China's population is rural . . . If medicine is to serve them it requires simple, effective techniques which can be used by relatively unskilled personnel in the remote areas.' 'The lack of penetration of China by western medicine shows that the people had less respect (not to say less money!) for western than for their own traditional medicine.'[39] In seventeenth-century England Culpeper tried to extend knowledge of local traditional medicines, and Dr Poynter has suggested that his criticisms of contemporary medical treatment have been justified by later botanical knowledge.[40] A preference for home-bred simples as against the apothecaries' imported drugs was expressed by Timothy Bright in 1580 and by many after him, including George Herbert. By that time it had become a respectable position among medical authorities. Culpeper exhorted his countrymen to 'betake them to their gardens and fields' rather than relying on drugs brought from foreign parts, to which English bodies were not adapted. (Tobacco is said to have been a contributory to the illness of which Culpeper himself died.) He recommended the drinking of milk, moderate diet, exercise, sleep, moderate sexual indulgence, cold baths and a whole series of common-sense remedies for common diseases and accidents.[41]

Given the shortage of doctors and the high fees charged by those who did practise, it was inevitable then that men and women lacking technical professional qualifications would practise physic – illegally before 1640, but in the revolutionary decades more freely and with the encouragement of radical politicians like Culpeper. 'The late years of tyranny', wrote John Heydon in 1664, 'admitted stocking-weavers, shoemakers, millers, masons, carpenters, bricklayers, gunsmiths, porters, butlers etc. to write and teach . . . physic' – and, he might have added, a lawyer's clerk like himself, whose main medical qualification (men said) was to have married Culpeper's widow.[42] 'All the nation are already physicians,' Culpeper declared. 'If you ail anything, everyone you meet, whether a man or a woman, will prescribe a medicine for it.' So they might as well be informed physicians. 'My writings may teach you, but it is yourselves must make yourselves physicians.'[43] One of John Cook's main charges against the College of Physicians was that they refused 'to teach ordinary medicines to poor people, as good drinks and possets made of herbs'.[44]

William Walwyn the Leveller expressed this as a general ideology: 'In natural things all things whatsoever that are necessary for the use of mankind, the use of them is to be understood easily without study or difficulty: every capacity is capable thereof; and not only so, but they are all likewise ready at hand, or easily to be had.'[45] Walwyn was writing of religion; but his later practice as a physician fitted well into the theory. 'The works of God,' Culpeper said in 1652, 'are common for everyone to view and for everyone to receive benefit by, and it is a sin in man to impropriate what God hath left common. If God hath left the medicine common, who gave man commission to impropriate?'[46] We may compare Winstanley's insistence that in every parish educational lectures should be given in law and medicine (among other subjects) and that all useful discoveries should be widely publicized. Culpeper foresaw an educated lay public well enough informed to practise a largely preventive medicine and to cure simple ailments. He and others would have envisaged more difficult medical problems being tackled, free of charge, by doctors who were the servants of the community, paid by the community. Doctors who were no longer mainly interested in fees for *curing* illness would co-operate the more willingly in preventive medical measures. Hugh Peter and some Levellers wanted physicians' fees to be regulated and reduced, 'and then help commanded upon a known price' for the poor.[47] John Cook, Henry Robinson, Gerrard Winstanley, Samuel Hering advocated state medicine, free for the poor, preventive as well as curative: Samuel Hartlib and his circle also favoured preventive medicine. Richard Overton, Peter Chamberlen and Sir William Petty supported

Henry Robinson's proposals for state-sponsored teaching hospitals; Chamberlen wanted the state to sponsor public baths.[48]

'The law of England is ancienter than books', cried John Cook, himself a lawyer of standing.[49] The radicals looked back to political traditions allegedly inherited from the free Anglo-Saxons, as mechanic preachers looked back to the days of the Apostles. John Warr thought that legal reform was part of a general religious revolution.[50] In exactly the same way a Hermeticist physician like Robert Fludd looked back to the *prisca theologia* and to the traditional wisdom attributed to Hermes Trismegistus. Radical medical reformers thought that medicine was not primarily to be learnt from books, but from the book of nature, by experiment.[51]

III

There is not the place for a full discussion of the importance of chemical medicine, vital though it is to our theme. From Paracelsus in the early sixteenth century to Van Helmont in the mid-seventeenth, chemists strongly emphasized the need for experiment, for working in laboratories with one's own hands, trying out new chemical combinations. This led to real discoveries. I quote Mr Charles Webster: 'Opposition to Galenic medicine and sympathy with chemical therapy was common to the whole medical reform movement of the Puritan Revolution . . . [It] represented a rival experimental tradition to the contemporaneous mechanical philosophy.' More Paracelsan and chemical books were published in English translation during the 1650s than in the whole preceding century.[52] Advocacy of chemistry linked Culpeper's circle with the chemical group which Samuel Hartlib organized, including Boyle, Petty, Plattes, John Hall, William Rand, Thomas Vaughan, George Starkey, William Sprigge, Henry Oldenburg. Chemical medicine was also supported by Gerrard Winstanley, Noah Biggs, John Webster, Marchamont Nedham, Henry Pinnell and a host of others.

So the medical reformers, in suggesting that every man could and should be his own doctor, were thinking on lines parallel to those who thought laymen should preach and those who wished

to elevate the juror over the judge. It is therefore not surprising
that many medical reformers were fiercely hostile to clergy and
lawyers. Culpeper, like William Lilly, used his almanacs as
vehicles for slashing attacks on both.[53] In 1650 Culpeper said of
the clergy, 'so long as they thought the Army would drive on
their designs, what encouragements did they give men to fight
[in the Civil War], . . . what forcing men to fight for fear of hell
and damnation!' But all changed when the rank and file of the
Army began to reject a state church and tithes. 'As for the
clergy,' he wrote in 1652, 'as they stand at state present, they
must down.' 'True religion will scarce ever flourish by public
authority', he had written in the preceding year, 'till Jesus
Christ be set upon his holy hill of Zion.'[54] 'Who are our jailors?'
he asked in *A Directory for mid-wives*. 'I say scholars.' (We recall
'the meaner sort's' class-conscious suspicion of 'the learned'
recorded by John Robinson.) 'His most public enemies were
physicians', said Culpeper's biographer; 'and his most private
ones divines.' Culpeper's father and maternal grandfather were
both clergymen.[55]

Culpeper was similarly on the side of the Levellers and their
allies in hostility to lawyers. 'William the Bastard having conquered this nation . . . brought in the Norman laws, written in
an unknown tongue, and this laid the foundations to their
future and our present slavery.' The English educational system
was devised to maintain the privileges of a ruling class descended from the conquerors;

'that it might come to be an extreme difficult thing to be a
linguist and understand Latin and Greek, they have imposed
such multiplicity of needless rules in the learning of the Latin
tongue that unless a man have gotten a very large estate he is
not able to bring up his son to understand Latin, a dozen
years expense of time will hardly do it as they have ordered
the matter, in which time, by whipping and cruel usage, the
brains of many are made so stupid that they are unfit for
study, but are fain to pin their faith upon the sleeve of that
monster, Tradition . . . The poor commonalty of England is
deprived of their birthright by this means . . . I hope, as the
rise of the Norman race was the beginning of our slavery, so
the consummation of it [by victory in the Civil War and the

execution of Charles I] will be the end. I hope that light which is now breaking out shall increase more and more to a perfect day.'[56]

And this light would affect medicine no less than politics and religion. 'If ever God ... shall cast again the tyrannical yoke of kingship upon the neck of the English nation, they will be deprived of all those blessed opportunities they now enjoy to improve their understandings in this art' of medicine.[57]

'Kings and magistrates thieve by authority', Culpeper wrote in his almanac for 1652, repeating a familiar radical theme. He often expressed himself in favour of the rule of the people against monarchy, once actually using the word 'democracy' in a favourable sense. He hoped that English liberty would within a few years be extended to 'all the nations in Europe'.[58]

IV

Culpeper is eminently quotable, but he was by no means the only medical reformer to align himself with the religious and political radicals against the three professions. Peter Chamberlen, son of Sarah Delaune, Gideon Delaune's sister, was himself a Fellow of the College of Physicians. This did not prevent him attacking them even earlier than Culpeper, on the same ground that they kept secret knowledge which was capable of saving thousands of lives. He was dismissed from his Fellowship in 1649. He himself preached to an Anabaptist congregation, and in 1652 defended lay preaching, denouncing the Presbyterian ministers of the state church as antichristian. He also attacked the law and lawyers, and thought judges should be elected. He too was a political radical who spoke up for the poor. '*Meum* and *tuum* [i.e. property] divide the world into factions, into atoms; and till the world return to its first simplicity or ... to a Christian Utopia ... covetousness will be the root of all evil.' In 1649 he advocated public works to relieve unemployment and pointed out that 'rich men are none of the greatest enemies to monarchy' – though he himself had been physician extraordinary to Charles I and was to be physician in ordinary to Charles II.[59] He was accused of extortionate charges, but there is independent evidence to support his own claim that he charged far less to the poor than to the rich.[60]

John Webster, chaplain and surgeon in the New Model Army, better known as critic of the universities, disapproved of the academic training of a professional clergy no less than he disapproved of the type of medical education dispensed at Oxford and Cambridge.[61] He attacked tithes and a state church ('better no ministry than a pretended one' were words which he attributed approvingly to William Erbery). He advocated the teaching of chemistry and more mathematics in the universities, as well as of astrology and natural magic; he wanted more application of the ideas of Bacon and Harvey as well as of Paracelsus, Dee, Fludd and Helmont. Webster too was a convinced radical Parliamentarian, who suffered for his activities on behalf of the cause, and was denounced as a Leveller by defenders of the universities. In dedicating his critique of the universities to John Lambert, Webster went out of his way to praise Lambert's share in 'redeeming the English liberty, almost drowned in the deluge of tyranny and self-interest'. 'The work of Christ is an overturning, overturning, overturning work,' he had said in 1653.[62]

As a doctor himself, Webster thought that Harvey's discoveries, which he admired, were of little use in practice. (This reminds us of Dr Poynter's remark, that Culpeper had far more influence on medical practice in the century after 1650 than Harvey or Sydenham.[63]) After the Restoration Webster wrote a courageous book against the belief in witches of Fellows of the Royal Society like Sir Thomas Browne and Joseph Glanvill. In this he drew interestingly on his own medical experience. By 1671, when he was said to have 'practised chemistry now a great while', Webster admitted that he had previously 'had too high an esteem of chemical medicines', though he still praised Paracelsus, Van Helmont and the Hermetic philosophy as well as the Royal Society. At Gresham College he had been a pupil of Hans Hunneades, the Hungarian chemist to whom Arthur Dee was said to have remitted the secrets of his father, John Dee. In 1677 Webster still cited Dee and Fludd with approval, as well as Bacon and Harvey, Hakewill and Galileo.[64]

We know very little about my next medical reformer, Noah Biggs, whose *Vanity of the Craft of Physick* was published in 1651; in it he praises 'that famous society and community of the R.C.' (Rosicrucians). Biggs's book is a curious hotch-potch, repro-

ducing almost *verbatim* but without acknowledgment, long
passages from other writers – for example John Hall's *An Humble
Motion to the Parliament of England concerning the Advancement of
Learning* and Milton's *Areopagitica*.[65] Biggs makes many familiar
criticisms. The diet recommended by physicians was too
expensive for the poor. Physicians 'seem to study only for
lucre of gain'. He called for medical reform in the light of
chemistry, for reform of the universities and a review of old
experiments and traditions. 'The divine goodness hath persuaded me that home-bred diseases have their remedies likewise
at home': so he opposed the importation of foreign drugs. Biggs
stressed sobriety as the cardinal point in diet, together with
thorough mastication. Otherwise we should follow our own
judgment in what we eat. Exercise, labour, rest, sleep and air,
plus 'the primitive method of healing noted in Scripture' by
herbal remedies: these build up the body, whereas 'the whole
bulk of the art of healing seems nowadays to be moved upon the
slender hinges of purgations, phlebotomy or blooding, . . . cup-
ping, baths, sweatings, . . . cauteries; and in short, upon no other
than the diminution of the strength and emaciation of the
body'.[66] ('There were a certain sort of physicians that were like
the bishops,' Culpeper observed; 'they had the keys of binding
and loosing, and nothing else.'[67]) Some of Biggs's points were
later elaborated by the Leveller William Walwyn.

It has long been known that Walwyn practised as a doctor
after the Restoration, and that in 1681 he published a small
volume called *Physick for Families*. In 1949 Dr Poynter showed
that an edition of this work had been published in 1669 over
the initials W.W., and that a tract of 1667 called *A Touchstone
for Physick*, also signed W.W., was by Walwyn too. Two earlier
tracts by W.W. can be shown on internal evidence to be by the
same author: one published in 1661 entitled *Healths new Store-
house Opened*, and another seven years earlier still, in 1654:
Spirits Moderated . . . Nor was even that the beginning of
Walwyn's medical career, for he claimed in 1654 to have been
'very intent and serious for many years in the study and consideration of the things appertaining to the great blessing of
health'. It looks as though he turned to medicine immediately
after the defeat of the Leveller movement in 1649. His words
'nor did I ever take so much satisfaction in mind in anything

wherein I ever exercised myself (next the things of everlasting concernment) as I have done in this employment' read like an epitaph on his political career.[68] The only political tract that Walwyn published between 1649 and 1654 was *Juries Justified* (1651). It is perhaps significant that after he took up lay medicine he should still be interested in defending the rights of laymen against professional lawyers.

In 1654 Walwyn said he had conducted many experiments into the effect of simples – i.e. herbs – which he concluded were 'very much over-boasted in books'. He decided that 'the way of chemistry and distillation was the most effectual of any for my purpose', which was as much preventive as curative – like that of his son-in-law and earlier political defender Dr Humphrey Brooke.[69] (Those who read Andrew Malleson's articles in the *Observer* early in 1973 will recall his argument that preventive medicine keeps us alive despite the harm that curative medicine does us.) In *Physick for Families* (1669) Walwyn attacked purgings, vomitings, bleedings, clysters, sweating, on lines made familiar by Culpeper, Biggs and George Starkey. Moderate exercise Walwyn thought better than purging. He recommended that diet should be left to everyone's own experience, and physic to the physicians when required: he himself could offer 'what might be of good avail upon the borders of both'. He advertised for sale up to thirty-three medicines designed as general specifics: we are reminded both of the quest for a universal medicine in the Hermetic tradition, and of Hartlib's and Boyle's interest in a universal medicine. By 1669 Walwyn – like John Webster – had lost his earlier confidence in chemical medicines. 'Chemistry hath lately abounded to its own disparagement, yielding nothing comparable to the noble countenance given unto it. For who now will not be a chemist, whether nature hath fitted him thereunto or not?' And he referred to chemistry's 'vapouring fancies, mysteries and riddles'. All doctors, he proclaimed, 'ought to be obliged to take the same remedy as at any time they prescribe, and in the same quantity'.[70]

V

The rise and fall of chemical medicine runs parallel to the rise and fall of the movement for medical reform, and may well conclude our story. Although in the 1640s and 1650s chemical medicine competed on equal terms with the mechanical philosophy, by the end of the century the latter had triumphed. The popular basis of alchemy, as of intellectual magic, proved first a source of strength but ultimately of weakness. In the upsurge of the Revolution a man like Culpeper was able to draw on the traditional lore of the herbal doctor and the cunning man, and to appeal at the same time to popular hostility towards 'lordlike' doctors. But as the Revolution ebbed, chemistry – always viewed sceptically by the professional physicians of the College – suffered for its association with political radicalism.

In the late 1650s William Rand – associate of Hartlib, Culpeper and Walwyn – tried to organize a College of Graduate Physicians, to protect respectable unlicensed practitioners against renewed persecution by the College of Physicians.[71] But after the restoration of Charles II in 1660, although some Fellows of the newly-founded Royal Society were alchemists, they did not share the popular democratic associations of the chemical medicine of Culpeper, Biggs, Webster and Rand, from which indeed the scientists of the Royal Society were busily dissociating themselves. The post-Restoration Society of Chemical Physicians, through which Marchamont Nedham and others tried to hold the chemists together in opposition to the College of Physicians, lacked the academic respectability of Rand's proposed *Graduate* College, and could not avoid the compromising company of the quacks and empirics, astrologers and magicians, whom the College of Physicians used to smear the whole chemical movement. Some of the practical achievements of Paracelsan and Helmontian chemistry were absorbed into orthodox medical practice; but the cosmic speculations and social applications of the radical medical reformers of the revolutionary decades were abandoned. The contemptuous dismissal of the Society of Chemical Physicians was self-validating: chemists were driven into the underworld where magic, alchemy and astrology came to be prized *because* of their irrationality, no longer as a possible source from which truth might be painfully sifted. Despite Boyle, chemistry languished for the next century. Sir Isaac Newton never published his voluminous alchemical writings.[72] The mechanical philosophy triumphed absolutely over the rival chemical tradition, for reasons which were social as well as intellectual.

After 1660 it was as fashionable to denounce 'enthusiasts in physic as in divinity',[73] to dismiss them both as fanatical lower-class extremists who were politically dangerous. From the fifties the reformers were disposed of by social sneers as much as by argument. Webster was denounced as a Leveller by Wilkins and Ward, future founders of the Royal Society. 'Had you been a right gentleman,' one of his critics told Culpeper, 'you would have scorned so much to vilify the gown' – just as well-bred men did not vilify the law.[74]

The different attitudes of hostility towards professionalism which we have been considering are linked theologically by the cardinal protestant tenet of the priesthood of all believers, the conviction that God speaks immediately to the conscience of each believer. The logical conclusion drawn in the seventeenth century was that the individual conscience was infallible: one should follow one's inner light wherever it led. The Bible in English is a useful guide, but it is to be interpreted by the enlightened conscience. Similarly natural reason must play on the texts of the law, and in medicine all men should be educated to interpret the Book of Nature from which – rather than from the books of learned men – wisdom is to be rediscovered. God reveals himself in his works no less than in his Word. In matters of diet we should trust our own judgment rather than any authority. If this doctrine looks back to Luther's priesthood of all believers, it also looks forward to the secularized democracy of the century of the common man. (The phrase 'the common man' was being used in the 1650s.)[75]

This radical doctrine holds it to be wrong to lock truth up in languages accessible only to the learned; it rejects the mumbo-jumbo of self-styled experts, the obfuscation of specialists. It can be a brash and ill-informed hostility to learning; it can also be a searching criticism of shams and pretensions. Professionalism is not always and only a defence of monopoly privilege at the expense of the poor: it is sometimes concerned with maintaining standards and advancing knowledge. But – I speak as a member of one of the professions to a professional audience – we can admit that both aspects coexist within the concept of a profession, even within most individual members of them: mumbo-jumbo aspects of professionalism are more likely to preponderate given monopoly than free competition. We can today perhaps appreciate better than preceding generations seventeenth-century anxieties about excessive specialization.

After the mid-seventeenth century Revolution professionalism had come to stay, in medicine no less than in divinity and law. The greatest change was perhaps in religion, where church courts lost their coercive power, and after 1689 the monopoly of the state church was opened to some competition. But – as with law and medicine – entry to the clerical profession remained restricted by the doctrinal tests which excluded nonconformists from the universities; and tithes remained as a tax on all Englishmen. But the assumptions of the society were profoundly secularized. John Cook put forward the remarkable view that lawyers were more necessary than physicians or divines, for medicine cares only for the bodies of men, divinity only for the souls of individuals, whereas justice makes possible the good life in society. 'Justice is as necessary as the sun in the firmament', as necessary to society as women.[76]

In medicine the College of Physicians' monopoly was not restored after 1660 in its pre-1640 form. Medical practice, Professor Roberts tells us, became 'a free economic activity like any other', its personnel and behaviour directed by the market, dependent on 'a numerous middle class, which not only expected medical care but was also able to pay for it, provided that the fees were not exorbitant'.[77] Entry to the profession became easier. Walwyn, who in 1654 described himself as 'a lover of useful studies', and in 1661 as 'health's student', by 1681 brazenly added 'physician' to his name on the title-page. Both he and Peter Chamberlen died relatively rich men in the 1680s: both defended the market and the practice of professional secrecy from which they profited. 'An arts man subsisting by his art,' declared Walwyn, 'being owner of it no longer than he keep it to himself, nothing can be more improper or more unwelcome than to ask discovering questions.' 'The draper is not bound to find cloth for all the naked because he hath enough in his shop, nor yet to afford it at the buyer's price,' wrote Chamberlen.[78] This sounds unattractive today, and even in the seventeenth century Hartlib, Boyle, Winstanley and others attacked professional secrecy. But the argument no doubt seemed valid to most men living in the triumphant market society: it is still used to justify private legal practice.

About the lower ranks in this society history tells us little but bare statistics. In 1715 three out of every four babies born in one poor London parish died almost immediately; an even higher proportion of Englishmen, a Quaker philanthropist told Parliament in the following year, were too poor to be able to afford medical advice or treatment.[79] During the brief period in which the press was free, Culpeper, Biggs, Chamberlen and others had spoken for this submerged 75 per cent. But now there was silence. All three professions, despite the efforts of mechanic preachers, of law reformers and of medical reformers, survived the Revolution – in the long run perhaps even more securely protected by the market than by Charles I's Privy Council.

Division of labour, they say, depends on the extent of the market. In seventeenth-century England only Gerrard Winstanley dared to suggest that lifetime professionalism could be got rid of if you abolished the market altogether by abolishing private property and wage-labour. Only so could the over-specialization, which he thought inimical to democracy, be eliminated. In the seventeenth century this was no more than a dream. But the same idea occurred to Karl Marx two centuries later, and in the century of the common man it is perhaps less obviously absurd than it used to seem. Most common men and women today are their own theologians, or have decided to do without divinity altogether. Law holds its own better; but it may be that medicine in our time is the most firmly established of the three traditional professions. That would have surprised as well as disappointed its seventeenth-century critics. They would have been less disappointed but even more surprised to observe that its keenest critics today come from within the medical and nursing professions.

PART IV

Change in Continuity: Some Social Attitudes

8

The Many-Headed Monster[1]

A rabble is . . . the greatest and most savage beast in the whole world . . . Nothing in the world delights them so much as the ruin of great persons.

> Samuel Butler, *Characters and Passages
> from Notebooks*, ed. A. R. Waller
> (Cambridge, 1908), p. 147.

I

Most writers about politics during the century before 1640 agreed that democracy was a bad thing: from Sir Philip Sidney and Sir Thomas Smith to a conservative Parliamentarian like Richard Baxter, a defender of the Good Old Cause like Henry Stubbe, or a detached observer like Francis Osborn.[2] 'The people' were fickle, unstable, incapable of rational thought: the headless multitude, the many-headed monster. The educated could find confirmation of this prejudice in classical Greek or Latin literature; they could also find it in current theology, Protestant and Catholic alike, which assumed the natural wickedness of the mass of the population. Government was a consequence of the Fall: democracy, by handing power to the sinful majority, would defeat the objects of government.

But of course the men of property did not need to go to church or university to learn class hostility: it was a simple fact of the world in which they lived, so obvious that it was rarely discussed. 1549 had shown their dependence on the central power of the monarchy.[3] 'So hated at this time was the name of worship or gentleman that the basest of the people, burning with more than hostile hatred, desired to extinguish and utterly cut off' the gentry. In Norfolk, where 'all have conceived a wonderful hate against gentlemen and taketh them all as their enemies', they were driven out of the county, and had to wait till the government sent foreign mercenaries to restore them. Meanwhile men were saying 'there are too many gentlemen in England by 500'; 'gentlemen have ruled aforetime, and they [i.e. the commons] will rule now'.[4] Norwich, second city of the kingdom, had been at the mercy of the peasantry too; in Cambridge the non-freemen seized the opportunity to assert their rights against the citizen oligarchy. Hence the class solidarity among gentlemen and merchants alike, which bridged the religious differences of the later sixteenth and seventeenth centuries.[5] In all countries of Western Europe the period of peasant revolts was the period of the formation of absolute monarchies.

In the famine year of 1596 there were anti-enclosure riots in Derbyshire, rumblings in Northants and Somerset, where men 'stick not to say boldly, They must not starve, they will not starve'. There was a minor rising in Oxfordshire, whose aim was 'to knock down the gentlemen and rich men'; the rebels hoped that they would be joined by the London apprentices, who had themselves been rioting. If 'the ruder sort' were 'privy to their own strength and liberty allowed them by the law', a Member of Parliament observed in 1597, they 'would be as unbridled and untamed beasts'.[6] In 1607, another year of bad harvests and high prices, men called 'Levellers' and 'Diggers' rose in Northamptonshire, Warwickshire and Leicestershire. There was support from craftsmen and the poorer sort of the town of Leicester, who for a time scared the ruling burgesses.[7] Shakespeare's *Coriolanus* first appeared on the stage in 1607.

The lean years 1628–31 again saw much violence. The Crown was forced to give up land which it had tried to claim in the Forest of Dean. The High Sheriff of Gloucestershire was 'soon and easily repulsed by . . . base and disorderly people'. In Kent and Rutlandshire there was seditious talk of threats of violence. In Wiltshire royal enclosure gave rise to 'extreme discontent' which expressed itself in 'popular revolts' which 'ushered in the Great Rebellion'.[8] There were also agrarian disturbances in Dorset, Worcestershire, Shropshire, and riots against the draining of the fens.

The idea that to be many-headed is the same as to be headless is easier to conceive metaphorically than literally. It relates to the theory of degree, to the conception of a graded society in which the feudal household and the family workshop or farm were the basic units. The many-headed monster was composed of masterless men, those for whom nobody responsible answered. Dread and hatred of the masses were often reflected in literature. In Sidney's *Arcadia*, whenever 'the many-headed multitude' appears, we are in for naturalistic violence that contrasts as sharply with the artificial scenes of shepherds' life as does the brutality of depopulating enclosure with the splendours of Penshurst which resulted from it. In Laconia there was permanent civil war and bitter hatred between 'the base multitude' and the gentry. In Arcadia the violence of 'the unruly sort of clowns' was wholly irrational: 'like a violent flood', they were 'carried, they themselves knew not whither'. 'Like enraged beasts', they 'show the right nature of a villein, never thinking his estate happy but when he is able to do hurt'. 'The mad multitude' was utterly disorganized; 'he only seemed to have most pre-eminence that was most rageful'.[9] Once liquor gave them Dutch courage, 'public affairs were mingled with private grudges, . . . railing was counted the fruit of freedom, . . . disdainful reproaches to great persons had put a shadow of greatness in their little minds'. They declared that 'their blood and sweat must maintain all, . . . the country was theirs and the government adherent to the country'.[10] 'They had the glorious shadow of a commonwealth with them.' 'So, to their minds (once past the bounds of obedience), more and more wickedness opened itself.' 'A popular licence is indeed the many-headed tyranny.' Naturally, when faced with such a 'rascal company', the chivalrous princes used their superior weapons to cut off vulgar arms, legs and heads in the most amusing manner.[11]

So far the gentle Sidney, who within limits was a liberal constitutionalist in his politics. The sweet Spenser had an equally virulent hatred and fear of the lower orders. I hasten to quote, to show that this is not putting it too strongly:

> 'Then as he spoke, lo! with outrageous cry
> A thousand villeins round about them swarmed
> Out of the rocks and caves adjoining nigh:
> Vile caitiff wretches, ragged, rude, deformed . . .'

In Book v (Of Justice) there is a curious passage on egalitarianism. It is the Giant speaking:

'For why, he said, they all unequal were,
And had encroached upon others' share;
Like as the sea (which plain he shewed there)
Had worn the earth, so did the fire, the air;
So all the rest did others' parts impair,
And so were realms and nations run awry.
All which he undertook for to repair,
In sort as they were formed anciently,
And all things would reduce unto equality.

Therefore the vulgar did about him flock,
And cluster thick unto his leasings vain,
Like foolish flies about an honey-crock,
In hope of him great benefit to gain
And uncontrolled freedom to obtain.'

Artegall, when he saw 'how he misled the simple people's train', talked Aristotelianism to the Giant. But the latter, reasonably enough, replied:

'Seest not how badly all things present be,
And each estate quite out of order go'th? . . .
Were it not good that wrong were then surceas'd
And from the most that some were given to the least?

Therefore I will throw down these mountains high,
And make them level with the lowly plain;
These tow'ring rocks, which reach unto the sky,
I will thrust down into the deepest main,
And, as they were, them equalize again.
Tyrants, that make men subject to their law,
I will suppress, that they no more may reign;
And lordings curb that commons over-awe,
And all the wealth of rich men to the poor will draw.'

Spenser must have heard someone saying that. Artegall's not unfamiliar reply was to introduce the will of the Almighty, in a passage of heartfelt eloquence. Talus then flung the Giant into the sea, and routed with his flail the popular revolt which followed, since Artegall was loth

'his noble hands t' imbrue
In the base blood of such a rascal crew.'[12]

The contempt for the lower orders shown by Shakespeare's Coriolanus, who 'stuck not to call' Roman citizens 'the many-headed multitude', need not necessarily represent the dramatist's point of view; nor need Sir Humphrey Stafford, who described Jack Cade's followers as 'rebellious hinds, the filth and scum of Kent'; 'a ragged multitude of hinds and peasants, rude and merciless'. What is interesting is the type of argument which Shakespeare puts into the mouths of the rebels: virtue and labour should be more regarded than birth; 'it was never merry world since gentlemen came up'; 'Adam was a gardener'. Prices are too high, lawyers and clerks fleece the poor. JPs 'call poor men before them about matters they were not able to answer'. Cade looked upon education as a class privilege, as indeed it often was: 'because they could not read, thou hast hanged them'. He proposed to burn all legal records, 'and henceforward all things shall be in common'. His supporters are patriotic, and accuse the aristocracy of treacherous relations with the national enemy – as Roman citizens might have accused Coriolanus – as well as of clothing their horses better than working-men. Cade's appeal was to the 'clouted shoon', as Lilburne's was to be later: 'for they are thrifty honest men'. In London 'the rascal people' joined the rebels, whilst 'the citizens fly and forsake their houses'. Cade was eventually overcome, he insisted, 'by famine, not by valour'.[13]

Shakespeare was clearly a good listener, and his attitude seems to have been relatively detached. So was that of Middleton, who puts talk of the inconstancy of 'that wide-throated beast, the multitude' into the mouth of a tyrant and murderer. But a more common attitude was that expressed in Barnabe Googe's contempt for 'crabbed clowns', 'dunghill dogs', 'peasants vile', when they presumed to rise in revolt. Characters in Dekker's plays referred to 'that wild beast multitude',

> 'this many-headed Cerberus,
> This pied chameleon, this beast multitude . . .,
> This heap of fools.'[14]

Such traditional contempt for 'the hydra-headed monster multitude', 'th' idiot multitude, that monster many-headed', was confirmed by Ramus, by Montaigne as translated by Florio in 1603, and by Du Bartas as translated by Sylvester.[15]

Massinger and Davenant both have references to 'the many-headed monster, the giddy multitude'. Joseph Beaumont spoke of 'the causeless-rebel multitude', John Collop of 'the beast, the rabble'.[16] Both Robert Burton, the anatomist and Sir Thomas Browne despised 'that great enemy of reason, virtue and religion, the multitude, that numerous piece of monstrosity which . . . confused together make but one great beast'. The mild Thomas Fuller said of 'the headless multitude' that the greatest cruelties 'might be expected from servile natures when they command'. 'The people', the Leveller Walwyn remarked ironically, 'is a pitiful, mean, helpless thing, as under school-masters in danger to be whipped and beaten in case they meddle without leave and license from their master.'[17]

II

This contemptuous attitude thinly concealed the fears of the propertied class. 'In time of peace,' asked Sir Richard Morison in the year of the Pilgrimage of Grace, 'be not all men almost at war with them that be rich?' Magistrates existed to keep rich and poor from conflict, Francis Thynne believed about the time of the rising of the Northern earls. Sir Thomas Smith in 1565, Sir Thomas Aston in 1641 and the Duke of Albemarle in 1671 all agreed that 'the poorer and meaner people . . . have no interest in the commonweal but the use of breath', and 'no account is made of them, but only to be ruled'. Parliament, consisting of the nobility and gentry, dispenses 'the rules of government; the plebeians submit to and obey them'. But, the Duke added with the experience of a revolutionary general, the multitude 'are always dangerous to the peace of a kingdom, and having nothing to lose, willingly embrace all means of innovation, in the hope of gaining something by other men's ruin'.[18] 'The rude multitude', if led by 'some daring Ket', was always capable of upsetting society, declared Ralph Knevet in 1628. 'The meaner sort of people', Sir John Oglander agreed in 1630, are 'always apt to rebel and mutiny . . . on the least occasion'. To prevent this the landed class – the armigerous – carried weapons; 'the meaner sort of people and servants' were normally excluded even from the militia.[19]

The state was the main support of the propertied class. 'If

there were not a king', James 1 reminded JPs in 1616, 'they would be less cared for than other men.' 'The authority of the king', Sir Thomas Wentworth agreed, 'is the keystone which closeth up the arch of order and government, which keepeth each part in due relation to the whole.' 'Without laws,' said a pamphlet of 1629, 'the beast with many heads will . . . be head of all', and society will be at the mercy of 'the rage of the harrowing multitude.' 'Happy is that commonwealth', mused the preacher of an assize sermon at Preston in 1632, 'where the bridle of government is put upon the people, which otherwise is as a beast with many heads.' But for sovereignty, a preacher at Paul's Cross confirmed in March, 1642, 'the honourable would be levelled with the base, . . . and all would be . . . huddled up in an unjust parity'. So obvious was the connection between law and property that there were those, from Sir Thomas More onwards, who saw every government as 'nothing but a certain conspiracy of rich men procuring their own commodities under the name and title of the commonwealth'. The law seemed to confirm this by deciding that 'an insurrection . . . for the enhancing of salaries and wages' or a combination to cast down enclosures, were both 'a levying of war against the King' and so liable to the terrible penalties of treason. But the view that 'all orders, policies, kingdoms and dominions' originated from the devil, or from pride and covetousness, and were nothing but 'cruel tyranny and oppression of the poor', was normally confined to 'the unlearned and ungodly people': we hear of this position only when their betters are refuting it.[20] Class distinctions in the administration of justice were usually taken for granted.[21] Fulke Greville was being unusually sympathetic to the lower classes (or unusually realistic) when he said in the House of Commons in 1593: 'If the feet knew their strength as well as we know their oppression, they would not bear as they do.' Ralegh too showed imagination when three years later he predicted that in case of Spanish invasion the poor would say 'Let the rich fight for themselves.' 'These hopeless people' would find looting more agreeable than dying to defend a country which paid them 8*d*. a day. Fifty years later a similar remark by Gerrard Winstanley the Digger was made in a very different context.[22]

'The poor hate the rich,' said Deloney in 1597, 'because they will not set them on work; and the rich hate the poor, because they seem burdensome.'[23] In the century before 1640 the standard of living of the mass of the population was steadily declining, whilst the wealth of the rich was visibly increasing. In a city like Exeter harsh poverty was the lot of more than half the population, who had no reserves to meet a crisis such as unemployment or famine. 'The fourth part of the inhabitants of most of the parishes of England are miserable poor people, and (harvest time excepted) without any subsistence,' said a pamphlet of 1641. This helps us to understand the panic fear of disturbance which government and propertied class showed, and the readiness with which the lower orders resorted to violence in famine years. One consequence of the economic and social changes of the period was vagabondage – roving bands of beggars who were past the possibility of working and who terrorized their betters, animating others 'to all contempt both of noblemen and gentlemen, continually buzzing into their ears that the rich men have gotten all into their hands and will starve the poor'. 'A rabble of rogues, cutpurses and the like mischievous men, slaves in nature though not in law', was the description given by Smyth of Nibley, looking back regretfully to the good old days of serfdom.[24]

The number of such 'able men that are abroad seeking the spoil and confusion of the land' was kept down by the wholesale massacres of the law-courts. Seventy-four persons were sentenced to death in Devon in 1598, 160 in Middlesex in fourteen months of 1614–15; fifty-seven of the latter escaped by pleading benefit of clergy, which helps to explain the hatred of education shown by Shakespeare's Jack Cade. Some were hanged for being without visible means of livelihood. But the beneficent efforts of the courts to solve the problem of vagabondage by hanging were hampered by the fact that 'most commonly the simple countrymen and women . . . would not procure a man's death for all the goods in the world', and so failed to prosecute. Hanging, however, was not the only solution. Edward Hext, whose report on vagabonds I have just quoted, left £1,000 to found an almshouse in Somerton. The switch in charitable giving from ecclesiastical to secular objects, notably to poor relief and education, which Professor Jordan has so fully documented, may testify to the social fears as well as to the generous sentiments of the rich. One of the arguments put forward in propaganda for colonizing Ireland in 1594, Virginia in 1612 (and on many similar occasions), was that 'the rank multitude' might be exported, 'the matter of sedition . . . removed out of the City'.[25]

III

It was the duty of the church to soften the bitterness of class hatred, to keep the lower orders peaceful and subordinate, to stress the religious considerations which united a hierarchical society against the economic facts which so visibly divided it, to console the desperate. The *Homilies* spoke clearly: 'It is an intolerable ignorance, madness and wickedness for subjects to make any murmuring, rebellion, resistance or withstanding, commotion or insurrection.' Lucifer was the author of rebellion. 'What a perilous thing were it to commit unto the subjects the judgment which prince is wise and godly, and his government good, and which is otherwise; as though the foot must judge of the head . . . Who are most ready to the greatest mischiefs but the worst men?'[26] Sir Thomas Browne was thus thoroughly orthodox in thinking it was 'no breach of charity' to call the multitude fools. 'It is . . . a point of our faith to believe so.'[27] That 'the greatest multitude' was 'for the most part always wicked' was accepted by all parties in the church. 'Take away gentlemen and rulers,' Archbishop Cranmer told the western rebels in 1549, 'and straightway . . . followeth barbarical confusion . . . A gentleman will ever show himself a gentleman and a villein a villein.' 'Take away kings, princes, rulers, magistrates, judges and such estates of God's order,' the *Homily of Obedience* echoed, 'no man shall ride or go by the way unrobbed, no man shall sleep in his own house or bed unkilled, no man shall keep his wife, children and possessions in quietness, all things shall be common.' Archbishop Parker, who in 1549 had been derided by the Norfolk rebels as a hireling, asked ten years later 'what Lord of the Council shall ride quietly-minded in the streets among desperate beasts', if it be 'referred to the judgment of the subject, of the tenant, and of the servant, to discuss what is tyranny, and to discern whether his prince, his landlord, his master is a tyrant?' At the beginning of her reign Elizabeth had not wished reformation to be made 'in compliance with the impulse of a furious multitude': the words are Bishop Jewell's. Archbishop Whitgift thought that 'the people . . . are commonly bent to novelties and to factions, and most ready to receive that doctrine that seemeth to be contrary to the present state, and that inclineth to liberty'. Bancroft agreed in being apprehensive of the results of a Presbyterian system of elections, 'considering the sinister affections of the people, and how easily they are divided and rent asunder'. Yet Presbyterians were not democrats either: Knox himself had no use for 'the rascal multitude', 'the godless multitude'.[28]

The sects, especially those which their enemies called Anabaptist, tended to express democratic political heresies as well as doctrinal heresies. Anabaptists, said Nashe comprehensively, were 'such as thought they knew as much of God's mind as richer men'. 'Every man is now counted an Anabaptist if he does not maintain monarchy to be *jure divino*', said Francis Cheynell in 1643. 'The Anabaptists are men that will not be shuffled out of their birthright as free-born people of England', wrote one of their defenders in 1655.[29] Anabaptists were regularly accused of advocating communism, and this clearly corresponded to a popular desire. Lever in 1550 thought that the addiction of the lower orders to communism resulted from lack of preaching and the oppression of the rich; forty years later Bishop Cooper was still denouncing Anabaptists who wanted communism and 'a general equality, most dangerous to the society of men'. The well-known passage in Spenser's *Mother Hubberds Tale*, in which the Fox advocates a division of landlord's land, attributed communism to laziness. But the Fox's rejection of wage-labour is interesting, since the point seems to have been made by some of the Oxfordshire rebels of 1596, and was to reappear in the programme of the Diggers in 1649–50. As late as 1631 it was being alleged that Puritanism led to communism.[30]

Presbyterians tried to curb the dangers of Anabaptism by preaching, discipline, Sabbatarianism, and an insistence on the religious duties of heads of households; and by emphasizing that revolt was never justified unless led by magistrates, who would come from the propertied class. Once the church had lost its magical controls – confession, absolution (by which 'the consciences of the people' were 'kept in so great awe', Aubrey said), indulgences, the sacraments – preaching seemed to middle-of-the-road men the best way of influencing the sinful multitude, congregational discipline of controlling it. Yet Presbyterians themselves were open to the charge that they were unleashing the many-headed monster. Marprelate's mockery of bishops shocked many conservatives; and no less a person than John Field declared, in despair of Parliament, 'it is the multitude and people that must bring the discipline to pass which we desire'.[31] This must have seemed little better than Browne's *Reformation without Tarrying for Anie.*

Bishops were held in 'loathsome contempt, hatred and disdain' by 'the most part of men', a bishop admitted in 1589. So they had reason to point out that 'if you had once made an equality . . . among the clergy, it would not be long ere you attempted the same among the laity'. The point was taken up by the Earl of Hertford in 1589 – in reaction, significantly, to the Marprelate Tracts: 'As they shoot at bishops now, so will they do at the nobility also, if they be suffered.'[32] On the eve of the Civil War, Edmund Waller looked upon episcopacy 'as a counter-scarp or outwork', and was especially anxious that it should not 'be taken by this assault of the people'. For then the 'mystery . . . that we must deny them nothing when they ask in troops' would be revealed.

> 'We may in the next place have as hard a task to defend our property . . . If by multiplying hands and petitions they prevail for an equality in things ecclesiastical, their next demand perhaps may be . . . the like equality in things temporal . . . You may be presented with a thousand instances of poor men that have received hard measure from their landlords.'[33]

The social case for episcopacy was most elaborately stated in a petition from the gentry of Cheshire in December, 1641: Presbyterianism 'must necessarily produce an extermination of nobility, gentry and order, if not of religion'. Presbyterianism, added Sir Thomas Aston, would be 'dangerous doctrine if once grounded in vulgar apprehensions'.

> 'The old seditious argument will be obvious to them, that we are all the sons of Adam, born free; some of them say the

> Gospel hath made them free. And law once subverted, it will appear good equity to such Chancellors to share the earth equally. They will plead Scripture for it, that we should all live by the sweat of our brows . . . The empty name of liberty, blown into vulgar ears, hath overturned many states.'

Aston admitted that gentlemen might be able to control Presbyterian elections at first, and 'keep the vulgar low enough'. But annual elections would amount to a civil war in every parish.[34]

IV

Conservatives always hated anything like an appeal to opinion outside the ruling class. James Morice, who had attacked the oath *ex officio*, was told in 1593 that 'her Majesty would have me to be admonished . . . if aught were amiss in the Church or Commonwealth, I should not straightway make it known to the common sort, but declare it to her Majesty or some of her Privy Council'. Burghley noted with disapproval in 1595 that 'some . . . do secretly entice the vulgar sort to be vehement in desiring' Puritan reforms. 'Nowadays there is no vulgar, but all statesmen', commented Bacon wryly, who did not love 'the word "people".'[35] It was indeed an ambiguous word. Both friends and foes of Presbyterianism pointed out that 'the people' who were to elect elders and ministers were not the rabble but heads of households, men of some small substance. It was only with the hindsight of 1652 that Marchamont Nedham went out of his way to emphasize that when he spoke of 'the people' he meant 'such as shall be duly chosen to represent the people successively in their supreme assemblies'.[36]

In 1629 the Commons really did begin to appeal to the people, in the three resolutions against popery, Arminianism, and tonnage and poundage. In 1640, even worse, the lower orders were encouraged to sign the Root and Branch Petition, and it was supported by popular demonstrations. In May 1641, the Protestation was issued to be taken by people all over the country, with the object of rallying support for Parliament. Two months later it was voted that all who refused the Protestation were unfit to bear office in church or commonwealth; and the Commons ordered this vote to be printed and sent down by MPs to their counties. The Grand Remonstrance of November 1641 was described by a royalist as 'that appeal to the people'. When Hampden proposed printing it, he was told 'You want to raise the people and get rid of the Lords'. During the debates Sir Edward Dering had protested against 'this descension from a Parliament to a people'. 'I did not dream that we should remonstrate downward, tell stories to the people, and talk of the King as of a third person.' 'I neither look for cure of our complaints from the common people, nor do desire to be cured by them.' 'Considering the necessity of a multitude', it was not good to wake a sleepy lion, Holles told the House of Lords early in February 1642, a few days after a petition had been presented by fifteen thousand labourers and men of 'the meanest rank and quality'.[37] Within four years the lion began to roar.

V

Historians, I believe, have consistently underestimated the significance of popular tumults in the immediate origins of Civil War.[38] As early as February 1641, Lord Digby was warning that it was unfit 'for a Parliament under a monarchy to give countenance to irregular and tumultuous assemblies of people, be it for never so good an end'. He foresaw untold dangers 'when either true or pretended stimulation of conscience hath once given a multitude agitation'. Fiennes replied by asking 'whether an act of will in us may not produce an act of will in the people?' A gentleman of Kent said at about the same time 'it is thought that things are already gone so far', and the poor driven to such necessity, that outrages could not be prevented. 'We must take care,' an MP warned in October, 'that the common people may not carve themselves out justice by their multitudes. Of this we have too frequent experience', he added, referring to anti-enclosure and other riots. In January 1642, Pym drew attention to the risk of 'tumults and insurrections of the meaner sort of people . . . Nothing is more sharp and pressing than necessity and want; what they cannot buy they will take.' There might be general insurrection by 'the multitude'.[39]

Already in 1639 Drummond of Hawthornden had anticipated a '*bellum servile*' in Scotland. He was the more delighted with Montrose's victories in 1645, as a result of which 'the many-headed monster' was 'near quelled'.[40] Similarly in England Archbishop Williams had warned the Parliamentarians that 'you will make so many masters to yourselves that we shall all be slaves'. 'When the beast did imagine it was loose from the chain of monarchy and laws, who could tie it up again?' Williams's biographer asked. James Howell in 1642 foresaw 'anarchical confusions and fearful calamities . . . unless with the pious care which is already taken to hinder the great Beast to break into the vineyard there be also a speedy course taken to fence her from other vermin and lesser animals (the *belluam multorum capitum*)'.[41]

In London there were demonstrations and riots at every major political crisis from May, 1640, onwards. In *Eikon Basilike* Charles I was made to emphasize the influence of such popular tumults on Parliament, 'like an earthquake, shaking the very foundations of all'. They were reinforced by 'the multitude, who from all the counties come daily in thousands with petitions to the Houses' and created panic among the 'popish and malignant' gentry. One of Fairfax's correspondents in January 1642 reflected that 'the insurrections of the apprentices (as all ungoverned multitudes) are of very dangerous consequence'. He consoled himself by the thought that 'God, who works miracles, can out of such violent actions bring comfortable effects'.[42] But would God always work a miracle? This was the vital question: men's answers to it might determine the side they took in the Civil War.

In Gloucestershire, God seemed to be on Parliament's side. For there the royal commission of array was 'crushed by the rude hand of the multitude before it saw the light, . . . by the meanest of the people'. 'That fury that took hold on the ignoble multitude' led them on to sack the house of the leading local royalist. 'Their insolency becomes intolerable', said the Parliamentarian historian of the siege of Gloucester. 'Nevertheless, they have produced good effects, and oft times a more undiscerned guidance of superior agents turns them to the terror of the enemy and inexplicable self-engagement upon the common people, which prudent men promote and maintain, yet no further than themselves can over-rule and moderate.' Thus, in Gloucestershire, God helped those who helped themselves, just as there were those who alleged that Pym and Pennington called up mobs in London when they needed them. But this was a dangerous game, especially as the economic situation deteriorated. There were riots against enclosure in Durham, Yorkshire, Huntingdonshire, Lincolnshire, Cambridgeshire, Norfolk, Hertfordshire, Middlesex, Somerset, Dorset, Wiltshire and Cornwall; forest riots in Northamptonshire, Essex, Surrey, Hampshire, Berkshire. In May 1642 the House of Commons heard with disapproval of rioters against enclosure in the fens who had also said that 'the King should shortly be no longer King there'. Even in Gloucestershire it was found that 'the needy multitude, besides their natural hatred of good order, were at the devotion of the rich men', who might not be Parliamentarians.[43]

'The rude multitude in divers counties took advantage of those civil and intestine broils to plunder and pillage the houses of the nobility, gentry and others.' Any rich man was liable to be labelled a malignant. In August 1642, 'the King having left the Parliament, and thereby a loose rein being put into the mouth of the unruly multitude', 'many thousands' turned out to sack the Countess of Rivers's house in Essex. At Milford 'no man appeared like a gentleman, but was made a prey to that ravenous crew . . . So monstrous is the beast when it holds the bridle in its teeth.' 'The rude people are come to such a head,' said Major Thomas Wade of Colchester, also in August, 'that we know not how to quiet them.' 'The gentry . . . have been our masters a long time', 'vulgar hearts' were saying in Oxfordshire; 'and now we may chance to master them.' Now the lower classes have learnt their strength, Sir Thomas Gardiner reflected, 'it shall go hard but they will use it'.[44]

'If we take not advantage of this time,' said an opponent of enclosure in Essex in April 1643, 'we shall never have the opportunity again.' In July a rioter in Northamptonshire hoped 'within this year to see never a gentleman in England'. In Chelmsford the common people were said to have determined that they would no longer be 'kept under blindness and ignorance', or yield themselves 'servants, nay slaves to the nobility and gentry'. A royalist in the Isle of Wight thought that in 1642–3 the gentry 'lived in slavery and submission to the unruly base multitude'; it was in the power of the commonalty 'not only to abuse but plunder any gentleman' – a state of affairs which he rightly said had never before been seen in England. Charles I in his Declaration of 23 October 1642 played on social anxieties by speaking of 'endeavours . . . to raise an implacable malice and hatred between the gentry and commonalty of the kingdom, . . . insomuch as the highways and villages have not been safe for gentlemen to pass through without violence or affront'. By January 1643 petitioners from Hertfordshire described how 'the greatest number of people now (breaking the bonds of law) submit not themselves to government but threaten and commit outrages'. They begged the House of Lords to protect them from 'the violence and fury of all unruly and dissolute multitudes'.[45]

It was 'under pretence of religion' that 'the lower sort of citizens . . . do challenge' liberty to themselves, Hobbes observed in 1651. The Parliamentarians, an enemy alleged, caused 'the very dregs and scum of every parish to petition against the orthodox clergy'. The preachers, indeed, in their attempt to win support for Parliament addressed themselves directly to the lower classes. Jeremiah Burroughs, for instance, said in the pulpit in 1641 that the bishops 'have slighted the people, the vulgar, as if their very souls were made to lie under them for them to trample upon; but they shall be ashamed for their envy at the people.'[46] There were many such sermons. Again the question of riding the storm arose. Edward Bowles, chaplain successively to Manchester and Fairfax, said in 1643: 'I am far from the monster of a democracy: that which I call to the people for is but a quick and regular motion in their own sphere.'[47] But would the people remain in what their betters thought their own sphere? In London and many of the home counties they were escaping from the control of ministers. James Howell associated 'those petty sectaries which swarm so in every corner' with 'the many-headed monster' which was laying England open to 'waste, spoil and scorn'. In April 1642 preachers were ominously quoting the lines

> 'When Adam delved and Eve span,
> Who was then the gentleman?'

So we can understand why Henry Oxinden, belatedly agreeing with Waller and his friends, declared in November 1643 that it was 'high time for all gentlemen to . . . endeavour rather to maintain episcopal government . . . with some diminution in temporalities . . . than to introduce I know not what presbyterial government, which will . . . equalize men of mean conditions with the gentry.' If the reins are let loose upon 'the multitude (that senseless and furious beast)', they will 'destroy all government, both in church and state', or 'bring in such a one wherein themselves . . . may be able to tyrannize over their betters, whom naturally they have ever hated and in their hearts despised'.[48]

'I would not have the King trample on the Parliament,' said Lord Savile in 1643, 'nor the Parliament lessen him so much as to make a way for the people to rule us all'. The remark goes far to explain Savile's frequent changes of side: and there were many like him. In the elections to the Short Parliament Serjeant Maynard found that 'fellows without shirts' challenged 'as good a voice as myself'. He would 'not easily suffer myself hereafter upon the persuasions of others to appear in any popular assemblies'. A participant in the Army Plot exposed in May 1641 explained that the conspirators feared lest 'some turbulent spirits, backed by rude and tumultuous mechanic persons . . . would have the total subversion of the government of the state'.[49] In Lancashire in November 1642, the royalist High Sheriff summoned the gentry of the county to appear for the King, 'who we know now suffers under the pride and insolency of a discontented people, also for the securing of our own lives and estates, which are now ready to be surprised by a heady multitude'. Even the official historian of Parliament admitted that 'some who were not bad men' objected to 'that extreme license which the common people, almost from the very beginning of the Parliament, took to themselves of reforming without authority, order or decency'.[50]

After Civil War started, such social anxieties were alleged by many who deserted Parliament. John Hotham in January 1643 thought that if war continued, 'the necessitous people of the whole kingdom will presently rise in mighty numbers' and ultimately 'set up for themselves, to the utter ruin of all the nobility and gentry of the kingdom'. 'If this unruly rout have once cast the rider, it will run like wildfire in the example through all the counties of England.' 'The nobility cannot fall if the King be victorious,' thought the Marquis of Newcastle, Hotham's correspondent, 'nor can they keep up their dignities if the King be overcome.'[51]

By 1644 Lord Willoughby believed that 'nobility and gentry are going down apace'. The Earl of Westmorland warned the Parliamentarian Colonel Harley against 'that monster parity', which 'so much now seeks to domineer'. Bulstrode Whitelocke was afraid that the ignoble would come to rule the noble. Even Parliament's general, the Earl of Essex, feared in December 1644 lest 'our posterity will say that to deliver them from the yoke of the King we have subjected them to that of the common people'. He announced that henceforth he would 'devote his life to redressing the audacity of the common people'.[52] It was rather late in the day for a royalist astrologer like George Wharton to console himself by reflecting that 'none but your seduced many-headed monster will credit' a Parliamentarian rival; by 1644 the stars in their courses seemed to be fighting against Charles I. Consternation among the more conservative was general. Nobody knew where the sectaries would stop, Thomas Edwards observed in 1646, but they threatened all civil government. 'The giddy-headed multitude' even called in question 'the saving doctrines of eternal truth' on which the Presbyterian clergy based its supremacy. There were social as well as religious reasons for opposing toleration.[53]

VI

On 8 June 1642 Sir Simonds D'Ewes noted in his diary that 'all right and property, all *meum* and *tuum*, must cease in a civil war, and we know not what advantage the meaner sort also may take to divide the spoils of the rich and noble amonst them.' Vulgar men were beginning already 'to allege that, all being of one mould, there is no reason that some should have so much and others so little'. Ten days later Charles I responded to this mood by warning Parliament to accept his terms lest 'at last the common people . . . set up for themselves'.[54] In 1643, six months after Hotham had also envisaged the possibility of the many-headed monster setting up against royalists and Parliamentarians alike, it seemed to be actually happening in Kent. On 28 July Sir Thomas Walsingham told the Commons that he had recently been captured by 'tumultuary people' near Tunbridge, 'most of them men of very mean and base condition'. These persons 'chiefly aimed at enriching themselves by the robbing and spoiling of such as were wealthy, intending to destroy the gentry'.[55] In 1645 George Smith thought that the tyranny and unfair taxation of Parliamentary committees 'put the people upon resolutions of setting up a third party'. In that year the Clubmen of Somerset formed just such a third party, and were asking 'whether the able and rich who will not join with us be not only counted ill-affected but liable to pay for the poor who do their county service?' The main centre of the Clubmen was Somerset, Dorset and Wiltshire; but there were similar movements in Devon, Hampshire, Sussex, Gloucestershire, Herefordshire, Shropshire, Worcestershire and Glamorganshire.[56] Discontent with the taxation, plunder and indiscipline which accompanied a prolonged war – the motives for the Clubman movement – forced upon Parliament the military and financial reorganization that produced the New Model Army, with its regular pay and strict discipline. The Clubmen were routed and dispersed.

But the hydra was no sooner suppressed here than it reappeared in the Army itself, and in 'the motley hundred-headed faction of the Levellers' in London. If no agreement could be reached with the Army, an MP said in July 1647, 'clubs and clouted shoes will in the end be too hard for both'. Lilburne boasted that his support came from 'the hobnails, clouted shoes, the private soldiers, the leather and woollen aprons'. At Putney in October 1647, Sexby protested that 'the poor and meaner of this kingdom' had won the war for Parliament, and Rainborough ominously added that the common soldier seemed to have 'fought to enslave himself, to give power to men of riches, men of estates, to make him a perpetual slave'. 'Is not all the controversy whose slaves the poor shall be: whether they shall be the King's vassals or the Presbyterians' or the Independent faction's?' asked a pamphleteer in January 1648. In May 1647 Overton had published *An Appeale From the degenerate Representative Body the Commons of England assembled at Westminster: To the Body Represented, the free people of England*. 'This way of petitioning by multitude of hands to the Parliament, which was formerly promoted by some of both Houses as a means to carry on their designs at that time', Whitelocke observed dryly, 'began now [1647] to be made use of and retained upon them, to their great trouble and danger'.[57]

The Independents repressed the Levellers forcibly; but the subtle distinction between the two groups was too much for men like Denzil Holles and Clement Walker. The former wrote from his exile in 1649:

> 'The wisest of men saw it to be a great evil that servants should ride on horses: an evil now both seen and felt in this unhappy kingdom. The meanest of men, the basest and vilest of the nation, the lowest of the people, have got the power into their hands; trampled upon the crown, baffled and ruined the Parliament, violated the laws; destroyed or suppressed the nobility and gentry of the kingdom; and now lord it over the persons and estates of all sorts and ranks of men.'

The object of the Rump, Walker alleged, was 'to raise the rascal multitude and schismatical rabble against all men of best quality in the kingdom'. Thus some supporters of Parliament now thought (perhaps always had thought) that monarchy and property were indissolubly connected: the stage was set for Charles 1's magnificent performance at his trial, and for the legend sedulously built up in *Eikon Basilike*, offering monarchy as the alternative to 'the insolencies of popular dictates and tumultuary impressions', and calling on Parliament to shake off 'this yoke of vulgar encroachment'. For long after the crushing of the Levellers, Oliver Cromwell was able to make the flesh of his Parliaments creep by recalling how Levellers had proposed 'to make the tenant as liberal a fortune as the landlord'.[58]

Oliver spoke to men easily convinced. 'We hate . . . confusion in the many-headed monster', proclaimed Nathaniel Fiennes and his father Lord Saye and Sele. Even a radical like John Webster appealed to intellectuals against the many-headed multitude.[59] 'There is no jewel which swine delight more to wear in their snouts than this of liberty', wrote John Gauden elegantly; though he had supported Parliament, he was to win a bishopric at the Restoration. 'In these degenerating times', said two royalists in 1657, 'the gentry had need to close nearer together, and make a bank and bulwark against that sea of democracy which is overrunning them'. In 1659–60 panic increased. 'We lay at the mercy and impulse of a giddy, hot-headed, bloody multitude', a Presbyterian believed. 'The rabble hate both magistrates and ministers', wrote Richard Baxter, and if they were not bridled 'they would presently have the blood of the godly', and also of 'the more wealthy and industrious', whom Baxter perhaps identified with the godly. No tyrant was 'so cruel as the many-headed tyrant; . . . it being the surest way to be always miserable, to be governed by them that are always naught, that is the multitude'.[60]

So Charles II came home again, and with him 'elective Parliaments, the bulwark of property.' The Army was disbanded, sectaries persecuted, the jewel of liberty torn from the snouts of the swinish multitude. 'It is certain that the greater number of men are bad', said the royalist Earl of Derby, explaining to his son why the people should be fooled for their own good; 'reason will never persuade a senseless multitude.'[61]

VII

I have established, I hope, the importance of the many-headed monster in the minds of contemporaries. One problem remains to be discussed: Why did that solidarity, which in the sixteenth century the monster helped to create among the propertied, break down after 1640? Similar arguments were used in 1640-1 to those used against Browne, Field, Marprelate and Hacket, and they helped greatly in the formation of a royalist party: but in 1641, unlike the 1590s, a significant section of those whom Parliaments represented, especially in the South and East of England, and in towns, remained unmoved by these arguments. What had changed?

I can offer only a few suggestions here. First, those whom contemporaries describe as the many-headed monster were politically outside the pale, could affect politics only by revolt or through religious organization. At the Reformation, for the first time since the rise of Christianity, a popular belief had broken through to secure political power. In the long-continuing economic, social and psychological crisis of the sixteenth and early seventeenth centuries, religious organization offered a means of controlling and directing upheavals of the masses. Calvinism is the most familiar form in which this discipline and direction was exercised for political purposes.[62] By 1640 Calvinism was strongly entrenched in England, though on the defensive. The possibility now existed that popular revolt could occur without escaping from the control of the lesser magistrates. There is no proof that men ever consciously calculated along these lines: but this was the world in which they lived.

Secondly, economics reinforced religion. This century of crisis for the lower orders in England had brought prosperity to the middle classes[63] who were the backbone of Puritanism – the merchants whose charitable legacies Professor Jordan has analysed, the yeomen whose rising expenditure on household goods Dr Hoskins has demonstrated. In 1604 William Stoughton had to argue very carefully that there would be enough 'men of occupations' to act as elders of Presbyterian churches: by 1640 this was no longer felt to be a problem. The century also saw the extension of the economic and intellectual hegemony of London. Sidney in 1580 had shrewdly observed (of Arcadia, but he must have learnt the lesson in England), 'the peasants would have the gentlemen destroyed; the citizens . . . would but have them reformed.' By 1640 many yeomen, the leading figures in the villages, had more in common with 'the citizens' than with 'the peasants', including an interest in the preservation of private property. The economic and social advance of the industrial areas reduced the fear of lower-class revolt that had held the rich united in the sixteenth century. At the same time two generations of Puritan preaching, under the patronage of gentlemen, especially in the South-East and the Midlands, had built up something in the nature of a political party.[64]

Thirdly, as the risks of loosing the many-headed monster lessened, so the provocation to do so increased. By 1640 Charles I's government had so alienated many members of the landed class that they were prepared for desperate measures. It may even be suggested that Laud *forced* an appeal to the people on the Puritans and their allies if they were not to surrender or emigrate. Official encouragement of the traditional rural sports, and Laud's ostentatious opposition to enclosure, could be interpreted as an attempt to rally the multitude to the defence of a static hierarchical society, just as Laud's attack on Puritan preaching, repetition of sermons, discipline and Sabbatarianism threatened the preachers' control over the monster. Finally, the presence in the North of England of a disciplined Scottish army in 1639 and 1640–1, and the possibility of its return thereafter, created a new situation. In 1628 Sir Robert Cotton had been anxious that Parliamentary opposition to the King should not be pushed too far, precisely because of the risks of triggering off revolt by 'the loose and needy multitude, . . . with a glorious pretence of religion and public safety, when their true end will be only rapine of the rich'.[65] This consideration may well have had its bearings on the behaviour of Wentworth and Noy in 1628–9, on the collapse of opposition to unparliamentary taxation in the 1630s, and on the Long Parliament's determination to blame 'evil councillors' rather than the King himself. In 1640 the Scottish presence seemed a reassurance against any danger that the English lower classes might get out of control. It was indeed only after the Scottish army had gone home that things went seriously wrong for the English gentry.

Whatever the reasons, men of property were more prepared in 1640–2 than at any time since 1536 to connive at, if not positively to foster, a popular revolt. There had been allegations of Puritan support for the rising in the West in 1628–31; in the Forest of Dean the Rev Peter Simon, nominee of the Haberdashers Company of London, was preaching the equality of all mankind; in the Fens Oliver Cromwell put himself at the head of rioting commoners. But all these were isolated incidents. It was different when in 1640–1 Pym and Pennington in London, and 'prudent men' in Gloucestershire, promoted and maintained popular tumults.[66] A middle-class intellectual like Milton felt in 1641 that human dignity was in far less danger from the sects than from the Laudians. I am not suggesting that London demonstrations, or riots against enclosures, were created by the Parliamentarians; but some of them at least were no longer afraid to take advantage of popular initiative. The counties in which there is clearest evidence that the 'rabble' was royalist – Worcestershire and Gloucestershire – were on the fringes of the area of London's hegemony, and were to produce Clubmen in 1645.[67]

If any of the Parliamentarian leaders did consciously gamble on letting loose the many-headed monster, relying on the ability of parsons, landlords and JPs to bring it back under control, the evidence indicates that they calculated rightly. Milton's growing disillusionment with the people, his sense that they were unfit for liberty, suggests that they were more responsive to conservative than to radical influences. Unless and until the Army could be used 'to teach peasants to understand liberty', as Hugh Peter wished,[68] manhood suffrage would probably have brought back the King. The real danger of the Levellers lay in the possibility that they might capture the Army.

Yet even the Levellers had a limited conception of who 'the people' were. They wished to extend the franchise from Ireton's men of property to all the freeborn, the heads of households. Only perhaps the Diggers would have given the vote to the really propertyless – servants and paupers. It is hardly surprising that the unfree were fickle allies for their betters. The common people were 'foolish and ignorant', often illiterate – in consequence, William Stoughton and John Milton agreed, of the failure of the bishops to educate them.[69] They were susceptible to irrational influences – magic, prophecies, anti-papist panics and witch panics, the lure of divine kingship (remember the long-standing peasant tradition of appealing to the king against local oppressors, which goes back to Wat Tyler and Ket). Yet even on rational grounds it was not self-evident that it was to their interest to support Parliament. What after all did the multitude get from the Revolution? Excise, free-quarter, pillage, conscription: not stable copyholds, abolition of tithes, or protection of industrial craftsmen against their employers. 'For the millions it did nothing', said a Chartist in 1837, looking back to the seventeenth-century English Revolution.[70]

The discipline which Puritans inculcated had long-term social and economic effects, as well as short-term political effects. It contributed to the establishment of labour discipline, of individualist habits suited to an industrial society, the antithesis of the communism which its opponents identified with idleness. There was perhaps a real consistency in the attitude of the many-headed monster which, from Spenser's Fox to Winstanley's utopia, rejected not only the gentry-controlled state and its law but also the wage-labour system; and opposed to them a backward-looking and idealized communism.[71]

9
A One-Class Society?[1]

Theories of social morality are always the product of a dominant group which identifies itself with the community as a whole, and which possesses facilities denied to subordinate groups or individuals for imposing its view of life on the community.

E. H. Carr, *The Twenty Years Crisis* (1939), p. 101.

I

The Cambridge Group for the History of Population and Social Structure has for some time been collecting information from county and parish sources all over Britain, sent in by enthusiastic volunteers. *The World We Have Lost* (1965), by Mr Peter Laslett, 'founder and director' of this group, draws on some of this material. It is high time that the rich resources of English local archives were applied to demographical and social problems, a field in which English scholarship lags badly behind that of France. A great deal of admirable sociological history of sixteenth- and seventeenth-century England has been written. A synthesis and critique of this work, underpinned by hard demographical statistics, could be of the greatest value, might indeed be a turning point away from current controversies which are too often insoluble for want of precisely this statistical information. One picks up Mr Laslett's book, therefore, with high hopes.

II

The author makes some interesting and important points, mostly in chapters 3–6. It is useful to be reminded that 'before the coming of the bicycle and the paved highway, there was a

205

fixed distance from the labourer's cottage beyond which a full day's work was out of the question' (p. 77). Mr Laslett's emphasis on the differences in physical health between the ruling class and others is vividly expressed: 'The privileged must have been taller, heavier, better developed and earlier to mature than the rest' (p. 89). There is much interesting evidence for starvation during the crisis of the 1620s, especially in London and in clothing areas of Lancashire (pp. 113–17, 123, 137). There is a passage which all historians must applaud, rejecting the sentimental view that 'we have lost some more humane, much more *natural* pattern of relationships than industrial society can offer' (p. 236); another in which Mr Laslett insists that English society cannot usefully be studied in isolation from Western European society or indeed from the societies of other continents (p. 231).

The author appears to envisage his audience as primarily non-academic. It needs to be told that 'history often provides useful knowledge which we could not have in any other way' (p. 229). 'It may see [*sic*.] extraordinary' to this audience that 'the peerage in England was for all purposes except the details of their status at one with the rest of the ruling segment, the gentry as a whole' (p. 40). The fact that a yeoman might be called 'Goodman', and his wife 'Goodwife (abbreviated Goody)' is repeated (pp. 38, 75). Seventeenth-century English is annotated for fear of incomprehension: 'Their use is [it is usual]' (p. 96); 'sack [sherry]' (p. 110). Technical terms like 'dowry', 'jointure' and 'oral culture' (pp. 188, 194) are defined. A point needing 'a little explanation' is that Parliament did not sit continuously in the seventeenth century (p. 165). Mr Laslett sometimes affects to share the simple-minded preconceptions of this audience ('Prone as we are to be sentimental about our ancestors, we are also quite prepared to believe that they were often wicked people' – p. 128). Lest he should be misinterpreted as suggesting that these wicked ancestors copulated anywhere but in bed, he gravely explains that 'the parlour was the bedroom before the ordinary man's house acquired an upstairs' (p. 132). So naive is Mr Laslett's reader that he is expected to find 'the continuing political leadership of the very rich and prestigious . . . a paradoxical feature of other democratic countries than our own, even of the United States' (p. 171). In what follows we must remember that Mr Laslett is presenting his own theories, and attacking those of others, before readers who are assumed to have little background knowledge or critical ability to assess these theories for themselves.

In addressing this innocent audience he does not err on the side of modesty. He claims to have established 'a new branch of history' (p. 230); his is 'a type of historical criticism previously unknown' (p. 237); 'sophisticated sociologism', as opposed to 'naif sociologism' (p. 232). This 'historian of the newer sort' makes the 'somewhat arrogant claim' to have made 'an addition to "scientific" knowledge' (pp. 239, 237). The sort of questions which Mr Laslett asks 'could have arisen from no previously established form of historical inquiry'. History, he believes, 'is about to claim a new and more important place in the sum of total human knowledge' (p. 240). The author thus expects us to treat very seriously the book in which this new branch of history is revealed.

He is severe with his less fortunate predecessors. Now a criticism of the deficiencies of historians, to be effective, should be specific, well informed, and accurate. Let us take first his own standards of scholarly accuracy. On page 165 he says: 'When Charles I's Long Parliament met in 1640, no less than eleven years had elapsed since the last foregathering' of MPs. 'The previous experience of 328 of the 547 members was confined to a few weeks of the Short Parliament of 1628–9.' For 'eleven years' we should read 'six months'. The Short Parliament met in April–May 1640, not 1628–9. The Parliament of 1628–9 lasted not 'a few weeks' but fifty; long enough to convince Charles I that parliaments were of the nature of cats: they ever grow cursed with age. The 328 MPs to whom Mr Laslett refers however did sit in the Short Parliament of 1640: their experience was eleven years more recent than he suggests.

Mr Laslett is no more accurate in his criticism of historians. He severely rebukes 'historians and other authorities' who quote Deloney's *Jack of Newbury* 'to argue that factories existed before the coming of modern industry'. He names two historians, George Unwin and S. R. (*sic*) Bindoff (pp. 153–4, 270). This seems a most reprehensible mistake of those eminent historians: one looks them up in some alarm. In neither of the passages to which Mr Laslett refers us is there any reference to a factory or anything like it. Unwin says Deloney's story is 'mainly mythological', 'a fantastically embroidered tradition'; Bindoff says 'so runs the legend'. Mr Laslett's strictures on 'literary evidence even when used by professional historians' turn out to be utterly without foundation.

Too often, indeed, the author seems to have no first-hand acquaintance with the work of 'the historians' whom he airily dismisses. He complains of 'the difficulties of deciding to compare rather than to recount, as historians ordinarily do' (p. 232), with no mention of the serious comparative work of Professors Rudé and Hobsbawm. He speaks of ' "the commercial revolution of the sixteenth and seventeenth centuries" ' as a recent phrase in the vocabulary of historians (p. 157), though any student of the period could have told him that Professor Davis revived this phrase exclusively for the period *after* the Civil War. Any student too could have told Mr Laslett that 'the middling sort of people' did not begin to 'enter into social descriptions *as early as* the eighteenth century' (p. 46; my italics) but at least two centuries earlier. Mr Laslett describes the conclusions about social mobility which he drew from two villages as 'striking and entirely unexpected', the result of 'the attempt now at last being made to understand the social structure of our peasant forefathers in something like numerical form' (p. 147). In fact the 'entirely unexpected' discovery confirms conclusions reached fifty years ago by the Russian historian A. N. Savine in studies of three manors.[2]

We all make mistakes: Professor Trevor-Roper was kind enough to point out a number of mine in a recent issue of *History and Theory*. But the founder of 'a new branch of history', who is so contemptuous of 'the loose discussions of historians' (p. 247), ought at least to avoid schoolboy errors. It is difficult to refute Mr Laslett's allegations against 'historians', because he rarely names the offenders. When for instance he writes, ironically one presumes, 'it is now supposed that the whole of the English gentry . . . was imbued with bourgeois values by the middle years of the seventeenth century' (p. 36), one can only guess by whom this is supposed. Not by Professor Macpherson, hinted at in the following sentence. Not by myself, mentioned in the preceding note. Not by Professors Tawney, Stone or Trevor-Roper. Not, so far as I am aware, by any historian. But

Mr Laslett's uninformed readers may well believe that he is attacking a view that really exists, as he is when he speaks of the English, French and Russian Revolutions as 'great historical realities in accepted parlance' (p. 150) – before the new sociologism came along. What is really intolerable is the author's condescending dismissal of 'generalizations' which 'have confidently been made about such things as the "rise of the gentry" or "the crisis of the nobility" and so on' (p. 193). One could question the taste of this even if Mr Laslett had done anywhere near as much serious historical research as Professors Tawney, Stone and Trevor-Roper.

III

Mr Laslett's statistics are drawn from parish registers. In presenting these to a popular audience it would surely have been wise, to say no more, to point out the difficulties inherent in the use of such evidence. There are many reasons for being unhappy about the reliability of parish registers. From at least the reign of Elizabeth many Puritans expressed disapproval of their own incumbent by arranging for their children to be born and baptized outside the parish; by bringing in a preacher from outside the parish in order to baptize them; by getting married or taking corpses to be buried outside the parish.[3] With the rise of organized dissent in the seventeenth century, we can be sure that such practices increased. Many dissenters would no doubt conform to some ceremonies out of timidity, escaping others as best they could. There were plenty of discouragements. In 1671 Colonel Titus proposed in the House of Commons that nonconformists should be prohibited from celebrating baptisms, marriages or funerals.[4] By the middle of the eighteenth century we are told of the 'perhaps no inconsiderable number among the lowest class of people who never are brought to be baptized at all'.[5] There must have been variations from parish to parish, according to the laziness or kindliness of the parson or parish clerk; and variations over time, as dissent became legally established and church courts lost their punitive powers. The point is that at the moment we have no idea how much to allow for such factors in any given region at any given time. Yet population statistics are still necessarily based on such a small sample of parishes that the variations here may be of very great significance.

Here is an example of what I have in mind. The Rev William Sweetapple, former member of my College, officiated in the parish of Fledborough from 1712 to 1753. In 1729 there was a sudden and dramatic increase in the number of marriages in his parish: from one every third year or so to more than twenty a year. Canon West is almost certainly right to explain this by Mr Sweetapple's sudden realization of the financial possibilities of clandestine marriages.[6] William Stukeley might almost have been thinking of the historian of population when he wrote in 1752: 'frequently the task of keeping a register book is committed to a parish clerk, illiterate, that can scarcely write, sottish or indolent', whose record is 'kept at random, without any reasonable proof or certainty'.[7]

Mr Laslett recognizes the existence of a problem here (pp. 102, 133–4, 261). But he never faces it squarely – indeed he could hardly have written his book if he had – and he seems to forget it altogether when he decides that bastardy was commoner in England than in France (pp. 135–6). This is not quite so surprising a conclusion as Mr Laslett thinks, once we reflect that many nonconformists' children might be regarded as illegitimate if their parents were not married in a parish church. But so far as England is concerned Mr Laslett's conclusion is based on one parish register for Westminster, another for Bristol. 'It would be unwise', he rightly says, 'to treat either figure very seriously.' Yet by the next page he is asserting 'with something approaching confidence' the conclusion quoted. With a similar light-heartedness he tells his uninformed readers that 'the truth seems to be that infantile mortality [in England] cannot have been higher under Queen Victoria than it was under the Stuarts' (p. 126). He may be right; but the *evidence* for this 'truth' comes from one Nottinghamshire parish, plus Graunt's study of the London bills of mortality, plus the conclusions of French demographers about rural *France*. This hotchpotch is then compared with statistics about Victorian England.[8]

IV

Speculations of dubious validity are on occasion put forward as manifest truth. In 'the world we have lost', 'it would seem impossible to cite statements which contemplated permissiveness of any sort in [sexual] matters except for those which made full use of poetic licence' or Restoration plays (p. 130). Before encouraging the simple-minded reader to rejoice at the morality of our forefathers, it would have been fair to remind him that there was ecclesiastical censorship for most of the period of which Mr Laslett speaks. During the breakdown of this censorship in the interregnum some Ranters at least expressed tolerably permissive opinions. The fact that 'witnesses in ecclesiastical courts . . . left no doubt that sexual intercourse outside marriage was universally condemned' is neither here nor there. Does the author really think that a man or woman who thought otherwise would have been well-advised to proclaim the fact in a church court? The evidence gives him the right to go no further than 'it was universally thought proper (or safe) to condemn intercourse outside marriage'.

But then Mr Laslett makes many unverifiable assumptions about 'the world we have lost'. He writes with bland confidence all of our ancestors were literal Christian believers, all of the time', and the vast majority good churchgoers (pp. 71–3). On his premise he raises 'one more of the paradoxes which urgently await systematic study by the sociological historian': how could a society so static and authoritarian in its attitude to social discipline' be 'so free and inventive in its political ideas and institutions'? If he had read the admirable sociological history of A. G. Dickens, or even the most obvious books on Puritanism, he could have answered that one from hard evidence, without the vague guessing to which he resorts on page 179.

There are signs everywhere that this book must have been rushed out hastily, despite the author's assurance that it 'has been six years in the making' (p. vii). Sentences occur of which the second is simply a repetition of the first (pp. 52, 165, 194, 233). There are phrases like 'our own world, the whole globe as it is now' (p. 149); 'the whole English Revolution as a whole' (p. 150). Figures are wrongly added up (p. 64). There are numerous misprints (pp. 40, 200, 258, for example), and several sentences which are simply ungrammatical (pp. 127, 238, 239). What is one to make of a new sophisticated historian who tells us that half . . . or even three-quarters' of those who lived alone were 'widowed women, *in the main*' (p. 96; my italics)? Or of houses which 'seem *always* to have been vacant, *especially* in the later seventeenth century' (p. 92; my italics)? Or of the alarming fact that 'wage-earning fathers died much more often' in the seventeenth century than now (pp. 120–1)?

Slipshod thinking occurs again in a phrase like 'we want contradictory things – a system of status and universal social equality' (p. 24). It is clear from the context that two different groups of people are concealed in 'we'. And when Mr Laslett writes that 'the English' still want to live in thatched cottages (p. 25), we can rescue him from absurdity only by assuming that he means 'some middle-class Englishmen'. It is a matter of observation that in scores of English villages thatched cottages are being vacated or sold to weekenders or commuters who can afford the considerable sums needed to modernize them. Their former occupants prefer to live in more comfortable if less romantic housing estates.

The sentimentality implicit in Mr Laslett's title extends to his view of the family. The day labourer who was provided with food in lieu of wages 'was made a member of the working family for that day by breaking bread with the permanent members. It was almost a sacramental matter' (p. 15). After pointing out that the household, with its children, servants and apprentices, was the basic economic unit in the sixteenth and seventeenth centuries, Mr Laslett continues 'every relationship could be seen as a love-relationship' (p. 5). Recalling the many stories of apprentices who had to be rescued from their brutal masters by JPs, one can only feel that Mr Laslett has a rather peculiar definition of the word love. 'Industrial societies', he believes, are 'less stable than their predecessors' because 'they lack the extraordinarily cohesive influence which familial relationships carry with them, that power of reconciling the frustrated and the discontented by emotional means' (p. 4). This is highly debatable, though it would be worth debating seriously. But again, when one reflects on the army of vagabonds, cut off from all social ties; on the large numbers of old people living and dying in isolation; on the broken homes and crimes by adolescents which the author himself reminds us are not peculiar to the twentieth century; on the early deaths, the remarriages, the hatreds and miseries that folktales about wicked stepmothers convey, one

wonders whether all the frustrated and discontented were re-
conciled by emotional means through 'familial relationships'.
It is at least not self-evident.

England before the Industrial Revolution was, in Mr Laslett's
curious phraseology, 'a one-class society'. Historians with 'a
faulty sense of proportion, which we can only now begin to
correct', used to speak of the ruling class. Mr Laslett agrees that
the tiny ruling minority, at most 5 per cent of the population,
'owned most of the wealth, wielded the power, and made all
the decisions, political, economic and social for the national
whole' (p. 26). Its members were stronger and physically fitter
than the rest (p. 89). There was 'enormous inequality' (p. 45).
'There is a sense', Mr Laslett concedes, 'in which the phrase
"class-conflict" might be appropriate to pre-industrial society,
even if it did contain only one class. For the conflict could be
between those who were included within it and everyone else'
(p. 23). Mr Laslett's 'one-class society' is a matter of definition.
He includes in his conception of class that it must be 'a community apart from the rest', 'sharing a common work situation'
(pp. 50–1); it must be 'nation-wide', 'capable of concerted
action over the whole area of society' (p. 22). For there to be
more than one class we must have '*unmistakable* evidence of
class-consciousness and *collective* resentment . . . amongst a group
of persons increasing in power, number and organization,
though *always* frustrated in their *expressed* aims' (p. 158; my
italics). If you build your conclusions into your definition like
that, then of course there have never been any classes except
ruling classes, at any stage of history. Mr Laslett in fact argues
that there was no 'solid middle class' in England in 1901 either
(p. 211).

'What does the word *England* mean, for the year 1640?' Mr
Laslett asks. 'The mass of Englishmen cannot be counted as
part of England for historical purposes' (p. 19) – whatever that
last phrase may mean. Sir Lewis Namier used to speak of Mr
Laslett's 'ruling minority' in eighteenth-century England as 'the
political nation'. But that great historian would never have
made the mistake of denying existence to those excluded from
politics. Mr Laslett is simply succumbing to the illusion of the
epoch which he is describing. That 'the minority lived for all
the rest' (p. 52) is no doubt what they themselves believed. It

has needed a lot of hard work by historians to demonstrate that the 'subsumption' of the lower orders in their betters was not a 'fact' but a piece of ideological propaganda.

Mr Laslett argues that 'the workers of the pre-industrial world' cannot 'be thought of as a community apart from the rest', since 'they did not all share a common work situation by any means, as does the working class in the contemporary industrial world' (pp. 50–1). This obvious fact has to my knowledge never been denied: there was no proletarian revolution in seventeenth-century England. But this is not the same thing as saying 'to exercise power ... you had to be a gentleman' (p. 27). That was true before 1640 and after 1660: it was not true for the intervening revolutionary decades. Mr Laslett claims that there were no significant social conflicts either within the landed class, which he regards as homogeneous and united, or between any of its members and 'the middling sort' (pp. 46–50). There is a mass of contemporary evidence for such social conflicts, however; they have been demonstrated in the work of the most respected historians of our generation (Tawney, Trevor-Roper, Stone, Ramsay, Ashton, etc., etc.). One can see why Mr Laslett finds the historian 'something of a nuisance to the sociological inquirer, just because it is his habit to ask questions of this blank and simple sort' – like 'What was it in Stuart society which led to political disaster and fighting' (p. 151)? Our author also holds the curious view that only the literate can participate in politics. (In a broadcast on 1 February 1966, Mr Laslett still further restricted this: 'In order to be a proper citizen you've got to *own* books' – my italics.) Historically this is absurd. The French, Russian and Chinese Revolutions, like the English, are inconceivable without the political action of illiterate masses, however much lead the literate may have given them. To say (as Mr Laslett did in the same broadcast) 'only the literate could communicate from one village to another' is as untrue of modern Africa or South-East Asia as it is of medieval England, or France in 1789.

V

The author treats the three centuries before the Industrial Revolution as a homogeneous period in which there was no significant change. He uses facts widely separated in time as though they were contemporaneous. Thus Sir Thomas Smith is said to have taken 'the minority view' because he thought in 1565 that apprenticeship derogated from gentry; the representatives of 'the majority view' all come from after the Civil War (pp. 42, 47, 249).[9] Mr Laslett cheerfully argues that the numbers of *Tudor* vagabonds may have been exaggerated because Gregory King thought there were only thirty thousand *in 1696* (p. 116). John Graunt's statement that very few starved in London between 1640 and 1661 is 'called in question' by evidence from 1557 (pp. 111–14, 262). Many other examples could be given of Mr Laslett's refusal to recognize the existence of change, and especially his determination to allow no break at what some historians have called the English Revolution. Only someone who has no grasp of how swiftly ideas were developing in mid-seventeenth-century England could see the Levellers as expressing 'boring common sense'.

To show that 'the notion of social revolution is not permissible' in seventeenth-century England (p. 164) is one of Mr Laslett's main propagandist concerns. He seems to think that the idea of an English Revolution is an invention of wicked post-Marxist historians. A little acquaintance with the literature would have revealed to him a book called *L'Histoire de la révolution d'Angleterre* published by Guizot when Marx was seven years old. In 1850 Marx fiercely attacked a lecture by Guizot, 'Pourquoi la révolution d'Angleterre a-t-elle réussi?' Mr Laslett might also have discovered *Lectures on the English Revolution* delivered by the innocent idealist philosopher T. H. Green in 1866. No serious historian since the seventeenth century has failed to agree either with Oliver Cromwell that there had been a revolution in England, or with Clarendon that there had been a great rebellion. In the late nineteenth century Gardiner invented the Puritan Revolution; over the past forty years historians have been returning to the seventeenth-century conception that the revolution was at least as much social as religious. Sadly for Mr Laslett's thesis, one of the most promising young American historians, Michael Walzer, has recently published a study, *The Revolution of the Saints*, which shows how revolutionary Calvinism broke through the bonds of patriarchal loyalties within which Mr Laslett wishes to confine all seventeenth-century Englishmen. Professor Walzer's book reopens the question of the links between ideology and social change whose existence Mr Laslett wishes to deny. If any historian were inclined to take *The World We Have Lost* seriously, a reading of *The Revolution of the Saints* (1965) would soon cure him.

Mr Laslett's 'more sophisticated' theory is that 'conflict . . . is a common enough form of social interaction' (p. 160). Historians have hitherto failed to notice that 'society at the same time had what might be called a conflict-mechanism built into it. This oversight is the more extraordinary,' Mr Laslett muses, since the *outcome* of what used to be called the English Revolution was the evolution of the parliamentary system for resolving conflicts (p. 162). Unless Mr Laslett means by this that there were no significant constitutional changes between 1640 and 1688, which is untrue, I am unable to attach any meaning to it at all. 'Collisions sometimes take place in social and political life, just as car collisions do, and there is a logical resemblance.' (p. 160) This trivial dictum disposes of the question. It would be 'a simple and over-dramatic question' to ask why in the 1640s, instead of the statistically normal number of collisions, we find most of the drivers deliberately aiming their cars at one another and piling up over miles of road (p. 161). 'Once the imagination is set free' by Mr Laslett's new formula, it can even see an analogy in 'Professor Gluckman's examination of African communities', which 'shows how a fight over the dynastic succession is a permanent feature of political life' (p. 162). Unliberated imaginations may not see the relevance of this to a society which was not primitive, to a war which was not dynastic, and to a problem which, so far from being permanent, was unique.[10]

A similar logic will also wish the French and Russian Revolutions out of existence (pp. 150, 160). Yet Mr Laslett does not deny the existence of all revolutions. He appears to think that one took place in England between 1943 and 1951. The components of this revolution are a reduction in the numbers of births per marriage, full employment, a welfare state, 'new towns, the nationalization of industries, the final democratization of the parliamentary system, and many other things'. Royalty and archbishops of Canterbury remain undecapitated; civil war has not yet broken out, the republic has not yet been proclaimed, the House of Lords is still with us; but – and this is the final crescendo of revolution as seen from suburban Cambridge – 'the price of domestic help had risen in the last twenty years more than almost any other item of household expenditure, but servants are still not to be had' (pp. 224–7).

VI

One would wish to conclude more in sorrow than in anger, since statistical demography has so important a role to play in the future development of English historical writing. Part of the explanation of Mr Laslett's unfortunate book is no doubt that he rushed into print far too quickly. In his Introduction he remarks that some of his conclusions will be called in question by recent work done by his colleagues in the Cambridge Group for the History of Population and Social Structure. They will indeed. If Mr Wrigley is right in believing that birth control was practised in the seventeenth century – and to a mere historian it seems likely *a priori* – then Mr Laslett's speculations in chapters 4 and 6 about the age of sexual maturity and the low fertility of young women will need revision; so will his thoughts about the children of the poor, and the confident statement at page 132 that 'by and large men and women . . . were chaste until marriage came . . . Thereafter . . . they only seem very rarely to have indulged themselves outside marriage.' This in its turn will throw further doubt on Mr Laslett's dicta about the influence of orthodox Christianity. The otherwise interesting speculation on page 108, that shortage of food necessitated late marriages and 'authoritarian sexual morals', will also need reconsideration. So will the view that rich women conceived more often than poor (p. 192). Large sociological conclusions have been founded on what now appear to be dubious hypotheses – for instance, the absence of 'any general approach of sexual licence' in seventeenth-century England (p. 141). Mr Laslett knew that it was necessary 'to think out again what is written in this book about births, marriages and deaths' and many other questions (p. ix). He might with advantage have done the thinking before publication.

But the most serious accusation against him is sheer ignorance. It is bad not to know that the Short Parliament met in 1640, but it is far worse, in an author who takes it upon himself to rebuke others, to be ignorant of the important sociological history written in England and the USA during the past twenty-five years. One thinks of Robert and T. S. Ashton, G. E. Aylmer, E. J. Buckatzsch, J. D. Chambers, D. C. Coleman, K. G. Davies, M. G. Davies, R. Davis, A. G. Dickens, A.Everitt, Mrs M. E. Finch, W. Haller, E. Hobsbawm, W. G. Hoskins, J. Hurstfield, W. K. Jordan, B. S. Manning, Miss D. Marshall, Mrs V. Pearl, G. Ramsay, G. Rudé, A. Simpson, L. Stone, R. H. Tawney, Mrs J. Thirsk, E. P. Thompson, H. R. Trevor-Roper, M. Walzer, C. Wilson. I deliberately include the names of historians with whom I disagree on many points of interpretation but whose solid scholarship compels respect. Mr Laslett cites seven of them in his notes, and refers to an eighth in his Introduction; but there is little internal evidence to suggest that he has read them with any comprehension.

A 'new critical history' should surely start from a modest and accurate appreciation of the very considerable volume of work done by sociological historians over the past generation; it should not be a vehicle for its author's prejudices and hobby-horses; it must be aware of the limitations as well as the strengths of statistical demography, and have some understanding of other relevant disciplines. One still hopes that the Cambridge Group may make an important contribution in this field, despite the disastrous disservice which one suspects this book has done them.[11]

Pottage for Freeborn Englishmen: Attitudes to Wage-Labour[1]

Wage-earning is not a career that men seek for its own sake.

E. H. Phelps Brown and Sheila Hopkins,
Economica, N.S., vol. xxiv (1957), p. 299.

I

Recent controversies between 'optimists' and 'pessimists' concerning the effects of the Industrial Revolution have dealt mainly with the standard of living. Insufficient emphasis, it seems to me, has been placed upon the 'ideological' hostility to the status of wage-labourer which many men and women felt in the eighteenth century. In our time, thanks to two centuries and more of trade union struggle, wage-labour has won a self-respecting place in the community, and it is difficult for us to think ourselves back to a world in which, as Sir John Clapham wrote of the French *cahiers* of grievances in 1789, 'the position of *journalier* is seldom referred to except as a kind of hell into which peasants may fall if things are not bettered'.[2] This attitude was almost universal in the England of the Industrial Revolution, and it derived from at least two centuries of history. My object here is to recall some of the economic facts and social and legal theories which underlay the attitude.

II

Significant changes in the status of wage-labour came with the rapid development of capitalism in the sixteenth century. Many of the wage-labourers (*servientes*) whom Professor Hilton records on Leicestershire estates in the late fourteenth and fifteenth centuries would have holdings of their own: they were not wholly dependent on wages for their existence. Indeed Froissart tells us that the rebels of 1381 demanded that 'if they laboured or did anything for their lords, they would have wages therefor as well as other'.[3] Wage-labour meant freedom by contrast with serfdom. But in the sixteenth century more and more of those who worked for wages were losing their land, and so were becoming wholly dependent on such earnings, together with their remaining rights in the common lands. The author of *A Discourse of the Common Weal* (1549) spoke of 'many a thousand cottagers in England . . . having no lands to live of their own but their handy labours and some refreshing upon the said commons'.[4]

The assumption that wages were supplementary to an agricultural holding kept wages low:[5] the rates which JPs authorized were rarely sufficient in themselves for the rearing of a family. Poor relief was therefore needed in addition: full-time wage-earners were assumed to be paupers. There are many complaints against the introduction of a new industry into an area, on the grounds that it would lead to an influx of socially undesirable down-and-outs. Thus in 1606 the tenants of Broseley, Shropshire, protested that the owner of a new colliery was spoiling the manor by introducing 'a number of lewd persons, the scums and dregs of many [counties], from whence they have been driven'.[6] Twelve years later Robert Reyce wrote of Suffolk that 'in those parts of this shire where the clothiers do dwell or have dwelt, there are found the greatest number of the poor'.[7] A similar remark was made two generations later. Industry creates poverty, for

> 'though it sets the poor on work where it finds them, yet it draws still more to the place; and their masters allow wages so mean that they are only preserved from starving whilst they can work; when age, sickness or death comes, themselves, their wives or their children are most commonly left upon the parish; which is the reason why those towns (as in the Weald of Kent) whence the clothing is departed, have fewer poor than they had before.'[8]

In these early days, when only the weakest would accept the

status of full-time wage-labourer, there was little or no protection against the sort of abuses which were still prevalent in the
eighteenth century – truck, delay in payment of wages and consequent indebtedness. In Sir Arthur Ingram's Yorkshire alum
works wages in James I's reign were often nine months in arrears.
The workers complained that they were grossly overworked,
paid in kind, with goods seriously overvalued, and that the con-
tractors were deliberately aiming to ruin their credit locally so
as to reduce them to complete economic dependence.[9] In such
circumstances men fought desperately to avoid the abyss of
wage-labour. In the Stannaries of Cornwall in the sixteenth and
early seventeenth centuries, 'miners as a rule preferred the illu-
sory independence of the tribute system rather than frank
acceptance of the wage system', though this made them fall ever
deeper into debt to usurious dealers. 'They have no profit of
their tin if they be hired men'; once the status of free miner was
lost, there was no hope of return.[10] 'Abandon hope all ye who
enter here' was written over the portals of wage-labour. Sir
William Monson in James I's reign described how mariners preferred the 'liberty' (his word) of service on a privateer, where
they shared in the profits and the risks, to the regular wages and
floggings of the King's ships.[11] Even on the outskirts of Edinburgh in the mid-seventeenth century wage-labourers were
deemed inferior in status to those who held the most minute
fragment of land to farm for themselves.[12]

Professor Nef pointed out that the rise of industrial specialization led to segregation from their communities of some wage-
labourers at least: this would be especially true of new industries
staffed by immigrants, and of miners, whose work made them
look and smell different from their neighbours. He also suggested that the falling standard of living of wage-labourers in
the sixteenth and early seventeenth centuries may have led to
differences in physical appearance – a greater incidence of
rickets among workers' children and an earlier loss of teeth in
adults.[13] This argument has been reinforced by Dr Joan Thirsk
and Professor Everitt, who suggest that we must distinguish
between the stable agricultural communities of the open-field
country, and the pastoral and forest areas – so much more widespread in the seventeenth century than now. Here squatters and
cottagers, often immigrants, lived apart from the traditional

communities, supplying labour for domestic industry and a general reserve of labour for agriculture or industry. Mobile, footloose, undisciplined, such immigrants were also often heretical: the Weald of Kent and the Forest of Dean, among many others, were traditional areas of popular religious radicalism. These areas may have supplied many of the rank and file of the New Model Army. Norden tells us of forest squatters who were 'given to little or no kind of labour, . . . dwelling very far from any church or chapel, and are as ignorant of God or of any civil course of life as the very savages amongst the infidels'.[14] Professor Notestein had suggested that farm labourers seldom went to church in the seventeenth century, because they had no suitable clothes.[15] In this way they too would be excluded from the communities in which they lived. (One wonders indeed whether the baptisms, marriages and deaths of all members of the reserve army of squatter-labourers were included in all parish registers; or whether these, our main source of statistical information for sixteenth- and seventeenth-century population, may not be far from complete, in some parishes at least, at this early date.)[16]

The Statute of Artificers of 1563 accentuated the isolation of the poorest classes, since by it any man or woman without an agricultural holding could be condemned to semi-servile labour in industry or agriculture, whilst the children of paupers were compulsorily apprenticed. No labourer was to leave his employment without his employer's consent, under penalty of imprisonment until he submitted. These provisions had the effect of depressing wages and lowering the status of all wage-labourers in town and country; and resistance was made impossible by the fact, which we have already noted, that a militant combination to raise wages was treasonable.[17] This outcast class was also liable to conscription for overseas service in army or navy. But wage-labourers were normally excluded from service in the militia, the internal police force of the propertied class.[18]

It is hardly surprising that the rank and file of many early colonizing expeditions was composed of wage-labourers, attracted by the prospect of winning the freehold land in America to which they could never aspire in England. Satirical verses of 1631 depict New England as the Land of Cokayne, that medieval utopia in which wealth came without work.[19] Conversely propagandists for colonization put forward the argument that 'swarms of our rank multitude' might be exported.[20] In 1622 a preacher told the Virginia Company of English labourers rising early, working all day and going late to bed. They 'are scarce able to put bread in their mouths at the week's end, and clothes on their backs at the year's end'. Such men, starving in the London streets, would form a useful labour supply for the plantations.[21]

III

Those entirely dependent on wage-labour were so badly off in the sixteenth and seventeenth centuries that 'neither contemporary nor modern economists can explain how they lived'.[22] Children had to be put to work so early in life that there was no chance of educating them.[23] Their poverty and helplessness was accompanied, as cause and effect, by an unfree status. Even the Levellers, the most radical of all seventeenth-century political groupings, would have excluded paupers and servants (i.e. wage-labourers) from the franchise, because they were unfree.[24] The Leveller franchise would have been restricted to 'freeborn Englishmen'. Wage-labourers and paupers had lost their birthright because they had become economically dependent on others: they had lost their property in their own persons and labour. Not only the Leveller Richard Overton but also the Parliamentarian Henry Parker equated loss of property in one's self with 'a condition of servility'. The republican James Harrington not only denied citizenship to servants but regarded them as a class outside the Commonwealth.[25] 'Servants', wrote John Eliot in New England in 1659, 'are not personally capable of interest in public political elections'; they are virtually comprehended in their master's covenant with God.[26] Gregory King made the same point from the economist's point of view when he excluded cottagers, paupers and labourers from those who contributed to the wealth of the nation. So did Karl Marx when he wrote 'it is already contained in the concept of *free labourer* that he is a *pauper*: virtual pauper.'[27]

There is plenty of confirmatory evidence for Professor Macpherson's argument that in the sixteenth and seventeenth century those in receipt of wages were regarded as unfree. For Sir Thomas Smith in 1565 the 'commonwealth consisteth only of freemen'. 'Day labourers' and others who have no free land 'have no voice nor authority in our commonwealth, and no account is made of them but only to be ruled'. Those who 'be hired for wages . . . be called servants'. Apprenticeship too was '*vera servitus*', though only temporary.[28] For William Harrison yeomen were 'freemen born English', who 'may dispend of their own free land in yearly revenue to the sum of 40*s*.[29] The author of *Haec-Vir* (1620) said women are as freeborn as men. In 1624 an MP attributed to Magna Carta, cap. 30, the statement 'he that hath no property in his goods is not free'.[30] In this sense Thomas Whythorne felt himself 'as freeborn as he who may spend thousands of yearly inheritance', despite the fact that he earned wages as a musician. For he differentiated sharply between 'the liberal arts', the arts of the freeborn, of gentlemen, and the 'drudgery' of 'servile and filthy trades'. Music was one of the former.[31] Samuel Rowlands in 1614 thought that a 'free-bred muse' would despise poets who wrote 'for gold or silver pay'.[32] Gosson denounced stage players as 'hirelings', and in 1615 one of the worst things that could be said against an actor was that 'his wages and dependence prove him to be a servant of the people'.[33] George Wither prided himself upon his 'freeborn lines' at a time when, in Day's words, 'verses though freemen born are bought and sold like slaves'. Robert Burton similarly described himself as 'a free man born'.[34]

The pejorative sense of 'hireling' and 'journeyman' is a comment on my theme. Bacon wanted 'to keep the plough in the hands' of freeholders, who were not 'mere hirelings' in a 'servile condition'.[35] Ralegh in his *History of the World* wrote of 'factious and hireling historians'.[36] Martin Marprelate denounced curates as 'journeymen hedge-priests'.[37] The separatist Henry Barrow thought all priests were 'the waged servants of Antichrist'.[38] 'Our souls', cried William Stoughton in 1604, 'and the souls of our wives and children and families, should be more dear . . . than that carelessly we would hazard all our birthrights upon the skill and ability of such a mess of hirelings.'[39] Milton and many others during the interregnum echoed this denunciation of 'hireling priests'. Even the episcopalian author of *Persecutio Undecima* (1648) spoke of the 'illiterate mechanics

... planted into churches in the hurly-burly days of Queen Elizabeth', who gathered in 'wages for their journey-work'.[40] Others generalized less selectively: 'journeyman-like he travels from place to place seeking to be set on work before he hath learnt his trade'; 'journeyman or chaplain'.[41]

All political theorists assumed that 'servants' should be excluded from the franchise; as they usually were in seventeenth-century English political practice.[42] In 1640 it was 'the sense of the house' of Commons that 'no beggar, or man that received relief, or is not sub (*sic*) to scot and lot, is capable of giving his voice in election of burgesses'.[43] George Wither's servant was satisfied to

> 'act an humble servant's part,
> Till God shall call me to be free.'[44]

'Will you be beggars still when you may be freemen?' the Diggers asked in 1650. (In Winstanley's commonwealth a certain type of offender might however become 'a servant for ever', losing 'his freedom in the commonwealth'.[45]) James Ussher attacked the idea of a social contract by asking 'Had women and children and servants and madmen and fools the freedom of suffrage, as well as men of age and fortunes and understanding?'[46] Parliament made similar social assumptions when in 1645 it legislated for the election of elders in its new Presbyterian church. They were to be chosen by members of congregations who were not 'servants that have no families'.[47] Fathers of families were regarded as virtually representing, *vis-à-vis* the state, their wives, children, apprentices, journeymen and servants, over whom within their families they had complete authority. A great deal of confusion was caused by advocates of a Presbyterian disciplinary system, like William Stoughton, who spoke of the 'birthright' of the people and yet specifically excluded 'the multitude' from the right to elect elders. It was Anabaptists who advocated equality of servants and masters, William Gouge alleged.[48] The right of the minister (or of the minister and ruling elders acting together) to exclude from the sacrament those whom they held to be the ungodly, and so to shut them out from full church membership, was thus also a way of keeping them unenfranchised – as in New England. One of the horrors of religious toleration for Presbyterians was

225

that it made a nonsense of this sort of discipline by depriving the state church of its monopoly and thus depriving the minister of his ultimate sanction – the right to exclude from the sacraments.

In 1647 it was argued that 'very many in the Army, the pretended representatives of the people' were 'servants and prentices not yet free', and so by definition *incapable* of representing anybody.[49] Thomas Hobbes used the parallel of household and state in order to emphasize that 'the subjection of them who institute a commonwealth amongst themselves is no less absolute than the subjection of servants'.[50] Richard Baxter thought that those (and those only) whose poverty was 'so great as to make them servants of others and deprive them of ingenious freedom' should be deprived of civil freedom.[51] The novelty indeed with 'freeborn John' Lilburne and the Levellers was that they proposed so wide an extension of the franchise, beyond freehold landed proprietors and men free of corporations, that the inclusion of wage-labourers had to be contemplated, at least as a logical possibility. Oliver Cromwell had to argue that it was absurd that 'men that have no interest but the interest of breathing' should have voices in elections. When he appreciated that the Levellers, even though agreeing to exclude children and servants, nevertheless proposed to regard those in receipt of alms as competent to elect – then Cromwell felt that 'this drive at a levelling and parity etc.' had gone too far and must be resisted.[52] Previously such persons had been deemed to be beyond the pale of the constitution. The only exception which I have found to the assumption that wage-labourers are unfree comes in strict legal terminology. In Hampden's Case Croke distinguished between 'bondmen, whose estates are at their lord's will', and 'freemen, whose property none may invade'; Ship Money was illegal because it constituted such an invasion.[53] Thomas Hooker in his *Synopsis Chorographical of Devonshire* (*c.* 1599–1600) describes 'the daily worker or labourer in the tin works' as '*liberi homines* and of a free condition . . . albeit their labours be of the most inferior in degree'. He was contrasting this liberty specifically with the unfreedom of serfs, so there may be no contradiction.[54]

Freedom in fact was a class concept. Drayton assumed that 'the freeborn' are the privileged.[55] 'Privileges . . . made our fathers freemen', Sir John Eliot told the Commons in 1628:[56] *libertas*, as Maitland put it, meant freedom to oppress others.[57] Charles i claimed 'the natural liberty all free men have' to choose his own advisers.[58] Rowland Vaughan in 1610 felt that 'being freeborn' gave him a superior nature as well as bluer blood.[59] In Scotland Patrick Gordon spoke of 'our nation (I mean the gentry, not the commons) having never been conquered, but always a freeborn people'. He distinguished between 'a freeborn gentleman and a servile or base-minded slave'.[60] In 1650 Robert Heath similarly contrasted 'freeborn birth' with 'peasant blood'.[61] Two years earlier Joseph Beaumont had asked 'Where is your freeborn subjects' liberty?'

> 'How are our servants by our madness thriven
> Into imperious lords! Whilst we are fain
> To be at charges towards our own plunder
> And keep an army up to keep us under!'[62]

Charles i claimed at his trial that 'any freeborn subject' should enjoy the protection of the law.[63] In 1642 the High Sheriff of Lancashire referred casually to 'under-tenants and all other servants'.[64] The Fifth Monarchist John Archer believed that in the approaching millennium only the elect would be freemen, the reprobate becoming their slaves.[65]

The *Oxford English Dictionary* defines 'free', among other things, as meaning 'noble, honourable, of gentle birth and breeding'.[66] Free men were freeholders: Parliament represented them only. It was royalist prisoners who in March 1659, as 'freeborn people of England', petitioned Parliament, 'the representative of the freeborn people of this nation', against being transported, put to forced labour and whipped.[67] Torture had been condemned by Sir Thomas Smith as 'taken for servile in England', and the Levellers regarded whipping as a punishment 'fit only for slaves or bondmen'.[68] 'Servants and labourers', a pamphlet of 1660 declared, 'are in the nature of vassals.'[69] In America, apart from Virginia between 1621 and 1655, servants had no vote unless they were freemen by virtue of being church members.[70]

The passage which I quoted from Stoughton in 1604 contained the idea of a 'birthright', though in the very act of proclaiming it he denied it to those who had been born poor.[71]

227

In the Putney Debates the Leveller Edward Sexby said that, small though his property was, he would give up his birthright to none.[72] The outstanding characteristic of a birthright at this period indeed seems to have been the ease with which it was lost. In Massinger's *The Bondman* (1623) Timoleon 'ever loved an equal freedom', and denounced as 'rebels to nature' those who 'would usurp on others' liberties'. But he recognized that when men

> 'have made forfeit of themselves
> By vicious courses, and their birthright lost,
> 'Tis not injustice they are marked for slaves.'[73]

The interregnum was a great restitutionist period. Men hoped to restore Anglo-Saxon freedom and Christian liberty. For Sir Simonds D'Ewes the right to a vote was 'the birthright of the subjects of England'.[74] For others the birthright was property. Both concepts were taken up and developed by the Levellers. Lilburne in December 1646 wrote that 'the only and sole legislative power is originally inherent in the people, and derivatively in their commission[er]s chosen by themselves by common consent, and no other. In which the poorest that lives hath as true a right to give a vote as well as the richest and greatest.'[75] *The Moderate* in 1649 declared that all men possessed the same birthright, including freedom. Only the sword had deprived 'the vulgar' of this birthright, settling 'upon a few a cursed propriety'.[76] It was time for restitution.

In 1645 an anti-monopolist tract argued that 'to bar any freeborn subject from the exercise of his invention and industry . . . is to deprive him of part of his birthright.'[77] In this case the restriction to 'freeborn subjects' was perhaps a saving clause; but it was not unreasonable for a Presbyterian like Thomas Case to argue in 1647 that if liberty were once granted to lower-class sectaries, 'they may in good time come to know also . . . that it is their birthright to be freed from the power of Parliaments and from the power of kings, and to take up arms against both when they shall not vote and act according to their humours.'[78] Some in the Army were already justifying his fears: the Nottinghamshire horse told Parliament in 1647 that victory in the Civil War should have purchased 'peace and liberty to the poor (yet freeborn) people of this kingdom'.[79] Soon Gerrard Winstanley was arguing that ownership of land was the birthright of every Englishman, though Culpeper retorted 'Who desires a community? We desire but our birthright.'[80] Mr Lindsay has plausibly argued that some such concept as Winstanley's lies behind Bunyan's horror of selling his birthright, as so many peasants had to sell their scraps of land, with disastrous consequences to themselves.[81]

In the 1640s and 1650s many besides Levellers wished to recover the birthrights of all Englishmen; some of these hoped to extend the number of those to be regarded as 'freeborn Englishmen', even at the expense of the property and privileges of the ruling class. George Smith, a gentlemen who supported first Presbyterians and then the Protectorate; Lawrence Clarkson, Ranter; William Erbery, Seeker; John Child, New Englander; John Webster, critic of the universities; the editor of Nicholas Culpeper the astrologer – all proclaimed themselves to be freeborn Englishmen. So did John Bachiler, Parliament's licenser of the press.[82] Milton spoke of 'freeborn Englishmen' and of 'freeborn Christians'; he also said that all *men* since Adam were born free.[83] Agricola Carpenter the Mortalist, who claimed to be 'a freeborn subject' with a 'freeborn soul', thought that 'an infidel is the best proficient in the school of nature', and looked for 'some wiser Columbus' to reveal 'an America of knowledge yet unfound out'.[84]

'Are there any Englishmen that are not freeborn?' a pamphlet of 1648 asked.[85] Sir Robert Filmer in 1652 argued that 'every man that is born, is so far from being freeborn, that by his very birth he becomes a subject to him that begets him'.[86] But this was no longer generally acceptable. Tithes, a petition of September 1647 had said, were 'contre le libertye des freebornmen'.[87] John Jones, urging that jurors should take over the main responsibility from judges in the law-courts, insisted that ploughmen were 'the best kind of freemen in England'.[88] 'The Anabaptists are men that will not be shuffled out of their birthright as freeborn people of England', wrote one of their defenders in 1655.[89] The Quaker Francis Howgill claimed in 1654 that he and Edward Burrough were 'freeborn Englishmen, and have served the commonwealth in faithfulness'.[90] The latter said in the following year that the Quakers were a freeborn people, who should not be banished or taken for guilty until proved so; in 1661 he described Quakers as freeborn, with a right to their lives, liberties and estates.[91] In 1656 George Fox said 'We are free men of England, freeborn; our rights and liberties are according to law and ought to be defended by it':[92] it was a familiar Quaker attitude. Lodowick Muggleton also called himself 'a freeborn Englishman'.[93] A pamphlet of 1659, written in reply to Harrington's *Oceana*, advocated an oligarchy consisting of those who adhered to the Good Old Cause, saying that for the time being only 'such as are freeborn in respect of their holy and righteous principles' should be enfranchised citizens.[94]

The word 'freeborn' in fact acquired a temporary notoriety as the catch-phrase of political radicals. In 1654 John Hall warned of the dangers, now 'there is not one of the meanest servants in a family, but is in his conceit one of the people, or one of the commons at least . . . So a freeborn subject, as he is, shall be free of master as well as prince.'[95] He might almost have been quoting James Nayler the Quaker, who in 1655 told Oliver he had counted 'nothing too dear to bring the government into your hands (for the liberty of freeborn men').[96] Marchamont Nedham, looking back from 1661 in his *Short History of the English Rebellion*, sang

> 'Farewell the glory of our land,
> For now the freeborn blades
> Our lives and our estates command,
> And ride us all like jades.'[97]

For the Restoration had changed everything, bringing back the domination of the truly freeborn, in the traditional sense. In February 1660 the gentry of Oxfordshire were asserting their right as 'freeborn Englishmen' to be represented in Parliament.[98] It was the birthright of the gentry, G.S. asserted in the same year, 'to choose and be chosen' MPs.[99] Sir George Sondes claimed that he 'never was so great a royalist as to forget I was a freeborn subject'.[100] Samuel Butler jeered at 'what freeborn consciences may do': no saint 'should be a slave to conscience'.[101] By 1669 'ranting like a freeborn subject' on behalf of 'privileges' was a subject for theatrical mockery.[102] Dryden in 1682 described the effects of Cromwell's rule as 'The freeborn subject sunk into a slave'.[103] When Cowley spoke of birds as freeborn, and Aphra Behn of 'freeborn lovers', the word was losing its former precision.[104] In Swift's *Discourse of the Contests and Dissensions between the Nobles in Athens and Rome* (1701), an elaborate series of parallels with recent English history, Servius Tullius (= Oliver Cromwell) was described as first introducing 'the custom of giving freedom to servants, so as to become citizens of equal privileges with the rest, which very much contributed to increase the power of the people'.[105] The history is absurd; the implications however made very good sense for Swift's audience.

IV

Although the Levellers did not think the poorest classes capable of exercising the right of freeborn Englishmen, there were those who did. But, significantly, such men opposed wage labour. In Spenser's *Mother Hubberd's Tale* (1591), the Ape asked the Fox:

> 'Shall we tie ourselves for certain years
> To any service?'

and the Fox replied

> 'Why should he that is at liberty
> Make himself bond? Since then we are free born
> Let us all servile base subjection scorn . . .
> And challenge to ourselves our portions due
> Of all the patrimony which a few
> Now hold in hugger-mugger in their hand
> And all the rest do rob.'

In the Golden Age, mankind's original condition of equality, there was not 'ought called mine or thine'. The Fox urged that the poor should spurn the drudgery of 'vile vassals, born to base vocation'. They should refuse to 'be of any occupation', should no longer work to enrich others.

> 'We will walk about the world at pleasure . . .
> Lords of the world; and so will wander free
> Whereso us listeth, uncontrolled of any . . .
> Free men some beggars call, but they be free,
> And they which call them so more beggars be;

> For they do swink and sweat to feed the other,
> Who live like lords of that which they do gather –
> And yet do never thank them for the same,
> But as their due by nature do it claim.'[106]

Spenser must have heard something like that from a sixteenth-century agitator. A not dissimilar attack on the principle of wage labour can be read into words used by one of the Oxfordshire rebels of 1596. ('Care not for work, for we shall have a merrier world shortly . . . I will work one day and play the other . . . Servants were so held in and kept like dogs that they would be ready to cut their masters' throats.')[107]

Just over fifty years later Gerrard Winstanley the Digger made a communist theory out of what must long have been muttered among the exploited poor. Wage-labour for him was slavery, a loss of man's birthright freedom. 'Israel shall neither take hire, nor give hire. And if so, then certainly none shall say, This is my land, work for me, and I'll give you wages.'[108] 'Whosoever shall help that man to labour his proper earth, as he calls it for wages, the hand of the Lord shall be upon such labourers, for they . . . hold the creation still under bondage.'[109]

> 'If the common people have no more freedom in England but only to live among their elder brothers and work for them for hire, what freedom then have they in England more than we have in Turkey or France? . . . The poor that have no land are left still in the straits of beggary, and are shut out of all livelihood but what they shall pick out of sore bondage, by working for others as masters over them.'

The Civil War would have been fought in vain, would have given freedom only to the gentry and clergy, if there were not a far more radical reform than the men of property were prepared to envisage.[110]

A truly free and communist commonwealth, on the other hand, Winstanley argued, would

> 'unite the hearts of Englishmen together in love, so that if a foreign enemy endeavour to come in we shall all with joint consent rise up to defend our inheritance, and shall be true to one another. Whereas now the poor see, if they fight and should conquer the enemy, yet either they or their children

are like to be slaves still, for the gentry will have all. And this is the cause why many run away and fail our armies in the time of need. And so through the gentry's hardness of heart against the poor the land may be left to a foreign enemy, for want of the poorers' love sticking to them. For, say they, we can as well live under a foreign enemy working for day wages as under our own brethren, with whom we ought to have equal freedom by the law of righteousness.'[111]

Winstanley, who described himself as a 'servant', stood forward as the spokesman of 'the common people, that are the gatherings together of Israel from under that bondage [of property in land, buying and selling and wage labour], and that say the earth is ours, not mine, let them labour together and eat bread together upon the commons, mountains and hills.'[112] This was a call to the cottager-squatter class, hitherto not regarded as free: to those who did not accept the protestant ethic or the doctrine of the dignity of labour.[113] In Winstanley's utopia there would be a law that 'No man shall either give hire, or take hire for his work, for this brings in kingly bondage. If any freeman want help, there are young people, or such as are common servants [i.e. those under penal sentence] to do it, by the Overseer's appointment. He that gives and he that takes hire for work shall both lose their freedom and become servants for twelve months.'[114] The Digger colony on St George's Hill was intended to be the first stage in a sort of general strike against wage-labour. As the Digger poet Robert Coster put it in December 1649,

'Rather than go with cap in hand and bended knee to gentlemen and farmers, begging and entreating to work with them for 8d. or 1od. a day, which doth give them an occasion to tyrannize over poor people (which are their fellow-creatures), if poor men would not go in such a slavish posture, but do as aforesaid, then rich farmers would be weary of renting so much land of the lords of manors'

and 'down would fall the lordiness' of the spirits of the latter.[115]

V

The Diggers were of course an extreme example and a small

group. But the other evidence collected here may help us to appreciate that their attitude towards wage-labour was not unique among their class, though their remedies no doubt were. By the end of the century, at least, life-long wage-labourers may well have been a majority of the population.[116]

In the same centuries as the working class showed this hatred of wage labour, Puritans and others were evolving a doctrine of the dignity of labour. This began as part of the protestant critique of idle monks and begging friars. It soon became a primitive version of the labour theory of value, which seems to have been held, among others, by Bishop Jewell, William Perkins, Dod and Clever, Arthur Dent, John Preston, Richard Baxter, Milton, Hobbes and Sir William Petty, as well as by Peter Chamberlen and Gerrard Winstanley. These Puritan theories, which I have tried to discuss elsewhere,[117] were aimed at free craftsmen: they take for granted that property in a man's own labour and person which wage labourers had lost. George Herbert's lines,

> 'A servant with this clause
> Makes drudgery divine;
> Who sweeps a room, as for thy laws,
> Makes that and the action fine,'[118]

represented a point of view more common among employers and independent craftsmen than among employees. When in 1697 James Puckle praised the inventiveness and technical skill of English artisans, when in 1751 Malachy Postlethwayt uttered his famous paean in praise of 'the ingenuity and dexterity of [England's] working artists and manufacturers, which have heretofore given credit and reputation to British wares in general', his reference was precisely to such free craftsmen, whose skill was 'owing to that freedom and liberty they enjoy to divert themselves in their own way'. 'Were they obliged to toil the year round, the whole six days in the week, in a repetition of the same work, might it not blunt their ingenuity and render them stupid instead of alert and dexterous?'[119] What is freedom but choice? Milton had asked. And Hobbes agreed for once in defining a free man as 'he that in those things which by his strength and wit he is able to do, is not hindered to do what he has a will to do'.[120] Craftsmanship was *free* craftsmanship: Tawney emphasized the contrast between having the status of wage-labourer thrust upon one and being able to choose between that and working on the land as a squatter. 'The former is slavery: the latter is freedom.'[121]

Theories of the dignity of labour had little appeal for those who had evolved out of serfdom into wage labour. Such men in the sixteenth century sympathized with vagabonds and refused to prosecute thieving beggars. In the eighteenth century their descendants read the literature of roguery which glorified highwaymen and pirates, non-working heroes like Robin Hood and Dick Turpin, and they gave moral support to condemned criminals at Tyburn. In 1650 Abiezer Coppe the Ranter pictured God Almighty as a highwayman, 'demanding restitution from the rich like some urban Robin Hood: "Thou hast many bags of money, and behold I (the Lord) come as a thief in the night, with my sword drawn in my hand, and like a thief as I am – I say Deliver your purse, deliver sirrah! deliver or I'll cut thy throat." '[122] Lower-class utopias from the Land of Cokayne onwards aim to abolish wage-labour altogether, or drastically to reduce the working day. This is the context in which we should see the numerous seventeenth-century references to the English national characteristic of hating labour more than death. According to a pamphlet printed in 1647, a Scot, a Dutchman and an Englishman had all been condemned to death when their lives were begged by a man who wanted to use their labour. The Scot and the Netherlander accepted: the Englishman 'desired he might be hanged first'.[123] In 1694 a French visitor referred to the Englishman's 'contempt of death and fear of labour'. Moll Flanders' last husband thought hanging preferable to transportation and forced labour in Virginia.[124]

VI

This historical perspective may help to explain the attitude of those men and women who in the eighteenth century hated going into factories. Even if our 'optimists' could prove that workers would have been economically better off in factories than outside, men still did not live by bread alone. The relations of employer and wage-labourer, wrote Dean Tucker in George II's reign, 'approach much nearer to that of a planter and slave in our American colonies than might be expected in such a country as England'.[125] Many factories looked like work-houses for paupers: they were certainly so regarded by many workers.[126] Self-respecting men fought against going into them, or sending their wives and children into them, just as today no one in his senses would go voluntarily into the army as an other rank if he could avoid it. Factory discipline must have seemed to the eighteenth-century craftsman equally irrational, equally irrelevant to his interests, equally unfree. He clung on to his birthright, his property in his own person and labour. Among the many complaints that the English poor would work only when prices were high, common from the seventeenth century onwards, I cite this published by a French visitor in 1770:

'Les bas artisans, les compagnons même portent encore plus loin ce qu'ils appellent l'indépendance anglaise: le seul défaut d'argent les ramène à l'atelier. Y sont-ils, ils se battent, pour ainsi dire, avec l'ouvrage: ils travaillent en furieux et comme gens fâchés de travailler. Ils aiment mieux travailler ainsi de toutes leurs forces, et se reposer de temps en temps, que de passer mollement et langoureusement la journée à l'ouvrage. Il gagne à cette ardeur qu'y apporte l'ouvrier: on en peut juger par la perfection de la main-d'oeuvre anglaise, soit dans les ouvrages en acier, soit dans tous les ouvrages de l'aiguille.'

This '*perfection de la main-d'oeuvre*' goes with '*l'amour de la liberté*', even in '*la dernière classe des artisans*'.[127]

One of Petty's favourite ideas for obtaining docile wage-labour had been to transfer the bulk of the populations of Ireland and the Scottish Highlands to England.[128] The early factories were in fact largely worked either by pauper children and women, or by Welshmen, Irishmen and Scots who lacked the English craftsman's 'notion, that as Englishmen they enjoy a birthright privilege of being more free and independent than in any country in Europe'. (This is perhaps one reason why Irishmen played such a large part in early English working-class movements of protest.) The anonymous author of *An Essay on Trade and Commerce* (1770) had little use for such a sentimental notion: 'the less the manufacturing poor have of it, certainly the better for themselves and the state . . . The cure will not be perfect till our manufacturing poor are contented to labour for

six days for the same sum which they now earn in four days.'
His remedy was a 'House of Terror' and 'ideal workhouse',
where 'the poor shall work fourteen hours a day'. This House of
Terror, Marx observed grimly, was realized a few years later,
and was called the factory.[129] 'We make a nation of helots and
have no free citizens', wrote Adam Ferguson in 1765, adding
that 'manufactures . . . prosper most where the mind is least
consulted, and where the workshop may, without any great
effort of imagination, be considered as an engine, the parts of
which are men.'[130] The antithesis of freedom was the stultifying
drudgery of those who had become cogs in someone else's
machine.

To Adam Smith it seemed obvious that a factory worker,
from the nature of his toil, was 'altogether incapable of judging
. . . the great and extensive interests of his country'. He contrasted the state of affairs in pre-industrial societies, where
'invention is kept alive, and the mind is not suffered to fall into
that drowsy stupidity which, in a civilized society, seems to
benumb the understanding of almost all the inferior ranks of
people . . . Every man, too, is in some measure a statesman, and
can form a tolerable judgment concerning the interest of the
society, and the conduct of those who govern it'. Smith –
interestingly enough in the high priest of *laissez-faire* – advocated
state interference to ensure minimum standards of education.[131]

Until 1875 the relations of wage-earners and employers were
regulated by the Master and Servant Acts, whose title is a
comment on my thesis. These placed wage-labourers in a wholly
inferior position to their employers.[132] We look back over two
centuries in which wage-labour has won freedom and self-
respect, and are astonished (or some historians are) at the
prejudices of those who were reluctant to enter the factories;
men and women then looked back over two centuries and more
of rejection of the slavery of wage-labour, of contemptuous pity
for its victims. Liberty still included the concept of property in
one's own labour (and that of one's family), of small proprietor-
ship, of an agricultural holding to ward off starvation in unemployment, sickness and old age. This tradition helps to explain
the overwhelming strength of the back-to-the-land movement
right into the nineteenth century, even among the Chartists.
To accept a merely wage status in the factories was a surrender

of one's birthright, a loss of independence, security, liberty. 'It takes centuries', observed Marx, 'ere the "free" labourer, thanks to the development of capitalistic production, agrees, i.e. is compelled by social conditions, to sell the whole of his active life, his very capacity for work, for the price of the necessaries of life, his birthright for a mess of pottage'.[133]

A historical approach suggests that Adam Smith and Marx got closer and more imaginatively to the heart of the matter than many recent historians who analyse so carefully the calory-content of the pottage. So did Wesley, who offered a birthright in heaven to those who had irretrievably lost it on earth. It was a long time before freeborn Englishmen could be convinced that the chains of factory discipline could in any way be justified. The acceptance of wage-labour as a permanent system was accompanied, significantly, by the abandonment of the backward-looking ideal of the birthright, and even of the concept of the freeborn Englishman itself.

Men as They Live Their Own History[1]

The working clothiers are unfortunately true to each other.

> The Lord Lieutenant of Somerset about
> machine-breakers, 1802, in G. D. H. Cole and
> R. Postgate, *The Common People, 1746–1938*
> (1938), p. 175.

Thirty or forty years ago the history of the origins of the English labour movement was being written by the Hammonds, G. D. H. Cole and a handful of enthusiastic amateurs. Today working-class history has become a respectable academic subject, enshrined in university syllabuses and studied for Ph.D.s: there is a Labour History Society. As with the present-day transformation of adult education from a vocation to a secure job with pension attached, the professionalization at least of early working-class history has brought loss as well as gain. The first generation, with more political enthusiasm than financial backing, concentrated on immediately obvious sources – radical and working-class press, memoirs, autobiographies. The new generation has turned to the archives. This is true especially of the pre-Chartist phase of working-class history, for which Home Office papers are particularly valuable. A conservative bias is common among administrative historians, and appears to derive from the nature of their sources (or from the temperament that is attracted to such sources). A reader of *The Black Dwarf* or of *The Northern Star* has to guard against being carried away by his sources' assumption that England was governed by fools or

239

knaves. But documents left in the Home Office archives were not written by men concerned to improve the administrative machine, still less to smash it: they took it for granted, and were concerned at most with oiling and tinkering.

There are as few Luddites among administrative historians as among administrators. Because of the great gulf fixed between the Home Office records and the working-class rebels depicted in them, the historian of the early working-class movement needs to keep his imagination about him if he is not to be choked in archive dust. (For the Chartist and post-Chartist period, when the sources are more voluminous and more varied, the concealed bias of the archives matters less.)

Sympathy for administrators has become almost fashionable since Tout and Namier put them on the historian's map. It is no doubt part of a general reaction against the romantic leftism of the 1930s. The tired, worldly-wise cynicism of the postwar generation knows how to appreciate the devoted labours of unromantic civil servants which keep society cohesive and functioning; it has less sympathy for the idealists and revolutionaries whose naive enthusiasms sometimes brought less rather than more happiness to those whom they hoped to serve. So (to quote a few recent examples) we are now told that the Pilgrim Fathers grossly exaggerated the persecutions which they suffered in England, of which no evidence survives in ecclesiastical archives: it was presumably for the fun of it that they risked their lives crossing the Atlantic and in the New England wilderness. Some historians enter so sympathetically into the predicament of the Inquisitors who had to deal with the obstinate and unreasonable Galileo that they almost forget that he was right and the Inquisitors wrong on an issue that mattered. Historians of early nineteenth-century England now appreciate so fully the difficulties of Lord Sidmouth and Lord Eldon, and of the yeomanry at Peterloo, that any evidence from Byron or Shelley can be treated with the contempt that poets deserve. A recent historian of Tudor England concludes that it is not 'at all apparent that the vast majority of those executed as traitors were not in fact guilty in law'.[2] When the G.P.U. archives are opened their evidence will no doubt force similar conclusions on the conscientious historian of the USSR in the 1930s.

A prejudice in favour of stability, law and order is a bias no less than that of the romantic rebels. To start with a determination to prove Engels wrong is not necessarily more conducive to clear thinking than to start determined to prove Engels right. No doubt some Christian historians have paid insufficient attention to Pilate's point of view on events leading to the Crucifixion but it would be over-compensating to take his as the only valid one. The historian, like the Ombudsman, should be at least as prepared to believe that the police can lie as that the objects of their attention will. A bias towards the status quo is dangerous because difficult to identify, especially by the man who holds it. A rebel knows he is a rebel; a conservative may think himself simply a good citizen. An academic historian enters imaginatively into the position of a stocking-frame owner or a Home Office official more easily than into that of a Luddite, a Cato Street conspirator or a devotee of Joanna Southcott; for he is likely to own some property, however inadequate, and to do some administration, however amateurish.

Moreover, the historian of the early labour movement knows that the events he is describing look forward in some sense to Mr Harold Wilson, towards whom his feelings are unlikely to be entirely neutral. All historians (except those who write about the very latest times) face problems when discussing the lower 50 per cent of the population who normally appear only in police records or as the objects of exhortation. Sustained historical imagination is needed to conceive, let alone to understand and convey to the reader, the way of thinking of the inarticulate, especially in times of revolutionary crisis. We need not postulate a crowd psychology: what the historian needs is rather the imaginative insight of a Carlyle or a Trotsky, among the great historians; insight which today can be reinforced by the research techniques of the modern school of historians of the French Revolution – Albert Soboul, Richard Cobb and George Rudé. The early students of the pre-Chartist working class tried to perform this difficult feat of understanding in order to reconstruct. Some of their successors, one feels, are less prepared to listen patiently to points of view with which they do not sympathize. Yet what else is the historian's job?

Mr E. P. Thompson's important book *The Making of the English Working Class* deals with the generation after 1790. It recaptures the imaginative sympathy of the pioneer historians while profiting by subsequent advances in knowledge and historical method. Mr Thompson is aware of, and applies, the latest techniques of plumage analysis; but he never allows his readers to forget the struggling bird. He thus concludes a review of that contentious subject, working-class standards of living during the industrial revolution:

'In fifty years . . . the working-class share of the national product had almost certainly fallen relative to the share of the property-owning and professional classes. The "average" working man remained very close to subsistence level at a time when he was surrounded by the evidence of the increase of national wealth, much of it transparently the product of his own labour, and passing, by equally transparent means, into the hands of his employers. In psychological terms, this felt very much like a decline in standards. His own share in the "benefits of economic progress" consisted of more potatoes, a few articles of cotton clothing for his family, soap and candles, some tea and sugar, and a great many articles in the *Economic History Review*.'

The snort at the end reveals the author's sympathies, but his preceding review of the evidence was sober and balanced, leading up to

'two propositions which, on a casual view, appear to be contradictory. Over the period 1790–1840 there was a slight improvement in average material standards. Over the same period there was intensified exploitation, greater insecurity, and increasing human misery. By 1840 most people were "better off" than their forerunners had been 50 years before, but they had suffered and continued to suffer this slight improvement as a catastrophic experience . . . The deep-rooted folk memory of a "golden age" or of "Merrie England" derives not from the notion that material goods were more plentiful in 1780 than in 1840 but from nostalgia for the pattern of work and leisure which obtained before the outer and inner disciplines of industrialism settled upon the working man.'

Mr Thompson accurately describes his book as 'a group of studies on related themes'. He has thus forestalled the criticism that important aspects of working-class life and politics, such as the naval mutinies of 1797, are either omitted or inadequately dealt with in this long book. Mr Thompson's strength lies in his ability to make sense of the apparently senseless. He declares:

'I am seeking to rescue the poor stockinger, the Luddite cropper, the "obsolete" hand-loom weaver, the "utopian" artisan, and even the deluded follower of Joanna Southcott, from the enormous condescension of posterity. Their crafts and traditions may have been dying. Their hostility to the new industrialism may have been backward-looking. Their communitarian ideals may have been fantasies. Their insurrectionary conspiracies may have been foolhardy. But they lived through these times of acute social disturbance, and we did not. Their aspirations were valid in terms of their own experience.'

Nowhere is this determination not to condescend better shown than in Mr Thompson's 130 pages on Luddism. This movement has usually been written off as one of blind, anarchic, 'backward-looking' violence, and contrasted with the more obviously political movements which followed. By working over the evidence, and by paying especially careful attention to dates, Mr Thompson makes a plausible case for supposing that 'far from being "primitive" ', Luddism 'exhibited, in Nottingham and Yorkshire, discipline and self-restraint of a high order':

'Anyone who has conducted a raffle or organized a darts tournament knows that scores of men cannot be assembled at night, from several districts, at a given point, disguised and armed with muskets, hammers and hatchets; formed into line; mustered by number; marched several miles to a successful attack, to the accompaniment of signal lights and rockets – and all with the organization of a spontaneous college "rag".'

Mr Thompson emphasizes for instance that the Luddites were highly selective in their chosen targets, were drawn from many social classes and had 'the backing of public opinion in the Midlands and the West Riding'. Previous historians, he argues, have too easily dismissed the evidence of informers and agents provocateurs – both the law-and-order school (unwilling to accept the existence of widespread revolutionary sentiment in

England) and the Fabian school (contrasting machine-breakers with later, more recognizable ancestors of the Labour Party).

> 'There is only one reason for believing that the various depositions in the Home Office papers as to [Luddism's] revolutionary features are false, and this is the assumption that any such evidence is *bound* to be false.'

Spies and provocateurs of course had their living to earn. But careful investigation and comparison of the depositions of informers suggest that they contain a harder core of truth than has been supposed.

Many of the Luddite leaders were men who had previously shown their mastery of orthodox trade union tactics, and of orthodox methods of political action such as petitioning.

> '[Luddism] commenced (1811) in Nottingham as a form of direct "trade union" enforcement, endorsed by the working community. As such it at once incurred outlawry, and its very situation drove it in a more insurrectionary direction . . . Small groups of democrats or Painites saw in Luddism a more general revolutionary opportunity.'

In Lancashire, where the Jacobinism of the 1790s had struck deeper roots and where Irish influences were stronger, and in the West Riding, Luddism gave way to revolutionary conspiracy. Although the Luddites themselves clouded the evidence about their movement, Mr Thompson suggests possible connections between the machine-breakers and Despard's conspiracy of 1802. He rehabilitates the latter as 'an incident of real significance in British political history', 'a last flaring up of the old Jacobinism'. The evidence linking

> 'the underground of 1802 and that of 1812 . . . comes . . . from so many different sources that if it is all to be discounted we must fall back upon some hypothesis which would strain credibility a great deal further – such as the existence of a veritable factory of falsehoods, turning out complementary fantasies, for the sole purpose of deluding the authorities.'

In the summer of 1812 there were more troops out in the disturbed areas than Wellington had under his command in the Peninsula. Mr Thompson also stresses the Luddites' constitutional grievances, suggesting that the movement in Yorkshire may have been triggered off by the failure of hopes that the Prince Regent would bring in a reforming ministry when the restrictions on his power came to an end. A Nottinghamshire magistrate reported in 1817:

> 'The Luddites are now principally engaged in politics and poaching. They are the principal leaders in the Hampden Clubs which are now formed in almost every village in the angle between Leicester, Derby and Newark.'

Luddism is a good example of Mr Thompson's method, and of his critical attitude towards both the Fabian school of historians (the Webbs, Graham Wallas, the Hammonds) and the more recent school of economic historians. The former, Mr Thompson thinks, followed Francis Place too closely, who had his own axes to grind. The latter fail to clothe their skeleton of statistics with flesh and blood. Mr Thompson, an extramural lecturer in the West Riding, is extremely well versed both in local and in central sources. If his fully documented and closely argued conclusions are to be refuted, it will have to be by equally cogent use of evidence. He shows a similar independence in his criticism of Dr Rudé's work. Temperamentally, Mr Thompson must have found Dr Rudé's conversion of 'the mob' into 'the revolutionary crowd' sympathetic; but his own evidence suggests that mobs were more often manipulated by the authorities than Dr Rudé supposed.

The same freshness characterizes Mr Thompson's estimate of religious influences. An early chapter traces the dissenting inheritance, and stresses the continuing power of millenarianism in the early working-class movements. (He breaks a lance here with Mr Norman Cohn, who dismissed 'chiliastically-minded movements' as having a 'chronically impaired sense of reality'. Mr Thompson could never find anything human as alien as that.) His section on 'the Chiliasm of Despair' leads to some shrewd and helpful pages about Joanna Southcott. Mr Thompson is critical of contemporary attitudes towards Wesleyanism:

> 'So much of the history of Methodism has, in recent years, been written by apologists or by fair-minded secularists trying to make allowances for a movement which they cannot

understand, that one notes with a sense of shock Lecky's judgment at the end of the nineteenth century: "A more appalling system of religious terrorism, one more fitted to unhinge a tottering intellect and to darken and embitter a sensitive nature, has seldom existed." '

Mr Thompson inclines to agree. His quotations on Methodist attitudes to sex are particularly horrifying. 'The worst kind of emotional bullying' is his phrase for Sunday school education. He notes 'the extraordinary correspondences between the virtues which Methodism inculcated in the working class and the desiderata of middle-class Utilitarianism'. 'Almost every line' of Blake's *The Everlasting Gospel* 'may be seen as a declaration of "mental war" against Methodism and Evangelicism'. (Mr Thompson's first book was on William Morris, and he still seems to think that poets can tell us as much about an age as statisticians.) But Mr Thompson also concludes 'what the orthodox Methodist minister intended is one thing; what actually happened in many communities may be another'. Methodism taught men how to organize: some used this knowledge for democratic purposes that would have horrified Wesley and Jabez Bunting.

Not all Mr Thompson's conclusions will be accepted. But his book is a portent. Just as new orthodoxies seemed to be settling down on the pre-Chartist period of working-class history, a fresh, lively mind has ranged over the whole field and shown that new scholarship is not incompatible with old enthusiasm and commitment. Only a few themes from this stimulating and provocative book have been mentioned: it manages even to say something new about Cobbett and Owen. Again and again, in a footnote or an aside, Mr Thompson gives us more to think about than many a Ph.D. thesis:

'Those writers today who rightly expose the human depreciation resulting from the commercial abuse of the media of communication seem to me to have matters out of proportion when they overlook the extent and character of mass indoctrination in earlier periods.'

Mr Thompson is very conscious of the sociologist looking over his shoulder. What, after all, is a class?

'If we stop history at a given point, then there are no classes but simply a multitude of individuals with a multitude of experiences. But if we watch these men over an adequate period of social change, we observe patterns in their relationships, their ideas and their institutions. Class is defined by men as they live their own history, and, in the end, this is its only definition. If I have shown insufficient understanding of the methodological preoccupations of certain sociologists, nevertheless I hope this book will be seen as a contribution to the understanding of class.'

It is that, but also much more. It deals with the decades in which England was transformed from a 'backward' to an industrialized economy. Mr Thompson's deeply humane imagination and controlled passion help us to recapture the agonies, heroisms and illusions of the working class as it made itself: no one interested in the history of the English people should fail to read his book. But since a large part of the population of the globe is at present experiencing just this transition, Mr Thompson's studies of Luddism, millenarianism and revolutionary conspiracy are of more than parochial significance: his refusal to condescend to the defeated may after all not be so quixotic. Outside the small group of fully industrialized countries, the subjects with which he deals may seem more relevant than the trade unionism of the later nineteenth century or the parliamentary politics of the twentieth. 'Causes which were lost in England' – it is Mr Thompson's own reflection – 'might in Asia or Africa, yet be won.'

PART V
Change out of Continuity

Sir Isaac Newton and His Society[1]

I see . . . humanity in deadly sleep . . .
For Bacon and Newton, sheath'd in dismal steel, their terrors hang
Like iron scourges over Albion . . .
I turn my eyes to the schools and universities of Europe
And there behold the loom of Locke, whose woof rages dire,
Wash'd by the water-wheels of Newton: black the cloth
In heavy wreathes folds over every nation: cruel works
Of many wheels I view, wheel without wheel, with cogs tyrannic
Moving by compulsion each other, not as those in Eden, which
Wheel within wheel, in freedom revolve in harmony and peace . . .

> May God us keep
> From single vision and Newton's sleep!

> William Blake, 'Jerusalem', and letter to
> Thomas Butts, 22 November 1802, in
> *Poetry and Prose* (Nonesuch ed.),
> pp. 574–5, 1068.

I

One way to approach the subject of Newton and his society would be to quote Professor Alexander Koyré: 'The social structure of England in the seventeenth century cannot explain Newton.' That seems final. But of course one must gloss Koyré by emphasizing the word 'explain'. A complete explanation of Newton cannot be given in social terms: nor indeed do I know of anyone who ever suggested that it could. The obverse of Professor Koyré's platitude (as it seems to me) is Professor Hall's remark that 'in a more backward technological setting the scientific revolution could not have occurred'.[2] The historian, *qua* historian, is not – or should not be – looking for single causal explanations, whether internal to science or external in the society. The historian's questions are 'Why here?', 'Why now?' If science were a self-evolving chain of intellectual development, then it would be irrelevant that it was Newton, living in post-revolutionary England, who won international fame by following up Galileo, a persecuted Italian, and Descartes, a Frenchman living in exile in the Dutch republic. But for the historian the where, when and why questions are vital. It is no more possible to treat the history of science as something uncontaminated by the world in which the scientists lived than it is to write the history of, say, philosophy or literature or the English constitution in isolation from the societies which gave birth to them.[3]

'Restrictivist' historians of science who emphasize the scientific revolution as an 'intellectual mutation' cannot side-step such questions. For, as Professor Hall emphasizes, the important thing in scientific advance is often the asking of new questions, approaching a given body of material from a fresh angle.[4] All the factors which precede and make possible such a breakthrough are therefore relevant. The real problem is not, how do men come to look at familiar facts in a different way? but how do they liberate themselves from looking at them in the old way? And here the history of the society, the intellectual environment in which the scientist lived, as well as the facts of his personal biography, may frequently be suggestive, if rarely conclusive. 'Restrictivist' historians of science wax facetious at the standard example, used perhaps too simply by the preceding generation: the influence of pumps on Harvey's discovery of the circulation of the blood. Yet there was, as we know, a great expansion in the use of pumps for mining and other purposes in Harvey's England: Harvey, we know, had watched water pumps, and himself compared the working of the heart to a water bellows. At least we can say, adapting Professor Hall, that in a society without pumps the circulation of the blood might not have been discovered. What I want to suggest about Newton is that his Puritan upbringing, combined with the post-revolutionary environment of Cambridge, and possibly certain psychological factors which are both personal and social, may have helped him to ask fresh questions and so to break through to his new synthesis.

The history of science is different from other forms of intellectual history, Professor Kuhn has well said, because science advances.[5] An accumulation of knowledge and understanding may lead to a measurable increase in control over the environment. In the history of philosophy or art or literature there is no such linear advance. This makes historians of science peculiarly liable to one of two diametrically opposed fallacies. The 'externalists' stress the environmental stimulus to scientific advance: 'restrictivists' reply by showing from individual biographies that some scientists, and these often the greatest, took a disinterested delight in their work. They in their turn stress the internal chain of intellectual development which links Newton with Galileo and both with the Schoolmen; they tend to play down (or at least fail to explain) the breaks or mutations in this chain.

The history of science is intellectual history, and most great scientists were disinterested pursuers of truth or intellectual satisfaction. But the particular kinds of truth they pursued, the forms of intellectual satisfaction they sought, are not unrelated to the general intellectual and moral climate in which they lived; and this climate is a changing social product which the historian, however inadequately, can attempt to analyse and explain. It is natural for scholars, convinced of their own disinterested search for truth and intellectual satisfaction, to see the same in their predecessors. It is equally natural for them to feel intellectually self-sufficient, to be unaware of the social pressures and assumptions which beset them personally, and so to ignore the effect of similar pressures and assumptions on the great scientists of the past. It is the self-perpetuating academic fallacy of purity against which all historians have consciously and continually to be on their guard.

II

Newton was born in 1642, 'the year of discoveries',[6] the year in which the English Civil War broke out. The first twenty-four years of his life witnessed a great revolution, culminating in the execution of Charles I and the proclamation of a republic. They saw the abolition of episcopacy, the execution of an archbishop of Canterbury, and a period of greater religious and political liberty than was to be seen again in England until the nineteenth century. The censorship broke down, church courts ceased to persecute. Hitherto proscribed sects preached and proselytized in public, and religious speculation ran riot, culminating in the democratic theories of the Levellers, the communism of Gerrard Winstanley and the Diggers, the scientific materialism of Hobbes and the economic determinism of Harrington. Books and pamphlets were published on a scale hitherto unprecedented on all subjects, including science, mathematics and medicine; for the natural sciences, too, benefited from Parliament's victory. Oldenburg rightly said in 1659 that science got more encouragement in England than in France.[7] Bacon was popular among the Parliamentarians, and from 1640 onwards began that climb to fame which soon caused him to be hailed as 'the dictator of philosophy' – an ascent which the Royal Society materially assisted.

The first two decades of Newton's life, then, saw a political revolution which was also a religious and intellectual revolution, the climax in England of a transformation in ways of thought which had been proceeding for a century and a half, and of which Renaissance, Reformation and the scientific revolution were all part. Protestantism, by its hostility to magic and ceremonial, its emphasis on experience against authority, on simplicity in theology, helped to prepare an intellectual climate receptive to science – not least in the covenant theology, so popular in Newton's Cambridge, with its rejection of arbitrary interference with law, its insistence that God normally works through second causes, not by miracles.[8] In England transubstantiation was publicly ridiculed from the pulpit; in Roman Catholic Europe the miracle of the mass was believed to be a daily event, to be treated with awe and reverence. In the 1660s Sprat was arguing, in defence of the Royal Society, that it was only doing for philosophy what the Reformation had done for religion. Samuel Butler, an enemy of the Society, was arguing at the same time that protestantism led to atheism.[9] Both saw connections between protestant and scientific revolutions.

But the years immediately before 1666 had seen a reaction. In 1660 Charles II, the House of Lords and the bishops came back to England. An ecclesiastical censorship was restored. Oxford and Cambridge were purged again. The scientists regrouped in London around Gresham College, and succeeded in winning the patronage of Charles II. But it was not all plain sailing. In the early years of its existence the Royal Society had continually to defend itself against the accusation that science led to atheism and social subversion – the latter charge made plausible by the Parliamentarian past of the leading scientists. 'The Act of Indemnity and Oblivion', the renegade Henry Stubbe sourly reminded his readers in 1670, had been 'necessary to many of the Royal Society.'[10] Next year Stubbe denounced Bacon's philosophy as the root cause of 'contempt of the ancient ecclesiastical and civil jurisdiction and the old government, as well as the governors of the realm'.[11] The fact that John Wilkins, the Society's secretary, conformed to the episcopal church in 1660 seemed less important to contemporaries than that he was Oliver Cromwell's brother-in-law and that he had been intruded by the Parliamentary Commissioners as Warden of Wadham, where he gathered around him the group which later formed the nucleus of the Royal Society. In 1667 his fellow Secretary, Henry Oldenburg, was arrested on suspicion of treasonable correspondence. Conservatives and turncoats in the universities and among the bishops attacked both science and the Royal Society.

III

The mechanical philosophy suffered from its very name. The word *mechanic* was ambiguous. In one sense it meant 'like a machine': the mechanical philosophy was what we should call the mechanistic philosophy. In this sense Oldenburg spoke of 'the mechanical or Cartesian philosophy'.[12] But not all English scientists were Cartesians, and this meaning crystallized only in the later seventeenth century. When Dudley North in 1691 said 'Knowledge in great measure is become mechanical' he thought it necessary to add a definition: 'built upon clear and evident truths'.[13] Long before Descartes wrote Bacon had been urging Englishmen to learn from mechanics, from artisans, and to draw a philosophy from their fumbling and uncoordinated but successful practice. 'The most acute and ingenious part of men being by custom and education engaged in empty speculations, the improvement of useful arts was left to the meaner sort of people, who had weaker parts and less opportunity to do it, and were therefore branded with the disgraceful name of mechanics.' But chance or well-designed experiments led them on. (I quote not from Bacon but from Thomas Sydenham, who like Sprat learnt his Baconianism at Wadham in the 1650s under Wilkins.[14])

Bacon too was only summing up a pre-existent ideology which held up to admiration 'expert artisans, or any sensible industrious practitioners, howsoever unlectured in schools or unlettered in books' (Gabriel Harvey, 1593). John Dee referred to himself as 'this mechanician'. We recall John Wilkins's *Mathematical Magick, or the Wonders that may be performed by Mechanical Geometry* (1648). Fulke Greville spoke of 'the grace and disgrace of . . . arithmetic, geometry, astronomy' as resting 'in the artisans' industry or vein'. We recall also Wallis's reference to mathematics in the 1630s as a 'mechanical' study, meaning by that 'the business of traders, merchants, seamen, carpenters, surveyors of lands and the like'. Marlowe expressed this ideology in heightened form in *Doctor Faustus*:

'O what a world of profit and delight,
Of power, of honour and omnipotence,
Is promised to the studious artisan!'

Here the artisan was also a magician. But then so too was Dee; so was Newton.

Keynes's description of Newton as 'the last of the magicians', which seemed so paradoxical when he enunciated it, now appears self-evident.[15] Andrew Ramsay in the eighteenth century saw Sir Isaac in the long line of the magi.[16] Newton's manuscripts contain many references to Hermes Trismegistus: he does not seem to have been shaken by Isaac Casaubon's demonstration that the allegedly ancient Hermetic writings dated in fact from the second or third centuries of the Christian era.[17] Newton possessed and studied a copy of the translation of the Rosicrucian manifestos.[18] He devoted an enormous amount of time and effort to the serious study of alchemy.

The Baconian emphasis was shared by many of the early Fellows of the Royal Society, and expressed most forcibly by Boyle – no magician, but anxious to learn from alchemists. Boyle insisted that scientists must 'converse with practitioners in their workhouses and shops', 'carry philosophic materials from the shops to the schools'; it was 'childish and unworthy of a philosopher' to refuse to learn from mechanics. Professor M. B. Hall is right to stress Boyle's good fortune in having not been subjected to the sort of academic education he would have got at a university before the Parliamentarian purges.[19] Hooke too consistently took counsel with skilled craftsmen. Cowley, in his *Ode to the Royal Society*, rejoiced that Bacon had directed our study 'the mechanic way', to things not words. Newton himself was a skilled craftsman, who had already constructed a water clock, sundials and a windmill while still a boy. Later he ground his own lenses, made his own grinding and polishing machines and his own telescopes, and conducted his own alchemical experiments. As late as the eighteenth century he was issuing specific and detailed instructions to Royal Society experimenters.

Yet the word 'mechanic' was not neutral. It had other overtones. It conveyed the idea of social vulgarity, and also sometimes of atheism. The Copernican theory, said an archdeacon in 1618, 'may go current in a mechanical tradesman's shop', but not with scholars and Christians. During the interregnum the word came into new prominence when applied as a pejorative adjective to 'mechanic preachers', those doctrinally heretical and socially subversive laymen of the lower classes who took advantage of religious toleration to air their own disturbing views. Such men appealed to their own experience, and the experiences of their auditors, to confute authority, just as the scientists appealed to experiment. ('Faithfulness to experiment is not so different a discipline from faithfulness to experience', wrote Professor Longuet-Higgins recently.[20] 'This I knew experimentally', said George Fox of his spiritual experiences in 1647.[21]) There is no need to labour the importance of the mechanic preachers, nor the consternation which they caused to their betters: this has been demonstrated in Professor Tyndall's admirable *John Bunyan, Mechanick Preacher*, analysing both the genus and its supreme exemplar, who was safely in jail from 1660 to 1672, with many of his fellows. From 1641 onwards it had been a familiar royalist sneer that Parliament's supporters were 'turbulent spirits, backed by rude and tumultuous mechanic persons', who 'would have the total subversion of the government of the state'; 'those whom many of our nation, in a contemptuous folly, term mechanics', wrote Marchamont Nedham defensively. Charles II in 1654 referred sneeringly to the Lord Protector Oliver Cromwell as 'a certain mechanic fellow'.[22] Many of the educational reforms proposed in the revolutionary decades were aimed at benefiting this class. Thus Petty proposed 'colleges of tradesmen', where able mechanicians should be subsidized while performing experiments; William Dell wanted better educational opportunities for 'townsmen's children'.

So there were dangerous ambiguities in the word 'mechanic', of which the Royal Society was painfully aware. (If its members ever forgot, Henry Stubbe was ready to remind them by denouncing them as 'pitiful Mechanicks', Samuel Butler as 'mechanical virtuosi'.)[23] Sprat in his *History*, in Baconian vein, spoke of 'mechanics and artificers (for whom the true natural philosophy should be primarily intended)', and defined the Society's ideal of prose style as 'the language of artisans, country-men and merchants'. But – consistently with his propagandist purpose – he was careful to insist that the technological problems of industry must be approached by 'men of freer lives', gentlemen, unencumbered by 'dull and unavoidable employments'. 'If mechanics alone were to make a philosophy, they would bring it all into their shops; and force it wholly to consist of springs and wheels and weights.' This was part of a campaign to make the Royal Society respectable. The atheist Hobbes and the radical Parliamentarian Samuel Hartlib were kept out. Anyone of the rank of baron or over was automatically eligible for a Fellowship. A number of courtiers and gentlemen were made Fellows, some of whom were genuinely interested in science, but many of whom were not. The Society prepared pretty tricks for Charles II, Newton had to pretend that James II could be interested in the *Principia*, and that epoch-making work was issued over the imprimatur of Samuel Pepys as president of the Royal Society – an estimable man, but hardly Newton's peer.

In the long run, this had of course deplorable consequences for science. Despite Boyle's insistence, a gentleman dilettante like Evelyn could not lower himself to 'conversing with mechanical, capricious persons'.[24] Even Seth Ward, intruded professor of astronomy at Oxford during the interregnum, thought that 'mechanic chemistry' was an unsuitable subject for the sons of the nobility and gentry to study at universities. But in the short run it was essential to free the scientists from the 'mechanic atheism' which Cudworth scented in Cartesianism,[25] and from the stigma of sedition which clung around the word 'mechanical'. 'Plebeians and mechanics', said a Restoration bishop, 'have philosophized themselves into principles of impiety, and read their lectures of atheism in the streets and highways'. Glanvill in his dedication to the Royal Society of *Scepsis Scientifica* in 1664 emphasized the Society's role in 'securing the foundations of religion against all attempts of mechanical atheism'; 'the mechanic philosophy yields no security to irreligion.'

But there was a narrow tightrope here. Boyle, the 'restorer of the mechanical philosophy', was opposed to occult qualities, wanted to expel mystery from the universe as far as was compatible with the retention of God. Wren had told a London audience in 1657: 'Neither need we fear to diminish a miracle by explaining it.'[26] 'What cannot be understood is no object of belief', Newton said. 'A man may imagine things that are false, but he can only understand things that are true.'[27] But there were still many who held the view denounced by Bacon 'in men of a devout policy' – 'an inclination to have the people depend upon God the more, when they are less acquainted with second causes; and to have no stirring in philosophy, lest it may lead to an innovation in divinity, or else should discover matter of further contradiction to divinity.' Experience of the interregnum had strengthened the prejudices of those who thought like that. And there were very real intellectual problems in combining scientific atomism with Christianity – problems which Boyle, the defenders of the Royal Society and Newton himself spent their lives trying to solve. Newton once referred, revealingly, to 'this notion of bodies having as it were a complete, absolute and independent reality in themselves, such as almost all of us, through negligence, are accustomed to have in our minds from childhood'. This was a main reason for atheism: we do not think of matter as created or dependent on the continuous action of the divine will.[28]

Professor Westfall has plausibly suggested that the violence of the scientists' attacks on atheism may spring from the fact that 'the virtuosi nourished the atheists within their own minds.'[29]

Given the general social anxiety of the Restoration period, how were men to frame a theory of the universe which would accommodate both God and the new science? The problem was acute, 'the vulgar opinion of the unity of the world being now exploded' (the words are those of Henry Oldenburg) 'and that doctrine thought absurd which teacheth the sun and all the heavenly host, which are so many times bigger than our earth, to be made only to enlighten us.' Mechanic philosophy, purged of the atheism and enthusiasm of the rude mechanicals, offered the best hope. Newton, whom Swift called 'an obscure mechanic',[30] ultimately supplied the acceptable answer; but he was only one of many trying to find it. The question would have been asked if Newton had never lived.

IV

We do not know how far Newton was aware of the great revolution which was going on while he was growing up, but it is difficult to think that it left him untouched. His county, Lincolnshire, was a centre of strong pro-Parliamentarian feeling. His mother was an Ayscough, and Edward Ayscough was MP for Lincolnshire in the Long Parliament, a staunch Parliamentarian. Newton's maternal uncle became rector of Burton Coggles in 1642; the stepfather whom his mother married was rector of another Lincolnshire parish.[31] Both apparently remained on good terms with the Parliamentary ecclesiastical authorities. Newton lived for many years at Grantham while attending its grammar school. Until 1655 the leading ecclesiastical figure in Grantham was its lecturer, John Angell, a noted Puritan.[32] After his death, the tone was set by two more Puritans, both ejected for nonconformity at the Restoration, both praised by Richard Baxter. Over the church porch was a library given to the town fifty years earlier by Francis Trigge, another eminent Puritan, who wrote a treatise on the Apocalypse.[33] Newton almost certainly used this library; he may even have acquired his interest in the mysteries of the Book of Revelation from it.

I emphasize these points because there used to be a mistaken impression, based on a poem which he was believed to have written, that Newton was in some sense a royalist. Even L. T.

More, Newton's best biographer, repeats this error. But this poem was not Newton's; he copied it from *Eikon Basilike* for his girl friend, Miss Storey. There is no evidence that Newton sympathized with the sentiments expressed in the poem. Even if he did regard Charles I as a martyr, this would not make him a royalist in any technical sense. Most of those who fought against Charles I in the Civil War deplored his execution: the Army had first to purge the Presbyterians from Parliament. Indeed the author of *Eikon Basilike* was himself a Presbyterian divine, a popular preacher before Parliament during the Civil War. It was only after the Restoration that he (like Wilkins and so many other Puritans) conformed to the episcopal church and took his reward in a bishopric.

Newton's whole education, then, was in the radical protestant tradition, and we may assume that his outlook was Puritan when he went up to Cambridge in 1661. This helps to make sense of his later beliefs and interests; he did not take to theology after a mental breakdown in the 1690s. Before 1661 he was learning Hebrew. In 1664–5, if not earlier, he was keeping notebooks on theology and on the ecclesiastical calendar.[34] He later argued that bishops and presbyters should be of equal status, and that elders should be elected by the people.[35] Newton conformed indeed to the restored episcopal church – as he had to do if he wanted an academic career. But he abandoned belief in the Trinity very early in life and resisted all pressure to be ordained. He seldom attended Trinity College chapel. He had a typically Puritan dislike of oaths, shared with Boyle and Ray. In Newton's scheme for tuition at Trinity he went out of his way to insist 'No oaths of office to be imposed on the lecturers. I do not know a greater abuse of religion than that sort of oaths.' In later life he was alleged to be 'hearty for the Baptists'.[36]

If Newton went up to Cambridge with Puritan inclinations, he can hardly have been happy in his first two years. John Wilkins had just been expelled from the mastership of Newton's college, despite the wishes of the fellows. We do not know how many fellows were ejected or forced to resign; the number may be of the order of twenty.[37] They included John Davis, Fellow, Librarian and Hebrew Lecturer, and William Disney from Newton's county of Lincolnshire. John Ray resigned in 1662, perhaps not before Newton had heard him preach sermons in the college chapel which were later written up as *The Wisdom of God manifested in the Works of the Creation* and *Miscellaneous Discourses concerning the Dissolution and Changes of the World*. Ray had originally preached his sermons as a layman, but after 1660 ordination was insisted on for all fellows after their first seven years.[38]

As early as 1660 Ray had deplored the lack of interest in experimental philosophy and mathematics at Cambridge,[39] and the expulsion and withdrawal of men like himself and Wilkins did not help. By 1669, when the university entertained Cosimo de' Medici with a Latin disputation, the subject was 'an examination of the experimental philosophy and a condemnation of the Copernican system'. Newton can hardly have found this a congenial atmosphere.

Nevertheless, the interregnum left its mark on Cambridge. Isaac Barrow, who came up to Trinity in 1647, spoke of mathematics as then 'neglected and all but unknown, even on the outward surface by most'. A decade earlier Wallis and Seth Ward had both left Cambridge in order to learn mathematics from William Oughtred, a country parson. 'The study of mathematics', Wallis said in an oft-quoted phrase, 'was at that time more cultivated in London than in the universities.' Wallis did not hear of the new philosophy till years after he went down. Barrow claimed to have introduced it to Cambridge, and in the 1650s there was rapid progress there, as in Oxford. By 1654 or 1655 we find Barrow congratulating his university on escaping from traditional servility to scholasticism. 'You have very recently begun to cultivate the mathematical sciences'; and natural philosophy (anatomy, medicine, chemistry) had lately started to be studied seriously. Barrow was one of the strongest early influences on Newton.[40]

Above all Cambridge had become interested in the Cartesian philosophy, and was the scene of the most elaborate attempt to adapt traditional Puritan covenant theology to accommodate the findings of the new science. This was the school misleadingly known as the Cambridge Platonists, which derived from Joseph Mede, whom we shall meet again when we discuss Newton's interest in the Apocalypse. Its members included Ralph Cudworth, Puritan and Parliamentarian, who had links with Newton; like Newton, he was accused of being unsound on the

Trinity. The outstanding figure among the Cambridge Platonists when Newton came up to Trinity was Henry More, old boy of Newton's school at Grantham and tutor to two of his teachers here. More – later a Fellow of the Royal Society, like Cudworth – was strongly influenced by Descartes. But in 1659 More published *The Immortality of the Soul*, in which, he said, 'I have demonstrated with evidence no less than mathematical, that there are substances incorporeal.'[41] He hoped to become the Galileo of a new science of the spirit world. Newton was an intimate associate of More's, became an adherent of the atomic philosophy in his undergraduate days, and was influenced by Descartes. But in the sixties More came to reject the Cartesian mechanical philosophy because it led to atheism[42]; and Newton followed suit.

V

If we try to think ourselves back into the position of men living in this post-revolutionary world, we can see that there were various intellectual possibilities.

(1) The older generation of revolutionaries, who had seen their hopes of building God's kingdom betrayed, necessarily withdrew from politics. Most of them, like George Fox and the Quakers, decided that it had been a mistake to try to build God's kingdom on earth. They turned pacifist, their religion became a religion of personal morality, not of social reform. They accepted the position of minority sects, asking only for freedom from persecution. Bunyan, writing in jail, saw his pilgrim oppressed by the burden of sin, and concerned only to get rid of it; even wife and children are secondary to that consideration. The toughest of all the revolutionaries, Milton, still wrestled with God and history to justify God's ways to men. He completed *Paradise Lost* in 1665, published it in 1667; even he looked for 'a Paradise within thee, happier far'.

(2) The more intellectual among the returned royalists, their high hopes equally disappointed, found consolation in a cynical and mocking materialist atheism, which was probably only skin deep. Many, like Rochester, abandoned it when they believed they were on their deathbeds. But at court, and among the court dramatists, sceptical Hobbism was fashionable, if only

to *épater* the bourgeois and the Puritans. 'There is nothing' wrote Samuel Butler, whose *Hudibras* was a best seller in 1662–3, 'that can prevail more to persuade a man to be an atheist as to see such unreasonable beasts pretend to religion.'[43] His reference was probably to mechanic preachers.

Oldham in 1682 wrote:

> 'There are, who disavow all Providence
> And think the world is only steered by chance;
> Make God at best an idle looker-on,
> A lazy monarch lolling on his throne.'[44]

(3) Others among the returned royalists found that their authoritarian leanings could best be expressed by a return to Catholicism. Laudianism was dead in Restoration England, despite the apparent importance of some former Laudians in 1660. The Revolution had made impossible any revival of the independent economic or political power of either church or crown. Henceforth both were subject to the ruling class in Parliament. Charles II and James II had to look for support from Catholic and absolutist France – or, still more desperately, from papist Ireland. Many men of authoritarian temperament were impressed by the achievements, military and cultural, of Louis XIV's France. Some ultimately were converted to Catholicism, like the former Trinity undergraduate Dryden; others, like Archbishop Sheldon, had abandoned the traditional Anglican doctrine that the Pope was Antichrist. Such men were in a dilemma in Restoration England, since most Englishmen regarded France as the national enemy. After 1688 this dilemma could be resolved by rallying to the protestant William and Mary. But there was a time earlier when Catholicism was both intellectually and politically attractive, to the horror of traditional protestant patriots. It was in this intellectual climate that Nell Gwyn claimed that, if she was a whore, at least she was a protestant whore – unlike her French rival, the Duchess of Portsmouth. Newton would have applauded the theological part of her claim.

(4) The main group of middle-of-the-road Parliamentarians adhered to a lay, secularized Puritanism. They accepted restored episcopacy in the Church, purged of Laudianism. They had no difficulty in joining hands with moderate and patriotic ex-

Cavaliers. Both were enemies of enthusiasm (remembering the mechanic preachers) and of Hobbist atheism; but they were even more opposed to the much more real danger of popery. Atheism had no respectable support; it was a fashion, a whim. It was perhaps more important as a charge to hurl at the Royal Society and the scientists than in itself; and even here Henry Stubbe thought it necessary to accuse the Society of opening the door to popery as well as to atheism.[45]

Newton was of the post-revolutionary generation, and so had not known the former enthusiasm and present guilt of the revolutionaries. His Puritan upbringing ensured that by and large he shared the outlook of my last group – Puritans with the temperature reduced.

Caution was a natural result of the shock of the Restoration. Pepys was afraid someone might remember that after Charles I's execution in 1649 he had said that the right text to preach from would be 'The memory of the wicked shall rot.'[46] Men like Dryden, Waller, Cudworth, Henry More, no less than scientists like Wilkins, Wallis, Seth Ward, Goddard and Petty, had complied with the revolutionary régimes far enough to be worried after 1660. Anyone with Puritan sympathies plus a reasonable desire to get on in the world would learn in the early sixties not to talk too much. Newton did want to get on, and he was cautious; yet there were limits beyond which he would not compromise. He refused to be ordained, and I think we must reasonably refer back to this period the very strong anti-papist feelings which he always showed. On principle he was very tolerant, but he would never extend toleration to papists or atheists – any more than Milton or Locke would.

This is something which Newton's liberal biographers have found rather shocking and have tended to underestimate. I have already stressed the patriotic reasons for opposing popery. In view of the crypto-popery in high places under Charles and James II, Newton's attitude was also anti-court. In one of his manuscripts he declared that idolatry (i.e. popery) was even more dangerous than atheism 'because apt by the authority of kings and under very specious pretences to insinuate itself into mankind'. He added, prudently, that he referred to pre-Christian kings who enjoined ancestor worship, but the application to Charles and James was clear enough.[47] 'Was it the interest

of the people to cheat themselves into slavery . . . or was it not
rather the business of the court to do it?' Newton asked in a
passage about Assyria which Professor Manuel very properly
relates to the conflict with James II.[48]

I should like to emphasize Newton's behaviour in 1687, when
in his first overt political action he led the anti-papal party in
Cambridge in opposition to James II's measures, at a time when
such action needed a great deal of courage. It is in this light too
I think that we should see his acceptance of public service after
1688. It need not have resulted merely from political or social
ambition. Perhaps Newton really did think something important
was at stake in the wars of the 1690s. If England had been
defeated, Catholicism and absolutism might have triumphed on
a world scale. Newton believed that the Pope was Antichrist,
for which he had sound Anglican backing; and all the best
interpreters of the biblical prophecies agreed that the 1690s
would be a climacteric decade: I return to this later. The Mint
was not just a reward – or only in the sense that the reward of
service is more service. We should think of Newton in the same
terms as of Milton, sacrificing his eyes in the service of the
English republic, or of Locke, going into exile with Shaftesbury
– and also taking office after 1688; or of the gentle John Ray,
who like Newton seldom referred to politics, which makes his
paean on 1688 all the more noteworthy: 'the yoke of slavery
has been broken . . . If only God grants us peace, we can rely
upon prosperity and real age of gold.'[49] In 1714 Newton tried
to get an act of Parliament passed declaring that Rome was a
false church.[50] It must have been with considerable pleasure
that in 1717 he used – to support a telescope – a maypole which
had just been taken down from the Strand. For its erection in
1661 had been a symbol of the victory of those 'popish elements'
in church and state whose final defeat in 1714–15 must have
delighted Newton.

VI

Nor was anti-popery irrelevant to Newton's science. Sir Isaac
congratulated himself on having been born an Englishman, not
subject to the Inquisition like Galileo, nor compelled to publish
abroad and accommodate his philosophy to papal dogma like

Descartes.[51] Descartes's writings were still on the Index of Prohibited Books, together with Copernicus's treatise. Newton's own dislike of mysteries and superstition is in the protestant as well as the scientific tradition. And it also relates to his anti-Trinitarianism. In his *Quaeries regarding the word ὁμοῶσιος* his object was just as much to draw attention to papal corruptions as to argue a positive case. Anti-Trinitarianism seemed to Newton the logical consequence of protestantism. He referred to Luther, Bullinger, Grotius and others when discussing papal corruptions of Scripture. But like so many others of protestant-ism's logical consequences, this one had been drawn mainly by the most radical and socially subversive lower-class sects.[52] In England from 1583 to 1612 a number of anti-Trinitarians were burnt, including (1589) Francis Ket, grandson of the leader of the Norfolk rebels in 1549 and Christopher Marlowe's friend; and in 1612 Edward Wightman and Bartholomew Legate, the last Englishmen burnt for religious heresy.

Anti-Trinitarianism seems to have been endemic in England, despite this persecution. One of the abortive Laudian canons of 1640 was directed against its prevalence among the 'younger or unsettled sort of people', and undergraduates were forbidden to own or read Socinian books. Like so many other heresies, anti-Trinitarianism flourished during the interregnum. In 1644 there was a Unitarian group in Coleman Street, that nest of heretics. In 1652 the first English translation of the Racovian Catechism was published; next year a life of Socinus appeared in English translation.[53] The most notorious anti-Trinitarian was John Bidle, son of a Gloucestershire tailor, who was in prison more often than not from 1645 onwards, and was the cause of a storm in the Parliament of 1654–5. Bidle was saved from savage punishment only by Cromwell's sending him, quite illegally, to the Scilly Isles. Released in 1658, he was arrested again after the Restoration and in 1662 died in prison at the age of forty-six.[54]

One reason for the virulent persecution was the notorious fact that denial of the divinity of Christ had often been associated with social heresies. At the trial of Servetus in 1553 the subversive consequences of his heresy were strongly emphasized. The doctrines of Socinianism, thought an Oxford don in 1636, 'are repugnant to our state and government'; he referred specifically to the pacifism and anarchism of its adherents.[55] 'The fear of Socinianism', wrote Sir John Suckling in 1641, 'renders every man that offers to give an account of religion by reason, suspected to have none at all.'[56] In 1651 John Pordage was accused both of anti-Trinitarianism and of saying there would soon be no government in England; the saints would take over the property of the wicked. Pordage may have had connections with William Everard the Digger.[57] Socinus was a Mortalist, Mede warned Hartlib; the chief English Mortalist was the Leveller leader, Richard Overton.[58]

Conservatives were alarmed by the spread of anti-Trinitarianism. Bishop Joseph Hall in 1648 thought that Socinians should be exempted from the toleration he was prepared to extend to all other Christians (now that he was no longer in a position to do so). Twelve years later the London Baptists were equally intolerant of Socinianism.[59] Nevertheless, anti-Trinitarians continued to exist, if only in small groups. But they were outlaws, specifically excluded from such toleration as was granted in 1689; in 1698 those who wrote or spoke against the Trinity were disabled from any office or employment. A Unitarian was executed in 1697, another imprisoned in 1703. In 1711 Newton's friend Whiston was expelled from Cambridge for Arianism. There was every reason for not proclaiming anti-Trinitarian sentiments. Milton and Locke shared Newton's caution in this respect.

VII

Newton's theology thus had radical associations. So had his studies of the Hebrew prophecies. Thanks to Professor Manuel among others, it is now recognized that this was a serious scholarly subject, occupying the best minds of the sixteenth and seventeenth centuries. Once grant, indeed, that the whole of the Bible is an inspired book and to be taken literally, it is difficult to see how a Christian could fail to be interested in trying to date the end of the world and the last judgment. Servetus had expected the end of the world to come soon. An official declaration of Elizabeth's government in 1589 spoke of 'this declining age of the world'.[60] Leading British mathematicians, from Napier through Oughtred to Newton, worked on he problem. Napier's *Plaine Discovery of the Whole Revelation of St. John* ran to twenty-one editions between 1593 and 1700.

The quest received especial stimulus and a new twist from the revolution of the 1640s: eighty tracts are said to have been published on the subject by 1649. 'The Second Coming is each day and hour to be expected', said one published in 1647.[61] 'Though men be of divers minds as to the precise time,' claimed another of 1653, 'yet all concur in the nighness and swiftness of its coming upon us.'[62] The *raison d'etre* of the sect of Muggletonians, the last witnesses, was that the end of the world was at hand. And many excited radicals thought it their duty to expedite the Second Coming of Christ by political action. 'Men variously impoverished by the long troubles,' observed the mathematician John Pell, 'full of discontents and tried by long expectation of amendment, must needs have great propensions to hearken to those that proclaim times of refreshing – a golden age – at hand.'[63] There were two not very significant military risings in London, in 1657 and 1661. Militant Fifth Monarchists were an embarrassment to the scholarly interpreters of the prophecies, just as plebeian atheists were an embarrassment to mechanic philosophers; but the two activities were quite distinct in each case.

In England the best known scholarly interpreters were Thomas Brightman and Joseph Mede. Brightman, a supporter of the Presbyterian discipline, published his *Revelation of St. John Illustrated* in 1615; it was in its fourth English edition by 1644. He thought that the saints' reign of a thousand years had begun in 1300, that the Reformation had been a great turning point, and that now 'truth doth get ground and strengthens every day more.'[64] The abomination would be set up in 1650, and the year 1695 should see the utter destruction of Turkish power by the conversion of the Jews. 'Then shall be indeed that golden age.'[65]

Mede was a botanist, an anatomist, a mathematician and an astronomer, as well as a precursor of the Cambridge Platonists. He regarded his mathematical studies as a preparation for divinity.[66] He too saw the years since about 1300 as a continuous upward movement whose phases were (1) the Albigensian and Waldensian heresies; (2) the Lutheran Reformation; (3) the reign of Elizabeth; (4) the Thirty Years' War; (5) would see the destruction of Rome – the Pope being of course Antichrist; (6) the destruction of the Turkish Empire and the conversion of the Jews; (7) the final judgement and the millennium.[67] Mede was a Fellow of Christ's College, Cambridge, the college of the great Puritan William Perkins. At the time of his election (1602, the year of 'our Mr Perkins's' death) Mede was 'thought to look too much to Geneva', and he was wary of publishing in the Laudian thirties; but he seems to have been a middle-of-the-road man.[68] In 1642 Mede's *Key of the Revelation* was published in English translation by order of the Long Parliament. The translator was Richard More, himself an MP and a Puritan writer, and the official character of the publication was enhanced by the inclusion of a preface by William Twisse, the Presbyterian minister who was Prolocutor of Parliament's Assembly of Divines gathered at Westminster, and who was so much of a Parliamentarian that in 1661 his remains were dug up from Westminster Abbey by royal command and thrown with others into a common pit. In 1635 William Twisse had said in a letter to his friend Mede 'This old world of ours is almost at an end.'[69] In his Preface Twisse, in Baconian vein, observed that the opening of the world by navigation and commerce met at one and the same time with an increase of scientific and biblical knowledge.

So though the Long Parliament encouraged this belief for its own propagandist purposes, perfectly sane and respectable scholars were taking the prophecies very seriously, and were concluding that they would soon be fulfilled. Milton spoke of Christ as 'shortly-expected king'; Henry More thought the ruin of Antichrist was near.[70] In 1651 a scholarly friend of Brian Duppa, future bishop, expected the end of the world within a year;[71] in 1655 the great mathematician William Oughtred, a royalist, had 'strong apprehensions of some extraordinary event to happen the following year, from the calculation of coincidence with the diluvian period'. Perhaps Jesus Christ would appear to judge the world.[72]

On dating testimony converged. Napier was believed to have predicted 1639 as the year of the destruction of the enemies of the church[73] – a prophecy which must have been noted when episcopacy was overthrown in his native Scotland in that year. Vavasor Powell thought '1650 . . . is to be the saints' year of ubilee.'[74] In Sweden and Germany the downfall of the Beast was widely expected in 1654 or 1655.[75] Not only Brightman and Mede had foretold great events for the 1650s; so too had Christopher Columbus, George Wither, Samuel Hartlib, Sir Henry Vane and Lady Eleanor Davies (though this volatile lady had predicted catastrophe for many earlier dates).[76]

Once the 1650s had passed, the next crucial period appeared likely to be the nineties. Brightman and Mede had both plumped for them. So did Nicholas of Cusa, Napier, Alsted, John Archer, William Lilly, Hanserd Knollys, Thomas Goodwin, Thomas Beverly the Behmenist and John Mason.[77] The 1690s saw Newton in the service of an English state now resolutely anti-popish. The French Huguenot Jurieu thought that the destruction of Antichrist would occur between 1710 and 1715, following the defeat and protestantization of France.[78] Mede and Whiston expected the world to end in 1715.

It is thus not so odd as it used to be thought that Newton's theological manuscripts are as bulky as his mathematical and scientific writings. Perry Miller was perhaps a little bold to conclude positively that, from about 1693, Newton wanted to find out exactly how close he was to the end of the world.[79] Newton held, cautiously, that the prophecies would not be fully understood 'before the last age of the world'. But 'amongst the interpreters of the last age', amongst whom he included Mede, there is scarce one of note who hath not made some discovery worth knowing.' 'The great successes of late interpreters' suggested to Newton that 'the last age, the age of opening these things', is 'now approaching'; that 'God is about opening these mysteries'. This gave him 'more encouragement than ever to look into' them.[80] The point to emphasize is that this was an area of investigation which had traditionally attracted mathematical chronologists; Newton would have been in good company if he wished to throw light on the end of the world as well as on its beginning. And a number of serious scholars whom Newton respected, including Mede, had thought that great events might begin in the nineties. But again it was a subject which had radical associations and overtones; caution was needed.

VIII

By 1665–6 the Restoration honeymoon, such as it was, was over
Charles II's genuine attempt to continue Cromwell's policy of
religious toleration had been defeated by Parliament. Between
1660 and 1662, 1,760 ministers were driven out of the church
The Conventicle Act of 1664 and the Five Mile Act of 1665
expelled them from the towns which were the main centres of
opposition. In 1665 England was involved in an aggressive
commercial war with the Dutch ('What matters this or that
reason? What we want is more of the trade the Dutch now have',
said the Duke of Albemarle, with soldierly frankness).[81] This
war was such a fiasco that men began to look back to the days
when Oliver Cromwell had led England to victory. The City
turned against Charles II as Dutch ships sailed up the Medway.
Even Dryden, even in 'Annus Mirabilis', said of the King

> 'He grieved the land he freed should be oppressed,
> And he less for it than usurpers do.'

(Dryden no doubt recalled his fulsome praise of Cromwell seven
years earlier, in 'Heroic Stanzas to the Glorious Memory of
Cromwell'.) Samuel Pepys, another former Cromwellian who
now looked back nostalgically, recorded in February 1666 that
his old patron the Earl of Sandwich feared there would be some
very great revolutions in the coming months. Pepys himself was
full of forebodings, and was getting money in against a foul day.[82]
Fifteen years earlier the famous William Lilly had quoted a
prophecy that 'in 1666 there will be no king here or pretending
to the crown of England.' The Plague in 1665 and the Great
Fire of London in 1666, together with the comets of 1664 and
1665, again made men think that the end of the world was at
hand. Lilly was in trouble for having predicted the Fire.[83]

In these troubled years 1665–6, Newton, away from it all, was
discovering the calculus, the nature of white light and universal
gravitation. He made another discovery when the Heralds
visited Lincolnshire in 1666: that whereas his father had never
claimed to be more than a yeoman, he, Isaac, was a gentleman.

I tread warily in discussing Newton's elusive personality.
There are some aspects of genius which it is futile to try to

explain. But if we recall that Shakespeare abandoned the theatre just as soon as he could afford to, and set himself up as a gentleman in his native Warwickshire, we shall perhaps be the less surprised by the young Newton's improvement on his illiterate father's social aspirations in 1666, or by Newton's apparent abandonment of science for more gentlemanly activities from the nineties.

By 1666, too, or soon afterwards, Newton had decided not to marry Miss Storey. Why? 'Her portion being not considerable,' Stukeley tells us, 'and he being a fellow of a college, it was incompatible with his fortunes to marry.'[84] The reasoning is ungallant and unromantic, but it makes sense. Marriage would either have necessitated ordination and taking a living (to which we know Newton's objections); or else would have condemned him to the kind of vagabond life, dependent on the charity of others, which a man like John Ray led for twenty years after 1660.

I feign no Freudian hypotheses. But the fact that Newton, a posthumous child, never had a father, is surely relevant. He saw little enough of his mother after he was two years old, living first with his grandmother and then with an apothecary at Grantham. Only for a couple of years between the ages of sixteen and eighteen did he live with his mother, now widowed for the second time. So the decision not to marry Miss Storey would seem finally to have cut love out of Newton's life. Newton's later complaisance to his niece's affair with Halifax, which so bothered nineteenth-century biographers, may have been simply due to his not noticing.

Newton's theology denied the sonship of Christ, and though the Father exists he is a *deus absconditus*, in no close personal relation with his creatures. He is the first cause of a universe lacking all secondary qualities, all warmth and light and colour. The eternal silence of those infinite spaces seems never to have frightened Newton. Professor Manuel comments on his history: 'Newton never wrote a history of men . . . The individuals mentioned in his histories . . . have no distinctive human qualities. . . . Nations are . . . neutral as astronomical bodies; they invade and they are in their turn conquered . . . An interest in man's creations for their own sake, the aesthetic and the sensuous, is totally absent in his writings.'[85]

It would be naïve to suppose that these things would have been different if Newton had married Miss Storey. But the decision not to, apparently so easily taken and accepted, on prudential economic grounds, fits in with all we know of Newton's personality – his careful and minute keeping of accounts from boyhood until he became a very rich man indeed. Fontenelle in his *Eloge* rightly singled out Newton's frugality and carefulness for very special mention.[86]

This leads on to consideration of Newton's caution. Again a little history dispels some of the legends that have grown up around it. Many men – like Pepys – had reason to be cautious in the Restoration period. Newton's reluctance to publish, moreover, was no more than was expected of someone who had aspirations to be thought a gentleman. The part played by Halley in getting the *Principia* published repeats almost verbatim Ent's description of his role in persuading Harvey to allow his *De Generatione Animalium* to be printed in 1651. One may suspect that both accounts are highly stylized, remembering how many seventeenth-century poets claimed to publish only under great pressure or after alleged attempts to pirate their poems. There were parallels among the scientists. Ralph Bathurst, physician, FRS, and President of Trinity College, Oxford, had a wife who 'scorns that he should be in print'.[87] Francis Willughby died reluctant to publish his *Ornithology*, which Ray issued posthumously.[88]

And of course in Newton's case there were very special reasons for caution. His anti-Trinitarian writings would have been dangerous to publish. For the same reason Milton, not normally averse to seeing himself in print, held back the *De Doctrina Christiana;* and Locke showed a similar reticence. Hobbes thought the bishops would like to burn him; Waller dared not praise Hobbes publicly. After 1688 Newton did once consider publishing his *Historical Account of Two Notable Corruptions of Scripture,* anonymously, in French, and on the continent; but he thought better even of that. His theological heresies had other consequences. Newton was firm enough in his convictions to refuse to be ordained; but not to risk leaving Cambridge. In 1675 the Royal Society induced Charles II to issue letters patent authorizing Newton to retain his fellowship although not a clergyman. By accepting this quite exceptional use of the dispensing power Newton gave hostages to fortune. Any scandal attaching to his name would certainly be made the occasion for drawing attention to his anomalous position, and might call the retention of his fellowship in question. This did not prevent Newton taking serious political risks in 1687, and all credit to him; but on that occasion his deepest convictions were stirred. On any lesser issue he would be likely to play safe. This, combined with a natural furtiveness of temperament, seems an entirely adequate explanation of his early reluctance to publish. By 1694 he was uninhibitedly discussing with David Gregory a whole range of projects for mathematical publications.[89]

IX

Many of Newton's attitudes can, I suggest, be related to the post-Restoration desire for order, an order which should be as uncomplicated as possible. Puritanism and Baconian science had for many years been preparing for this ordered simplicity which Newton triumphantly achieved in the *Principia*, where the watchmaker God, 'very well skilled in mechanics and geometry', presided over an abstract mathematical universe.[90] Similarly, Newton thought, there is a natural religion, 'one law for all nations, dictated . . . to all mankind by the light of reason'.[91] The same simplification informs Newton's anti-Trinitarianism, with its denial of the mystery of the Incarnation. Newton thought he found in the writings of Joseph Mede a single key which would likewise dispel the apparent mystery of the biblical prophecies. 'The prophets', Newton believed, 'wrote in a language as certain and definite in its significance as any vulgar language.' The heavens, the sun and moon, signify kings and rulers; the earth signifies inferior people; hades or hell 'the lowest and most miserable of the people'.[92] ('In Newton's pragmatization of myth and reduction of prophecy to plain history', said Professor Manuel, we can see 'a reflection of the new realities of middle-class society' – the society which triumphed in England after the revolution of the mid-century.)[93] Similarly Mr Forbes and Mr Sherwood Taylor have suggested that in Newton's alchemical experiments he may have hoped to find a key to the presumed common language of the alchemical writings, and a synthesis of the micro-structure of matter which would have been the counterpart to his celestial and terrestrial mechanics.[94] In his concern with spelling reform, which goes back to his pre-Cambridge days, Newton wanted to find a 'real character' which should replace Latin and be truly international because as abstract as mathematics. This was an interest he shared with Wallis, Evelyn, Wilkins and many other Fellows of the Royal Society.[95] The quest for a simplified order in all intellectual spheres was very topical.

It is not unreasonable to compare Hobbes's simplification of the universe to matter and motion, of political science to individuals accepting sovereign power in the interests of order; or the literary classicism which was invented by the defeated royalists during the interregnum, yearning for decorum and order, and which became fashionable in the Restoration years of French influence, with the order-loving Dryden as its high priest.[96]

And yet – and yet. As has often been pointed out, Newton was not wholly a Newtonian. Though he stripped the universe of secondary qualities, his experiments with colours enabled eighteenth-century landscape painters and poets to paint far more brightly than before. Contradictions lurk in the heart of his universe. In his desire to refute the Cartesian mechanism, Newton, like Pascal, postulated an irrational God behind the irrational force of gravity, a *deus absconditus* but very real. 'A continual miracle is needed to prevent the sun and the fixed stars from rushing together through gravity.'[97] 'A Being eternal, infinite, all-wise and most perfect, *without dominion*, is not God but only Nature', Newton wrote.[98] Newton's God is as arbitrary as Hobbes's sovereign. Newton brought back into physics the notion of 'attraction' which Boyle had devoted so much energy to expelling.[99] (It is ironical that the lectures in which Bentley used Newton's new 'occult qualities' to confute atheism should have been endowed by Boyle; and not untypical of the difficulties in which seventeenth-century scientists found themselves in their determination to have both God and science.)

'Those things which men understand by improper and contradictious phrases', Newton assured the too impetuous Dr Bentley, 'may be sometimes really in nature without any contradiction at all.'[100] Newton accepted, dogmatically, experimental science and biblical revelation as equally self-validating. 'Religion and philosophy are to be preserved distinct. We are not to introduce divine revelations into philosophy, nor philosophical opinions into religion.'[101] Science deals with second causes. The experimental method itself assumes that there is an intelligible order in nature which is law-abiding, 'simple and always consonant to itself'.[102] The first cause is a matter of revelation. Perhaps one day, when the Baconian programme has been completed, science and revelation can be linked. Newton never doubted that there was an ultimate mechanical cause of gravitation, though he could not discover it experimentally. But he had realized that this was a far longer-term programme than Bacon had ever dreamed. 'The great ocean of truth lay all undiscovered' before the 'boy playing on the seashore, . . . now and then finding a smoother pebble or a prettier shell than ordinary.'[103] Newton may have worried lest the ocean itself might be annihilated before it was fully explored; but in fact the hope of linking science and revelation was abandoned before the explorers were out of sight of land.

13
Conclusion

All continuity of history means is after all perpetual change.

> William Morris, Address to the Twelfth Annual Meeting
> of the Society for the Protection of Ancient Buildings,
> quoted by E. P. Thompson, *William Morris: Romantic to
> Revolutionary* (1955), p. 277.

I

This book has been about change and continuity. We started with witches and cunning men in the dark corners of England: we end with Sir Isaac Newton, the high priest of modern science. Change then, clearly enough: but also continuity, more than historians used to recognize. For Newton was also an alchemist, a magus, a student of biblical prophecy. Similarly in our study of changing concepts of reason we started with Hooker (Aquinas in sixteenth-century dress) and we ended with John Locke, the high priest of modern utilitarian ethics and politics. But again qualifications must be made: Dr Locke believed that a patient could be cured of pain in the kidneys by burying her urine in a stone jug; he too made computations from Daniel with a view to dating the end of the world.[1] Newton and Locke are not our intellectual contemporaries, despite first appearances. They belong firmly in the seventeenth century.

Historians have become fully conscious of facts like these only fairly recently, after a period in which 'progress' was seen as a linear development, heralded by great men 'in advance of their time'. Yet the historian in recognizing the existence of continuity is not, or should not be, denying the fact of change: he should rather emphasize its dialectical character. For change, sharp and sudden change, did in fact occur. Newton and Locke

278

did open up a new intellectual world, however much their own thinking remained rooted in the past; the conquest of the North and West of England by the New Model Army was a decisive breach with the past, even though elements in those dark corners welcomed the conquerors when they came. The English Revolution of the seventeenth century is not less a revolution because it was not made by conscious revolutionaries.

This needs saying, because even so competent a historian as Perez Zagorin seems to think that since the word 'revolution' did not have its modern meaning in the seventeenth century, we should not use it to describe what happened in England at the crisis of that century.[2] But apples dropped to the ground before Newton formulated the law of gravity: revolutions happen without men consciously willing them. I cannot accept the logic of a historian who recently declared: 'We cannot usefully indulge in grand generalizations about the causes of the Civil War when a detailed examination of the decade or so before the rebellions reveals how little men thought of the consequences of their actions.'[3] This is rather like arguing that a plane cannot have crashed because we know that neither the pilot nor any of his passengers wanted it to. The idea of consciously making a revolution arrives late in human history, is perhaps not fully formulated until *The Communist Manifesto*. But it would be unwise to argue that there were no revolutions before 1848.

In this, as in so many other ways, we have perhaps been put on the wrong track by the unfortunate phrase 'the Puritan Revolution'. For this implied, or could appear to imply, a revolution made by Puritans in order to establish a Puritan society. It assumes an element of conscious will among an identifiable group of those who made the revolution. Most historians reject the Puritan Revolution these days, and interpret the events of 1640–60 in more sociological terms. There is no reason why such interpretations need make any assumptions about purpose. The object indeed of a sociological interpretation should be to account for events which cannot be explained in terms of human intentions. In particular the Marxist conception of a bourgeois revolution, which I find the most helpful model for understanding the English Revolution, does not mean a revolution made by the bourgeoisie. I quote Isaac Deutscher's remarks on bourgeois revolution:

'The traditional view, widely accepted by Marxists and anti-Marxists alike, is that in such revolutions, in Western Europe, the bourgeoisie played the leading part, stood at the head of the insurgent people, and seized power . . . It seems to me that this conception, to whatever authorities it may be attributed, is schematic and historically unreal . . . Capitalist entrepreneurs, merchants and bankers were not conspicuous among the leaders of the Puritans or the commanders of the Ironsides, in the Jacobin Club or at the head of the crowds that stormed the Bastille or invaded the Tuileries. Nor did they seize the reins of government during the revolution, or for a long time afterwards, either in England or in France . . . Yet the bourgeois character of these revolutions will not appear at all mythical if we approach them with a broader criterion and view their general impact on society. Their most substantial and enduring achievement was to sweep away the social and political institutions that had hindered the growth of bourgeois property and of the social relationships that went with it . . . Bourgeois revolution creates the conditions in which bourgeois property can flourish. In this, rather than in the particular alignments during the struggle, lies its *differentia specifica*.'[4]

The point was made – about Ireland – by Lenin in 1916. He wrote: 'Those who imagine that in one place an army will line up and say "We are for socialism", and in another place another army will say "We are for imperialism", and that this will be the social revolution' does not understand what revolution is. 'Whoever expects a "pure" social revolution will never live to see it.'[5] So far indeed were London Levellers and the rank and file of the New Model Army from fighting to make a world safe for capitalist farmers and merchants to make profits in that they protested loudly when they realized that such a world was in fact coming into existence. 'It is evident,' declared Overton, 'a change of our bondage is the utmost is intended us.' 'Great men in the City and Army have made you but the stairs by which they have mounted to honour, wealth and power,' added Walwyn. 'The only quarrel . . . is . . . whose slaves the people shall be.' Sexby told the Grandees that they would 'have had fewer under your command to have commanded' if the rank and file had been forewarned what the outcome would be.[6] Yet the overthrow of prerogative courts, of arbitrary taxation and imprisonment, the abolition of feudal tenures (but retaining insecurity of tenure for copyholders), the Navigation Act, the imperialist foreign policy of the 1650s, the opening up of the North and West to London trade and London ideas – none of these were accidents. For many years before 1645 the gentry had pressed for abolition of feudal tenures; merchants had advocated something like a Navigation Act for a generation before 1651. The idea of an aggressive colonial foreign policy was at least as old as Hakluyt. The attempt to limit the independence of the crown dominates the constitutional history of the reigns of the first two Stuarts. I have tried to show in chapter 1 the importance of the campaign to enlighten the dark corners. None of these separately caused the Revolution; but together they determined its shape. The Revolution was caused, ultimately, by economic developments which could not be absorbed within the old régime.

Those who benefited by these developments tried to absorb themselves. Rich merchants, just because they were rich, bought their way into the state machine, into monopolies, into customs farming: as the natural rulers of their communities they looked to the crown to protect them against the lower classes whom they exploited and excluded from political influence. They were loyal to the crown, through all the choppings and changings of Tudor religious policy, on principles which Hobbes was the first to enunciate: so long as the crown protected them. But only a privileged minority could thus identify with the old régime: those excluded from privileges which were by definition limited had less hesitation in appealing for support to the lower classes as the old régime proved less and less capable of protecting their interests by advancing the total wealth of the economy.[7] This I think is what Professor Tawney meant – if the phrase is correctly attributed to him – when he said: 'Bourgeois revolution? Of course it was a bourgeois revolution. The trouble is the bourgeoisie was on both sides.'

The Revolution came because more and more sections of the community felt dissatisfied with government performance in relation to possible opportunities. Among the propertied classes this dissatisfaction related especially to taxation: not so much to the amount levied, in impositions or Ship Money, as to the fact that the taxpayers were not consulted, so that taxation was not geared to policies of which they approved and for which they would have been prepared to pay. They paid, handsomely and voluntarily, after 1640 and again after 1688. The lower classes may not have been worse off in the 1630s than they had been throughout history – though this is arguable – but they were increasingly conscious of a contrast between what was and what might be. 'This is the bondage the poor complain of,' declared Winstanley, 'that they are kept poor by their brethren in a land where there is so much plenty for everyone, if covetousness and pride did not rule as king in one brother over another.'[8]

II

Here we come to what has been the main subject of this book – ideas. Revolutions are made by men and women, whether conscious or unconscious of what they are doing: shifts in ideas are therefore necessary if a revolution is to take place. In chapter 3 I suggested ways in which protestantism, the religion of the heart, made advocacy of social change easier, just as protestants by encouraging Bible-reading also created the public for Leveller pamphlets, though that was far from being their intention; just as protestant theologians by denouncing, often in crude materialist terms, the miracle of the mass, helped to create a mental climate more favourable to the rise of rational science.

Old ideas with new content – Christianity, reason – developed side by side with old institutions whose content was changing. One of the illusions against which English historians have to struggle especially hard – just because our Revolution was not made by conscious revolutionaries – is that institutions which retain the same name remain the same institutions – whether monarchy, Parliament, common law or universities. We know as soon as we reflect on it that this is not true: the monarchy of George I was manifestly very different from that of Henry VIII. But we have continually to remind ourselves of the consequences of change within continuity.

The fact that the same words can signify different things at different times should help us also to grasp that the same ideas can point to different conclusions for different classes at the same time. Many of the essays in this collection try to illustrate this class differential, as I have tried to illustrate it in some of my earlier writings ('The Norman Yoke' in *Puritanism and Revolution*, *Antichrist in Seventeenth-Century England*). Mr Laslett's vision of seventeenth-century England as a 'one-class society'[9] is a particularly extreme example of acceptance at its face value of the propaganda of a past ruling class. But all historians, always, by the nature of the surviving evidence, tend to find ruling-class views the easiest to recapture in any society: the viewpoint of the underdog has to be reconstructed painfully and piecemeal. Yet if we are to understand the past we must try to reconstruct it. The views of the radical critics of the universities did not prevail in the seventeenth century (though in many respects they have done since), the views of the radical critics of the medical profession have not yet prevailed and perhaps never should; hatred of wage-labour did not stop the onward march of capitalism, which in time has brought an improved living standard for all of us. But a trend of thought is not worth studying only if it is successful. The abysmal decline of Oxford and Cambridge in the eighteenth century encourages us at least to try to understand what their seventeenth-century critics were about; and only the most Pecksniffian Pangloss can think that the freeborn Englishmen of my chapter 10 are totally answered by global figures of an increased GNP. When we know more about Chinese medicine we may even feel a little less superior to the medical reformers.

All knowledge of the past should help to humanize us, in so far as it is knowledge about human beings and not about abstractions. Dismissing interregnum critics of the universities as 'the lunatic fringe', 'extremists', 'religious fanatics', deprives us of the experience of entering into the struggles of men and women trying to make their world a better place. Dismissing the opponents of wage-labour as lazy short-sighted enemies of progress blinds us to the loss which has accompanied the gain that industrialization has brought. But the human beings in this book are not only mechanic sectaries or obscure squatters in woodland and fen. They include Arise Evans, who started from the primitive society of early seventeenth-century Merionethshire and ultimately made himself at home in the sophisticated London world of journalism and the mechanical philosophy; they include Sir Isaac Newton, one of the greatest and best-documented of English intellectuals, who was also in danger of becoming an abstraction until historians started to take seriously the fact that he thought alchemy and biblical chronology as important as promulgating the laws of physics or managing the Mint. He too may help us to understand our own times better by understanding the past.

Some chapters in this book, especially in Parts III and IV, pursue a line of thought traced more connectedly in my *The World Turned Upside Down*: since capitalism, the protestant ethic, Newtonian physics, so long taken for granted by our civilization, are now at last coming under general and widespread criticism, it is worth going back to consider seriously and afresh the arguments of those who opposed them before they had won universal acceptance. The secret life and suppressed thoughts of the great Sir Isaac may supply their own comment on the public abstract figure of 'the founder of modern science' whom Blake hated so much. That is why history has to be rewritten in each generation: each new act in the human drama necessarily shifts our attitude towards the earlier acts. So there is a dialectic of continuity and change not only in the seventeenth century itself, but also in our awareness of the seventeenth century. We ourselves are shaped by the past; but from our vantage point in the present we are continually reshaping the past which shapes us.

Notes

PART I   CHANGING RELATIONSHIPS: LONDON AND THE OUTLYING
          REGIONS

Chapter 1   *Puritans and 'the Dark Corners of the Land'*

1   Originally published in two parts: (i) 'Puritans and "the Dark
     Corners of the Land" ', *T.R.H.S.*, 5th Series, XIII (1963);
     (ii) 'Propagating the Gospel', in *Historical Essays, 1600–1750,
     presented to David Ogg*, ed. H. E. Bell and R. L. Ollard (1963).

2   F. J. Fisher, 'The Development of the London Food Market,
     1540–1640', *Ec.H.R.*, V, no. 2 (1935), pp. 47–9.

3   T. C. Mendenhall, *The Shrewsbury Drapers and the Welsh Wool
     Trade in the Sixteenth and Seventeenth Centuries* (Oxford, 1953), pp.
     227–30; G. D. Ramsay, *The Wiltshire Woollen Industry in the
     Sixteenth and Seventeenth Centuries* (Oxford, 1943), pp. 107–8;
     H. Heaton, *The Yorkshire Woollen and Worsted Industries* (Oxford,
     1920), chapter V.

4   D. Williams, *A History of Modern Wales* (1950), p. 90.

5   *C.S.P.D., 1645–47*, p. 258; J. and T. W. Webb, *Memorials of
     the Civil War . . . in Herefordshire* (1879), I, pp. 203, 242–3;
     ii, p. 46.

6   *Reliquiae Baxterianae*, ed. M. Sylvester (1696), p. 89; cf. pp. 30,
     40–1.

7   E[dward] B[ush], *A Sermon preached at Pauls Crosse, 1571* (1576),
     Sig. f. iv, quoted by H. G. Owen, 'Tradition and Reform:
     Ecclesiastical Controversy in an Elizabethan London Parish',
     The Guildhall Miscellany, II, no. 2 (1961), p. 66.

8   G. Mattingly, *Catherine of Aragon* (1963), pp. 287–9.

9   G. Burnet, *The History of the Reformation . . .*, II (1825), p. 275.

10   J. O. W. Haweis, *Sketches of the Reformation and Elizabethan Age*
     (1844), pp. 84–102.

11   *Correspondence of Matthew Parker* (Parker Soc., 1853), p. 119.

12   *Ibid.*, p. 123.

13   *Visitation Acts and Injunctions of the Period of the Reformation*, ed.
     W. H. Frere and W.P. M. Kennedy (Alcuin Club Collections,

XVI), p. 261; J. Lynch, 'Philip II and the Papacy', *T.R.H.S.*, 5th Series, xi (1961), p. 35. For Bishop Sandys of Worcester's account of the unreliability of Wales in 1569, see J. Strype, *Annals of the Reformation . . .* I (ii) (Oxford, 1824), p. 328.

14 *C.S.P.D., 1566–79*, p. 65; R. Reid, 'The Rebellion of the Earls, 1569', *T.R.H.S.*, New series, XX (1906), pp. 183–4, 190. The archbishop of York in 1535 had estimated that there were not twelve preachers in the whole of his diocese: many benefices were so poor that no learned man would take them (ed. Sir H. Ellis, *Original Letters Illustrative of English History*, 3rd Series, II (1846), p. 338).

15 J. Strype, *The History of the Life and Acts of . . . Grindal . . .* (Oxford, 1821), p. 562. It was unfortunate for Grindal's case, but illuminating, that Halifax remained, throughout the period we are considering, a centre of religious radicalism, as it had earlier been a centre of Lollardy (A. G. Dickens, *Lollards and Protestants in the Diocese of York, 1509–58*, Oxford, 1959, pp. 247–8). It was later to produce a series of eminent scientists (my *Intellectual Origins of the English Revolution*, Oxford, 1965, pp. 37, 54, 266). The sympathy which Grindal showed for 'prophesyings', the attempt to train preaching ministers, probably sprang from his experience in the North. Those held at Halifax (and no doubt elsewhere) during his archbishopric helped to train a group of Puritans who had profound effects on the West Riding (R. L. Arundale, 'Edmund Grindal and the Northern Province', *Church Quarterly Rev.* CLX (1959), pp. 197–8). Nevertheless in 1578 Grindal's successor Sandys was still blaming the clergy of the diocese of York for their inability to instruct the people (W. P. M. Kennedy, *Parish Life under Queen Elizabeth* (1914), p. 36).

16 Kennedy, *op. cit.*, p. 36.

17 *C.S.P.D., 1547–80*, p. 180.

18 W. Gilpin, *The Life of Bernard Gilpin*, 2nd ed. (1753), pp. 172, 176; B. Gilpin, 'A Sermon preached in the Court at Greenwich, 1552', *ibid.*, p. 279.

19 E. Grindal, *The Remains* (Parker Soc., 1843), pp. 325–6; cf. J. Strype, *The History of the Life . . . of . . . Grindal*, p. 251.

20 *V.C.H., Cumberland*, II, pp. 69–70, 74–8, 90; *V.C.H., Durham*, II, pp. 35–6, 39.

21 Quoted in J. G. Miall, *Congregationalism in Yorkshire* (1868), p. 38.

22 W. Bradford, *History of Plymouth Plantation*, ed. C. Deane (Massachusetts Hist. Soc. Collections, 1856), pp. xvi–xvii; *C.S.P.D., 1598–1601*, p. 362; K. V. Thomas, *Religion and the*

Decline of Magic (1971), p. 165. Cf. *Elizabethan Journals*, ed. G. B. Harrison (New York, 1965), I, pp. 95–6, 112–15, for lack of religious education in the North in the 1590s.

23 J. Penry, *Three Treatises concerning Wales*, ed. D. Williams (Cardiff, 1960), pp. 29, 32–9, 62; cf. Strype, *The Life . . . of . . . Whitgift* (Oxford, 1822), III, pp. 309–11. For the poverty of the Welsh clergy, see T. Richards, *A History of the Puritan Movement in Wales, 1639–53* (1920), chapter I, *passim*.

24 G. Williams, 'The Elizabethan Settlement of Religion in Wales and the Marches', *Journal Hist. Soc. of the Church in Wales*, II (1950), p. 68.

25 D. R. Thomas, *The Life and Work of Bishop Davies and William Salesbury* (Oswestry, 1902), p. 27; G. Williams, 'Richard Davies, Bishop of St David's, 1561–81', *Trans. Hon. Soc. Cymmrodorion*, 1948, pp. 157–8.

26 Kennedy, *op. cit.*, p. 36; cf. Kennedy, *Elizabethan Episcopal Administration* (Alcuin Club Collections, XXV, 1924), I, pp. cxci–cci.

27 Quoted by Penry Williams, 'The Welsh Borderland under Queen Elizabeth', *Welsh Hist. Rev.*, I, no. 1 (1960), p. 29.

28 Quoted by F. Jones, 'An Approach to Welsh Genealogy', *Trans. Hon. Soc. Cymmrodorion*, 1948, p. 390; cf. J. Waddington, *John Penry* (1854), p. 13.

29 Strype, *The History of the Life and Acts of . . . Grindal . . .*, p. 401. For much similar information about vice in Wales, to which the mountain air was thought to contribute, see Penry Williams, *The Council in the Marches of Wales under Elizabeth I* (Cardiff, 1958), chapter IV.

30 G. Gruffydd, 'Bishop Francis Godwin's Injunctions for the Diocese of Llandaff, 1603', *Journal Hist. Soc. of the Church in Wales*, IV (1954), p. 16.

31 *Salisbury MSS* (Hist. MSS Comm.), XI, p. 460.

32 A. H. Dodd, *A History of Wrexham* (Wrexham, 1957), pp. 51–2.

33 *Rowland Vaughan, His Booke*, ed. Ellen B. Wood (1897), pp. 40, 43–4.

34 *Archaeologia Cambrensis*, 3rd Series, IX (1863), pp. 283–5.

35 Dodd, 'Wales in the Parliaments of Charles I', *Trans. Hon. Soc. Cymmrodorion*, 1945, p. 29; cf. E. A. Barnard, 'Lewis Bayly, Bishop of Bangor, and Thomas Bayly, his son', *ibid.*, 1928–9, p. 122.

36 Dodd, *Studies in Stuart Wales* (Cardiff, 1952), p. 53; cf. J. Lewis, *The Parliament Explained to Wales, 1646* (reprint, Cardiff, 1907), p. 30.

37 W. Laud, *Works* (Oxford, 1847–60), V, pp. 335, 359. The archbishop personally confirmed the report for St David's, which he had briefly visited during his five years' tenure of that see.

38 *Portland MSS* (Hist. MSS Comm.), III, p. 71.

39 T. Rees, *History of Protestant Nonconformity in Wales*, 2nd ed. (1883), p. 68. See p. 28 above.

40 T. Richards, *History of the Puritan Movement in Wales . . .* (1920), pp. 15, 51.

41 *Reliquiae Baxterianæ*, pp. 2, 40. It was only after the Civil War, Baxter tells us, that preachers ceased to be despised and reviled (*ibid.*, p. 86).

42 *Portland MSS* (Hist. MSS Comm.), III, p. 79.

43 In *Letters of the Lady Brilliana Harley*, ed. T. T. Lewis (Camden Soc., 1854), pp. 227–8. The same petition opposed the import of Spanish wool, in the interest of Herefordshire wool-growers.

44 S. Clarke, *The Lives of Sundry Eminent Persons* (1683), p. 4.

45 *The Fortescue Papers*, ed. S. R. Gardiner (Camden Soc., 1871), pp. 180–3. John Packer, whom the bishop was thanking for watering the soil, was also providing preaching in the diocese of Coventry and Lichfield.

46 Kennedy, *Parish Life under Queen Elizabeth*, p. 37.

47 I owe all these points to the generosity of Mr John Addy.

48 J. Aubrey, *Remaines of Judaisme and Gentilisme* (1881), pp. 36, 159, 247; Arise Evans, *An Eccho to the Voice from Heaven* (?1653), pp. 9, 16, 34–5. See chapter 2 below.

49 B. Jonson, *Plays* (Everyman ed.), II, pp. 649–50, 265.

50 Quoted in D. Campbell, *The Puritan in Holland, England and America* (1892), II, p. 35. I have not been able to trace Campbell's reference to Strype.

51 *C.S.P., Rome, 1558–71*, p. 68.

52 V. J. K. Brook, *A Life of Archbishop Parker* (Oxford, 1962), pp. 210–12; *V.C.H., Cumberland*, II, p. 82; *V.C.H., Durham*, II, p. 39.

53 J. A. Froude, *English Seamen in the Sixteenth Century* (1901), p. 148; cf. *C.S.P., Rome, 1558–71*, p. 68.

54 A. J. Loomie, *The Spanish Elizabethans* (New York, 1963), p. 203.

55 A. H. Dodd, 'North Wales in the Essex Revolt of 1601', *E.H.R.*, LIX (1944), pp. 354, 357; D. Mathew, *The Celtic Peoples and Renaissance Europe* (1933), chapter 12. Stanley had Welsh as well as northern connections. For Welsh participation in plots see also Loomie, *op. cit.*, pp. 83–92, 114–15, 191.

56 Dodd, *op. cit.*, pp. 357, 363, 369–70; 'The Spanish Treason, the Gunpowder Plot, and the Catholic Refugees', *E.H.R.*, LIII

(1938), pp. 629, 635; Mathew, *op. cit.*, chapters 18–19, 22. There were never more than a thousand popish recusants reported from Wales after 1605 (Dodd, *Studies in Stuart Wales*, p. 44). But we may doubt whether this is anything like the total of Catholic sympathizers. In Northumberland the number of recusants was said to be increasing in 1616 (*C.S.P.D., 1611–18*, p. 358).

57 *Salisbury MSS* (Hist. MSS Comm.), XVII, pp. 235, 258–9, 304–6, 360–1. I owe this reference and the information about the vicar to the kindness of Mr R. Mathias.

58 W. Bradshaw, *Humble Motives for Association to Maintain Religion Established* (1601), p. 35; R. C. Richardson, *Puritanism in north-west England* (Manchester University Press, 1972), p. 146.

59 H. Heaton, *Yorkshire Woollen and Worsted Industries*, pp. 183–4. For John Favour's ministry at Halifax (1593–1623) see W. K. Jordan, *The Charities of Rural England, 1480–1660* (1961), pp. 323–6.

60 *Yorkshire Archaeol. and Topographical Journal*, VII (1882), pp. 287–8.

61 There were, of course, dark corners outside the North, Wales and Cornwall (for which see *The Seconde Parte of a Register*, ed. A. Peel (Cambridge, 1915), II, pp. 174–6). In 1686 the bishop of Chichester said that no bishop had been seen in Rye in the century and a half since the Reformation until his visitation of that year (Agnes Strickland, *The Lives of the Seven Bishops* 1866, p. 127).

62 R. Hitchcock, *A Politic Plat* (1580), in E. Arber, *An English Garner* (1897), II, pp. 141, 153.

63 See my *Puritanism and Revolution* (1958), p. 234.

64 Z. Cawdrey, *A Discourse of Patronage* (1675), p. 45.

65 D. Williams, *A History of Modern Wales*, pp. 112–14.

66 John Addy, *The Archdeacon and Ecclesiastical Discipline in York-shire, 1598–1714* (St Anthony's Hall Papers, York, 1963), p. 13.

67 Penry, *Three Treatises*, p. 37.

68 R. Howell, *Newcastle upon Tyne and the Puritan Revolution* (Oxford, 1967), p. 80.

69 F. Peck, *Desiderata Curiosa* (1779), p. 151.

70 Penry, *Three Treatises*, p. 39. We must bear such facts in mind when we hear contemporaries or historians speak of 'over-production of graduates' at this time. As with the total population, the surplus was relative, not absolute. Given a different economic structure and government policy, it could have been absorbed.

71 A. F. Scott Pearson, *Thomas Cartwright and Elizabethan Puritan-*

ism, *1535–1603* (Cambridge, 1925), p. 234. I owe this reference to my former pupil, Mr A. J. V. Cheetham.

72　*C.S.P.D.*, *1638–9*, p. 434.

73　W. Vaughan, *The Spirit of Detraction* (1611), pp. 92–4; cf. pp. 106–10, 249; *V.C.H.*, *Cumberland*, ii, p. 89; *V.C.H.*, *Durham*, II, p. 35.

74　W. J. Kaye, 'An Ecclesiastical Survey of the Province and Diocese of York, 1603', *Yorkshire Archaeol. Journal*, XXXI (1934), pp. 421–2. But at this date there were proportionately more preachers in the province of York than in that of Canterbury. Bishop Davies of St David's complained that impropriations held clerical stipends down, and so preachers could be got only by pluralism (G. Williams, 'Richard Davies', p. 157). For impropriations in the North, see R. Sibbes, *Works* (Edinburgh, 1862–4), VII, p. 470, and my *Economic Problems of the Church* (Oxford, 1956), pp. 139–41.

75　Gruffydd, 'Bishop Francis Godwin's Injunctions', p. 16.

76　Peck, *Desiderata Curiosa*, p. 94; cf. Bishop Richard Davies's remark that the Queen's impropriations were the worst of all in his diocese (Thomas, *Bishop Davies and William Salesbury*, p. 28).

77　Parker, *Correspondence*, p. 222; V. J. K. Brook, *A Life of Archbishop Parker*, pp. 151–2.

78　E. Sanders, *A View of the State of Religion in the Diocese of St David's*, pp. 65–8. (I quote the 1949 reprint of this book, originally published in 1721.) For other impropriations held by members of the hierarchy in Wales, see Richards, *History of the Puritan Movement in Wales*, pp. 3–5.

79　Penry, *Three Treatises*, pp. 38–40, 155–6.

80　*Ibid.*, p. 65.

81　F. Peck, *Desiderata Curiosa*, p. 113.

82　I owe this information to the kindness of Mr John Addy.

83　Quoted in W. Addison, *Worthy Dr Fuller* (1951), p. 285; cf. T. Fuller, *Worthies* (1840), II, p. 520, and S. B. Babbage, *Puritanism and Richard Bancroft* (1962), p. 243: Bancroft on popery in Lancashire. Cf. P. Collinson, *The Elizabethan Puritan Movement* (1967), especially pp. 406–7, 498.

84　E. Axon, 'The King's Preachers in Lancashire, 1599–1845', *Trans. Lancashire and Cheshire Antiq. Soc.*, LVI, pp. 68–103; R. Halley, *Lancashire: its Puritanism and Nonconformity* (Manchester, 1869), I, pp. 65–6. Cf. W. Harrison, King's Preacher, *The Difference of Hearers* (1614), *passim*. It would be interesting to know more about the third preacher, who appears to have anticipated the antinomianism of some of the itinerant ministers of the interregnum. See pp. 37–41 above.

85 C. Burges, *A Sermon preached to the Hon. House of Commons* (1641), p. 78.

86 F. Bacon, *Works*, ed. J. Spedding (1868–74), X, p. 124; XI, p. 254. Bacon proposed that 'reading ministers, if they have rich benefices', should be charged to finance the scheme, which would be enough to damn it in the bishops' eyes.

87 R. G. Usher, *The Reconstruction of the English Church* (New York, 1910), II, pp. 352–3; Strype, *Life of Whitgift*, III, p. 405; *V.C.H.*, *Lancashire*, II, p. 59. Mr Marchant explains the lenient treatment which Puritan ministers received in the diocese of York, down to the late 1620s, by their usefulness as preachers (R. A. Marchant, *The Puritans and the Church Courts in the Diocese of York, 1560–1642* 1960, pp. 24, 140–4, 183). Here again the Laudians seemed to be the innovators.

88 M. H. Curtis, 'The Hampton Court Conference and its aftermath', *History*, XLVI (1961), pp. 12, 15; Usher, *op. cit.*, I, p. 331; Dodd, *Studies in Stuart Wales*, p. 41.

89 Penry, *Three Treatises*, pp. 40–1, 56.

90 Dodd, *Studies in Stuart Wales*, p. 62. This was still a small proportion of the total population. There was not one Bible in 500 families, said Vavasor Powell in 1646; scarce one among twenty families, said the translator of Perkins, more cautiously, three years later (Richards, *History of the Puritan Movement in Wales*, p. 11).

91 Dodd, *loc. cit.* Heylyn also promoted the publication of a Welsh dictionary. Middleton's brother had published in 1603 the first Welsh metrical version of the Psalms (J. Ballinger, *The Bible in Wales* (1906), p. 24).

92 The phrase is John Shaw's (*Yorkshire Diaries and Autobiographies in the 17th and 18th Centuries* (Surtees Soc., 1875), p. 128).

93 Ballinger, *op. cit.*, p. 29. John White was author of *The First Century of Scandalous Malignant Priests* (1643). He was great-grandfather of John and Charles Wesley. Richard Baxter hoped to meet John White in Heaven, together with Lord Brooke, John Hampden and John Pym.

94 J. Preston, *A Sermon Preached . . . before the Commons House, 2 July 1625*, printed with *The Saints Qualification*, 2nd ed. (1634), pp. 298–9. Sir Edward Coke followed this point up in the debate of 1625: 'Where prophecy ceases the people perish. A great part of the realm without teaching. To petition the King to have this in some sort remedied . . .' (*House of Lords MSS*, XI p. 206).

95 I. Morgan, *Prince Charles's Puritan Chaplain* (1957), pp. 118, 181; see also my *Economic Problems of the Church*, p. 257. In the 1630s there were long disputes over this lectureship, in which the Privy Council intervened (*C.S.P.D.*, *1637–38*, pp. 58–9). For Heylyn's other benefactions to Shropshire, see W. K. Jordan, *The Charities of London, 1480–1660* (1960), pp. 198, 288, 374.

96 Fuller, *Church History* (1842), III, p. 371.

97 *Activities of the Puritan Faction of the Church of England, 1625–33*, ed. I. M. Calder (1957), pp. xvi–xxii, 10, 85; Calder, 'A Seventeenth Century Attempt to purify the Anglican Church', *American Hist. Rev.*, LIII (1947–8), p. 766. The vicar at Bridgnorth, where Richard Baxter was lecturer, got an augmentation from the Feoffees. For Presteign (the largest purchase which the Feoffees made) see W. H. Howse, 'A Contest for a Radnorshire Rectory in the Seventeenth Century', *Journal Hist. Soc. of the Church in Wales*, VII (1957), pp. 70–8; Calder, 'The St Antholin Lectures', *Church Quarterly Rev.*, CLX (1959), pp. 52–6.

98 See my *Economic Problems of the Church*, pp. 267–71, and references there given; *Letters of John Chamberlain*, ed. N. E. McClure (Philadelphia, 1939), II, p. 408; Jordan, *The Charities of London*, pp. 153–4, 236–7, 285–6; G. M. Griffiths, 'Educational Activity in the Diocese of St Asaph', *Journal Hist. Soc. of the Church in Wales*, III (1953), pp. 64–77. Cf. T. S. Willan, *Studies in Elizabethan Foreign Trade* (Manchester, 1959), pp. 195–6.

99 E. A. Beller, 'A Seventeenth Century Miscellany', *Huntington Library Quarterly*, VI (1942–3), p. 217, quoting Samuel Annesley.

100 The lecturer appointed to Berwick proved so 'factious' that in 1639 Charles I asked the Company to suspend him. For other similar activities by London companies, see Jordan, *The Charities of London*, pp. 231–2, 236, 286–7.

101 See my *Economic Problems of the Church*, p. 268; D. Williams Whitney, 'London Puritanism: the Haberdashers' Company', *Church History*, XXXIII, pp. 4–6.

102 *City of Exeter MSS.* (Hist. MSS Comm.), pp. 195–6: the bishop of Carlisle to the mayor of Exeter, 10 October 1633. See Jordan, *The Social Institutions of Lancashire* (Chetham Soc., 1962), pp. 51–114, for Lancashire and other merchants endowing preaching 'to water the dry and barren places of the county of Lancaster' (p. 82).

103 *C.S.P.D.*, *1631–3*, p. 36. The Haberdashers later gave a lectureship to the vicar of Monmouth (Richards, *A History of the Puritan Movement in Wales*, p. 41).

104 Jordan, *Philanthropy in England, 1480–1660* (1959), pp. 253, 314.

105 *Ibid.*, pp. 252, 282, 289, 364; Jordan, *The Charities of Rural England, 1480–1660*, pp. 220–1, 418, 422–6. For London donations to Yorkshire, see Jordan, *The Charities of London, passim*, especially pp. 110, 288, 290; *The Charities of Rural England*, especially pp. 218, 233–42, 300, 309, 324–49, 377–9, 406–15, 432. For donations to other northern, Welsh and Marcher counties, see Jordan, *The Social Institutions of Lancashire, passim*; *The Charities of London*, especially pp. 117, 149, 153–4, 184, 198, 204, 220–42, 263, 283–90, 344, 348–9, 374, 382. For donations from other southern counties, see *ibid.*, pp. 162, 234, 244, 317, 331–2, 337, 354.

106 Parker, *Correspondence*, p. 188. Some bishops nevertheless managed to do so.

107 Jordan, *The Charities of Rural England*, p. 332, quoting from the funeral sermon by Edmund Layfielde on William Fawcett of London, *The Soules Solace* (1633). In addition to rebuilding a chapel at Halton Gill, building a school, augmenting the schoolmaster's salary and providing for the poor, Fawcett endowed two sermons for each anniversary of the Gunpowder Plot.

108 Jordan, *The Charities of Rural England*, pp. 406, 411–15.

109 *C.S.P.D., 1629–31*, p. 473. For lack of preaching on the Border, see C. M. L. Bouch, *Prelates and People of the Lake Counties . . .* (Kendal, 1948), pp. 17, 244–5, 258.

110 Quoted in R. Barclay, *The Inner Life of the Religious Societies of the Commonwealth* (1876), p. 260. The merchants of Sunderland supported Parliament in the Civil War, the 'ancient and opulent' gentry families outside were royalist (P. Gregg, *Freeborn John: A Biography of John Lilburne* (1961), p. 97). See Howell, *op. cit.*, pp. 65–71, 218, for shortage of preaching in Northumberland in the early seventeenth century and consequent ignorance.

111 W. London, *A Catalogue of the Most Vendible Books in England* (1657), Sig. B. These were the four counties later covered by Parliament's Commission for Propagating the Gospel.

112 Jordan, *The Charities of London*, pp. 249–50; twenty-four of forty-five unendowed schools set up outside London and Middlesex were in seven western counties extending from Cumberland to Herefordshire. Over 18 per cent of Londoners who made benefactions in the Welsh border region were not western-born. In Wales the percentage was 29 (*ibid.*, p. 313).

113 *Ibid.*, p. 426.

114   L. Stone, 'The Educational Revolution', *P. and P.*, no. 28, p. 47.

115   J. Brinsley, *A Consolation for our Grammar Schools* (1622), Sig. *3, pp. 14–15.

116   J. A. Manning, *Memoirs of Sir Benjamin Rudyerd* (1841), pp. 135–8. Cf. P. Smart, Preface to *A Short Treatise of Altars* (1629): there was very little preaching 'in most parishes, if not all the country towns of Wales, and too many in England', especially in the North (*The Acts of the High Commission Court within the Diocese of Durham*, ed. W. H. D. Longstaffe (Surtees Soc.,1858), p. 204).

117   *The Hireling Ministry None of Christs* (1652), quoted in Perry Miller, *Roger Williams* (Indianapolis, 1953), p. 200; cf. *Mr Peters Last Report of the English Wars* (1646), p. 5.

118   G. H. Turnbull, 'Letters written by John Dury in Sweden, 1636–38', *Särtryck ur Kyrhistorisk Årsskrift* (Uppsala, 1949), pp. 209–10.

119   R. Sibbes, *Works*, VII, p. 27; cf. p. 470, and my *Economic Problems of the Church*, p. 245.

120   Mendenhall, *The Shrewsbury Drapers and the Welsh Wool Trade*, pp. 43–4.

121   Gruffydd, 'Bishop Francis Godwin's Injunctions', p. 17.

122   Harrison, *The Difference of Hearers*, *passim*; Richard James, *Iter Lancastrense*, ed. T. Corser (Chetham Soc., 1845), pp. 10–11, 59; *Political Ballads published in England during the Commonwealth*, ed. T. Wright (Percy Soc., 1841), p. 127; K. M. Briggs, *Pale Hecate's Team* (1962), p. 112. For ignorance of Jesus Christ in Lancashire, see *Yorkshire Diaries and Autobiographies in the 17th and 18th Centuries*, pp. 138–9.

123   John White, *The Way to the True Church*, in *Works* (1624), pp. 111–12; first published 1608. I owe this reference to Dr R. C. Richardson's *Puritanism in north-west England*.

124   Rees, *Protestant Nonconformity in Wales*, pp. 43, 47. For further evidence concerning maypoles in the Welsh marches, church ales in Somerset, Devon, Cornwall and Herefordshire, sports in Lancashire, Somerset and the Welsh marches, see my *Society and Puritanism in Pre-Revolutionary England* (Panther ed.), pp. 179–89.

125   Laud, *Works*, v, p. 320.

126   Rees, *op. cit.*, p. 41. The Llanfaches Puritans were in touch with those of Bristol as well as of London (*The Records of the Church of Christ in Broadmead, Bristol, 1640–87*, ed. E. B. Underhill (Hanserd Knollys Soc., 1847), pp. 9, 27–30, 37). For other examples of episcopal suppression, see Richards, *The Puritan*

Movement in Wales, pp. 26–8. Many of the ejected ministers joined the Parliamentary armies during the Civil War, or found preferment in London (*ibid.*, pp. 75–6).

27 Marchant, *The Puritans and the Church Courts . . .*, p. 87; cf. pp. 129, 186.

28 For Scots in Northumberland see Howell, *op. cit.*, pp. 77–119.

29 *C.S.P.D.*, *1636–37*, p. 545.

30 *Massachusetts Hist. Soc. Publications*, 4th Series, VI (1863), p. 458. Jacie was born in Yorkshire.

31 *The Life and Death of Mr Henry Jessey* (1671), pp. 6, 9–10. He had previously contemplated emigrating to New England.

32 Bacon, *Works*, x, p. 381.

33 P. Williams, 'The Welsh Borderland under Elizabeth', p. 29.

34 Sir J. F. Rees, *Studies in Welsh History* (Cardiff, 1947), p. 84. Pembroke was the only Welsh county to be mentioned in an act against enclosures – 39 Eliz., c. 2 (I owe this point to Sir J. F. Rees).

35 Dodd, *A History of Wrexham*, pp. 51–3; cf. pp. 37–40, and Dodd, 'Welsh and English in East Denbighshire', *Trans. Hon. Soc. Cymmrodorion*, 1940, p. 48; A. N. Palmer, *The History of the Parish Church of Wrexham* (Wrexham, 1887), pp. 73–4.

36 Dodd, *A History of Wrexham*, pp. 51–2, 167; G. F. Nuttall, *The Welsh Saints* (Cardiff, 1957), p. 75. It was also in 1603 that an alderman of Chester left money to endow a grammar school in Wrexham (L. S. Knight, 'Welsh Schools from A.D. 1000 to A.D. 1600', *Archaeologia Cambrensis*, 6th Series, XIX (1919), pp. 8–9).

37 T. Froysell, *The Beloved Disciple* (1658), funeral sermon on Sir Robert Harley, in *Letters of Lady Brilliana Harley*, p. xxxiii; cf. *ibid.*, p. 207. For Rowland Vaughan's rather ineffective attempts to get a preaching minister in his part of Herefordshire, see Wood, *Rowland Vaughan, His Booke*, pp. 38–40. Cf. also D. Mathew, 'Wales and England in the Seventeenth Century', *Trans. Hon. Soc. Cymmrodorion*, 1955, p. 38. A similar situation prevailed in Cornwall, where Lord Robartes, the Bullers, Rouses and Boscawens befriended Puritans and were Parliamentarians; but they too were a minority among the landed class (M. Coate, *Cornwall in the Great Civil War and Interregnum*, *1642–60* (Oxford, 1933), p. 327).

38 Howell, *op. cit.*, p. 92.

39 Marchant, *The Puritans and the Church Courts . . .*, p. 97.

40 Claire Cross, *The Puritan Earl* (1966), pp. 130–3.

41 *C.S.P.D.*, *1639–40*, p. 519. I owe this reference to Mr M. E. James.

142   *Op. cit.*, ed. C. W. Sutton, *Chetham Miscellany*, I (Chetham Soc. 1902), p. 18.

143   Ed. G. Ormerod, *Tracts on Military Proceedings in Lancashire* (Chetham Soc., 1844), p. 4.

144   Dodd, 'Wales and the Scottish Succession', *Trans. Hon. Soc. Cymmrodorion*, 1937, p. 209; 'Wales in the Parliaments of Charles 1', *ibid.*, 1945, p. 16; *ibid.*, 1946–7, pp. 71–2.

145   Halley, *Lancashire: its Puritanism and Nonconformity*, I, p. 283.

146   See p. 18 above.

147   R. Sibbes, *The Bruised Reed . . .* (1838), pp. 11, 40, 103; *Reliquiae Baxterianae*, p. 31.

148   Peck, *Desiderata Curiosa*, p. 430; F. H. Sunderland, *Marmaduke, Lord Langdale . . .* (1926), p. 69.

149   J. Corbet, *An Historicall Relation of the Military Government of Gloucester . . .* (1645), reprinted in *Bibliotheca Gloucestrensis* (Gloucester, 1823), i, p. 10. Cf. *ibid.*, p. 27: 'Those miserable Welshmen . . . were partly constrained to take up arms, partly allured with the hope of plunder'. There was 'inveterate hatred . . . between Welshmen and the citizens of Gloucester'.

150   Quoted in N. Tucker, *North Wales in the Civil War* (Denbigh, 1958), p. 9.

151   Thomas Hall, *Funebria Florae, The Downfall of May-Games*, 2nd ed. (1661), p. 34. Hall was curate of King's Norton, Worcestershire. The first edition of his pamphlet appeared in 1660.

152   See p. 15 above.

153   J. Gauden, *The Love of Truth and Peace* (1641), p. 24.

154   *C.J.*, II, p. 54.

155   *Ibid.*, II, p. 189.

156   E. Calamy, *Gods free Mercy to England* (1642), p. 50.

157   T. Goodwin, *Zerubbabels Encouragement to Finish the Temple* (1642), p. 41; O. Sedgwick, *England's Preservation* (1642), p. 25; Hill, *The Trade of Truth* (1642), pp. 54–6.

158   A. Perne, *Gospell Courage* (1643), p. 13; F. Cheynell, *Sions Memento* (1643), p. 4.

159   J. Greene, *Nehemiah's Teares and Prayers* (1644), p. 21; H. Hall, *Heaven Ravished* (1644), pp. 25, 30; G. Hickes, *The Glory and Beauty of Gods Portion* (1644), p. 21; H. Scudder, *Gods warning to England* (1644), p. 20; T. Thorowgood, *Moderation Justified* (1645), p. 15.

160   *Tracts on Liberty in the Puritan Revolution, 1638–1647*, ed. W. Haller (Columbia University Press, 1933), II, p. 15; Milton, *Complete Prose Works* (Yale ed.), I, p. 952; ed. C. W. Sutton, *Miscellany*, vol. I (Chetham Soc., 1902).

161 Quoted by John Stoughton, *History of Religion in England* (1881), I, p. 247.

162 J. Geree, *The Down-Fall of Anti-Christ* (1641), Sig. Bv–B4; H. Peter, *Gods Doing and Mans Duty* (1646), p. 111.

163 Ed. G. W. Johnson, *Fairfax Correspondence* (1848), II, pp. 271–80.

164 Ed. A. F. Mitchell and J. Struthers, *Minutes of the Sessions of the Westminster Assembly of Divines* (1874), p. 67.

165 *C.J.*, III, p. 565.

166 Richards, *op. cit.*, p. 46. Fairfax had in February 1644 similarly been given a free hand to place 'able and learned divines' in the North (ed. C. H. Firth and R. S. Rait, *Acts and Ordinances of the Interregnum* (1911), I, pp. 391–2).

167 Firth and Rait, *op. cit.*, I, pp. 846–7. A similar ordinance of April 1645 had provided for the maintenance of preaching ministers in York, Durham, Carlisle, Newcastle, Berwick (*ibid.*, I, pp. 669–71).

168 Ed. A. H. Dodd, *A History of Wrexham*, pp. 57–8; Richards, *op. cit.*, pp. 40, 65.

169 *C.J.*, IV, pp. 242, 622, 707. This was not confirmed by ordinance (i.e. with the concurrence of the Lords) for fifteen months (*L.J.*, VIII, pp. 463, 569), since the Westminster Assembly complained that the ministers had not received its authorization (Mitchell and Struthers, *op. cit.*, pp. 267, 301–2). Symonds ultimately got their blessing, but not apparently the others. Thomas Edwards was worried that such men should be sent into Wales (*Gangraena*, Part III (1646), pp. 163, 241–2). It is the recurrent story of the radicals being prepared to take on the tasks of evangelization which others shirked. Vavasor Powell managed to obtain a certificate from the Assembly, after some argument (*The Life and Death of Mr. V. Powell*, 1671, pp. 15–16).

170 A. Clark, *Raglan Castle and the Civil War in Monmouthshire* (1953), p. 63.

171 J. R. Phillips, *Memoirs of the Civil War in Wales and the Marches* (1874), I, ch. vi, *passim*; II, pp. 129, 139, 246, 268, 273–4, 279–281; *Portland MSS* (Hist. MSS Comm.), I, pp. 256, 294; E. Andriette, *Devon and Exeter in the Civil War* (Newton Abbot, 1971), p. 170; D. Underdown, *Somerset in the Civil War and Interregnum* (Newton Abbot, 1973), pp. 106–15.

172 Phillips, *op. cit.*, II, pp. 377–8.

173 Phillips, *op. cit.*, I, pp. 319–21; *C.J.*, IV, pp. 342, 622. There is no evidence that this order was ever carried out (Richards, *op. cit.*, p. 79).

174   J. Lewis, *The Parliament explained to Wales*, pp. 4, 6. I quote from the 1907 reprint.

175   Quoted in Richards, *op. cit.*, pp. 9, 79.

176   Lewis, *op. cit.*, pp. 34–5.

177   H. Palmer, *The Duty and Honour of Church-Restorers* (1646), pp. 27, 42–4.

178   J. Strickland, *Mercy Rejoycing against Judgement* (1645), Sig. A 3v–A 4v; Jeremiah Burroughs, *A Sermon Preached before . . . The House of Peeres* (1646), p. 48; H. Peter, *Gods Doings and Mans Duty* (1646), Sig. A 2.

179   Howell, *op. cit.*, pp. 218–22.

180   *Fairfax Correspondence*, III, pp. 337–8.

181   Ed. C. E. Surman, *The Register-Booke of the Fourth Classis in the Province of London, 1646–49* (Harleian Soc. Publications, LXXXII–III, 1952–3), pp. 20–8 and *passim*.

182   See *Writings and Speeches of Oliver Cromwell*, ed. W. C. Abbott (Harvard, 1937–47), I, p. 508: Cromwell asked to thank the citizens presenting one such petition; Robert Johnson, Eboraicus, *Lux and Lex* (1647), p. 28; Vavasor Powell, *Christ Exalted above all Creatures* (1651), p. 96.

183   H. Peter, *Gods Doings and Mans Duty* (1646), p. 44.

184   *Mr. Peters Last Report of the English Wars* (1646), p. 13.

185   J. Owen, *A Vision of Unchangeable free mercy* (1646), p. 44.

186   W. Cradock, *The Saints Fulnesse of Joy* (1646), p. 34.

187   Lewis, *op. cit.*, pp. 30, 33. Ten years later Lewis assumed that 'hardly . . . half the people of Wales would be granted to belong to Christ', though by that time he had moderated his destructive zeal (J[ohn] L[ewis], *Some seasonable and moderate Thoughts in order to the furtherance and promoting the affaires of Religion and the Gospel especially in Wales* (1656), p. 8. Contrast p. 41 above.) Cf. John Jones's question to Morgan Llwyd in 1651: 'Where more ignorance, where more hatred to the people of God, where the word saint more scorned . . . than in Merionethshire?' (ed. J. Mayer, 'Inedited Letters of Cromwell, Col. Jones, Bradshaw and Other Regicides', *Trans. Hist. Soc. Lancs. and Cheshire*, New Series, I, p. 185). Cf. pp. 40, 50 above.

188   For examples in Wales, see Richards, *op. cit.*, pp. 38–42, 47–52, 63–70.

189   *Ibid.*, p. 2.

190   See my *Puritanism and Revolution* (1958), pp. 168–83.

191   F. Cheynell, *An Account Given to Parliament By the Ministers sent by them to Oxford* (1647), p. 34; *The Scottish Dove*, nos. 56 and 58, 1645, quoted by W. Lamont, *Godly Rule* (1969), p. 112.

192   Peter, *Gods Doings and Mans Duty*, pp. 43–4.

93 My italics.

94 *Mr. Peters Last Report of the English Wars*, pp. 12–13; cf. p. 8.

95 Quoted in *Puritanism and Liberty*, ed. A. S. P. Woodhouse (1938), p. 246; *Mercurius Politicus*, no. 23, 7–14 November 1650, pp. 381–2.

96 H. Peter, *A Word for the Army* (1647), in *Harleian Miscellany* (1744–6), V, p. 573.

97 Peter, *Good Work for a good Magistrate* (1651), pp. 6–14. When Durham University was established in 1657 it was instructed to maintain two itinerant ministers (*V.C.H., Durham*, II, p. 53).

98 R. P. Stearns, *The Strenuous Puritan* (Urbana, 1954), pp. 362–3.

99 W. Dell, *Several Sermons and Discourses* (1709), p. 79.

200 T. Edwards, *Gangraena*, Part I, pp. 123–5. I have discussed this point at greater length in my *The World Turned Upside Down* (1972), chapter 5 *passim*. See also p. 40 above.

201 Quoted in Ballinger, *The Bible in Wales*, p. 30. Cf. J. Lewis, *The Parliament explained to Wales*, p. 31.

202 Quoted in Rees, *Protestant Nonconformity in Wales*, p. 67.

203 *Ibid.*, p. 77.

204 Professor Trevor-Roper notes that the Commissioners for the Propagation of the Gospel inherited the zeal of pre-revolutionary London merchants (*Ec.H.R.*, New Series, XIV, p. 140).

205 *The Petition of the Six Counties of South Wales* (1652), p. 3; cf. p. 29 – the speech of Col. Edward Freeman when presenting the Petition. A Petition in favour of the Propagators was said to have been signed by 19,000 people, as against the 15,000 claimed for the 1652 Petition (*ibid.*, p. 9; *Mercurius Cambro-Britannicus*, 1652, p. 14). Neither figure is to be taken too seriously; but the Petition of the Six Counties came later, and might be expected to wish to claim more than its rival. The petitioners were certainly not deterred by excessive scrupulosity. Even Anthony Wood said that the Act for the Propagation of the Gospel in Wales was 'so really intended, by the pious care and charity of those members of Parliament' (*Athenae Oxonienses* (1817), III, col. 913).

206 J. Walker, *Sufferings of the Clergy* (1714), pp. 147–50. The text of the Act for the Propagation of the Gospel in the Four Northern Counties has not survived, but it was presumably similar. Each act originated in response to petitions in the area in question, whether spontaneous or not. See Howell, *op. cit.*, pp. 231–55, for the working of the Act in the North.

207 Rees, *op. cit.*, p. 74; cf. Richards, *Religious Developments in Wales, 1654–1662*, pp. 419–20.

208 The proceedings of the Commission for North Wales are

printed in *An Act for the Propagation of the Gospel in Wales, 1649* (Cymdeithas Llên Cymru, 1908), pp. 18–32.

209   D. Williams, *op. cit.*, pp. 115–16; Dodd, *A History of Wrexham*, p. 148.

210   Harrison, it is worth noting, came from Newcastle-under-Lyme.

211   Richards, *History of Puritan Movement in Wales*, p. x. Dr Richards sees the Propagators as carrying out Penry's suggestions for reform (*ibid.*, p. 1).

212   H. Cary, *Memorials of the Great Civil War in England* (1842), II, p. 279. Cf. *C.S.P.D., 1656–57*, pp. 55–6, for the unreliability of Welsh juries.

213   V. Powell, *The Bird in the Cage* (2nd ed., 1662), p. 9. See Richards, *op. cit.*, pp. 171–5, 220, for favourable comments on the activities of the itinerants. There was, after all, gospel precedent for itinerant ministers.

214   Alexander Griffith, *Strena Vavasoriensis*, 1654 (1915), p. 1; *The Life and Death of Mr. V. Powell*, p. 108.

215   Abbott, *Writings and Speeches of Oliver Cromwell*, II, p. 572.

216   S. R. Gardiner, *History of the Commonwealth and Protectorate* (1903), II, pp. 250–1.

217   *Thurloe State Papers* (1742), IV, pp. 373–4.

218   Abbott, *Writings and Speeches of Oliver Cromwell*, III, p. 13.

219   *Ibid.*, p. 57.

220   B. Whitelocke, *Memorials of the English Affairs* (1682), p. 518. Whitelocke's experience of the problems of preaching in Wales dates at least from 1628, when he encountered the vicar of Mostyn, who could not preach in English (R. H. Whitelocke, *Memoirs, Biographical and Historical, of Bulstrode Whitelocke*, 1860, p. 51).

221   Powell, *The Bird in the Cage*, Sig. B.3; Ballinger, *The Bible in Wales*, pp. 10–32. Powell and Cradock were responsible for these editions.

222   H. R. Trevor-Roper, 'Oliver Cromwell and his Parliaments', in *Essays Presented to Sir Lewis Namier*, ed. R. Pares and A. J. P. Taylor (1956), p. 21.

223   Ed. J. A. Bradney, *The Diary of Walter Powell, 1603–54* (1907), p. 40.

224   The best discussion of the significance of this is in D. Masson, *Life of John Milton* IV (1877), pp. 387–98.

225   Dr T. Ranger made a similar point very well about Strafford's rule in Ireland ('Strafford in Ireland: a Revaluation', *P. and P.* no. 19, 1961).

226   E.g. by Rees, *op. cit.*, pp. 74–90, and Richards, *op. cit.*, especially pp. 184 and 247–61.

227 Rees, *op. cit.*, p. 75. Walker's accusations against the Propagators in *The Sufferings of the Clergy* are based almost entirely on Griffith.

228 Richards, *op. cit.*, p. 216; A. G. Veysey, 'Colonel Philip Jones, 1618–74', *Trans. Hon. Soc. Cymmrodorion*, 1966, pp. 316–40; A. N. Palmer, *A History of the Older Nonconformity of Wrexham* (1889), p. 4.

229 Firth and Rait, *op. cit.*, II, pp. 990–3; *C.J.*, VII, p. 448; ed. J. T. Rutt, *Burton's Parliamentary Diary* (1828), III, pp. 82–4; cf. *Harleian Miscellany* (1744–6), VI, p. 490.

230 Richards, *op. cit.*, pp. 215–17, 245–69, 272–3; *C.S.P.D., 1660–61*, pp. 4, 260; R. S. Bosher, *The Making of the Restoration Settlement* (1951), p. 233. For Vavasor Powell's asseverations about his own incorruptibility, see his *Brief Narrative* prefixed to *The Bird in the Cage*, Sig. B2–2v.

231 A. Wood, *Athenae Oxonienses*, III, col. 913.

232 Dodd, *A History of Wrexham*, p. 60.

233 Richards, *op. cit.*, p. 94.

234 *Mercurius Cambro-Britannicus*, p. 8. Cf. the observations of John Jones on the necessity of breaking the great men in Scotland, quoted on pp. 42–3 above.

235 Griffith, *Strena Vavasoriensis* (1654), p. 10. I quote from the reprint of 1915.

236 *Thurloe State Papers*, II, p. 129; cf. *Strena Vavasoriensis*, p. 27.

237 C. Walker, *History of Independency*, Part II (1649), pp. 156–7.

238 Griffith, *Strena Vavasoriensis*, p. 5.

239 Richards, *op. cit.*, p. 8; cf. pp. 21, 45–6.

240 Rutt, *Parliamentary Diary of Thomas Burton*, III, pp. 80–4; K. H. D. Haley, *The First Earl of Shaftesbury* (Oxford, 1968), p. 97.

241 *A Relation of a Dispute between Dr. Griffith and Mr. V. Powell* (1653), p. 16; [G. Griffith], *A Welsh Narrative Corrected* (1653), p. 22.

242 [A. Griffith], *The Petition of the Six Counties of South Wales* (1652), pp. 15–16.

243 *Mercurius Politicus*, no. 180, 17–24 November 1653, pp. 2881–2.

244 [G. Griffith], *A Bold Challenge of an Itinerant Preacher Modestly Answered* (1652), *passim*; *A Welsh Narrative Corrected*, *passim*.

245 Morgan Llwyd, *The Book of the Three Birds* (1653), quoted by Palmer, *A History of the Older Nonconformity of Wrexham*, p. 18.

246 *The Testimony of William Erbery* (1658), p. 75.

247 Griffith, *Strena Vavasoriensis*, pp. 20–1, 12.

248 *Thurloe State Papers*, II, p. 124.

249 Richards, *op. cit.*, p. 253.

250 Richards, *Wales under the Penal Code, 1662–87* (1925), pp. 167–9

251 W. Laud, *Works* (Oxford, 1847–60), V, p. 329.

252 Lewis, *Some seasonable and modest Thoughts*, pp. 14–17. Contras his *Parliament explained to Wales*, p. 30.

253 J. Taylor, *A Short Relation of a Long Journey* (1652), p. 23. Th royalist Taylor wished to suggest that the Parliamentarian were responsible for this state of affairs, as indeed they no doubt were for closing the churches. But the use made of the churchyard was highly traditional, and had been encouraged by James's and Charles's Book of Sports.

254 J. Musgrave, *A True and Exact Relation* (1650), pp. 36, 47.

255 Halley, *op. cit.*, II, p. 186.

256 *V.C.H., Durham*, II, p. 51; cf. A. C. Gibson, 'Original Corres-pondence of the Lord President Bradshaw', *Trans. Hist. Soc. of Lancs. and Cheshire*, New Series, II, p. 66.

257 Jordan, *Philanthropy in England, 1480–1660*, p. 320; Howell, *op. cit.*, pp. 270–1.

258 Ed. E. B. Underhill, *Records of the Churches of Christ gathered at Fenstanton, Warboys and Hexham, 1644–1720* (Hanserd Knollys Soc., 1854), pp. 304, 365. The Propagators' licence to preach seems still to have been regarded as valid by the congregation in June 1654.

259 Jordan, *The Charities of Rural England*, p. 362.

260 *V.C.H., Durham*, II, p. 53.

261 *Mercurius Politicus*, no. 174, pp. 2788–91.

262 *C.J.*, VI, p. 416.

263 Ed. C. H. Firth, *Scotland and the Protectorate* (Scottish History Soc., 1899), p. 394; cf. Owen, *Works* (1850–5), VIII, pp. 235–7; ed. P. Toon, *Correspondence of John Owen* (1970), pp. 36–7, 59; Richards, *Puritan Movement in Wales*, p. 146. For concern with the promotion of religion in Scotland, see also *C.S.P.D., 1654*, pp. 83–4; *1655*, p. 108; *1657–8*, p. 367; cf. H. R. Trevor-Roper, 'Scotland and the Puritan Revolution', in *Historical Essays, 1600–1750, presented to David Ogg*, pp. 115–21.

264 B. Capp, *The Fifth Monarchists* (1972), p. 190.

265 See pp. 15, 18 above.

266 Rees, *Protestant Nonconformity in Wales*, pp. 90–3.

267 Underhill, *Broadmead Records*, p. 37; Edwards, *Gangraena*, Part I, p. 125; Part II, p. 122; Richards, *op. cit.*, pp. 77, 151–2, 206.

268 E. Pagitt, *Heresiography* (5th ed., 1654), p. 136; cf. my *The World Turned Upside Down*, chapter 10 *passim*.

269 *An Account of the Convincement . . . of . . . Richard Davies* (1928), pp. 5, 27. For Quaker permeation by 1656 of neglected parishes

in Cornwall, see M. Coate, *Cornwall in the Great Civil War*, pp. 347–8.

70 Underhill, *Broadmead Records*, pp. 515–17; Richards, *op. cit.*, pp. 217–18.

71 Mayer, 'Inedited Letters', p. 185; G. F. Nuttall, *The Holy Spirit in Puritan Faith and Experience* (1946), p. 111. See pp. 50, 298, note 187 above.

72 'To the Camp of the Lord in England' (1655), in *The Memorable Works of . . . Edward Burroughs* (1672), p. 66. There is a similar apocalyptic attitude to the North and West in Erbery's *A Whirlewind from the South* and *The Children of the West*, in *The Testimony of William Erbery* (pp. 126–40). See p. 41 above.

273 Ed. Rutt, *Burton's Parliamentary Diary*, I, pp. 155–6.

274 Lewis, *Some seasonable and modest Thoughts*, pp. 10–12. Contrast his *Parliament explained to Wales*, pp. 33–5.

275 Owen, *Works*, VIII, p. 452; cf. Toon, *The Correspondence of John Owen*, p. 80.

276 *The Testimony of William Erbery*, *passim*; cf. Richards, *Puritan Movement in Wales*, pp. 214–15.

277 *The Testimony of William Erbery*, p. 147; cf. pp. 50–4.

278 *Ibid.*, pp. 126, 137, 140.

279 [W. Sprigge], *A Modest Plea for an Equal Common-Wealth* (1659), p. 36.

280 Ed. A. Peel, *The Notebook of John Penry* (Camden Soc., 1944), pp. 85–93.

281 Ed. Underhill, *The Records of the Church of Christ meeting in Broadmead, Bristol, 1640–87*, p. 39.

282 Peter, *Good Work for a good Magistrate*, p. 11.

283 Ed. T. Shankland, J. Miles's *An Antidote against the Infection of the Times*, 1656 (Welsh Baptist Historical Soc., 1904), pp. 25–35. Cf. Richards, *Wales under the Indulgence (1672–5)*, p. 232.

284 Griffith, *Strena Vavasoriensis*, pp. 18–19.

285 *Thurloe State Papers*, IV, pp. 334–5, 565.

286 Matthew Poole, *A Model for the Maintaining of Students of Choice Abilities at the University* (1658), p. 13; cf. Sig. A 2, p. 4.

287 Abbott, *op. cit.*, III, p. 511.

288 Mayer, 'Inedited Letters', p. 190. Jones's remarks about Scotland are relevant. 'It is the interest of the Commonwealth of England to break the interest of the great men in Scotland, and to settle the interest of the common people upon a different foot from the interests of their lords and masters . . . The great men will never be faithful to you so long as you propound freedom to the people and relief against their tyranny.' But, Jones added in this startlingly naked class

analysis, Scotland lacked a bourgeoisie which could be given a vested interest in the new régime. 'The people will hardly comprehend the excellency of a Commonwealth and a free people . . . they having no money to buy lands in England' (*ibid.*, p. 192).

289 Powell, *Bird in the Cage*, Sig. B.3–3v.

290 Mayer, 'Inedited Letters', p. 227.

291 Howell, *op. cit.*, pp. 329–30, 348.

292 P. J. Wallis and W. E. Tate, 'A Register of Old Yorkshire Grammar Schools', *Researches and Studies of Leeds Institute of Education*, XIII (1956), pp. 1–41; P. J. Wallis, 'A Preliminary Register of Old Schools in Lancashire and Cheshire', *Trans. of the Historic Soc. of Lancashire and Cheshire*, CXX (1968), pp. 1–21 For a more pessimistic view of educational achievements in Yorkshire and Lancashire see J. E. Stephens, 'Investment and intervention in education during the Interregnum', *British Journal of Educational Studies*, XV (1967), pp. 253–62; C. D Rogers, 'Education in Lancashire and Cheshire, 1640–1660' *Trans. of the Historic Soc. of Lancashire and Cheshire*, CXXIII pp. 39–56.

293 Phillips, *Civil War in Wales*, I, p. 24; Richards, *Puritan Movement in Wales*, pp. 223–4. For education in the North under the Propagators, see W. A. L. Vincent, *The State and School Education, 1640–60* (1950), pp. 21, 54, 135; Halley, *Lancashire: its Puritanism and Nonconformity*, I, p. 176; *Yorkshire Archaeological Soc. Miscellanea*, VI, pp. 23–4.

294 H. Peter, *Good Work for a Good Magistrate* (1651), pp. 1–3; Dell, *Several Sermons and Discourses*, pp. 644–5.

295 Lewis, *Some seasonable and moderate Thoughts*, p. 30.

296 Abbot, *op. cit.*, II, p. 397.

297 *Thurloe State Papers*, IV, p. 442.

298 Some appear to have declined under the Protectorate (Richards, *Religious Developments in Wales, 1654–62*, pp. 54–5).

299 There were voluntary associations in Cumberland, Cheshire, Shropshire, Worcestershire, Somerset, Dorset, Wiltshire, Devon, Cornwall, North Wales, Ireland; and in London, Essex, Cambridgeshire, Norfolk, Hampshire and Nottinghamshire. The Cumberland Association (of Presbyterians and Independents) seems to have been formed as a direct result of the spread of Quakerism (*V.C.H.*, *Cumberland*, II, pp. 94–5).

300 J. Phillips, *History of Pembrokeshire* (1909), pp. 549–50; Richards, *Wales under the Penal Code*, p. 46; cf. Dodd, *Studies in Stuart Wales*, p. 63 for Wales as a whole.

301 E. Calamy, *An Account of the Ministers . . . Ejected or Silenced*

after the Restoration in 1660 (1713), pp. 8–13; J. Tillotson, 'A Sermon Preached at the Funeral of the Reverend Mr. Thomas Gouge', 1681, in *Sermons on Several Subjects and Occasions* (1748), II, p. 104; A. G. Mathews, *Calamy Revised* (1934), pp. 229–30.

302 For the deplorable state of education in the diocese of St David's in the early eighteenth century, see Erasmus Sanders, *A View of the State of Religion in the Diocese of St. David's* (1721), p. 32. For Wales generally, see Richards, *Wales under the Penal Code*, pp. 62–70.

303 Calamy, *op. cit.*, p. 10, referring to W. Wynne's edition of Powell's *History of Wales* (1697).

304 Calamy, *op. cit.*, p. 720. Wharton in 1662 had settled lands sufficient to pay for 1,050 Bibles and catechisms to be distributed, mainly in the North of England (Ballinger, *op. cit.*, p. 37).

305 Williams, *op. cit.*, pp. 114–15, 119.

306 R. Pilkington, *Robert Boyle* (1959), p. 16.

307 G. Holmes, *The Trial of Dr. Sacheverell* (1973), pp. 234–8, 243–54.

Chapter 2   Arise Evans: Welshman in London

1 John Taylor tells us of Barmouth in 1652 that it is 'so plentifully furnished with want of provisions that it is able to famish a hundred men and horses' (quoted by W. J. Hughes, *Wales and the Welsh in English Literature from Shakespeare to Scott* (Wrexham, 1924), p. 43).

2 A. Evans, *An Eccho to the Voice from Heaven* (1653), p. 1.

3 For impropriations see pp. 13–14 above.

4 Evans, *An Eccho*, p. 27; T. C. Mendenhall, *The Shrewsbury Drapers and the Welsh Wool Trade in the Sixteenth and Seventeenth Centuries* (Oxford, 1953), pp. 37, 133–5.

5 A. H. Dodd, *Studies in Stuart Wales* (Cardiff, 1952), pp. 104–5; David Williams, *A History of Modern Wales* (1950), p. 98. For Wrexham see p. 22 above.

6 Mendenhall, *op. cit.*, pp. 194–5.

7 L. Owen, 'The Population of Wales in the Sixteenth and Seventeenth Centuries', *Trans. Hon. Soc. Cymmrodorion*, 1958, p. 111.

8 T. Richards, *Religious Developments in Wales* (1923), pp. 248–9; see p. 40 above.

9 D. Mathew, 'Wales and England in the early 17th century', *Trans. Hon. Soc. Cymmrodorion*, 1955, pp. 41–5; W. J. Hughes, *Wales and the Welsh in English Literature* (Wrexham, 1924), p.

13; J. Cule, 'A Note on Hugo Glynn and the Statute Barring Welshmen from Gonville and Caius College', *National Library of Wales Journal*, XVI, pp. 185–90; C. Grant Robertson, *All Souls College* (1899), p. 77; J. O. Bartley, *Teague, Shenkin and Sawney* (Cork, 1954), *passim*. Ordinary Welshmen were familiar in London, as Elizabethan and Jacobean drama demonstrates. They are depicted with greater friendliness than Scots or Irishmen, and are more fully developed as characters.

10 I restrain myself from speculating on the possible influence of Shakespeare's possible Welsh grandmother, or on the Welsh origins of Milton's mother's family (F. J. Harries, *Shakespeare and the Welsh* (1919), p. 73 and *passim*; ed. H. Darbishire, *The Early Lives of Milton*, 1932, p. 52).

11 See my *The World Turned Upside Down*, p. 65.

12 J. Hacket, *Scrinia Reserata* (1692), p. 7; Abbott, *Writings and Speeches of Oliver Cromwell*, I, pp. 500–1.

13 Evans, *An Eccho*, pp. 10–11; *A Rule from Heaven* (1659), pp. 22–3; see pp. 55–7 above.

14 *Ibid.*, pp. 13–22, 25–8, 107–12.

15 *Ibid.*, pp. 28–36.

16 *Ibid.*, pp. 37–48.

17 T. Spencer, 'The History of an Unfortunate Lady', *Harvard Studies and Notes in Philology and Literature*, X, pp. 43–59.

18 Evans, *The Bloudy Vision of John Farley* (1653), Sig. A 3v; *An Eccho*, pp. 49–53, 57, 63, 121–2.

19 Edwards, *Gangraena*, Part II (1646), p. 173. Edwards regarded Arise as a sectary, but did not think he was mad.

20 *An Eccho*, pp. 62–9. For Love see G. D. Owen, 'The Conspiracy of Christopher Love', *Trans. Hon. Soc. Cymmrodorion*, 1966, pp. 89–107.

21 *An Eccho*, pp. 71–2, 88–92, 104–5, 115–23; *A Voice From Heaven to the Common-Wealth of England* (1652), p. 2; *The Bloudy Vision of John Farley*, Sig. A 3v.

22 *A Voice From Heaven*, pp. 11, 70; *An Eccho*, To the Reader; *The Bloudy Vision*, p. 22; ed. G. H. Sabine, *The Works of Gerrard Winstanley* (Cornell University Press, 1941), p. 614.

23 *A Voice From Heaven*, pp. 26–7, 49; *An Eccho*, pp. 50, 101, 104; *The Voice of King Charls the Father to Charls the Son* (1655), pp. 28–9; *To the Most High and Mighty Prince Charles II . . . an Epistle* (1660), p. 9.

24 Ed. C. H. Josten, *Elias Ashmole (1617–1692)* (Oxford, 1966), II, pp. 641–2.

25 *To His Excellency the Lord General and his Honourable Councel of the Army* (1653).

26 *An Eccho*, p. 75, Sig. K–K2; *The Bloudy Vision*, Sig. A 8; *An Epistle*, pp. 18–19.

27 *An Eccho, passim*; *The Bloudy Vision*, Sig. A 3v.

28 Evans, *The Euroclydon Winde* (1654), pp. 74, 77; *A Message from God . . . to his Highness the Lord Protector* (1654), pp. 10–12. The title of the former pamphlet derives from Acts 27.14: 'There arose against it [St Paul's ship *en route* for Rome] a tempestuous wind, called Euroclydon'.

29 *The Voice of King Charls*, pp. 7–8; *The Euroclydon Winde*, p. 38; cf. pp. 65–82.

30 *An Epistle*, p. 13.

31 See Thomas Pugh, *British and Out-landish Prophecies* (1658), p. 152.

32 *The Euroclydon Winde*, Sig. B; *The Voice of King Charls*, Sig. A7–7v, pp. 2, 10–11; *The Voice of Michael the Archangel* (1654), p. 1; *The Voice of the Iron Rod* (1655), Sig. A 2v, pp. 10–11; *An Epistle*, pp. 16–17; cf. *A Rule from Heaven*, pp. 17–19.

33 *The Faithful Scout*, no. 246, p. 1962.

34 *An Eccho*, p. 84; *The Voice of King Charls*, pp. 20–1. 'My former book' was presumably *The Bloudy Vision of John Farley*.

35 *Light for the Jews* (1656), pp. 5–8, 11, 20, 39.

36 *A Rule from Heaven*. See pp. 68–9 above.

37 *An Epistle*, pp. 15–16, 20–1, 27–33.

38 *An Eccho*, p. 17.

39 *A Bloudy Vision*, Sig. A 8; *The Declaration of Arise Evans* (1654), p. 6. For mechanick preachers see W. Y. Tindall, *John Bunyan, Mechanick Preacher* (New York, 1934), *passim*.

40 *A Voice From Heaven*, pp. 26–7, 33, 45, 74–5.

41 Josten, *Elias Ashmole*, I, pp. 21–2.

42 W. M. Lamont, *Godly Rule* (1969), *passim*; cf. my *Antichrist in Seventeenth-Century England* (Oxford, 1971), *passim*.

43 Cf. K. V. Thomas, *Religion and the Decline of Magic* (1971), *passim*.

44 *The Bloudy Vision*, p. 23.

45 *A Rule from Heaven*, pp. 1–11; *An Epistle*, pp. 13–14, 60 sqq.; *An Eccho*, p. 13; *The Voice of King Charls*, pp. 13–14.

46 *A Voice From Heaven*, p. 51; *An Eccho*, p. 102.

47 *The Bloudy Vision*, Sig. A 3v–4.

48 *A friendly Admonition for Astrologers*, in *The Bloudy Vision*, p. 39; *The Declaration of Arise Evans*, pp. 7–8.

49 *A Voice From Heaven*, pp. 10–11; *An Eccho*, pp. 124–30; *The Declaration of Arise Evans*, pp. 7–8; *The Voice of King Charls*, p. 41; *An Epistle*, p. 9; *The Euroclydon Winde*, pp. 82–6; cf. *King Charls his Starre* (1654), pp. 37, 43. A manuscript insertion in

the Bodleian copy of this pamphlet attributes it to Arise Evans.

50   *An Eccho*, pp. 7–9; *The Bloudy Vision*, p. 62; *The Voice of King Charls*, pp. 7–8, 10–11. I am grateful to Dr Kenneth Morgan for checking the Welsh.

51   *An Eccho*, pp. 65, 109.

52   G. Fox, *Journal* (1902), I, pp. 281, 448; cf. Nuttall, *op. cit.*, p. 111.

53   *An Eccho*, pp. 9, 16, 34–5. Cf. Thomas, *op. cit.*, pp. 118–19, 544.

54   *A Rule from Heaven*, pp. 1–17, 23–4. This pamphlet is unique among Evans's writings in appealing to the Agitators and the rank and file of the Army. See p. 68 above.

55   *A Voice From Heaven*, pp. 19, 37; cf. *An Eccho*, To the Reader, where Evans defends his apparent denial of the existence of any church outside England; *The Bloudy Vision*, p. 38.

56   Cf. Evans's friends who in 1633 had advised him against prophesying because he was no minister (p. 52 above).

57   *The Voice of the Iron Rod*, p. 3; *The Euroclydon Winde*, pp. 26–7; *A Voice From Heaven*, pp. 53–4.

58   See my *The World Turned Upside Down*, especially chapter 8.

59   *A Voice From Heaven*, p. 75; *An Eccho*, To the Reader, and p. 48.

60   *The Bloudy Vision*, pp. 18–20; *An Epistle*, p. 42; cf. *The Voice of Michael the Archangel*, pp. 2, 20.

61   *The Bloudy Vision*, pp. 63–4; cf. *The Voice of Michael the Archangel*, p. 23. The text is not quite clear: it might have been Charles 1 who was to go to New England.

62   *An Eccho*, pp. 53, 91–2, 104; *The Voice of the Iron Rod*, p. 5.

63   *The Bloudy Vision*, Sig. A 6v, pp. 49–72; cf. *The Voice of King Charls*, p. 25.

64   *The Voice of the Iron Rod*, p. 5; *The Voice of King Charls*, pp. 44–53; *An Epistle*, pp. 53–5; *Light for the Jews, passim*; *A Rule from Heaven*, p. 48.

65   *A Voice from Heaven*, pp. 63–72; *The Bloudy Vision*, title-page and pp. 20–1, 38, 51–4, 59–63. Cf. M. Griffith, *God and the King* (1660), p. 84.

66   *The Bloudy Vision*, p. 60; *An Echo*, p. 3.

67   *The Voice of Michael the Archangel*, p. 15.

68   *An Epistle*, p. 51.

69   *An Eccho*, pp. 39–40; cf. pp. 52, 121.

70   *The Voice of King Charls*, Sig. B–B2, pp. 30–5. Defoe almost echoes Evans: Charles 1 'had the misfortune to be the first King of England, and perhaps in the world, that ever established wickedness by a law' (ed. H. Morley, *The Earlier Life and Works of Daniel Defoe* (1899), p. 166).

71   *The Bloudy Vision*, pp. 23–4; *An Eccho*, p. 100.

72   *The Bloudy Vision*, pp. 23–6; *A Voice From Heaven*, pp. 24, 38–9; *The Voice of King Charls*, pp. 17–18.

73   *A Voice From Heaven*, pp. 29–30; *The Voice of King Charls*, pp. 4–5, 14–15.

74   *An Eccho*, p. 133.

75   *The Voice of King Charls*, Sig. A 8v; cf. A 4v–8, and *An Epistle*, p. 70. Evans always favoured reconciliation – cf. *An Eccho*, p. 81; *The Voice of King Charls*, Sig. A 4v; *A Rule from Heaven*, p. 46.

76   *An Eccho*, p. 80; cf. *The Voice of King Charls*, Sig. B 2.

77   *A Rule from Heaven*, pp. 55–6; *The Bloudy Vision*, p. 60.

78   *The Bloudy Vision*, Sig. A 4v–5.

79   *The Euroclydon Winde*, pp. 3–4; *An Eccho*, p. 87; *The Bloudy Vision*, Sig. A 5–5v.

80   *An Eccho*, pp. 71–2; *The Bloudy Vision*, pp. 20–1, 26–7.

81   *The Voice of King Charls*, Sig. A7–8, B, B2, B4v, pp. 2–3, 6.

82   *The Bloudy Vision*, pp. 69–70; *An Eccho*, p. 76.

83   *A Rule from Heaven*, pp. 45, 50, 57 and *passim*. For Wildman see Woodhouse, *Puritanism and Liberty* (1938), pp. 439–43.

84   But at the end of the tract Evans somehow seems to want Charles II restored as well; apparently there would be two kings (*ibid.*, p. 59).

85   *Ibid.*, pp. 29–35, 40, 46, 50–1, 57.

86   Cyrano de Bergerac, *L'Autre Monde* (Paris, 1959), p. 235. A translation of Cyrano's *The Government of the World in the Moon* was published in 1659. Cyrano did not take the pauper king from Francis Godwin's *The Man in the Moon* (1638), by the French translation of which (1648) he is said to have been influenced. Bishop Godwin's moon was ruled by a quite traditional king and queen.

87   *The Euroclydon Winde*, Sig. A2, pp. 69–70; *The Voice of King Charls*, *passim*.

88   *A Message from God*, pp. 1–7; W. Gostelow, *Charls Stuart and Oliver Cromwell United* (1655), pp. 286–8 and *passim*; *The Faithful Scout*, no. 246 (21–8 September 1655), p. 1962. For Gostelow see p. 71 above.

89   *A Message from God*, pp. 11–12; *The Voice of the Iron Rod*, pp. 5–6. The title of the latter pamphlet picks up a reference to Micah 6:9 made by the Lord Protector in his speech dissolving his first Parliament, and fuses it with Revelation 12:5 and 19:15 (Abbott, *Writings and Speeches of Oliver Cromwell*, III, p. 583).

90   *An Epistle*, pp. 15–16.

91   Ed. E. B. Underhill, *The Records of a Church of Christ Meeting in Broadmead, Bristol, 1640–1687* (Hanserd Knollys Soc., 1847),

pp. 59–60. For a possible visit by Evans to Bath see p. 57 above.

92 Josten, *Elias Ashmole*, II, pp. 641–2; George Smith, *Gods Unchangeableness* (1655), p. 46. In 1660 John Phillips, Milton's nephew, mocked Arise Evans for being 'a false prophet 40 years' (*Montelion 1660, Or, The Prophetical Almanack* (1660), Sig. A 5).

93 *The Euroclydon Winde*, Sig. A 5v–6. I have come across no evidence for the existence of these translations.

94 W. Gostelow, *op. cit.*, especially pp. 63, 73, 82, 99, 189, 286–8. Gostelow also believed that the Jews should 'now know the Lord, receive mercy and go into their own land' (*The Coming of God in Mercy, in Vengeance* (1658), Sig. E8). Evans quoted Gostelow in 1655 (*The Voice of King Charls*, p. 141).

95 R. Loveday, *Lovedays Letters* (1659), pp. 174–5.

96 V. L. Pearl, 'The "Royal Independents" in the English Civil War', *T.R.H.S.*, 1968, pp. 69–96.

97 *The Bloudy Vision*, pp. 6–13; *King Charls his Starre*, p. 43.

98 *The Bloudy Vision*, p. 31. The reference is to *Eikonoklastes*, Milton's critique of *Eikon Basilike*.

99 No John Farley is recorded as a delinquent in the *Calendar of the Committee for Compounding*. John Farley, Grocer of London, compounded on behalf of a Cambridge surgeon, and himself bought up claims to Irish land. A Henry Farley is described as of Cambridge (*op. cit.*, II, pp. 1399, 1629; *C. S. P. Ireland – Adventurers, 1642–59*, p. 4, etc; K. S. Bottigheimer, *English Money and Irish Land: the Cromwellian Settlement* (Oxford, 1971), p. 154. Cf. G. Aylmer, *The State's Servants*, 1974, p. 439: a Captain Farley at Rye in 1651.

100 *An Epistle*, pp. 10–11; *C.S.P.D., 1651–2*, p. 160; *Thurloe State Papers* (1742), VII, p. 264. I owe this reference to the kindness of Professor G. E. Aylmer, who tells me that Satterthwayt did not hold this office in 1641–2. The Clerk of the Nichills made a note of returns by sheriffs in cases where the party named in a writ had no goods upon which a levy could be made: the clerk of nil returns.

101 Crofton had spoken up for the King under the Commonwealth, and attacked Fifth Monarchists; but he defended the Covenant and denounced bishops after the Restoration, even declaring in a moment of excitement that the power of the people was above that of the king. Sir Samuel's support seems to have involved no more than 'good offices' in enabling him to preach on one occasion in an Anglican pulpit in London (C. E. Whiting, *Studies in Puritanism, . . . 1660–1688* (1931), pp. 160, 484–91).

102 *An Epistle*, p. 19; *C.S.P.D.*, *1648–9*, p. 308; A. B. Beaven, *The Aldermen of the City of London* (1908), I, pp. 184, 332, 341; II, pp. 92, 187; J. R. Woodhead, *The Rulers of London, 1660–1689* (London and Middlesex Archaeological Soc., 1968), p. 156; Pepys, *Diary*, ed. H. B. Wheatley (1946), V, p. 406.

103 *A Message from God*, p. 12.

104 *A Voice From Heaven*, p. 49; *An Eccho*, pp. 50, 101, 104; *The Bloudy Vision*, pp. 63–4; *The Voice of King Charls*, pp. 28–9; *An Epistle*, p. 9.

105 *A Voice From Heaven*, pp. 33, 46; *A Rule from Heaven*, p. 49; *An Epistle*, pp. 21–3, 32–3. Lilly, interestingly enough, regarded Speaker Lenthall as 'ever my friend' (*Life and Times* (1715), p. 69).

106 *An Epistle*, pp. 76–7; *The Voice of King Charls*, p. 25.

107 *A Rule from Heaven*, p. 47; *An Epistle*, p. 35; Josten, *Elias Ashmole*, II, pp. 778–9; J. Aubrey, *Miscellanies* (1890), p. 128.

108 J. Brown, *Charisma Basilicon* (1684), pp. 162–4; J. Jortin, *Remarks on Ecclesiastical History* (2nd ed., 1767), I, pp. 249–55. Mr Knight, the King's surgeon, however said that Arise Evans's disease was not the King's Evil (*An Epistle*, p. 35). See also M. Shepherd, 'The Case of Arise Evans: An Historico-Psychiatric Study', *Psychological Medicine*, 1975.

PART II   CHANGE IN CONTINUITY: SOME FUNDAMENTAL IDEAS

Chapter 3   Protestantism and the Rise of Capitalism

1 Originally published in *Essays in the Economic and Social History of Tudor and Stuart England, in Honour of R. H. Tawney*, ed. F. J. Fisher (1961).

2 R. H. Tawney, *Religion and the Rise of Capitalism* (Penguin ed.), pp. 101–3.

3 By 'the capitalist spirit' I mean something more specific than a love of money, which can be found in earlier ages. I mean an ethos which, within the framework of a market economy, *emphasizes* productive industry, frugality and accumulation, as good in themselves. On this definition, banks and usury are not central to the problem, since they existed before the rise of capitalism. (See R. H. Hilton, 'Capitalism – What's in a name?', *P. and P.* (1952), no. 1.)

4 Ed. B. L. Woolf, *Reformation Writings of Martin Luther* (1952–6), II, p. 110; cf. pp. 121–3, 293; Luther, *Commentary on Galatians* (English translation, 1807), II, p. 216; cf. pp. 148, 270. In discussing theology, I have by preference quoted Luther, since

he initiated the protestant breakthrough, more often than Calvin: for my concern here is with the *theological* distinction between protestantism and catholicism. I do not wish to imply that Lutheranism, as it came to exist in Germany and Scandinavia, contributed significantly to the capitalist spirit.

5 William Tyndale, *An Answer to Sir Thomas More's Dialogue* (Parker Soc., 1850), pp. 202–3; J. Foxe, *The Acts and Monuments*, ed. J. Pratt (4th ed., n.d.), I, pp. xxii–iii, 61, 74–6, 85–6.

6 Ed. E. Cardwell, *A History of Conferences* (Oxford, 1840), p. 90.

7 F. A. Gasquet and E. Bishop, *Edward VI and the Book of Common Prayer* (1890), p. 418.

8 Luther, *Galatians*, I, p. 230; cf. II, pp. 299–300.

9 Luther, *Reformation Writings*, II, p. 214.

10 Loyola, *Spiritual Exercises*, part ii, no. 13; Luther, *Galatians*, I, p. 284; Tyndale, *Answer to More*, p. 51; Jean Calvin, *Institutes of the Christian Religion*, trans. H. Beveridge (1949), I, pp. 72–5.

11 Luther, *Thirty-four Sermons* (Dublin, 1747), pp. 76–7.

12 Tyndale, *Doctrinal Treatises* (Parker Soc., 1848), p. 280.

13 N. O. Brown, *Life against Death* (1959), chapter XIV, *passim*. The Cathari, who also thought the world was the devil's, drew the conclusion that what happened there was a matter of indifference: trade and usury were therefore permissible.

14 Luther, *The Bondage of the Will* (1823), p. 23; *Reformation Writings*, I, p. 259; Calvin, *Institutes*, I, p. 29.

15 Calvin, *Institutes*, I, p. 555.

16 Calvin, *Institutes*, II, pp. 75, 465; I, pp. 534, 551; cf. II, p. 101, and Foxe, *op. cit.*, I, p. 77.

17 Calvin, *Institutes*, II, p. 180.

18 Luther, *Reformation Writings*, I, p. 314; Tyndale, *Doctrinal Treatises*, pp. 118–19; *Expositions of Scripture* (Parker Soc., 1849), pp. 80–1.

19 Luther, *Reformation Writings*, I, p. 255.

20 Contrast Professor Boxer's agreeable account of a Jesuit who turned Protestant and married twice. He subsequently pleaded to the Inquisition that the ceremonies, being protestant, were invalid, and so he had been guilty only of 'a sin of the flesh'. His plea was accepted (C. R. Boxer, *Salvador de Sá and the Struggle for Brazil, 1602–86* (1952), pp. 197–8).

21 Sir Walter Raleigh, *History of the World* (Edinburgh, 1820), I, p. 78; H. R. Trevor-Roper, *Archbishop Laud*, p. 209.

22 Luther, *Reformation Writings*, I, p. 180.

23 R. Hooker, *Of the Laws of Ecclesiastical Polity* (Everyman ed.), I, p. xiii; Tyndale, *Doctrinal Treatises*, pp. 105, 362; *Answer to More*, pp. 6–7.

24 R. G. Usher, *The Reconstruction of the English Church* (New York, 1910), II, p. 124; R. Greenham, *Workes* (1612), p. 653.

25 Luther, *Reformation Writings*, I, pp. 370, 268, 270. The Puritan representatives at the Hampton Court Conference in 1604 were supplied in advance with arguments against the ceremonial observances they objected to. 'Whatsoever is not contained in the Word is burdensome to the conscience of Christians, who are set at liberty by Christ' (*Montague MSS.*, Hist. MSS Comm., p. 37.)

26 Calvin, *Institutes*, II, p. 70.

27 Thomas Taylor, *Works* (1653), pp. 166–7.

28 Richard Sibbes, *The Saints Cordials* (1629), p. 92.

29 Tyndale, *Doctrinal Treatises*, p. 407; Sibbes, *The Saints Cordials*, pp. 41–2.

30 J. Hall, *Works* (1625), p. 93; Abbott, *Writings and Speeches of Oliver Cromwell*, IV, p. 513.

31 Luther, *Thirty-four Sermons*, p. 281; *Reformation Writings*, II, pp. 115–16; Calvin, *Institutes*, II, p. 683; Tyndale, *Answer to More*, p. 114; Clarkson, *A Single Eye* (1650); cf. my *The World Turned Upside Down*, pp. 172–3.

32 J. Knox, *History of the Reformation* (Glasgow, 1832), p. 162.

33 Quoted by Tawney, *Religion and the Rise of Capitalism*, p. 213.

34 John Donne, *Complete Poetry and Selected Prose* (Nonesuch ed.), p. 285.

35 Calvin, *Institutes*, I, p. 445.

36 W. Perkins, *Workes* (1616–1617), I, p. 769.

37 Hooker, *Of the Laws of Ecclesiastical Polity* (Everyman ed.), I, p. 406. My italics.

38 Ed. G. Bullough, *Poems and Drama of Fulke Greville* (n.d.), II, p. 137.

39 *Thirty-four Sermons*, p. 215 and *passim*; cf. *Reformation Writings*, I, pp. 375–6; II, pp. 110–11, 121; Tyndale, *Doctrinal Treatises*, pp. 100–2; *Expositions*, pp. 125–6; *Answer to More*, p. 173.

40 Cf. *Thirty-four Sermons*, p. 211; *Reformation Writings*, I, p. 276; J. Dod and R. Clever, *A Plain and Familiar Exposition of the Ten Commandments* (19th ed., 1662), p. 190.

41 See my essay on 'William Perkins and the Poor', in *Puritanism and Revolution*, p. 234; and a communication by V. G. Kiernan in *P. and P.* (1953), no. 3, especially pp. 49–51.

42 T. Fuller, *The Holy State* (1648), p. 144; Perkins, *Workes*, I, p. 755.

43 Dod and Clever, *A Plaine and Familiar Exposition of the Proverbs of Salomon* (1612), chapter IX, pp. 65–6; chapter XVIII, pp. 10–11; cf. chapter XIII, pp. 70–3.

44 Bullinger, *Decades* (Parker Soc., 1849–52), III, pp. 32–3. The first sentence was considerably elaborated by the translator. In the original it ran '*displicit [Deo] supina rei familiaris neglegentia*'.

45 J. Preston, *Sinnes Overthrow* (4th ed., 1641), pp. 254–9; T. Taylor, *A Commentary Upon the Epistle of St. Paul to Titus* (1658), p. 183.

46 Greenham, *Workes*, p. 20; Sibbes, *The Returning Backslider* (1639), pp. 451–2; Perkins, *Workes*, II, p. 125.

47 T. Adams, *Workes* (1630), p. 389.

48 W. Gouge, *A Commentary on the Whole Epistle to the Hebrews* (1866–7), III, pp. 293–5; cf. Greenham, *Workes*, p. 784; Dod and Clever, *A godly forme of household government* (2nd ed., 1614), Sig. E. 6v–7; T. Taylor, *Works* (1653), p. 477.

49 Adams, *Workes*, p. 862; J. Hall, *Works* (1808), V, pp. 103–4; T. Hobbes, *English Works*, ed. Sir W. Molesworth (1839–45), VI, pp. 194–5.

50 Dod and Clever, *Proverbs*, XI, pp. 2–3; XX, p. 132; Greenham, *Workes*, p. 620.

51 Cf. Bullinger, *Decades*, III, pp. 41–2. Roman Catholic casuistry, on the other hand, by its emphasis on the formal and external, made release from the sin of usury depend to some extent on methods of accountancy (H. M. Robertson, *Aspects of the Rise of Economic Individualism*, Cambridge, 1933, p. 164).

52 R. Hakluyt, *Principal Navigations* (Everyman ed.), VI, pp. 3–4; *Divers Voyages* (1582), Dedication to Sir Philip Sidney.

53 Perry Miller, *Errand into the Wilderness* (Harvard, 1956), pp. 99–140.

54 M. Maclure, *The Paul's Cross Sermons, 1534–1642* (1958), p. 126.

55 Augustine, *De Spiritu et Litera*, 5; *The City of God* (Everyman ed.), II, p. 353. Cf. Samuel Butler's shrewd observation, 'The Stoical necessity and Presbyterian predestination are the same' (*Characters and Passages from Notebooks* (Cambridge),1908, p.279).

56 The failure of full-scale capitalism to develop in fourteenth-century Florence may be connected with a lack of thoroughgoing heresy to unite its citizens against the Church. The heretical possibilities in the early Franciscan movement were tamed by the Papacy: the big bourgeosie who came to rule Florence needed the Papacy, for this and economic reasons (Hilton, 'Capitalism – What's in a name?', *P. and P.* (1952), no. 1).

57 Calvin, *Institutes*, II, p. 135; Brown, *Life against Death*, chapter XIV, *passim*.

58 R. M. Kingdon, *Geneva and the Coming of the Wars of Religion in France, 1555–1563* (Geneva, 1956), p. 56 and *passim*.

59 Samuel Johnson, *A Journey to the Western Islands*, Raasay.
60 John Marlowe, *The Puritan Tradition in England* (1956), p. 133.

Chapter 4 'Reason' and 'Reasonableness'

1 The Hobhouse Memorial Lecture, 1969, originally published in *The British Journal of Sociology*, XX (1969), no. 3.
2 L. T. Hobhouse, *The Metaphysical Theory of the State* (1918), p. 126; *Elements of Social Justice* (1922), p. 57.
3 Quoted by F. Raab, *The English Face of Machiavelli* (1964), p. 148.
4 G. Winstanley, *A Watchword to the City of London and the Armie*, in *The Works of Gerrard Winstanley*, ed. G. H. Sabine (Cornell University Press, 1941), p. 316.
5 Woodhouse, *Puritanism and Liberty*, pp. 73, 91.
6 Winstanley, *The Law of Freedom in a Platform*, in Sabine, *op. cit.*, pp. 519, 595.
7 Ed. W. Notestein, F. H. Relf and H. Simpson, *Commons Debates, 1621* (Yale, 1935), II, p. 351.
8 Ed. G. M. Story and Helen Gardner, *The Sonnets of William Alabaster* (Oxford, 1959), p. 24.
9 See my *God's Englishman* (1970), pp. 169–71.
10 Abbott, *Writings and Speeches of Oliver Cromwell*, III, pp. 590–2. Cf. pp. 215, 279 above.
11 *Op. cit.* (Göteborg, 1957), p. 337 and *passim*.
12 Ed. R. H. Tawney, *A Discourse upon Usury by Thomas Wilson* (1935), p. 121.
13 F. Hutcheson, *Enquiry into the Original of our Ideas of Beauty and Virtue* (1725), p. 164.
14 D. Hume, *Essays* (World's Classics), p. 52.
15 R. Capel, *Tentations, Their Nature and Cure* (1658), I, p. 16. First published in 1633.
16 Tawney, *The Agrarian Problem in the Sixteenth Century* (1912), pp. 124–5. Cf. my *Economic Problems of the Church*, p. 325.
17 *The Copyholders Plea* (1653), quoted by Margaret James, *Social Problems and Policy in the Puritan Revolution* (1930), p. 95.
18 R. Overton, *An Appeale to all Englishmen* (1647), p. 32. This is part of what the radicals intended by demanding codification of the law.
19 J. Cotton, *Abstract of the Laws of New England* (1641), quoted by E. A. J. Johnson, *American Economic Thought in the 17th Century* (1932), p. 208.
20 Ed. A. E. Bland, P. A. Brown and R. H. Tawney, *English Economic History: Select Documents* (1914), p. 309.

21 *Op. cit.*, ed. E. Cardwell (Oxford, 1850), p. 260.

22 J. Hall, *Works* (Oxford, 1837–9), VIII, p. 53.

23 W. Perkins, *Works* (1609–13), I, p. 769; cf. my *Puritanism and Revolution*, p. 230.

24 W. Ames, *Conscience with the Power and Cases Thereof* (1639), pp. 241–3. Cf. W. Letwin, *The Origins of Scientific Economics* (1963), pp. 81–2, who regards 1640 as the dividing line in acceptance of usury.

25 R. Baxter, *A Christian Directory* (1673), Part IV, p. 129.

26 Sir John Hayward, *An Answer to the First Part of a Certain Conference Concerning Succession* (1603), Sig. A 4; cf. John Davies of Hereford, *Humours Heaven on Earth* (1609), in *Complete Works*, ed. A. B. Grosart (1878), I, p. 28. See also chapter 3 above.

27 *Acts of the Privy Council, 1630–1631*, p. 7.

28 Hobbes, *Leviathan* (Everyman ed.), pp. 74–6; *Elements of Law*, ed. F. Tönnies (Cambridge, 1928), pp. 65, 72.

29 See my *Intellectual Origins of the English Revolution*, pp. 250–4.

30 J. Rushworth, *Historical Collections* (1659–1701), II, p. 602. This view of the origin of Chancery was repeated by John Warr, *The Corruption and Deficiency of the Laws of England* (1649), in *Harleian Miscellany* (1744–6), III, p. 246.

31 S. Rutherford, *Lex, Rex* (1644), pp. 117–18, 184, 230–2.

32 Ed. E. R. Foster, *Proceedings in Parliament, 1610* (Yale, 1966), II, p. 178.

33 Peter Ramus, *The Art of Logick* (1626), Sig. A 5v; Preface by Antony Wotton.

34 Translated by Benjamin Farrington in *The Philosophy of Francis Bacon* (Liverpool, 1964), p. 99.

35 Ed. N. E. McClure, *The Letters of John Chamberlain* (American Philosophical Soc., Memoirs, XII, Part I, 1939), II, p. 372.

36 William Thomas, quoted in *Complete Prose Works of John Milton* (Yale ed.), I, p. 569.

37 Quoted by M. A. Judson, *The Crisis of the Constitution* (Rutgers, 1949), p. 296; cf. *Debates in the House of Commons in 1625*, ed. S. R. Gardiner (Camden Soc., 1873), pp. 110–11; J. Forster, *Sir John Eliot* (1865), I, pp. 152–3.

38 Prynne, *The Soveraigne Power of Parliaments and Kingdomes* (1643), I, p. 105, II, p. 23, and *passim*.

39 Milton, *The Tenure of Kings and Magistrates* (1649), in *Complete Prose Works*, III, p. 257.

40 J. Fidoe, T. Jeans and W. Shaw, *Parliament Justified* (1648 [–9]), p. 15. For Fidoe see A. G. Mathews, *Calamy Revised*, pp. 194–5.

41 Milton, *Complete Prose Works*, I, p. 561; II, pp. 222–5; III, p 464.

42   F. A. Yates, *Giordano Bruno and the Hermetic Tradition* (1964);
     A. G. Debus, *The English Paracelsans* (1965); P. M. Rattansi,
     'Paracelsus and the Puritan Revolution', *Ambix*, XI, pp. 24–32;
     C. Webster, 'English Medical Reformers of the Puritan
     Revolution', *Ambix*, XIV, pp. 16–41.

43   H. Haydn, *The Counter-Renaissance* (New York, 1950), *passim*.

44   Ed. A. Peel and L. H. Carlson, *The Writings of Robert Harrison
     and Robert Browne* (1953), pp. 177, 18.

45   Ralegh, *History of the World* (Edinburgh, 1820), I, pp. viii,
     xlii.

46   G. Hakewill, *An Apologie or Declaration of the Power and Providence
     of God* (1635), II, pp. 7, 57, 129. First published 1627.

47   J. Selden, *Table Talk*, s.v. Reason. Cf. my *Intellectual Origins*,
     p. 302.

48   J. Hall, *Works*, VIII, p. 40.

49   *Op. cit.*, p. 196; cf. p. 343.

50   J. Wilkins, *Mathematicall Magick* (1648), p. 2.

51   R. Hooker, *Of the Laws of Ecclesiastical Polity* (Oxford), I, pp.
     151–2, 193; cf. 407–9.

52   *Ibid.*, I, pp. 134, 298–314, 419; II, p. 685; cf. D. Little,
     Religion, Order and Law: a Study in Pre-Revolutionary England
     (Oxford, 1970), pp. 158–62. Sir Richard Fanshawe in 'A
     Canto of the Progress of Learning' (1648) equates reason with
     hierarchy (*Shorter Poems and Translations*, ed. N. W. Bawcutt
     (Liverpool, 1964), pp. 20–1, 93–5). Cf. my *Society and
     Puritanism*, pp. 234–5.

53   Cf. S. L. Bethell, *The Cultural Revolution of the Seventeenth
     Century* (1950), pp. 55, 63.

54   Rattansi, 'Paracelsus and the Puritan Revolution', p. 26.

55   M. Luther, *The Bondage of the Will*, p. 374; *A Commentary on
     St. Paul's Epistle to the Galatians*, pp. 239–42.

56   J. Knox, *Works* (1846–64), V, p. 392.

57   W. Sclater, *An Exposition with Notes upon the First Epistle to the
     Thessalonians* (1619), p. 392. In 1647 the Scottish General
     Assembly of the Kirk summed up a century of wisdom in the
     words: 'There is in the hearts of all the children of men an
     inclination to error, especially to those errors that are most
     plausible to the flesh and savour of carnal liberty' (ed. A. F.
     Mitchell and J. Christie, *The Records of the Commissioners of the
     General Assemblies of the Church of Scotland*, Scottish History Soc.,
     1892, I, p. 292.)

58   W. Laud, *Works* (Oxford, 1849), II, p. 280.

59   Ed. L. H. Carlson, *The Writings of Henry Barrow, 1587–90*
     (1962), pp. 241–2, 556–9.

60   Hakewill, *op. cit.*, II, p. 162.

61   Woodhouse, *op. cit.*, p. 56.

62   Hobhouse, *Morals in Evolution* (1908), p. 156.

63   J. Udall, *A Demonstration of Discipline*, 1588, ed. Arber (1880), p. 1; T. Hooker, *The Soules Humiliation* (1638), pp. 147–8.

64   Sidrach Simpson, *Reformation's Preservation* (1643), p. 26; A. Burges, *The Difficulty of, and the Encouragements to a Reformation* (1643), p. 13; John Bond, *Salvation in a Mystery* (1644), p. 8; Peter Sterry, *The Spirits Conviction of Sinne* (1645), p. 10; *The Teachings of Christ In The Soule* (1648), pp. 23–8.

65   J. Lilburne, *Strength out of Weaknesse* (1649), p. 14.

66   [H. Parker], *Jus Populi* (1644), p. 57.

67   Milton, *Complete Prose Works*, I, p. 699; II, pp. 588, 623.

68   J. Wilkins, *A Discourse concerning A New Planet* (1640), p. 28.

69   J. Calvin, *A Commentary on Genesis*, trans. J. King (1847), I, pp. 85–7, 141, 177, 256.

70   Cf. D. C. Allen, *The Legend of Noah* (Urbana, 1963), chapter III; D. Bush, *Science and English Poetry* (Oxford, 1967), p. 59; my *The World Turned Upside Down*, chapter 11.

71   G. L. Mosse, *The Holy Pretence* (Oxford, 1957), *passim.*

72   T. Taylor, *Christian Practice*, p. 77, in *Works* (1653).

73   Abbott, *Writings and Speeches of Oliver Cromwell*, I, pp. 696, 519; II, pp. 189–90.

74   P. Rossi, *Francis Bacon: from Magic to Science*, trans. S. Rabinovitch (1968), pp. 17, 38–9, 148–9, 190, 222–3 and *passim.*

75   F. A. Yates, 'The Hermetic Tradition in Renaissance Science', in *Art, Science and History in the Renaissance*, ed. C. S. Singleton (Johns Hopkins, 1968), pp. 267–8.

76   Ed. J. Crossley, 'Autobiographical Tracts of Dr. John Dee', in *Chetham Miscellany*, I (1851), p. 63.

77   P. Zagorin, *A History of Political Thought in the English Revolution* (1954), p. 28.

78   See chapter 3 above.

79   Ed. P. Laslett, *John Locke: Two Treatises of Government* (Cambridge, 1960), p. 83. The idea goes back to Marx (*A Contribution to the Critique of Political Economy*, trans. N. L. Stone (New York, 1904), p. 267).

80   F. Greville, *The Remains*, ed. G. A. Wilkes (Oxford, 1965), p. 231; Donne, *Elegie XVIII.*

81   Joseph Sedgwick, *Learnings Necessity* (1653), p. 37, quoted by R. F. Jones, 'The Humanistic Defence of Learning in the Mid-Seventeenth Century', in *Reason and the Imagination*, ed. J. A. Mazzeo (1962), p. 76. I quote via Professor Jones because

the text is obscure; I think this reading of Sedgwick is right, but I am glad to have his confirmation.

82 B. Whichcote, *Moral and Religious Aphorisms* (1930), p. 54. First published 1703.

83 Winstanley, *The Law of Freedom* (1652), in Sabine, *op. cit.*, pp. 564–6.

84 T. Sprat, *The History of the Royal Society of London* (1667), p. 62.

85 J. Glanvill, *Plus Ultra* (1668), p. 52; cf. p. 89. Cf. also Hobbes, *Leviathan*, p. 179, and my *Intellectual Origins*, pp. 184–5.

86 Jordan, *Philanthropy in England, 1480–1660*, and associated works, *passim*.

87 [W. Walwyn], *The Compassionate Samaritane*, in Haller, *Tracts on Liberty in the Puritan Revolution, 1638–47*, III, pp. 68–9; cf. *The Writings of Henry Barrow, 1590–1*, ed. L. H. Carlson (1966), pp. 73, 191.

88 Quoted by C. Webster, 'English Medical Reformers of the Puritan Revolution', pp. 26–7. Much other interesting material is to be found in this article on the analogy between experience and experiment. See also my *Intellectual Origins*, pp. 112–15, 294–7. For *Macaria* see Webster, 'The Authorship and Significance of *Macaria*', *P. and P.*, no. 56, pp. 34–48.

89 T. H. H. Rae, *John Dury* (Marburg, 1970), pp. 121–2, quoting Dury's 'Note concerning Mr. Kinner'. Cf. my *Intellectual Origins*, p. 122.

90 Agricola Carpenter, *Pseuchographia Anthropomagica* (1652), pp. 17, 22.

91 R. Barclay, *An Apology for the True Christian Religion* (1678), p. 38. Cf. pp. 135, 127 above.

92 P. Miller, *The New England Mind: from Colony to Province* (Harvard, 1953), p. 428; cf. D. P. Walker, *The Decline of Hell* (Chicago, 1964), *passim*.

93 R. Greville, Lord Brooke, *A Discourse opening the Nature of that Episcopacie which is exercised in England* (1641), in Haller, *Tracts on Liberty*, II, p. 57.

94 Milton, *Works* (Columbia ed.), XI, p. 7; XIV, p. 29; XV, pp. 206–7.

95 Woodhouse, *op. cit.*, p. 324.

96 Winstanley, *The Saints Paradice* (1648), pp. 78, 122–4; *Truth Lifting up its Head above Scandals* (1649) and *The True Levellers Standard Advanced* (1649), the last two in Sabine, *op. cit.*, pp. 105, 251.

97 J. Cook, *King Charles His Case* (1649), in *Somers Tracts* (1748–51), IV, p. 183.

98 H. Neville, *Plato Redivivus* (c. 1681), in *Two English Republican*

Tracts, ed. C. Robbins (Cambridge, 1969), p. 128; J. Warr, *Administrations Civil and Spiritual, passim*, quoted in my *The World Turned Upside Down*, pp. 219–20. For Coke see my *Intellectual Origins of the English Revolution*, pp. 250–4.

99   William Dillingham, *Prove all things, Hold Fast that which is good* (1656), pp. 14–15; P. W. Thomas, *Sir John Berkenhead, 1617–1679* (Oxford, 1969), pp. 166–7, 206–7.

100   Hobbes, *Leviathan*, pp. 18–19, 81–3; *Elements of Law*, p. 150; *English Works*, IV, pp. xiii–xiv.

101   J. Harrington, *The Oceana and Other Works* (1737), pp. 46–7.

102   J. Taylor, *Ductor Dubitantium*, in *The Whole Works* (1836), III, pp. 183–96.

103   H. More, *An Apology* (1664), chapters I, VII and VIII; Whichcote, *op. cit., passim*.

104   Underhill, *Fenstanton Records*, pp. 20–1, 93–4.

105   H. G. Van Leeuwen, *The Problem of Certainty in English Thought* (The Hague, 1963), pp. 37, 46, 65, 69, 130, 139–42.

106   M. Oakeshott, *Rationalism in Politics* (1967), pp. 17–18; Perry Miller, *op. cit.*, p. 430.

107   Hobbes, *Elements of Law*, pp. 63–4.

108   J. Reeve, *A Transcendent Spiritual Treatise* (1711), pp. 34, 38 (first published 1652); L. Muggleton, *The Acts of the Witnesses* (1764), pp. 37–9 (first published 1699, written 1677).

109   W. Chillingworth, *Works* (1727), p. 68; cf. my *Intellectual Origins*, p. 254.

110   I owe this point to Mr R. R. Orr.

111   P. Worsley, *The Trumpet Shall Sound* (1957), p. 272.

112   A. G. Dickens, *Lollards and Protestants in the Diocese of York, 1509–1558* (Oxford, 1959), *passim*.

113   R. Overton, *Mans Mortalitie* (Liverpool, 1968), p. 21 (first published 1643); G. Fox, *Journal* (1902), I, pp. 430–1; *Gospel-Truth Demonstrated* (1706), pp. 1088–1089. Cf. Samuel Butler, *Characters and Passages from Notebooks*, p. 320: surprising company for Overton and Fox!

114   C. B. Macpherson, *The Political Theory of Possessive Individualism* (Oxford, 1962), pp. 245–6; cf. my *Society and Puritanism*, p. 401.

115   R. S. Westfall, *Science and Religion in Seventeenth Century England* (Yale, 1958), p. 219; cf. pp. 107–11 and p. 259 above.

116   See p. 256 above.

117   N. O. Brown, *Life Against Death* (1959), Part Five; F. E. Manuel, *A Portrait of Isaac Newton* (Harvard, 1968).

118   Cf. F. A. Yates, 'The Hermetic Tradition in Renaissance Science', pp. 273–4.

119 Bacon, *Of the Advancement of Learning*, in *Works*, ed. J. Spedding, R. L. Ellis and D. D. Heath (1870), III, pp. 394–5.

PART III CONTINUITY IN CHANGE: DIVINITY, LAW, MEDICINE

Chapter 5   The Radical Critics of Oxford and Cambridge in the 1650s

1   A lecture delivered at Johns Hopkins University in May 1970; originally published in *Universities in Politics*, ed. J. W. Baldwin and R. Goldthwaite (Johns Hopkins University Press, 1972).

2   Pell to Sir Charles Cavendish, *A Collection of Letters Illustrative of the Progress of Science in England*, ed. J. O. Halliwell (1965 reprint), p. 80. Cf. Francis Osborn's ironical reference to 'the black art of mathematics', and Thomas Hobbes on geometry as an 'art diabolical' (my *Intellectual Origins of the English Revolution*, p. 55).

3   K. Dewhurst, *Dr. Thomas Sydenham (1628–1689)* (Oxford, 1966), p. 17; cf. my *Intellectual Origins*, chapter II, especially pp. 53, 64 and pp. 303–4.

4   J. Webster, *Academiarum Examen* (1654); [J. Wilkins and S. Ward], *Vindiciae Academiarum* (1654).

5   See my *Intellectual Origins*, pp. 301–2.

6   Hobbes, *Leviathan* (Penguin), pp. 728, 384; *Behemoth*, in *English Works*, ed. Molesworth, VI, p. 347; cf. pp. 184–5, 215–20, 230–4, 276–82.

7   J. Bramhall, *Works* (Oxford, 1842–5), III, p. 478.

8   George Kendall, *A Vindication of the Doctrine Commonly Received in the Reformed Churches* (1653), Epistle and p. 3; cf. J. Trapp, *A Commentary on the New Testament* (1958), p. 460: 'bemisted with the fog of superstition'. First published 1647. For the stultifying effect of the enforced conformity of the 1630s, see for example Joseph Mede, *Works* (1672), pp. 865–6.

9   *The Grand Remonstrance*, in *Constitutional Documents of the Puritan Revolution, 1625–60*, ed. S. R. Gardiner (Oxford, 1906), pp. 229–30. In April 1645 *Mercurius Politicus* noted of an ordinance about Cambridge that it confuted royalist slanders that Parliament was opposed to learning (no. 79, pp. 723–4). Cf. Henry Burton, *Englands Bondage and Hope of Deliverance* (1641), p. 29, quoted by J. F. Wilson, *Pulpit in Parliament* (Princeton, 1969), pp. 49–50.

10 T. May, *History of the Parliament* (1647), III, p. 79.

11 M. B. Rex, *University Representation in England, 1640–1690* (1954), pp. 58–60, chapters VI and VIII, *passim*.

12 [W. Walwyn], *The Compassionate Samaritane* (1644), in Haller, *Tracts on Liberty*, III, p. 82.

13 N. Culpeper, *A Directory for Mid-wives* (1651), Epistle to the Reader; *A Physicall Directory* (1651), Sig. Av.

14 H. Peter, *A Word for the Armie* (1647); *Good Work for a Good Magistrate* (1651), pp. 1–3.

15 B. S. Capp, 'Extreme Millenarianism', in *Puritans, the Millennium and the Future of Israel*, ed. Peter Toon (Cambridge, 1970), pp. 86–7.

16 See W. Y. Tindall, *John Bunyan, Mechanick Preacher* (New York, 1964), *passim*.

17 *The Cry of a Stone, Or a Relation of Something spoken in Whitehall by Anna Trapnel* (1654), pp. 42–3.

18 See my *Economic Problems of the Church*, chapter 5.

19 Margaret James, 'The Political Importance of the Tithes Controversy in the English Revolution, 1640–60', *History*, XXVI, pp. 1–18.

20 T. Hall, *The Pulpit Guarded with XX Arguments* (1651), Epistle and p. 22; *An Apologie for the Ministry and its Maintenance* (1660), pp. 56–7; R. B[oreman], *The Triumph of Learning over Ignorance* (1653), in *Harleian Miscellany* (1744–6), I, pp. 494–5.

21 H. Kaminsky, 'The University of Prague in the Hussite Revolution: The Role of the Masters', in *Universities in Politics*, pp. 79–106.

22 F. Osborn, *Letters . . . To Colonel William Draper*, p. 7, in *Miscellaneous Works* (1722), II.

23 [Anon.], *A Vindication of Learning From unjust Aspersions* (1646), pp. 1–2, 20; R. B[oreman], *The Country-Mans Catechisme: Or, the Churches Plea for Tithes* (1652), pp. 3–4; *The Triumph of Learning over Ignorance*, p. 499; Edward Waterhouse, *An Humble Apologie for Learning and Learned Men* (1653), especially pp. 91–110.

24 Walwyn, *The Compassionate Samaritane*, in Haller, *Tracts on Liberty*, III, p. 83.

25 See my *Economic Problems of the Church*, chapter X.

26 J. Milton, *Works* (Columbia ed.), VI, pp. 65, 101–5.

27 New universities were proposed for London, Durham, York, Bristol, Exeter, Norwich, Manchester, Shrewsbury, Ludlow, Cornwall, Wales, the Isle of Man (see my *Intellectual Origins*, pp. 108–9, 124; R. L. Greaves, *The Puritan Revolution and Educational Thought* (Rutgers, 1969), pp. 55–6). For scholarships see Greaves, *op. cit.*, pp. 59–60. Cf. G. Snell, *The Right Teaching of Useful Knowledge* (1649), pp. 311–27; [W. Sprigge], *A Modest Plea for an Equal Commonwealth* (1659), pp. 49–52.

28 W. Hartley, *The Prerogative Priests Passing-Bell* (1651), p. 6.

29 M. R[ande = Mary Cary], *12 Proposals To the Supreme Governours of the three Nations now assembled at Westminster* (1653), p. 7.

30 C. Webster, *Samuel Hartlib and the Advancement of Learning* (Cambridge, 1970), p. 191.

31 Cf. *Rump: Or an Exact Collection Of the Choycest Poems and Songs Relating to the Late Times* (1662), I, p. 15: suggesting, ironically, that universities must be overthrown because they 'maintain the language of the Beast'.

32 Kaminsky, *op. cit.*, p. 105; J. M. Headley, *Luther's View of Church History* (Yale, 1963), pp. 207–8. See W. Lamont, *Godly Rule* (1969), *passim*, and my *Antichrist in Seventeenth-Century England, passim.*

33 H. Schulz, *Milton and Forbidden Knowledge* (New York, 1955), pp. 186–7.

34 Ed. Peel and Carlson, *Writings of Robert Harrison and Robert Browne*, pp. 530–1; ed. Carlson, *Writings of John Greenwood* (1962), I, pp. 268–9; *Writings of Henry Barrow, 1587–1590*, pp. 344–53, 534–41; *1590–1591*, pp. 191, 211–24.

35 S. E. Morison, *The Founding of Harvard College* (Harvard, 1935), p. 176.

36 Samuel How, *The Sufficiency of the Spirit's Teaching* (8th ed., 1792), pp. 36, 40–1, 51.

37 Brooke, *A Discourse Opening the Nature of that Episcopacie which is exercised in England* (1642), p. 106, in Haller, *Tracts on Liberty*, II, p. 150. Brooke is ostensibly stating the views of others.

38 R. Williams, *The Bloudy Tenent of Persecution* (1644) (Hanserd Knollys Soc., 1848), pp. 263–5; *The Hireling Ministry None of Christs* (1652), pp. 14–17.

39 H. Denne, *Grace, Mercy and Peace* (1645), in *Fenstanton Records*, ed. Underhill, p. 377; Horne, *A Consideration of Infant Baptism* (1654), pp. 157–60.

40 [R. Overton], *The Araignement of Mr. Persecution* (1645), p. 40, in Haller, *Tracts on Liberty*, III, p. 250; cf. p. 228.

41 E. Chillenden, *Preaching without Ordination* (1647), p. 6.

42 H. Peter, *Good Work for a Good Magistrate* (1651).

43 Milton, *Works* (Columbia ed.), VI, p. 93; cf. p. 96, and *Prose Works* (Yale ed.), VI, pp. 572–3.

44 R. Norwood, *The Form of an Excommunication made by Mr. Sydrach Sympson . . . against Captain Robert Norwood* (1651), pp. 33–4.

45 R. Crab, *Dagons-Downfall* (1657), p. 2. For Crab see my *Puritanism and Revolution*, pp. 314–22.

46 H. Stubbe, *A Light Shining out of Darknes* (1659), pp. 145, 150; cf. pp. 92–106, 109–10, 139–50, 161–3.

47 R. Coppin, *Truths Testimony* (1655), p. 16.

48 John Spittlehouse, *The First Addresses to his Excellencie the Lord Generall* (1653), pp. 12–16; J. Canne, *The Time of the End* (1657), Sig. A 4v–6v.

49 R. F[arnsworth], *Antichrists Man of War* (1655), pp. 53, 55; G. Fox, *The Lambs Officer* (1659), p. 3; S. Fisher, *The Testimony of Truth Exalted* (1679), p. 298, cf. pp. 589–90. Cf. G. Fox, *Journal* (1902), I, pp. 7, 11, 236–7, 386; Greaves, *op. cit.*, pp. 24, 122–3, 133–6.

50 Abbott, *Writings and Speeches of Oliver Cromwell*, II, p. 73.

51 [Sprigge], *A Modest Plea for an Equal Commonwealth*, p. 45; cf. my *Intellectual Origins*, pp. 311–14.

52 H. Stubbe, *A Light Shining out of Darknes*, pp. 206–7.

53 J. Hall, *The Advancement of Learning* (1649), Dedication to Parliament; Dury, *A Supplement to the Reformed School*, pp. 6–7, 11–12, in *The Reformed Library-Keeper* (1650); Biggs, *The Vanity of the Craft of Physick* (1651), Sig. b 3–3v., pp. 229–30.

54 The Epistle Dedicatory to Webster's *Academiarum Examen* is dated 21 October 1653; cf. his *The Saints Guardian*, where the Epistle is dated 28 April 1653. Cf. also Samuel Hartlib's *True and Ready Way to Learn the Latin Tongue* (1654), written in 1653 and dedicated to Francis Rous, Speaker of the Barebones Parliament. Hartlib's *Some Proposals towards the Advancement of Learning*, written in 1653 but never published, presumably because of the dissolution of the Barebones Parliament, is printed by C. Webster in *Samuel Hartlib and the Advancement of Learning*, pp. 166–92. See also John Nickolls, *Original Letters and Papers of State Addressed to Oliver Cromwell* (1743), pp. 99–102, 129.

55 J. Owen, *Works* (1850–3), X, pp. 493–4; cf. *The Correspondence of John Owen*, ed. P. Toon (1970), pp. 59–61, 65, 79, 101. Cf. also T. Fuller, *Comfort in Calamity* (1654), in M. Fuller, *Pulpit Sparks* (1886), p. 242; [Anon.], *A True State of the Case of the Commonwealth* (1654), p. 16; G. Kendall, *op. cit.*, p. 3; *C.S.P., Venetian, 1653–1654*, p. 160; Anthony Wood, *History and Antiquities of the University of Oxford*, ed. J. Gutch (1786–92), II, p. 657; *Life and Times, I (1632–63)*, ed. A. Clark (Oxford Historical Soc., 1891), pp. 292–6; L. M. Payne, 'Sir Charles Scarborough's Harveian Oration, 1662', *Journal of the History of Medicine*, XII, p. 163.

56 D. Masson, *Life of Milton*, IV (1859–80), pp. 566–8.

57 Hartley, *The Prerogative Priests Passing-Bell*, pp. 9–10; W.

Sheppard, *The Peoples Priviledge and Duty Guarded Against the Pulpit Preachers Incroachment* (1652), p. 1; Webster, *Academiarum Examen*, Sig. A 4v, B 1v; [Wilkins and Ward], *Vindiciae Academiarum*, pp. 6, 23, 43, 48; T. Hall, *Vindiciae Literarum* (1654), pp. 198–9.

58   Abbott, *op. cit.*, IV, p. 273.

59   *Vindiciae Academiarum*, pp. 3–4; Evelyn, *Diary*, 10 December 1656; cf. Edward Leigh, *A Treatise of Religion and Learning* (1656), pp. 65–7, 91–7; Edward Reynolds, *A Sermon Touching the Use of Humane Learning* (1658); T. Blake, *Vindiciae Foederis* (2nd ed., 1658), pp. 173–8.

60   See H. R. Trevor-Roper, 'William Dell', *E.H.R.*, LXII, pp. 377–9.

61   *L.J.*, VIII, pp. 401, 403, 418; Dell, *The Building, Beauty, Teaching and Establishment of the truly Christian and Spiritual Church*, in *Several Sermons*, p. 68. The passage quoted is not in the printed text of the sermon: see [Anon.], *A Vindication of certain Citizens* (1646), pp. 6–9.

62   Dell, *op. cit.*, p. 158; Wilson, *Pulpit in Parliament*, pp. 88, 92.

63   E. C. Walker, *William Dell* (Cambridge, 1970), p. 94; T. Edwards, *Gangraena*, Part I, pp. 45, 63–4, 213, 262; S. Rutherford, *A Survey of Antinomianism*, pp. 187, 209, printed with *A Survey of the Spirituall Antichrist* (1648).

64   A. G. Matthews, *Calamy Revised*, pp. 161–2; Walker, *op. cit.*, pp. 115–16.

65   Dell, *op. cit.*, pp. 246, 251; B. Worden, *The Rump* (1974), p. 319.

66   Walker, *op. cit.*, pp. 105, 165.

67   Dell, *op. cit.*, pp. 642–8.

68   *Ibid.*, pp. 403–4, 642–8.

69   Fox added, however, 'Happy would Dell have been if he had lived what he spoke' (*The Great Mistery of the Great Whore Unfolded* (1659), p. 154). Nevertheless, among the Quaker books advertised at the end of William Sewell's *The History of the . . . Quakers* in 1722 and of Joseph Besse's *Sufferings of . . . Quakers* in 1733, Dell's writings are included.

70   Dell, *Several Sermons*, pp. 91, 388, 398, 402–3. Dell quoted Luther in support. Cf. p. 273.

71   *Ibid.*, pp. 390–2, 395–6, 467; cf. p. 375.

72   *Ibid.*, pp. 273–7, 297–300, 397.

73   *Ibid.*, pp. 407, 419.

74   *Ibid.*, p. 368. Dell cited Wyclif, Hus, Luther, Calvin, Tyndale, Latimer and Ridley against universities (*ibid.*, pp. 522–3, 573, 576–8, 582, 590–5, 600, 610–12, 619–22, 628–38).

75 *Ibid.*, pp. 381–2.
76 *Ibid.*, pp. 246, 466–9, 481, 483–4; cf. pp. 477–9.
77 Defined as 'an unlawful mixing of philosophy with the outward letter of the word' (p. 489); 'a dead word . . . out of the books and writings of men' (p. 640).
78 *Ibid.*, pp. 487–93.
79 *Ibid.*, pp. 495–513; cf. pp. 397, 615–16; the last sentence is attributed to Dell in *A Vindication of certaine Citizens*, p. 9.
80 *Ibid.*, pp. 550–5, 558–60, 574, 603–8, 615–18, 626, 641.
81 *Ibid.*, pp. 516–18, 525–6.
82 *Ibid.*, pp. 516, 525–31, 535–8, 544, 602–3, 617.
83 J. Sedgwick, *Learnings Necessity to an able Minister of the Gospel*, in *A Sermon Preached at St. Maries, in the University of Cambridge* (1653), p. 39.
84 Dell, *op. cit.*, pp. 371, 585, 597–9, 638.
85 *Ibid.*, pp. 575, 580, 613.
86 G. F. T. Jones, *Saw-Pit Wharton* (Sydney, 1967), p. 212; Dell, *The Increase of Popery in England* (1681), p. 2 and Postscript, pp. 2–3, 18–19.
87 Sabine, *Works of Gerrard Winstanley*, pp. 213–14.
88 *Ibid.*, pp. 237–42.
89 *Ibid.*, pp. 474–6; cf. p. 463.
90 *Ibid.*, pp. 239–40.
91 Cf. P. M. Rattansi, 'The Intellectual Origins of the Royal Society', *Notes and Records of the Royal Society of London*, Vol. 23, pp. 129–43.
92 Sabine, *op. cit.*, pp. 562–6.
93 *Ibid.*, pp. 568–70.
94 *Ibid.*, p. 271.
95 *Ibid.*, p. 241.
96 *Ibid.*, pp. 562–6, 576–8; cf. p. 593; Dell, *Sermons*, pp. 642–8.
97 Dell, *Sermons*, p. 647; Sabine, *op. cit.*, p. 570.
98 J. Pope, *The Unveiling of Antichrist* (1646), p. 14; How, *op. cit.*, p. 51.
99 Dell, *op. cit.*, p. 79.
100 Clarendon, *Life* (1759), II, p. 39.
101 [Anon.], *Sundry Things from several Hands concerning the University of Oxford* (1659), in *Harleian Miscellany*, VI, pp. 80–4. Cf. *Leybourn-Popham MSS* (Hist. MSS Comm.), pp. 4–5 – a petition to Parliament in 1642 from 'divers' of Oxford. See also [W. Sprigge], *A Modest Plea*, pp. 21–3, 31, 50.
102 Milton, *Areopagitica* (1644), in *Complete Prose Works* (Yale ed.), II, p. 544.
103 They have been treated much more sympathetically by

American than by English historians: see Martha Ornstein, *The Role of Scientific Societies in the Seventeenth Century* (Chicago, 1928), p. 245; Greaves, *op. cit.*, p. 168.

104 Greaves, *op. cit.*, pp. 137–8, 146. Cf. chapter 7 above.

Chapter 6   The Inns of Court

1 Originally published as a review article in the *History of Education Quarterly*, XII, no. 4 (New York, 1972).

2 Wilfrid R. Prest, *The Inns of Court under Elizabeth I and the Early Stuarts, 1590–1640* (1972), p. 26.

3 *Ibid.*, pp. 27–8.

4 *Ibid.*, pp. 30–2.

5 Ed. F. Bamford, *A Royalist's Notebook* (1936), p. 14.

6 Williams, *The Council in the Marches of Wales under Elizabeth I*, pp. 61–4, 321.

7 Ed. F. J. Fisher, *Sir Thomas Wilson's State of England (1600)*, *Camden Miscellany*, vol. 16 (1936), pp. 24–5; Hakewill, *An Apologie for the Providence of God*, p. 548; Whitelocke, *Memorials of the English Affairs*, pp. 416–17; G. Albion, *Charles I and the Court of Rome* (1936), pp. 176–7.

8 R. W. Turner, *The Equity of Redemption* (Cambridge, 1931), p. 30.

9 Kenneth Charlton, *Education in Renaissance England* (London, 1965), p. 188. It is embarrassing to have to explain that to say this is not to claim Coke as a protagonist of laissez-faire. But since the view is attributed to me by Barbara Malament ('The "Economic Liberalism" of Sir Edward Coke', *Yale Law Review*, 75, pp. 1321–58), I must make it clear that I do not hold and have never held it. To demonstrate, as her article convincingly does, that Coke did not believe in laissez-faire is rather like proving that Adam Smith did not advocate a welfare state.

10 W. J. Jones, *The Elizabethan Court of Chancery* (Oxford, 1967), pp. 497–8; cf. p. 321.

11 M. G. Davies, *The Enforcement of English Apprenticeship* (Harvard, 1956), p. 151.

12 Jones, *Court of Chancery*, pp. 461–2; R. Stock, *A Commentary upon the Prophecy of Malachi* (Edinburgh, 1865), p. 165. This last work was first published posthumously in 1641. Stock died in 1626.

13 Ed. G. B. Harrison, *De Maisse's Journal (1597)* (1931), p. 12. In the French fashion De Maisse presumably included the gentry in the word 'nobility'.

14 John Hare, *Englands Proper and onely way to an Establishment in Honour, Peace and Happinesse* (1648), p. 6.

15 R. Burton, *The Anatomy of Melancholy* (Everyman ed.), I, pp. 102–3; cf. pp. 83–5.

16 M. R[ande = Cary], *12 Proposals* (1653), p. 11; see my *Intellectual Origins of the English Revolution*, pp. 260–3; *The World Turned Upside Down*, pp. 216–18.

17 F. W. Jessup, *Sir Roger Twysden, 1597–1672* (1965), p. 16.

18 William London, *A Catalogue of the Most Vendible Books in England* (1657), Sig. G 2v–G 3.

19 P. Styles, 'Politics and Historical Research', in *English Historical Scholarship in the 16th and 17th Centuries*, ed. L. Fox (Dugdale Society, 1956), p. 70.

20 J. Rushworth, *Trial of Strafford* (1680), p. 662.

21 Lawrence Stone, 'The Educational Revolution in England, 1560–1640', *P. and P.*, no. 28, p. 28. (Mr D. H. Pennington supplied the figures.)

22 My *Intellectual Origins*, pp. 301–14. See also Mark Curtis, *Oxford and Cambridge in Transition, 1558–1642* (Oxford, 1959), *passim*.

23 Prest, *The Inns of Court*, p. 153.

24 *Ibid.*, pp. 153–7.

25 *Ibid.*, p. 168.

26 *Ibid.*, pp. 159–67.

27 *Ibid.*, pp. 196–7.

28 *Ibid.*, pp. 204–15, 223; cf. pp. 38 and 53.

29 *Ibid.*, pp. 41–3.

30 *Ibid.*, pp. 100–14. This appears to conflict with the findings of Messrs Brunton and Pennington, that in the Long Parliament the average age of supporters of the King was significantly lower than that of supporters of Parliament; and with Professor Aylmer's similar conclusion about civil servants (D. Brunton and D. H. Pennington, *Members of the Long Parliament* (1954), pp. 15–16; G. E. Aylmer, *The King's Servants* (1961), pp. 393–4). The apparent contradiction reinforces the point that MPs and civil servants were very special groups, and that no general conclusions should be drawn from them about the population as a whole, or even about the landed class as a whole, as some historians have rashly done (see my *The World Turned Upside Down*, pp. 151–2).

31 Prest, *The Inns of Court*, pp. 236–7.

32 *Ibid.*, pp. 170–3.

33 A. Warren, *A New Plea for the Old Law* (1653), quoted in D. Veall, *Popular Movements for Law Reform, 1640–1660* (Oxford, 1970), p. 124.

34 Davenant, *Shorter Poems and Songs* (Oxford, 1972), p. 83.

35 Prest, *The Inns of Court*, pp. 44–6.

Chapter 7   *The Medical Profession and Its Radical Critics*

1   The Gideon Delaune Lecture, delivered at Apothecaries' Hall,
London, 11 May 1973.

2   F. N. L. Poynter, 'William Walwyn, "Health's Student" ',
British Medical Journal, II; 'Nicholas Culpeper and his Books',
Journal of the History of Medicine, XVII; R. S. Roberts, 'The
Personnel and Practice of Medicine in Tudor and Stuart
England', *Medical History*, VI, no. 4 and VII, no. 3; C. Webster,
'English Medical Reformers and the Puritan Revolution: A
Background to the "Society of Chymical Physitians" ', *Ambix*,
XIV.

3   R. S. Roberts, review of Sir George Clark's *A History of the
Royal College of Physicians of London*, I, in *History of Science* (1966),
V, p. 91; John Cook, *Unum Necessarium: Or, The Poore Mans Case*
(1648), p. 61; cf. L. Stone, *The Crisis of the Aristocracy, 1558–
1641* (Oxford, 1965), p. 357.

4   *D.N.B.* His age was said to be ninety-seven.

5   J. H. Raach, 'Five Early Seventeenth Century English Country
Physicians', *Journal of the History of Medicine*, XX, pp. 214–15;
H. Brinkelow, *The Complaynt of Roderick Mors* (?1542). Cf. my
Intellectual Origins of the English Revolution, pp. 80–1.

6   G. Starkey, *Pyrotechny Asserted and Illustrated* (1658), p. 94.

7   John Robinson, *Essayes; Or, Observations Divine and Morall* (2nd
ed., 1638), pp. 300–3.

8   G. N. Clark, *A History of the Royal College of Physicians* (Oxford,
1964), I, p. 195; cf. N. Biggs, *The Vanity of the Craft of Physick*
(1651), p. 213.

9   Cook, *op. cit.*, pp. 61–3.

10   C. Wall, H. C. Cameron and E. A. Underwood, *A History of
the Worshipful Society of Apothecaries* (Oxford, 1963), *passim*; my
Intellectual Origins of the English Revolution, pp. 80–3, 237.

11   George Fox, *Journal* (1902), I, pp. 29–30.

12   Cook, *Monarchy No Creature of Gods making* (1652), Sig. C 4v;
cf. John Stoughton, *Choice Sermons* (1640), pp. 87–8.

13   Ed. John Nickolls, *Original Letters and Papers of State Addressed to
Oliver Cromwell* (1743), pp. 101, 129–30. This suggestion had
been made by Robert Burton: see p. 152 above.

14   *A Treatise of Taxes and Contributions* (1662), in *Economic Writings
of Sir William Petty*, ed. C. H. Hull (Cambridge, 1899), I, pp.
23–9; L. Muggleton, *The Acts of the Witnesses* (1764), pp. 110–13.

15   John Heydon, *The Harmony of the World* (1662), Sig. c 6.

16   C. Goodall, *The College of Physicians Vindicated* (1676), Sig. A 4v–
5v, pp. 1–2, 22–3; *The Royal College of Physicians* (1684), Sig. A 4.

17 J. Webster, *The Saints Guardian* (1654), pp. 2, 26–7; cf. his *Academiarum Examen* (1654), pp. 10–18.

18 Cf. p. 130 above and chapter 5 *passim*.

19 John Jones, *The Judges Judged out of their own Mouths* (1650), p. 56; *The Jurors Judges of Law and Fact* (1650), *passim*.

20 G. Fox, *Several Papers Given Forth* (1660), pp. 32–3.

21 B. S. Capp, *The Fifth Monarchy Men* (1972), p. 160; *Walwins Wiles*, in Haller and Davies, *op. cit.*, p. 303.

22 Sabine, *Writings of Gerrard Winstanley*, pp. 512, 282, 572–3.

23 J. Warr, *Administrations Civil and Spiritual* (1648), pp. 3–5; Jones, *The Jurors Judges of Law and Fact*, p. 92. Cf. chapter 6 above.

24 See my *Intellectual Origins*, p. 35; cf. Robert Burton, quoted on p. 152 above.

25 Jones, *The Jurors Judges of Law and Fact*, p. 81.

26 Biggs, *op. cit.*, Sig. B 1, p. 3. See pp. 172–3 above.

27 Culpeper, *Medicaments for the Poor* (1656), Sig. B 4; *A Physicall Directory* (1651), Sig. A 2v, pp. 344–5; *Galens Art of Physick* (1657), Sig. A 7–B 3.

28 *Medicaments for the Poor*, Sig. B 4; *Galens Art of Physick*, Sig. B 4.

29 My *Intellectual Origins*, p. 261; J. Heydon, *A New Method of Rosie Crucian physick* (1658), p. 49.

30 Ed. C. B. Robinson, *Rural Economy in Yorkshire in 1641* (Surtees Soc., 1857), pp. 150–1; M. Ashley, *John Wildman* (1947), p. 10.

31 C. Webster, 'Medical Reformers', p. 22; G. Herbert, *A Priest to the Temple*, chapter XXIII.

32 See epigraph to this chapter.

33 R. Barclay, *The Inner Life of the Religious Societies of the Commonwealth* (1876), Appendix to chapter VI, p. xiv.

34 Milton, *Works* (Columbia ed.), VI, pp. 80–1; Fox, *Journal*, I, p. 28.

35 Robinson, *op. cit.*, p. 303.

36 R. Mandrou, *Des humanistes aux hommes de science* (Paris, 1973), p. 115.

37 Quoted by H. S. Bennett, *English Books and Readers, 1558–1603* (Cambridge, 1965), pp. 183–4.

38 Culpeper, *A Physicall Directory* (1650), Sig. B 2, p. 242; (1651), Sig. A 2–2v.

39 Peter Fisher, 'Medicine: the best of both worlds', in *China Now*, no. 28 (January 1973), pp. 4, 8.

40 Poynter, 'Nicholas Culpeper and his Books', p. 157.

41 *Culpepers School of Physick* (1659), Sig. C 7, pp. 3–29, 41, 277–400.

42 Heydon, *The Wise-Mans Crown: Or, The Glory of the Rosie-Cross* (1664), Sig. C 3v; cf. *The Harmony of the World*, Sig. C 6; *Theomagia* (1666), p. 125.

43 Culpeper, *A Physicall Directory* (1649), Sig. A 2; *Semeotica Urania or an Astrological Judgment of Divines* (1651), p. 190.

44 Cook, *The Poore Mans Case*, p. 65.

45 Walwyn, *The Power of Love* (1643), pp. 1–2.

46 *Galens Art of Physick*, Sig. B 3.

47 Peter, *Good Work for a Good Magistrate* (1651), p. 33; Wolfe, *op. cit.*, p. 308.

48 Ed. C. Webster, *Samuel Hartlib and the Advancement of Learning*, p. 180; Webster, 'English Medical Reformers', p. 23; my *The World Turned Upside Down*, p. 240.

49 Cook, *Monarchy No Creature of Gods making*, Sig. e 3.

50 Warr, *Administrations Civil and Spiritual, passim.*

51 S. Hutin, *Robert Fludd (1574–1637)* (Paris, 1972), 3me. Partie, II, *passim.*

52 Webster, 'Medical Reformers', pp. 40–1; A. G. Debus, *Science and Education in the Seventeenth Century* (1970), p. 33.

53 Cf. Lilly's attacks on 'proud malicious clergymen', e.g. in *Astrological Predictions* (1654), *passim.*

54 Culpeper, *A Physicall Directory* (1650), Sig. Bv; *An Ephemeris for the Year 1652*, p. 18; *An Ephemeris for the yeer 1651*, Sig. G 3v–4v; cf. H 2v, T iv.

55 Culpeper, *A Directory for Mid-wives* (1651), Epistle to the Reader; *A Physicall Directory* (1651), Sig. A–Av; *Culpepers School of Physick*, Sig. B 6v, C.

56 Culpeper, *A Physicall Directory* (1650), Sig. B–Bv; cf. *An Ephemeris for The Year 1654*, *An Ephemeris for The Year 1656*, *passim.*

57 *Mr. Culpepers treatise of Aurum Potabile . . . to which is added Mr. Culpepers Ghost* (1656), p. 2.

58 *An Ephemeris for the Year 1652*, Sig. C 3, cf. p. 20; *The Fall of Monarchie* (1652), pp. 17, 72, 75; *An Ephemeris for the Year . . . 1653*, p. 24; *An Ephemeris for The Year 1654*, pp. 26–7; *An Ephemeris for The Year 1655*, Sig. C 3; cf. *A Physicall Directory* (1649), Sig. A.

59 *The Disputes Between Mr. Cranford and Dr. Chamberlen* (1652), *passim*; Chamberlen, *Legislative Power in Problemes* (?1659), p. 6; J. H. Aveling, *The Chamberlens and the Midwifery Forceps* (1882), p. 54; Chamberlen, *The Poore Mans Advocate* (1649), p. 21.

60 Aveling, *op. cit.*, pp. 55–6; ed. C. Severn, *Diary of the Rev. John Ward* (1839), p. 107.

61 Webster, *Academiarum Examen*, pp. 2–3, 10–18; *The Saints Guide*, Sig. B, pp. 1–6, 13–27.

62 *The Testimony of William Erbery* (1658), pp. 263–4; *C.S.P.D.*, *1653–4*, p. 302; T. Hall, *Vindiciae Literarum* (1655), p. 199;

Webster, *Academiarum Examen*, *passim*; *The Vail of the Covering, Spread over all Nations* (1713), p. 6 (first published 1653).

63 Poynter, 'Nicholas Culpeper and his Books', p. 153.

64 Webster, *The Displaying of Supposed Witchcraft* (1677), p. 259 and *passim*; *Metallographia: Or, An History of Metals* (1671), Sig. Bv–B 2v, pp. 3–9, 34–5, 319–23, and *passim*; ed. A. R. and M. B. Hall, *The Correspondence of Henry Oldenburg* (Wisconsin, 1965), VII, pp. 534–5; ed. C. H. Josten, *Elias Ashmole, 1617–1692* (Oxford, 1966), II, p. 763.

65 Biggs, *op. cit.*, p. 45, Sig. B, a 4. See Hall, *op. cit.* (1649), p. 27; Milton, *Complete Prose Works* (Yale ed.), II, p. 493.

66 Biggs, *op. cit.*, Sig. b 3–4, pp. 57–64, 200–31.

67 *Culpepers School of Physick*, Sig. C 5.

68 W.W., *Spirits Moderated, And so qualified, As to maintain the true Natural Heat and Radical Moisture of the Body* (1654), pp. 1, 25–6; Poynter, ' William Walwyn, "Health's Student" ', *passim*.

69 *Spirits Moderated*, pp. 2–4; H. Brooke, *A Commentary of Health* (1650), p. 1; Poynter, *op. cit.*, pp. 482–3.

70 *Spirits Moderated*, pp. 14, 4–5; *Physick for Families* (1669), pp. 6–20, 102, 113; (1681 ed.), pp. 4, 19–41.

71 C. Webster, 'English Medical Reformers', pp. 31–9.

72 See chapter 12 above.

73 Thomas, *Religion and the Decline of Magic*, p. 270.

74 Philastrogus, *Lillies Ape Whipt* (?1652), p. 3; *The World Turned Upside Down*, pp. 237, 244. For the law see chapter 6 above.

75 W. Lilly, *An Astrological Prediction* (1653), Sig. B 3v; but cf. Lambarde, quoted by G. R. Elton, *Studies in Tudor and Stuart Politics and Government* (Cambridge, 1974), I, p. 266.

76 Cook, *The Poore Mans Case*, p. 68.

77 Roberts, 'Personnel and Practice of Medicine', *Medical History*, VIII, p. 228.

78 Aveling, *The Chamberlens*, p. 56; W.W., *A Touchstone for Physick* (1667), p. 48.

79 C. Wilson, 'The Other Face of Mercantilism', *T.R.H.S.*, 1959, p. 91; A. Ruth Fry, *John Bellers, 1654–1725* (1935), p. 110.

PART IV CHANGE IN CONTINUITY: SOME SOCIAL ATTITUDES

Chapter 8 *The Many-Headed Monster*

1 Originally published in *From the Renaissance to the Counter-Reformation: Essays in Honor of Garrett Mattingly*, ed. C. H. Carter (New York, 1965).

2 For Stubbe, see his *Essay in Defence of the Good Old Cause* (1659)

and *A Letter to an Officer of the Army* (1659). For Osborn, see his *Miscellaneous Works* (1722), I, pp, 182–3.

3 In 1536 the gentry of Cumberland had put themselves at the head of a similar popular revolt, whose original intention was 'to destroy the gentry', as the generals were to put themselves at the head of the mutinous New Model Army in 1647 (Tawney, *The Agrarian Problem in the Sixteenth Century*, pp. 318–19).

4 A. Neville, *De Furoribus Norfolciensium* (1575), quoted by R. Groves, *Rebels' Oak* (n.d.), p. 50; Protector Somerset, quoted by G. Burnet, *History of the Reformation* (1825), IV, p. 202; R. H. Tawney and E. Power, *Tudor Economic Documents* (1924), I, p. 47; T. Cranmer, *Miscellaneous Writings and Letters* (Parker Soc., 1846), p. 190.

5 *V.C.H.*, *Cambridge*, pp. 14–15, 67; cf. W. T. McCaffrey, *Exeter, 1540–1640* (Harvard, 1958), p. 190.

6 F. Aydelotte, *Elizabethan Rogues and Vagabonds* (Oxford, 1913), p. 169; Tawney, *Agrarian Problem*, p. 320; *C.S.P.D.*, *1595–7*, pp. 316–19, 343–4; J. Nalson, *An Impartial Collection* (1683), II, p. 166; Bland, Brown and Tawney, *English Economic History: Select Documents*, p. 271. Cf. p. 187 above.

7 Tawney, *Agrarian Problem*, pp. 338–9; E. F. Gay, 'The Midland Revolt and the Inquisitions of Depopulation of 1607', *T.R.H.S.*, New Series, XVIII (1904), p. 214; *V.C.H.*, *Leicestershire*, IV, p. 108; cf. L. A. Parker, 'The Agrarian Revolution at Cotesbach', in *Studies in Leicestershire Agrarian History*, ed. W. G. Hoskins (Leicestershire Archaeological Society, 1949), p. 73.

8 D. G. C. Allan, 'The Rising in the West, 1628–31', *Ec.H.R.*, second series, V, pp. 83–5; Bland, Brown and Tawney, *op. cit.*, pp. 390–1; *C.S.P.D.*, *1629–31*, p. 387; E. Kerridge, 'The Revolts in Wiltshire against Charles I', *Wiltshire Archaeological and Natural History Magazine*, LVII (1958–60), pp. 66–72.

9 Ed. A. Feuillerat, *The Complete Works of Sir Philip Sidney*, I (Cambridge, 1922), pp. 318–19, 30, 34, 311; IV (1962), pp. 118–19, 125. For enclosure at Penshurst, see Tawney, *Agrarian Problem*, p. 194.

10 Cf. Shakespeare, *Coriolanus*, III, i: TRIBUNE SOCINIUS: What is the city but the people?

11 Sidney, *Works*, I, pp. 322–4, 201, 312–13; IV, pp. 120–2, 286–8. An almost identical attitude is shown in Sackville's *Gorboduc* (1561), where again the inconstancy of the rebellious people and their violence and desperation are stressed, as well as the ruthless suppression by sword and noose.

12 Spenser, *Faerie Queene*, book II, canto 9, stanza 13; book V, canto 2, stanzas 32–52, cf. book IV, canto i, stanza 28. In one

of the most openly political passages in the whole poem, Artegall was called upon for help by Burbon, 'Against these peasants which have me oppress'd'. Talus and the knight of justice 'made cruel havoc of the baser crew . . . The rascal many soon they overthrew' (book v, canto 11, stanzas 57–9). Cf. pp. 231–2 above.

13   Shakespeare, *Coriolanus*, II, iii; II *Henry VI*, IV, *passim*. Cf. the very similar 'causes of sedition' which Robert Crowley had seen in 1549 (*Select Works* (Early English Text Soc., 1872), pp. 132–3, 141–3, 164).

14   Middleton, *The Mayor of Queenborough*, in *Plays* (Mermaid Series), II, p. 302 (first printed 1661); B. Googe, 'An Epitaph on the Lord Sheffield's Death', *Eglogs, Epytaphs and Sonettes*, ed. E. Arber (1871), pp. 69–70 (first published 1563); T. Dekker, *Dramatic Works*, ed. F. Bowers (Cambridge, 1953–61), I, p. 119; IV, pp. 177–8. Both Dekker's plays probably date from 1599–1600. Cf. the clowns who revolt in *The Sun's Darling* (?1623–4), *ibid.*, IV, pp. 57–9.

15   W. J. Ong, *Ramus: Method and the Decay of Dialogue* (Harvard, 1958), p. 253; Montaigne, *Essays* (World's Classics), III, p. 55; J. Sylvester, *Complete Works*, ed. A. B. Grosart (1880), I, p. 207; II, p. 55.

16   P. Massinger, *Plays*, ed. F. Cunningham (1897), pp. 49, 207, 329; Sir W. Davenant, *Gondibert*, ed. D. A. Gladish (Oxford, 1971), pp. 16, 34–5, 38; cf. Davenant, *Shorter Poems and Songs*, ed. A. M. Gibbs (Oxford, 1972), pp. 83, 147; J. Beaumont, *Psyche* (1648), in *Complete Poems*, ed. Grosart (1880), I, p. 149; John Collop, *Poems*, ed. C. Hilberry (Wisconsin, 1962), p. 35.

17   R. Burton, *Anatomy of Melancholy* (Everyman ed.), I, p. 78; Browne, *Religio Medici* (1642), in *Works* (Bohn ed., 1852), II, pp. 415–16; T. Fuller, *The Holy Warre* (fourth edition, 1651), p. 113; Walwyn, *The Fountain of Slaunder* (1649), p. 19.

18   Quoted by W. G. Zeeveld, *Foundations of Tudor Policy* (Harvard, 1948), p. 216; F. Thynne, *The Debate between Pride and Lowliness*, ed. J. P. Collier (1841), p. 14; Sir T. Smith, *The Commonwealth of England*, ed. L. Alston (Cambridge, 1906), Book I, chapter 24; Sir T. Aston, *A Remonstrance against Presbytery* (1641), Sig. B 4; G. Monck, Duke of Albemarle, *Observations Upon Military and Political Affairs* (1671), p. 146.

19   R. Knevet, *Shorter Poems*, ed. A. M. Charles (Ohio State University Press, 1966), pp. 125–6; ed. F. Bamford, *A Royalist's Notebook*, p. 61; L. Boynton, *The Elizabethan Militia, 1558–1638* (1967), pp. 62, 108–11, 220–1.

20   Ed. J. R. Tanner, *Constitutional Documents of the Reign of James I*

(Cambridge, 1930), p. 21; C. V. Wedgwood, *Thomas Went-worth, First Earl of Strafford* (1961), p. 74; R. C. Richardson, *Puritanism in north-west England*, p. 147; [Anon.], *Leather* (1629), in *An English Garner*, ed. E. Arber (1895–7), VI, p. 211; Richard Gardiner, quoted by M. Maclure, *The Paul's Cross Sermons*, p. 115; Sir Thomas More, *Utopia* (Everyman ed.), p. 112; Sir E. Coke, *III Institutes* (1648), pp. 9–10; Bishop Hooper, *Later Writings* (Parker Soc., 1852), p. 78. I am indebted to Mr Conrad Russell for the reference to Coke.

21 I have given some illustrations of this point in my *Society and Puritanism in Pre-Revolutionary England* (1964), pp. 385–7.

22 *Parliamentary History of England* (1806), I, p. 822; cf. F. Greville, *The Remaines*, ed. G. A. Wilkes (Oxford, 1965), pp. 122, 185, 188–95; N. L. Williams, *Sir Walter Ralegh* (1962), p. 139. For Winstanley see Sabine, *op. cit.*, p. 414. Cf. p. 233 above.

23 T. Deloney, *Jack of Newberrie*, in *Shorter Novels: Elizabethan and Jacobean* (Everyman ed.), p. 50. Deloney ostensibly referred to clothiers in Henry VIII's reign; but the relevance to the year in which he published is obvious.

24 McCaffrey, *Exeter*, pp. 116–17, 247–9; [Anon.], *Considerations Touching Trade, with the Advance of the Kings Revenues* (1641), p. 15; Aydelotte, *op. cit.*, p. 171; J. Smyth, *A Description of the Hundred of Berkeley* (Gloucester, 1885), p. 43.

25 Aydelotte, *op. cit.*, pp. 169, 171; L. Radzinowicz, *A History of English Criminal Law . . . from 1750* (1948), I, pp. 140–1; B. Osborne, *Justices of the Peace, 1361–1848* (Shaftesbury, Dorset, 1960), pp. 83, 24; W. K. Jordan, *The Forming of the Charitable Institutions of the West of England* (Trans. American Philosophical Soc., New Series, L, Part 8, 1960), p. 56; E. G. R. Taylor, *Late Tudor and Early Stuart Geography* (1934), p. 163; D. B. Quinn, *The Elizabethans and the Irish* (Cornell, 1966), p. 157; cf. A. L. Rowse, *Shakespeare's Southampton* (1965), p. 241, and p. 223 above.

26 *Sermons or Homilies* (Oxford, 1802), pp. 93, 469, 473.

27 Browne, *op. cit.*, II, pp. 415–16. Browne was careful to add that he referred not exclusively to 'the base and minor sort of people'; there was also a rabble amongst the gentry.

28 T. Becon, *Prayers and other pieces* (Parker Soc., 1844), p. 243; Cranmer, *Miscellaneous Writings and Letters* (Parker Soc., 1846), pp. 193–6; *Sermons or Homilies*, p. 88; M. Parker, *Correspondence* (Parker Soc., 1853), p. 61, cf. p. 437; *Zurich Letters, 1558–1579* (Parker Soc., 1842), p. 18; J. Whitgift, *Works* (Parker Soc., 1851), I, p. 466; ed. A. Peel, *Tracts Ascribed to Richard Bancroft* (Cambridge, 1953); p. 83; J. Knox, *The History of the Reformation in Scotland* (Glasgow, 1832), pp. 115, 131, 237, 225.

29 T. Nashe, *The Unfortunate Traveller* (1594), in *Shorter Novels: Elizabethan and Jacobean*, p. 275; F. Cheynell, *The Rise, Growth and Danger of Socinianisme* (1643), p. 57; [J. Sturgion], *Queries for His Highness to Answer* (1655), quoted by D. B. Heriot, 'Anabaptism in England during the 17th Century', *Trans. Congregational Hist. Soc.*, XIII (1937–9), p. 29.

30 T. Lever, *Sermons*, ed. Arber (1901), pp. 28–9; T. Cooper, *An Admonition to the People of England*, ed. Arber (1895), p. 148; Spenser, *op. cit.*, p. 514; cf. my *Puritanism and Revolution*, p. 52; *C.S.P.D.*, *1595–7*, p. 344; ed. P. A. Kennedy, 'Verses on the Puritan Settlement in North America, 1631', in *A Nottinghamshire Miscellany*, Thoroton Soc., Record Series, XXI (1961), pp. 38–9. Cf. pp. 231–2 above.

31 See my *Society and Puritanism*, chapters 2, 5–6, 13, and pp. 240–1; J. Aubrey, *Miscellanies* (5th ed., 1890), p. 213 (written in 1670); T. Becon, *The Catechism* (Parker Soc., 1844), pp. 595–8; H. C. White, *Social Criticism in Popular Religious Literature of the Sixteenth Century* (New York, 1944), chapter III, *passim*; A. F. Scott Pearson, *Thomas Cartwright and Elizabethan Puritanism* (Cambridge, 1925), pp. 252–3.

32 Cooper, *Admonition*, p. 9; cf. pp. 102–3, 118–19, 139, 168–9; Whitgift, *Works*, II, p. 398; cf. Sir J. E. Neale, *Elizabeth I and her Parliaments, 1584–1601* (1957), p. 274; W. Pierce, *An Historical Introduction to the Marprelate Tracts* (1908), p. 182.

33 Ed. W. Notestein, *Journal of Sir Simonds D'Ewes* (Yale, 1923), pp. 339–40; *Old Parliamentary History* (London, 1763), IX, pp. 388–9; cf. Clarendon, *History of the Rebellion* (1888), II, p. 512; *Life* (1759), I, pp. 81, 96–7.

34 Aston, *op. cit.*, Sigs. b 4, I 4v–K, M 4. Both friends and foes of Presbyterianism pointed out that 'the people' who were to elect elders and ministers were not the rabble but heads of households, men of some small substance (see my *Society and Puritanism*, chapter 13).

35 C. Read, *Lord Burghley and Queen Elizabeth* (1960), pp. 470, 509; C. D. Bowen, *Francis Bacon* (1963), pp. 141, 21.

36 See my *Society and Puritanism*, chapter 13, *passim*; *Mercurius Politicus*, no. 78, 27 November–4 December 1651, p. 1237.

37 F. Guizot, *History of the English Revolution* (1884), p. 120; Sir E. Dering, *A Collection of Speeches* (1642), pp. 108–9, 118; V. Pearl, *London and the Outbreak of the Puritan Revolution* (Oxford, 1961), pp. 226–7; [B. Ryves], *Angliae Ruina* (1647), p. 176.

38 With the important exception of Mr Brian Manning's article, 'The Nobles, the People and the Constitution', *P. and P.*, IX,

1956, pp. 42–64; and more recently, *The Origins of the English Civil War*, ed. C. Russell (1973), pp. 242–4.

39 Nalson, *op. cit.*, I, pp. 749, 753; ed. D. Gardiner, *The Oxinden Letters, 1607–1642* (1933), p. 286; 'An honourable and worthy speech . . . by Mr. Smith', *Harleian Miscellany* (1744–6), V, p. 251; Rushworth, *Historical Collections*, IV, p. 509.

40 D. Masson, *Drummond of Hawthornden* (1873), pp. 306, 405.

41 J. Hacket, *Scrinia Reserata* (1693), II, pp. 165, 198; J. Howell, *Instructions for Forreine Travell*, ed. Arber (1869), p. 78 (first published 1642); cf. Sir John Denham, *The Sophy* (1641), Act IV, scene i.

42 *Eikon Basilike*, chapter IV *passim*; W. K. Jordan, *The Development of Religious Toleration in England* (1932–40), III, pp. 39–40; *Fairfax Correspondence*, II, p. 295.

43 J. Corbet, *An Historicall Relation of the Military Government of Gloucester* (1645), in *Bibliotheca Gloucestrensis* (Gloucester, 1823), I, pp. 8, 14; S. I. Arkhangelsky, *Peasant Movements in England in the 1640s and 1650s* (Moscow, 1960, in Russian), *passim*. Sir S. D'Ewes, *Diary*, Harleian MS. 163 f. 135 v. I owe this reference to the kindness of Mr Robert Clifton.

44 D'Ewes, quoted by A. Kingston, *Hertfordshire during the Great Civil War* (1894), p. 36; 'The Life of Mr. Arthur Wilson', in Peck, *Desiderata Curiosa*, pp. 474–5; Kingston, *East Anglia and the Great Civil War* (1897), p. 64; F. P. Verney, *Memoirs of the Verney Family* (1893), II, p. 69.

45 *L.J.*, V, p. 42; [Ryves], *Angliae Ruina*, pp. 96, 26–7; Bamford, *A Royalist's Notebook*, pp. 104–6; Rushworth, *op. cit.*, V, p. 41: see p. 48 for Parliament's indignant reply; Kingston, *Hertfordshire*, p. 30.

46 J. Burroughes, *Sions Joy* (1641), p. 34.

47 T. Hobbes, *English Works*, II, p. 79; 'A Letter from Mercurius Civicus to Mercurius Rusticus' (1643), *Somers Tracts* (1748–51), V, p. 415; [E. Bowles], *Plaine English* (1643), pp. 25–6. I owe this reference, and much other help and advice, to the generosity of Professor C. M. Williams.

48 Howell, *op. cit.*, p. 78; *Portland MSS.* (Hist. MSS Comm.), III, p. 86; ed. D. Gardiner, *The Oxinden and Peyton Letters, 1642–1670* (1937), pp. 36–7; cf. R. C. Goffin, *The Life and Poems of William Cartwright* (Cambridge, 1918), p. 142.

49 *C.S.P.D., 1641–3*, p. 445; Hist. MSS Comm., *Seventh Report*, I, p. 549; *The Examination of Sir John Coniers by a Committee of the House of Lords*, quoted by Manning, *op. cit.*, p. 61: the explanation may of course not have been the true one; but the speaker clearly expected it to impress his audience.

50 Ed. S. M. Ffarington, *Farington Papers* (Chetham Soc., 1856), p. 88; T. May, *History of the Parliament* (1647), I, pp. 113–14.

51 *Portland MSS.*, I, p. 87: cf. the similar reasons given by Robert Kirle for his change of side (J. and T. W. Webb, *Memorials of the Civil War in Herefordshire* (1879), II, pp. 350–3); Margaret, Duchess of Newcastle, *The Life of William Cavendish, Duke of Newcastle*, ed. C. H. Firth (1907), p. 94.

52 Hist. MSS Comm., *Fourth Report*, I, p. 268; ed. T. T. Lewis, *Letters of Lady Brilliana Harley* (Camden Soc., 1854), p. 214; J. H. Hexter, *The Reign of King Pym* (Harvard, 1941), p. 8; *C.S.P. Venetian, 1643–7*, p. 162.

53 G. Naworth (Wharton), *Mercurio-Coelico Mastix* (1644), p. 2; T. Edwards, *Gangraena*, Part I, pp. 115–18, Part III, pp. 261–2; [Anon.], *A Modell of the Government of the Church under the Gospell, by Presbyters* (1646), p. 2.

54 P. Zagorin, *The Court and the Country* (New York, 1970), p. 323; Rushworth, *Historical Collections*, V, p. 732.

55 Harleian MS. 165 f. 131. I owe this reference to Professor C. M. Williams.

56 G. Smith, *Englands Pressures* (1645), p. 9; A. R. Bayley, *The Great Civil War in Dorset* (Taunton, 1910), pp. 478–9, cf. p. 110; Arkhangelsky, *op. cit.*, *passim*; cf. George Downing to John Winthrop on the dangers of a third party in March 1648 (Massachusetts Hist. Soc. Collections, VI (1863), p. 541).

57 T.B., *The Engagement Vindicated* (1650), p. 11; Cary, *Memorials of the Great Civil War*, I, p. 293; J. Lilburne, *The Upright Mans Vindication* (1653), p. 15; *A Declaration of Some Proceedings of Lieut. Colonel John Lilburne* (1648), p. 52; Woodhouse, *Puritanism and Liberty*, pp. 70–1; Whitelocke, *Memorials of the English Affairs* (Oxford, 1853), II, pp. 128–9.

58 *Memorial of Denzil, Lord Holles*, in *Select Tracts*, ed. F. Maseres (1815), I, p. 191; C. Walker, *History of Independencie* (1661), part II, p. 156, part I, p. 59, cf. pp. 140–1; ed. Petrie, *Letters of Charles I*, p. 270; Abbott, *Writings and Speeches of Oliver Cromwell*, III, p. 435, cf. p. 584, IV, p. 267.

59 *Vindiciae Veritatis* (1654), quoted by V. Pearl, 'The "royal Independents" in the English Civil War', *T.R.H.S.*, 1968, p. 95 (the pamphlet was written in 1648); J. Webster, *Academiarum Examen*, Sig. A3; cf. H. Power, *Experimental Philosophy* (1664), p. 184; 'this numerous piece of monstrosity (the multitude)'. Power appears to quote the passage from Sir Thomas Browne cited in note 17 above.

60 J. Gauden, *Hieraspites* (1653), p. 437; *Verney Memoirs*, III, p. 199; H. Newcome, *Autobiography*, ed. R. Parkinson (Chetham Soc.,

1852), p. 119; R. Baxter, *The Holy Commonwealth* (1659), pp. 227, 93, 103, 203; *A Christian Directory* (1673), IV, p. 19.

61 *Thurloe State Papers*, I, p. 747; [Anon.], *The History of the House of Stanley* (Liverpool, 1799), pp. 216–17.

62 Cf. H. G. Koenigsberger, 'The Organization of Revolutionary Parties in France and the Netherlands during the 16th Century', *Journal of Modern History*, XXVII (1955), pp. 335–51; M. Walzer, 'Puritanism as a Revolutionary Ideology', *History and Theory*, III (1963), pp. 59–90.

63 I use the phrase advisedly, *pace* Professor Hexter. I do not know how else briefly to describe those whom I go on to discuss.

64 Jordan, *Philanthropy in England, 1480–1660, passim*, and related works; W. G. Hoskins, *Essays in Leicestershire History* (Liverpool, 1950), pp. 123–83; my *Society and Puritanism*, pp. 223–4, 230–1, 236; F. J. Fisher, 'The Development of the London Food Market', *Ec.H.R.*, V (1935); cf. chapter 1 above; Sidney, *op. cit.*, I, p. 315; Haller, *The Rise of Puritanism* (Columbia University Press, 1938), *passim*; Walzer, *op. cit., passim*.

65 [Sir R. Cotton], *The Danger wherein the Kingdome now standeth and the Remedies* (1628), p. 19.

66 Allan, *op. cit., passim*; cf. my *Economic Problems of the Church*, pp. 61–2.

67 *Reliquiae Baxterianae*, p. 89; Corbet, *op. cit.*, I, p. 14.

68 *Mr. Peters Last Report of the English Wars* (1646), p. 6.

69 Woodhouse, *op. cit.*, pp. 53–63; Macpherson, *The Political Theory of Possessive Individualism*, chapter 3; W. Stoughton, *An Assertion for true and Christian Church-Policie* (Middelburg, 1604), pp. 240–7; Milton, *Complete Prose Works* (Yale ed., 1953), I, pp. 932–3.

70 Bronterre O'Brien, *London Mercury*, 7 May 1837, quoted in Max Morris, *From Cobbett to the Chartists* (1948), p. 161.

71 See chapter 10 above.

Chapter 9   A One-Class Society?

1 Originally published as a review of Mr Laslett's *The World We Have Lost*, in *History and Theory*, vol. VI, 1967.

2 A. N. Savine, 'Istoriya dvukh Manorov' ('The History of Two Manors'), *Zhurnal Ministerstva Narodnago Prosveshcheniya* (*Journal of the Ministry of Education*), Petrograd, New Series, part 62 (1916), pp. 193–240; 'Istoriya odnogo Vostochnogo Manora' ('The History of an East Anglian Manor'), in *Sbornik v chest' M. K. Lyubavskogo* (*Essays in Honour of M. K. Lyubavsky*), Petrograd, pp. 251–79. Similar conclusions were reached by Professor

V. M. Lavrovsky in an article based on Savine's notes of another manor (*Izvestiya Akademii Nauk* [ION] – *Bulletin of the Academy of Sciences, Historical and Philosophical Series* – III, no. 3, 1946). Mr Laslett may be excused for not reading Russian; but Lavrovsky's article at least was summarized in the *Ec.H.R.* twenty years ago (XVI (1946), pp. 125–9). Mr Laslett does not even mention the pioneering statistical work on parish registers of the late John Buckatzsch ('Occupations in the Parish Registers of Sheffield, 1655–1719', *Ec.H.R.*, Second Series, I (1949), pp. 145–50; 'Places of Origin of a Group of Immigrants into Sheffield, 1624–1799', *ibid.*, Second Series II (1950), pp. 303–6).

3   Collinson, *The Elizabethan Puritan Movement*, pp. 143, 370–1, 374 and *passim*; A. M. Everitt, *The Community of Kent and the Great Rebellion* (Leicester, 1966), p. 225; Richardson, *Puritanism in north-west England*, p. 27 and *passim*; H. Barbour, *The Quakers in Puritan England* (Yale, 1964), p. 176; E. J. I. Allen, *The State of the Church in the Diocese of Peterborough, 1601–1642* (Oxford University B.Litt. thesis, 1972), pp. 65–7, 99–100, 113–15.

4   D. T. Witcombe, *Charles II and the Caroline House of Commons, 1663–1674* (Manchester, 1966), p. 121.

5   Thomas, *Religion and the Decline of Magic*, p. 166.

6   F. H. West, *Sparrows of the Spirit* (no date or place), pp. 36–7.

7   Ed. A Hastings White, *Memoirs of Sir Isaac Newton's Life by William Stukeley* (1752) (1936), pp. 25–6.

8   Further discussion of parish registers, published since this chapter was written, will be found in J. T. Krause, 'Changes in English Fertility and Mortality, 1781–1830', *Ec.H.R.*, 2nd Series, XI; ed. D. V. Glass and D. E. C. Eversley, *Population in History* (1965), especially pp. 170–2, 383–91; M. W. Flinn, 'Population in History', *Ec.H.R.*, 2nd Series, XX; E. A. Wrigley, 'London's Importance, 1650–1750', *P. and P.*, no. 37, p. 46 and *passim*; Wrigley, *Population and History* (1969); T. H. Hollingsworth, *Historical Demography* (1969), chapter 5.

9   For a historian's approach to this question, see L. Stone, 'Social Mobility in England, 1520–1700', *P. and P.*, no. 33, pp. 27–8; cf. p. 53.

10 I intend no disrespect to Professor Gluckman's exciting work by questioning Mr Laslett's analogy.

11 See also the following, published since this chapter was written: P. J. Greven, Junior, *Four Generations: Population, Land and Family in Colonial Andover, Massachusetts* (Cornell, 1970), especially p. 267; R. S. Schofield, 'Historical Demography: some possibilities and some limitations', *T.R.H.S.*, 1971, pp. 119–32; G. E. Aylmer, Introduction to *The Interregnum: the Quest for Settlement*,

1646–1660, ed. Aylmer (1972), pp. 1, 3–4; P. Clark, 'The migrant in Kentish Towns, 1580–1640', in *Crisis and Order in English Towns, 1500–1700*, ed. P. Clark and P. Slack (1972), p. 154; a review of a new edition of *The World We Have Lost* in *The Times Literary Supplement*, 4 May 1973; F. G. Emmison, *Elizabethan Life: Morals and Church Courts* (1973), pp. 76–7, 100, 102; R. Mandrou, *Louis XIV en son temps* (Paris, 1973), p. 381.

Chapter 10   *Pottage for Freeborn Englishmen: Attitudes to Wage-Labour*

1   Originally published in *Socialism, Capitalism and Economic Growth: Essays presented to Maurice Dobb*, ed. C. H. Feinstein (Cambridge, 1967).

2   Sir John Clapham, *A Concise Economic History of Modern Britain from the earliest times to 1750* (Cambridge, 1951), p. 212.

3   Froissart, *Chronicle*, translated by Sir John Bourchier, Lord Berners (1901–3), III, p. 224.

4   Ed. E. Lamond, *A Discourse of the Common Weal of this Realm of England* (Cambridge, 1893), pp. 49–50; cf. E. Lipson, *An Economic History of England* (1943), II, pp. 66–8; T. G. Barnes, *Somerset, 1625–40* (Oxford, 1961), p. 3.

5   Adam Smith, *The Wealth of Nations* (World's Classics), I, pp. 131–2.

6   Quoted by J. U. Nef, *War and Human Progress* (1950), p. 231.

7   Robert Reyce, *The Breviary of Suffolk (1618)*, ed. Lord F. Hervey (1902), p. 57.

8   [Anon.], *Reasons for a Limited Exportation of Wooll* (1677), quoted by A. Clark, *Working Life of Women in the Seventeenth Century* (1919), p. 149.

9   A. F. Upton, *Sir Arthur Ingram* (Oxford, 1961), pp. 112, 128–32.

10   G. R. Lewis, *The Stannaries: A Study of the English Tin Mines* (Harvard, 1924), pp. 211, 198.

11   Ed. M. Oppenheim, *The Naval Tracts of Sir William Monson* (Naval Records Soc., II, 1902), p. 237.

12   T. C. Smout, *A History of the Scottish People, 1560–1830* (1969), p. 134. The same was true of Aberdeenshire fifty years later.

13   Nef, *op. cit.*, p. 229.

14   Ed. J. Thirsk, *The Agrarian History of England and Wales, 1500–1640* (Cambridge, 1967), pp. 112, 411–12, 463 and *passim*.

15   W. Notestein, *The English People on the Eve of Colonization* (New York, 1954), p. 85.

16   See pp. 209–10 above.

17   See pp. 152, 186–7 above.

18 Ed. F. J. Fisher, *Sir Thomas Wilson's State of England (1600)*, Camden Miscellany, XVI (1936), p. 20; L. Boynton, *The Elizabethan Militia* (1962), pp. 108–9. Cf. p. 186 above.

19 P. A. Kennedy, 'Documents from the Nottinghamshire County Record Office', *A Nottinghamshire Miscellany*, Thoroton Soc. Record Series, XXI, p. 38; for the 'virtual social revolution' which free land meant, see S. C. Powell, *Puritan Village* (New York, 1965), especially pp. 107–8.

20 W. Strachey, *For the Colony of Virginia Britannica* (1612), quoted by E. G. R. Taylor, *Late Tudor and Early Stuart Geography* (1934), p. 163.

21 P. Copland, *Virginias God be Thanked* (1622), quoted by P. Miller, *Errand into the Wilderness* (1956), p. 110. Cf. p. 189 above.

22 D. Ogg, *England in the Reign of Charles II* (Oxford, 1955), I, p. 55.

23 R. Crowley, *Select Works* (Early English Text Society, 1872), p. 166; J. Simon, *Education and Society in Tudor England* (Cambridge, 1966), pp. 195, 217.

24 C. B. Macpherson, *The Political Theory of Possessive Individualism*, chapter 4, *passim*. In the section which follows I draw heavily on this brilliant book. Some have queried Professor Macpherson's identification of 'servants' with wage-labourers; but no evidence from seventeenth-century usage has yet been produced which refutes him.

25 H. Parker, *Observations upon some of his Majesties late Answers and Expresses* (1642), in Haller, *Tracts on Liberty*, II, p. 186; Macpherson, *op. cit.*, pp. 122–3, 140–1, 182–3.

26 J. Eliot, *The Christian Commonwealth* (1659), pp. 5–6.

27 K. Marx, *Grundrisse: Foundations of the Critique of Political Economy* (Penguin ed.), p. 604; cf. pp. 735–7, 769, 845.

28 Ed. L. Alston, *De Republica Anglorum, A Discourse of the Commonwealth of England* (Cambridge, 1906), pp. 20–2, 46, 138; cf. T. Fuller, *The Holy State* (1648), p. 112.

29 W. Harrison, *Description of England*, in R. Holinshed, *Chronicles* (1577), Sig. D iv.

30 [Anon.], *Haec-Vir* (1620), Sig. B3; *C.J.*, I, p. 759.

31 Ed. J. M. Osborn, *The Autobiography of Thomas Whythorne* (Oxford, 1961), pp. 212, 237, 248, 251.

32 S. Rowlands, *Complete Works* (Hunterian Club, 1880), II, p. 5; cf. W. Browne, *Poems* (Muses Library), I, p. 317.

33 S. Gosson, *School of Abuse*, 1579 (Shakespeare Soc., 1841), p. 29; J. Cocke, *A Common Player* (1615), quoted by E. K. Chambers, *The Elizabethan Stage* (Oxford, 1923), IV, p. 256; cf. *A Health to the Gentlemanly Profession of Serving Men* (1598),

quoted by M. C. Bradbrook, *The Rise of the Common Player* (1962), p. 43; Dover Wilson in *The Cambridge History of English Literature* (Cambridge, 1950), p. 399.

34   G. Wither, 'Wither's Motto', in *Juvenilia* (1621), Spenser Soc. reprint, II, p. 200; J. Day, *Works*, ed. R. Jeffs (1963), p. 568; Burton, *Anatomy of Melancholy* (Everyman ed.), I, p. 15.

35   Bacon, Essay XXIX.

36   Sir Walter Ralegh, *The History of the World*, quoted in *Oxford English Dictionary* under 'hireling'.

37   M. Marprelate, *The Epistle*, ed. Arber (1895), p. 30. First published 1588.

38   H. Barrow, *A Briefe Discovery of the False Church* (1590), in *The Writings of Henry Barrow*, ed. L. H. Carlson (1962), p. 505.

39   W. Stoughton, *An Assertion for true and Christian Church-Policie* (1604), pp. 238–9.

40   [Anon.], *Persecutio Undecima* (1648), p. 6.

41   J. Stephens, *Satyrical Essayes* (1615), p. 424; E. Hickeringill, *Priest-craft* (1705), II, vi, p. 62. Both quoted in *Oxford English Dictionary*, under 'journeyman'.

42   See M. F. Keeler, *The Long Parliament, 1640–1* (American Philosophical Soc., 1954), p. 33; K. H. D. Haley, *The First Earl of Shaftesbury*, p. 244.

43   M. R. Freer, 'The Election at Great Marlow in 1640', *Journal of Modern History*, XIV, p. 435.

44   G. Wither, *Hallelujah* (1857), p. 294: first published 1641.

45   Sabine, *Writings of Gerrard Winstanley*, pp. 408, 592; cf. pp. 288, 542, 586, 598, cf. pp. 232–3 above.

46   J. Ussher, *The Power communicated by God to the Prince* (3rd ed., 1710), Sig. D 6v–7.

47   Firth and Rait, *Acts and Ordinances of the Interregnum*, I, p. 749.

48   See my *Society and Puritanism in Pre-Revolutionary England*, pp. 437, 446–50, 456, 459–63.

49   [Anon.], *The Case of the Army Soberly Discussed* (1647), p. 6.

50   Hobbes, *Elements of Law*, p. 105.

51   Baxter, *The Holy Commonwealth* (1659), pp. 218–19.

52   Woodhouse, *Puritanism and Liberty*, p. 59; D. Underdown, 'The Parliamentary Diary of John Boys', *Bulletin of the Institute of Historical Research*, XXXIX, p. 152.

53   Ed. S. R. Gardiner, *Camden Miscellany*, VII (1875), pp. 1–3.

54   W. J. Blake, 'Hooker's Synopsis Chorographical of Devonshire', *Reports and Transactions of the Devonshire Association for the Advancement of Science, Literature and Art*, XLVII, p. 342; cf. John Ponet, *A Short Treatise of Politique Power* (1642), p. 23 (first published 1556). The importance of the distinction

between servants and villeins was still being stressed by Edward Chamberlayne in his *Angliae Notitia* (1669), pp. 515–16.

55 M. Drayton, *The Barons Warres*, in *Poems* (1619) (Scolar Press reprint, 1969), p. 6.

56 Quoted by C. V. Wedgwood, *Thomas Wentworth, First Earl of Strafford* (1961), p. 62.

57 I have been unable to trace this sentence, which is quoted by G. G. Coulton, *Medieval Panorama* (Cambridge, 1945), p. 56.

58 Edward, Earl of Clarendon, *The History of the Rebellion*, ed. W. D. Macray (Oxford, 1888), I, p. 437.

59 Ed. E. B. Wood, *Rowland Vaughan His Book* (1897), p. 153.

60 P. Gordon, *A Short Abridgment of Britanes Distemper* (Spalding Club, Edinburgh, 1844), pp. 76, 78.

61 R. Heath, 'To one blaming my high-minded Love', *Clarastella* (1650), p. 13.

62 J. Beaumont, *Psyche* (1648), in *Complete Poems*, ed. Grosart (1880), I, p. 87; II, p. 146; cf. Denham, *The Sophy*, Act IV, scene i.

63 *State Trials*, IV, pp. 1086–7.

64 Ed. S. M. ffarington, *The Farington Papers* (Chetham Soc., 1856), p. 89.

65 J. Archer, *The Personall Reigne of Christ upon Earth* (1641), *passim*.

66 Milton indeed translated Job 12:21: 'he pours contempt on the freeborn', where both the Geneva and the Authorized Version have 'he poureth contempt upon princes' (Milton, *Complete Prose*, Yale ed., VI, p. 786).

67 Rutt, *Parliamentary Diary of Thomas Burton*, IV, pp. 255–7.

68 Smith, *op. cit.*, p. 105; *To the . . . Supreme Authority of this Nation, the Commons of England in Parliament Assembled* (1649), in *Leveller Manifestoes of the Puritan Revolution*, ed. D. M. Wolfe (New York, 1944), p. 329.

69 [Anon.], *A Discourse for a King and a Parliament* (1660), pp. 1–2.

70 R. C. Simmons, 'Godliness, Property and the Franchise in Puritan Massachusetts', *Journal of American History*, LV, pp. 495–511; cf. *Puritan Political Ideas*, ed. E. S. Morgan (New York, 1965), pp. 165–7, quoting John Cotton.

71 See p. 225 above, and my *Society and Puritanism*, p. 459.

72 Woodhouse, *op. cit.*, p. 69.

73 Ed. F. Cunningham, *The Plays of Philip Massinger* (1897), p. 102.

74 Ed. W. Notestein, *The Journal of Sir Simonds D'Ewes* (Yale, 1923), p. 43; cf. p. 431.

75 Wolfe, *op. cit.*, p. 14; cf. Haller, *Tracts on Liberty*, III, p. 266.

76 *The Moderate*, no. 61, 4–11 September 1649, quoted by R. Howell, 'Reconsidering the Levellers: the evidence of *The Moderate*', *P. and P.*, no. 46, p. 75.

77 [Anon.], *A Discourse Consisting of Motives for the Enlargement and Freedome of Trade, Especially that of Cloth* (1645), p. 3. We may compare the MP who in 1610 said that for the King by patent 'to prohibit some of his subjects' to labour 'were unlawful and an absurd commandment because it is directly against the law of God' (E. R. Foster, *Proceedings in Parliament, 1610*, II, p. 160).

78 T. Case, *Spiritual Whordome* (1647), p. 34, quoted by A. Barker, *Milton and the Puritan Dilemma* (Toronto, 1942), p. 142.

79 Rushworth, *op. cit.*, VI, p. 624.

80 Sabine, *op. cit.*, pp. 560, 580; cf. pp. 260, 272; N. Culpeper, *The Fall of Monarchie* (1652), p. 16; cf. his *A Physicall Directory* (1651), Sig. B. The 1661 manifesto of Venner's Fifth Monarchy revolt demanded 'our birthrights'.

81 J. Lindsay, *John Bunyan* (1937), chapters 8 and 9 *passim*.

82 G. Smith, *Gods Unchangeableness* (1655), Sig. Av; L. Clarkson, *A Generall Charge* (1647), title-page; *The Lost Sheep Found*, p. 14; *The Testimony of William Erbery* (1658), p. 310; J. Child, *New Englands Jonas* (1647), p. 8; Webster, *Academiarum Examen*, Sig. B iv; *Culpeper's School of Physick* (1659), title-page.

83 Milton, *Complete Prose Works* (Yale ed.), I, pp. 585, 669, 728, 624; II, p. 485; III, pp. 204, 206, 411, 454; IV, p. 387.

84 Agricola Carpenter, *Pseuchographia Anthropomagica: Or, A Magicall Description of the Soul* (1652), pp. 5, 11–12, 22, 24.

85 [Anon.], *A Declaration of Some Proceedings* (1648), in Haller and Davies, *op. cit.*, p. 344.

86 Ed. P. Laslett, *Patriarcha and Other Political Works of Sir Robert Filmer* (Oxford, 1949), p. 232.

87 Underdown, 'The Parliamentary Diary of John Boys, 1647–8', p. 148.

88 J. Jones, *The Jurors Judges of Law and Fact* (1650), p. 93.

89 [J. Sturgion], *Queries for His Highness to Answer* (1655), quoted by D. B. Heriot, 'Anabaptism in England during the 17th century', *Trans. of the Congregational Hist. Soc.*, XIII (1937–9), p. 29; cf. *Thurloe State Papers*, V, p. 230 (1656).

90 [J. Besse], *Sufferings of the . . . Quakers*, p. 11.

91 E. Burrough, *The Memorable Works of a Son of Thunder and Consolation* (1672), pp. 85, 89, 773, 813; cf. pp. 563–4: 'birthright'.

92 Fox, *Journal*, I, p. 287; cf. Sewell, *History of the . . . Quakers*, p. 95 (Miles Halhead in 1654) and Besse, *Sufferings of the . . . Quakers*, I, pp. 133, 450.

93 L. Muggleton, *The Acts of the Witnesses of the Spirit* (1764), p. 160.

94 *A Needful Corrective or Ballance in Popular Government*, quoted by V. Rowe, *Sir Henry Vane* (1970), p. 227. Miss Rowe attributes this pamphlet to Vane.

95 J. Hall (of Richmond), *Of Government and Obedience* (1654), p. 102; cf. p. 110.

96 J. Nayler, *A Collection of Sundry Books* (1716), I, p. 187.

97 In *Harleian Miscellany* (1744–6), II, p. 503.

98 Ed. W. L. Sachse, *The Diurnal of Thomas Rugge* (Camden Soc., Third Series, XCI, pp. 40–1).

99 G.S., *The Dignity of Kingship Asserted* (1660), pp. 171–2. W. R. Parker, who edited a reprint in 1942, attributed this pamphlet to George Starkey.

100 *Harleian Miscellany* (1808–13), X, p. 55. Sondes had been a pupil of John Preston.

101 S. Butler, *Hudibras*, part II, canto 2.

102 J. Lacy, *The Dumb Lady*, in *Dramatic Works* (1875), pp. 18–19. Not published until 1672, but probably acted in 1669.

103 J. Dryden, *The Medal* (1682), in *Poetical Works* (Globe ed., 1886), p. 130.

104 A. Cowley, *Essays, Plays and Sundry Verses*, ed. A. R. Waller (Cambridge, 1906), p. 389; A. Behn, *Works*, ed. M. Summers (1915), VI, p. 141; cf. IV, p. 34.

105 J. Swift, *Works* (Edinburgh, 1814), III, p. 283.

106 E. Spenser, *Works* (Globe ed., 1924), p. 514. For the freedom of beggars see my *The World Turned Upside Down*, p. 39; cf. pp. 183–4, 190 above.

107 *C.S.P.D., 1595–97*, pp. 317, 343–5.

108 G. Winstanley, *The True Levellers Standard Advanced* (1649), p. 17, in Sabine, *op. cit.*, p. 261.

109 Winstanley, *The New Law of Righteousness* (1649), p. 55, in Sabine, *op. cit.*, p. 195; cf. *ibid.*, p. 262.

110 Winstanley, *A Letter to the Lord Fairfax and his Councell of War* (1649), p. 9, in Sabine, *op. cit.*, p. 288.

111 Winstanley, *An Appeale to all Englishmen* (1650), broadside, in Sabine, *op. cit.*, p. 414.

112 *Ibid.*, pp. 393, 195–6.

113 See my *The World Turned Upside Down*, chapter 16.

114 Winstanley, *The Law of Freedom in a Platform* (1652), p. 85, in Sabine, *op. cit.*, p. 595.

115 R. Coster, *A Mite Cast into the Common Treasury* (1649), p. 3, in Sabine, *op. cit.*, pp. 656–7.

116 Clapham, *op. cit.*, pp. 212–13; Macpherson, *op. cit.*, pp. 286–90.

117 Most of these names are quoted in my *Society and Puritanism in Pre-Revolutionary England*, chapter 4, especially pp. 133–44; *Puritanism and Revolution*, pp. 235–7; *The World Turned Upside Down*, chapter 16. See also J. Milton, *Complete Prose Works* (Yale ed.), I, p. 804; T. Hobbes, *English Works*, VI, p. 321; *Economic Writings of Sir William Petty*, ed. Hull, I, pp. 43–9, 181–2; p. 94 above.

118 G. Herbert, 'The Elixer', *Works*, ed. R. A. Willmott (n.d.), p. 196.

119 J. Puckle, *A New Dialogue* (1967), p. 20; M. Postlethwayt, *The Universal Dictionary of Trade and Commerce* (4th ed., 1774), p. xiv.

120 T. Hobbes, *Leviathan* (Everyman ed.), p. 110. The contrast between 'free' individuals shaping their own morality, and the lower classes who have hard work and morality thrust upon them, is one of the themes of Richardson's *Clarissa Harlowe*. See my *Puritanism and Revolution*, especially pp. 363–4.

121 Ed. J. M. Winter and D. M. Joslin, *R. H. Tawney's Commonplace Book* (Cambridge, 1972), p. 75.

122 Abiezer Coppe, *The Fiery Flying Roll* (1650), II, p.2, quoted, with useful comments, by A. L. Morton, *The World of the Ranters* (1970), p. 87. Morton's *The English Utopia* (1952) is also relevant.

123 [Anon.], *The Worth of a Penny* (1647), quoted by Margaret James, *Social Policy during the Puritan Revolution*, p. 282. When Voltimar in Dekker's *The Welsh Embassador* (*c.* 1624) was threatened with the galleys, he cried 'No, to'th gallows, upon a ladder a man may talk freely and never be sent to prison' (Dekker, *Dramatic Works*, ed. Bowers, IV, p. 331).

124 B. L. de Muralt, *Lettres sur les Anglais et les Francais*, quoted by L. Radzinowicz, *A History of English Criminal Law* (1948), I, p. 720; L. Ziff, *Puritanism in America* (Oxford, 1973), p. 206. Muralt's *Letters* were written in 1694 though first published in 1725.

125 Josiah Tucker, *Instructions for Travellers* (1757), p. 25.

126 S. Pollard, 'Factory Discipline in the Industrial Revolution', *Ec.H.R.*, Second Series, XVI, p. 254; cf. C. M. Andrews, *The Colonial Period of American History* (Yale, 1964), IV, p. 302.

127 Grosley, *Londres* (Lausanne, 2nd ed., 1774), I, pp. 203–4. I owe this reference to the kindness of Professor André Parreaux, who cites it in his *Daily Life in England in the Reign of George III*, trans. Carola Congreve (1969), p. 116.

128 Sir W. Petty, *Political Arithmetick* (1690), in *Economic Writings*, I, pp. 285–90.

129 K. Marx, *Capital*, ed. D. Torr (1946), I, pp. 261–3.
130 A. Ferguson, *An Essay on the History of Civil Society* (3rd ed., Edinburgh, 1768), pp. 309, 303.
131 Adam Smith, *The Wealth of Nations*, II, pp. 417–24.
132 D. Simon, 'Master and Servant', in *Democracy and the Labour Movement*, ed. J. Saville (1954), pp. 160–200. Domestic servants have until very recently stood in the relation of children to their employers (A. Harding, *A Social History of English Law*, Penguin ed., p. 248).
133 Marx, *Capital*, I, p. 256.

Chapter 11   *Men as They Live Their Own History*

1 Originally published as a review of E. P. Thompson, *The Making of the English Working Class*, in *The Times Literary Supplement*, 12 December 1963.
2 Ed. G. R. Elton, *The Tudor Constitution* (Cambridge, 1960), p. 81. For Professor Elton's retort, see *The Times Literary Supplement*, 2 January 1964.

PART V   CHANGE OUT OF CONTINUITY

Chapter 12   *Sir Isaac Newton and His Society*

1 Originally given as a paper at the Tercentenary Conference on Newton's Annus Mirabilis at the University of Texas, 1966. First published in the *Texas Quarterly*, X, no. 3, 1967.
2 Ed. M. Claggett, *Critical Problems in the History of Science* (Madison, 1959), pp. 855, 12.
3 For examples of the egregious misunderstanding into which ignorance of the historical context has led commentators on Thomas Hobbes, see Quentin Skinner, 'The Ideological Context of Hobbes's Political Thought', *Historical Journal*, IX (1966), especially pp. 313–17.
4 A. R. Hall, 'Merton Revisited', *History of Science*, II (1963), *passim*; C. Webster, 'The Authorship and Significance of *Macaria*', *P. and P.*, no. 56, pp. 44–8.
5 T. S. Kuhn, *The Structure of Scientific Revolutions* (Chicago, 1962), p. 159.
6 *Harleian Miscellany* (1744–6), VI, p. 119.
7 Ed. A. R. and M. B. Hall, *The Correspondence of Henry Oldenburg*, I, p. 278.
8 Perry Miller, 'The Marrow of Puritan Divinity', *Publications of the Colonial Society of Massachusetts*, XXXII (1935), p. 266.
9 T. Sprat, *History of the Royal Society* (1667), pp. 371–2; S. Butler, *Characters and Passages from Notebooks*, p. 458. Sprat's

comparison was pretty trite by this date: see my *Intellectual Origins of the English Revolution*, pp. 25–6, which gives sources for quotations unidentified above.

10 H. Stubbe, *Legends no Histories* (1670), Sig. +2.

11 H. Stubbe, *The Lord Bacons Relation of the Sweating-sickness examined* (1671), Preface.

12 Oldenburg, *Correspondence*, II, p. 630.

13 North, *Discourses upon Trade* (1691), in J. R. McCulloch, *Early English Tracts on Commerce* (1952), p. 511.

14 Sydenham, *De Arte Medica* (1669), in K. Dewhurst, *Dr. Thomas Sydenham* (Wellcome Historical Medical Library, 1966), p. 82.

15 My *Intellectual Origins*, pp. 15, 18, 64; Lord Keynes, 'Newton the Man', in the Royal Society's *Newton Tercentenary Celebrations* (Cambridge, 1947), p. 27; Keynes, *Collected Writings*, X, *Essays in Biography* (1972), pp. 363–4.

16 D. P. Walker, *The Ancient Theology* (1972), pp. 258, 263. Mr Walker thinks Newton would have agreed with Ramsay.

17 I owe this point to Professor F. E. Manuel's forthcoming Fremantle Lectures, *The Religion of Isaac Newton*.

18 F. Yates, *The Rosicrucian Enlightment* (1972), pp. 200–2.

19 M. Boas, 'The Establishment of the Mechanical Philosophy', *Osiris*, X (1952), p. 418.

20 *The Times Literary Supplement*, 25 October 1963.

21 G. Fox, *Journal*, I, p. 11.

22 Sir John Coniers, quoted by B. Manning, 'The Nobles, the People and the Constitution', *P. and P.*, No. 9, p. 61; *Mercurius Britannicus*, No. 107, November 24–December 1, 1645 (I owe this reference to the kindness of Mr Ian McCalman); C. H. Firth, *Oliver Cromwell* (World's Classics), p. 430.

23 Stubbe, *Legends no Histories*, Sig. +iv; S. Butler, *Hudibras*, part III, canto I.

24 R. Boyle, *Works* (1772), V, p. 397.

25 J. Tulloch, *Rational Theology and Christian Philosophy in England in the 17th century* (1874), II, pp. 278–9.

26 C. Wren, *Parentalia* (1700), p. 201.

27 Ed. H. McLachlan, *Sir Isaac Newton's Theological Manuscripts* (Liverpool, 1950), p. 17.

28 Ed. A. R. and M. B. Hall, *Unpublished Scientific Papers of Isaac Newton* (Cambridge, 1961), p. 197.

29 R. S. Westfall, *Science and Religion in 17th century England* (Yale, 1958), pp. 107–11, 205–6, 219–20.

30 Oldenburg to Samuel Hartlib, *Correspondence of Henry Oldenburg*, I, p. 277; F. E. Manuel, *A Portrait of Isaac Newton* (Harvard, 1968), p. 440.

31 See C. W. Foster, 'Sir Isaac Newton's Family', *Associated Architectural Societies' Reports and Papers*, XXXIX (1928), pp. 1–62.

32 See Joan Simon, 'The Two John Angels', *Transactions of the Leicestershire Archaeological and Historical Society*, XXXI (1955), pp. 38–41.

33 H. McLachlan, *The Religious Opinions of Milton, Locke and Newton* (Manchester, 1941), p. 119.

34 Sir D. Brewster, *Memoirs of the Life, Writings and Discoveries of Sir Isaac Newton* (Edinburgh, 1955), II, p. 318; F. E. Manuel, *Isaac Newton, Historian* (Cambridge, 1963), pp. 16, 268.

35 H. McLachlan, *Sir Isaac Newton's Theological Manuscripts*, pp. 55, 137.

36 W. W. Rouse Ball, *Cambridge Notes* (Cambridge, 1921), p. 258; Brewster, *op. cit.*, II, p. 338. The source for the last quotation (Whiston) is not of the most reliable.

37 H. M. Innes, *Fellows of Trinity College* (Cambridge, 1941), *passim*.

38 C. E. Raven, *John Ray* (2nd ed., 1950), pp. 57–8, 441, 461, 457. Ray reluctantly agreed to be ordained in December 1660, when he still hoped for a reasonable religious settlement.

39 *Ibid.*, p. 28 and *passim*.

40 I. Barrow, *Theological Works* (ed. A. Napier, 1859), IX, pp. 41–7; cf. R. H. Kargon, *Atomism in England from Hariot to Newton* (Oxford, 1966), pp. 78–9 and Chapter XI, *passim*.

41 H. More, *The Immortality of the Soul* (1659), *passim*; *Collection of Several Philosophical Writings* (1662), p. xv.

42 Hall and Hall, *Unpublished Scientific Papers of Isaac Newton*, pp. 75, 187; A. R. Hall, 'Sir Isaac Newton's Note-Book, 1661–5', *Cambridge Historical Journal*, IX (1948), pp. 243–4; Boas, 'The Establishment of the Mechanical Philosophy', p. 505.

43 Butler, *Characters and Passages from Notebooks*, p. 466.

44 J. Oldham, *Poems* (Centaur Press, 1960), p. 178.

45 Stubbe, *Legends no Histories*, Sig.*

46 Pepys, *Diary*, ed. H. B. Wheatley (1946), I, p. 253.

47 McLachlan, *Sir Isaac Newton's Theological Manuscripts*, pp. 49–51, 131–2. Cf. Pepys's fear of Catholicism in the early sixties – all the more significant in a man who was later himself to be accused of papist leanings.

48 Manuel, *Isaac Newton, Historian*, p. 116.

49 Raven, *John Ray*, pp. 251–2.

50 Brewster, *op. cit.*, II, pp. 351–2.

51 Manuel, *A Portrait of Isaac Newton*, p. 267.

52 E. M. Wilbur, *A History of Unitarianism* (Harvard, 1946), chapter 2 and *passim*.

53 [Anon.], *The Life of that Incomparable man Faustus Socinus* (1653).

54 J. Bidle, *The Apostolical and True Opinion concerning the Holy Trinity* (1653), *passim*. I have used the 1691 edition, which contains a *Life of Bidle*.

55 Ed. F. S. Boas, *The Diary of Thomas Crosfield* (1935), pp. 85–6.

56 Sir J. Suckling, *An Account of Religion by Reason* (1641), Preface. Cf. F. Osborn, *Advice to a Son* (1656): the Socinians are 'looked upon as the most chemical and rational part of our many divisions' (in *Miscellaneous Works*, 11th ed. (1722), p. 91).

57 J. Pordage, *Innocence appearing through the dark Mists of Pretended Guilt* (1655), *passim*; cf. G. P. Gooch, *The History of English Democratic Ideas in the 17th century* (Cambridge, 1927), p. 266. Pordage denied the accusations. See my *The World Turned Upside Down*, pp. 228–30.

58 J. Mede, *Works*, ed. J. Worthington (1664), II, p. 1082; [Richard Overton], *Mans Mortalitie*, *passim*.

59 J. Hall, *Pax Terris* (1648); J. Waddington, *Congregational History, 1567–1700* (1874), p. 559.

60 H. S. Bennett, *English Books and Readers, 1558 to 1603* (Cambridge, 1965), p. 225.

61 [Anon.], *Doomes-Day* (1647), p. 6. I have discussed these matters at greater length in my *Antichrist in Seventeenth-Century England*, *passim*.

62 J. Rogers, *Sagrir* (1653). By 1666 the Fifth Monarchy, Rogers predicted, 'must be visible in all the earth'.

63 John Pell to Secretary Thurloe, March 1655, in *The Protectorate of Oliver Cromwell*, ed. R. Vaughan (1839), I, p. 156.

64 T. Brightman, *The Revelation of St. John Illustrated* (4th ed., 1644), pp. 378–81, 520, 824; cf. pp. 109–12, 124–5, 136–7, 157 and *passim*.

65 Brightman, *A most Comfortable Exposition of the last and most difficult pages of the Prophecies of Daniel* (1644), pp. 966–7; *A Commentary on Canticles* (1644), p. 1077 (pagination of these last two is continuous with Brightman's *Revelation*, with which they are bound).

66 Mede, *Works*, I, pp. x, lxv.

67 Mede, *The Key of The Revelation* (2nd ed., 1656), pp. 114–25; *Works*, I, pp. xlviii–li.

68 Mede, *Works*, I, pp. lxv, xxxiv; II, pp. 978, 995.

69 Mede, *Works*, II, p. 979; cf. pp. 1006–7.

70 H. More, *Theological Works* (1708), p. 633.

71 Ed. Sir Gyles Isham, *The Correspondence of Bishop Brian Duppa*

and *Sir Justinian Isham, 1650–60* (Northamptonshire Record Society, 1955), p. 37.

72 Ed. E. S. de Beer, *The Diary of John Evelyn* (Oxford, 1955), III, p. 158. The flood was believed to have occurred in the year 1655 or 1656 from the creation.

73 [Anon.], *The Popes Spectacles* (1623), p. 1083.

74 V. Powell, *Saving Faith* (1651), p. 92.

75 M. Roberts, review in *Journal of Ecclesiastical History*, VIII (1957), pp. 112–15.

76 Brightman, *Daniel*, p. 967; Mede, *Remaines on some Passages in Revelation* (1650), p. 33; J. Merrien, *Christopher Columbus* (1958), p. 223; Wither, *Campo-Musae* (1643); Hartlib, *Clavis Apocalyptica* (1651); my *Puritanism and Revolution* (1958), p. 327; I owe Lady Eleanor Davies to the kindness of Professor Ivan Roots.

77 J. Trapp, *Commentary of the New Testament* (1958, first published 1647), pp. 250, 420; W. Lilly, *A Prophecy of the White King* (1644), p. 5; my *Puritanism and Revolution*, p. 329; G. F. Nuttall, *The Holy Spirit in Puritan Faith and Experience* (1946), p. 109; D. P. Walker, *The Decline of Hell*, p. 245.

78 G. H. Dodge, *The Political Theory of the Huguenots of the Dispersion* (Columbia University Press, 1947), pp. 35–8.

79 P. Miller, *Errand into the Wilderness*, p. 228.

80 Newton, *Opera Quae Exstant Omnia*, ed. S. Horsley (1775), V, pp. 448, 450, 474.

81 A. T. Mahan, *The Influence of Sea Power upon History, 1660–1783* (1890), p. 107.

82 Pepys, *Diary*, IV, p. 366, V, pp. 218, 283–4, 328, VI, p. 113.

83 W. Lilly, *The Lord Merlins Prophecy Concerning the King of Scots* (1651), p. 4; *Monarchy or no Monarchy in England* (1651), *passim*.

84 E. Turnor, *Collections for the History of the Town and Soke of Grantham* (1806), p. 179.

85 Manuel, *Isaac Newton, Historian*, pp. 137–8, 193.

86 *The Elogium of Sir Isaac Newton, by Monsieur Fontenelle* (1728), p. 32.

87 A. Wood, *Athenae Oxonienses*, I, *Life of Wood* (Ecclesiastical History Society, Oxford, 1848), p. 188.

88 *Op. cit.*, Preface.

89 Ed. H. W. Turnbull, *Correspondence of Sir Isaac Newton* (1959–), III, pp. 335–6, 338.

90 Newton, *Opera Quae Exstant Omnia*, V, p. 432.

91 McLachlan, *Sir Isaac Newton's Theological Manuscripts*, p. 52. Wilkins has been described as 'the English godfather of natural or moral religion' (G. McColley, 'The Ross-Wilkins Controversy', *Annals of Science*, III, pp. 155, 186).

92   McLachlan, *Sir Isaac Newton's Theological Manuscripts*, pp. 119–21; Newton, *Opera Quae Exstant Omnia*, V, pp. 306–10; cf. T. Brightman, *The Revelation of St. John Illustrated*, pp. 232–3, 273–92; J. Mede, *Works*, I, Sig.* xxx 4; J. Mede, *The Key of the Revelation* (1656), Sig. A4; H. More's dictionary of prophetical language in *A Modest Enquiry into the Mystery of Iniquity* (1664), pp. 226–59.

93   Manuel, *Isaac Newton, Historian*, p. 121.

94   R. J. Forbes, 'Was Newton an Alchemist?', *Chymia*, II (1949), pp. 35–6; F. Sherwood Taylor, 'An Alchemical Work of Sir Isaac Newton', *Ambix*, V (1956), p. 64; cf. I. B. Cohen, 'Newton in the Light of Recent Scholarship', *Isis*, LI (1960), pp. 503–4.

95   R. W. V. Elliott, 'Isaac Newton's "Of an Universall Language"', *Modern Language Review*, LII (1957), pp. 1–18; cf. Elliott, 'Isaac Newton as Phonetician', *ibid.*, XLIX (1954), pp. 5–12.

96   P. W. Thomas, *Sir John Berkenhead, 1617–1679*, chapters V and VI.

97   *Correspondence of Sir Isaac Newton*, III, pp. 334, 336, 355; cf. A. J. Snow, *Matter and Gravity in Newton's Physical Philosophy* (Oxford, 1926), *passim*.

98   Hall and Hall, *Unpublished Scientific Papers of Isaac Newton*, p. 363 (my italics).

99   Boas, 'The Establishment of the Mechanical Philosophy', pp. 420–2, 479, 489 and *passim*; cf. Turnor, *Collections for the History of the Town and Soke of Grantham*, pp. 172–3.

100   Newton, *Opera Quae Exstant Omnia*, IV, p. 439.

101   McLachlan, *Sir Isaac Newton's Theological Manuscripts*, p. 58.

102   Newton, *Mathematical Principles of Natural Philosophy*, transl. A. Motte, ed. F. Cajori (University of California Press, 1934), pp. 398–9.

103   L. T. More, *Isaac Newton: A Biography* (New York, 1962), p. 664. The famous phrase curiously recalls one of Donne's sermons: 'Divers men may walk by the sea-side and, the same beams of the sun giving light to them all, one gathereth by the benefit of that light pebbles or speckled shells for curious vanity, and another gathers precious pearl or medicinal amber by the same light.' (Ed. G. R. Potter and E. M. Simpson, *The Sermons of John Donne*, III (California University Press, 1957), p. 359.) It is not very likely that Newton read Donne, even Donne's sermons: a possible source is the Hermeticist John Everard (1575–?c. 1650), who said that most of us are busy 'playing with cockle-shells and pebble-stones that lie on the

outcoasts of the kingdom' and do not put back to the infinite sea (*Gospel Treasures Opened*, posthumously published in 1653, pp. 423–5, quoted by R. M. Jones, *Spiritual Reformers of the Sixteenth and Seventeenth Centuries* (1928), p. 249. For Everard see my *The World Turned Upside Down*, pp. 149, 210.) But a more plausible source perhaps is *Paradise Regained*, Book IV:

collecting toys
And trifles for choice matters, worth a sponge;
As children gathering pebbles on the shore.

Chapter 13   Conclusion

1 K. Dewhurst, *John Locke (1632–1704)*, *Physician and Philosopher* (1963), p. 204; for the computations I am indebted to Professor Frank Manuel.
2 P. Zagorin, *The Court and the Country* (1970), pp. 10–18.
3 L. M. Hill, 'County Government in Caroline England, 1625–1640', in *The Origins of the English Civil War*, ed. C. Russell (1973), p. 66.
4 I. Deutscher, *The Unfinished Revolution: Russia 1917–1967* (Oxford, 1967), pp. 21–2. Deutscher was criticizing me amongst others: rightly, I think, though there is still perhaps more to be said about class divisions in the Civil War line-up.
5 Lenin, *Selected Works* (Moscow, 1935), V, p. 303.
6 D. M. Wolfe, *Leveller Manifestoes of the Puritan Revolution* (New York, 1944), p. 124; ed. W. Haller and G.Davies, *The Leveller Tracts, 1647–1653* (Columbia University Press, 1944), p. 145; Woodhouse, *Puritanism and Liberty*, p. 74; cf. Rainborough, quoted on p. 199 above.
7 See pp. 201–4 above.
8 Sabine, *The Works of Gerrard Winstanley*, p. 558.
9 See pp. 213–14 above.

Index